Sustainable Development Goals Series

The **Sustainable Development Goals Series** is Springer Nature's inaugural cross-imprint book series that addresses and supports the United Nations' seventeen Sustainable Development Goals. The series fosters comprehensive research focused on these global targets and endeavours to address some of society's greatest grand challenges. The SDGs are inherently multidisciplinary, and they bring people working across different fields together and working towards a common goal. In this spirit, the Sustainable Development Goals series is the first at Springer Nature to publish books under both the Springer and Palgrave Macmillan imprints, bringing the strengths of our imprints together.

The Sustainable Development Goals Series is organized into eighteen subseries: one subseries based around each of the seventeen respective Sustainable Development Goals, and an eighteenth subseries, "Connecting the Goals," which serves as a home for volumes addressing multiple goals or studying the SDGs as a whole. Each subseries is guided by an expert Subseries Advisor with years or decades of experience studying and addressing core components of their respective Goal.

The SDG Series has a remit as broad as the SDGs themselves, and contributions are welcome from scientists, academics, policymakers, and researchers working in fields related to any of the seventeen goals. If you are interested in contributing a monograph or curated volume to the series, please contact the Publishers: Zachary Romano [Springer; zachary.romano@springer.com] and Rachael Ballard [Palgrave Macmillan; rachael.ballard@palgrave.com].

More information about this series at
https://link.springer.com/bookseries/15486

Emma Charlene Lubaale ·
Ashwanee Budoo-Scholtz
Editors

Violence Against Women and Criminal Justice in Africa: Volume I

Legislation, Limitations and Culture

palgrave
macmillan

Editors
Emma Charlene Lubaale
Faculty of Law
Rhodes University
Grahamstown/Makhanda, South Africa

Ashwanee Budoo-Scholtz
Faculty of Law, Centre for Human Rights
University of Pretoria
Pretoria, Hatfield, South Africa

ISSN 2523-3084 ISSN 2523-3092 (electronic)
Sustainable Development Goals Series
ISBN 978-3-030-75948-3 ISBN 978-3-030-75949-0 (eBook)
https://doi.org/10.1007/978-3-030-75949-0

Cover illustration: Korndanai Vitthayanukarun/EyeEm

This Palgrave Macmillan imprint is published by the registered company Springer Nature Switzerland AG
The registered company address is: Gewerbestrasse 11, 6330 Cham, Switzerland

To,

Every woman survivor of violence who is denied justice.

Foreword

Violence against women and girls is perhaps one of the most critical issues dominating discussions on the agendas of states across the African continent. This scourge is neither new nor unique to the African continent. Over the past few decades, however, it has become an increasingly public issue across states in Africa. The pervasiveness of violence against women and girls has seen some states label the scourge a national crisis warranting immediate redress. It can be considered as one of the main challenges to the realisation of women's rights in Africa.

Criminal justice systems in Africa have a fundamental role to play in the eradication of violence against women. Disheartening, however, progress has been extremely slow in as far as holding perpetrators of such violence to account is concerned. A significant number of cases, if at all reported, hardly make it through the criminal justice system. All considered, it is indisputable that violence against women and girls on the African continent has reached alarming levels. It is equally irrefutable that criminal justice responses are generally wanting. But also undeniable is the fact that most African states have made multiple reforms to national laws. Many have also committed themselves to international obligations by way of ratification of treaties relevant to addressing the scourge of violence against women and girls. Even so, these strides have not generally translated into better criminal accountability across justice systems in Africa. The challenges and prospects of criminal justice for women and girls in Africa, despite these reforms, have hardly been the subject of scholarly discussion.

The two edited volumes of this publication fill in this scholarly gap. They echo the provisions of article 4 of the Protocol to the African Charter on Human and Peoples' Rights (Maputo Protocol) that requires States parties to adopt and enforce laws, including punishing perpetrators, to ensure the elimination of violence against women. The contributions present a comprehensive and rigorous overview of the salient features and major developments in Africa's criminal justice systems in as far as justice for women is concerned, while also focusing on vulnerable women. They offer a unique insight into the practical challenges of advancing justice for women in cases of violence in the different regions in Africa.

As someone who has been engaged on women's rights on the continent, including on the issue of violence against women, I believe that the publication of these two volumes is timely and that the recommendations therein, if implemented, can ensure more accountability for violence against women in the criminal justice systems of African countries.

Yaoundé, Cameroon

Commissioner Lucy Asuagbor
Outgoing Special Rapporteur on
the Rights of Women in Africa

Acknowledgements

The editors wish to express their appreciation to all authors for their patience and dedication in this process, with them having to work with close deadlines. The chapters in this Volume could not have been finalised without the independent reviewers' insightful comments. Special thanks go to the editorial team at Palgrave Macmillan, especially to Naveen Dass and Josephine Taylor, in ensuring that the publication was on time. Emma thanks the Research Office of Rhodes University and the National Research Foundation (Funding to EC Lubaale, Grant No: 127504) for funding her trips to Pretoria from Grahamstown so that she can have working sessions on the book with Ashwanee. Ashwanee is grateful for the financial support of the Centre for Human Rights, Faculty of Law, University of Pretoria, which assisted her in securing an editorial assistant, Janet Gbom, whose work is also acknowledged.

Contents

Notes on Contributors

Yousra Abourabi is an assistant professor at Sciences Po Rabat, International University of Rabat in Morocco. She holds a Ph.D. in International Relations from the University of Lyon. Her research focuses on the Moroccan political system, its foreign policy and the challenges of African governance (environment, migration, security). She recently has published the book 'Maroc', edited by De Boeck.

Ashwanee Budoo-Scholtz is the programme manager of the Master's in Human Rights and Democratisation in Africa at the Centre for Human Rights, Faculty of Law, University of Pretoria. She holds a doctorate and master's degree in law from the University of Pretoria and a bachelor's degree in law from the University of Mauritius. Her research, teaching and training areas are the African human rights system, with a focus on women's and girls' rights. She was previously a project coordinator of the Women's Rights of the Centre for Human Rights. In this role, she worked with and supported the research and standard-setting functions of the African Commission on Human and Peoples' Rights' Special Rapporteur on the Rights of Women in Africa (e.g. the general comment on child marriage adopted by the African Commission and the African Committee of Experts on the Rights and Welfare of the Child, the African Commission's report on child marriage and state reporting workshops). Dr. Budoo-Scholtz is a member of the Editorial Committee of the African Human Rights Yearbook and the Global Campus Human Rights Preparedness. She has a proven track record in conducting research, with publications in peer-reviewed journals and chapters in books.

Lizelle Ramaccio Calvino holds a doctorate in Law from the University of Zululand. She is currently a Senior Lecturer at the Faculty of Law f the University of University. Her current research interests include, among others, the rights of women and children.

Shivani Georgijevic holds the position of Lecturer in Law at the University of Mauritius. Prior to joining her current position, she taught at the Université de Bordeaux. She is currently the Link Coordinator of the collaboration between the University of Mauritius and Université Paris Nanterre. She has also served as Consultant for a number of projects for the Mauritian Government and non-governmental organisations. Mrs Georgijevic holds an L.L.M. in International Law with International Relations from the University of Kent and a B.A. (Hons) from the University of Mauritius. She is currently a Ph.D. student at the Université de Bordeaux.

Mothibi A. Kholofelo is a holder of Ph.D. in Criminology from the University of Limpopo. Currently, she is an Associate Professor at the Tshwane University of Technology. She is also the secretary for Criminological Society of Africa and an editorial member for Acta Criminologica Journal. Her areas in research are crime prevention, policing, safety and security, domestic violence and victimology.

Annette Lansink holds law degrees from universities in South Africa and the Netherlands. She is the former Dean of the School of Law at the University of Venda and has extensive experience in higher education and contributed to the transformation of the university in numerous leadership roles. Her research interests are in the areas of public international law, human rights and gender. She was Rapporteur on women and migration for the global International Law Association's Committee on Feminism and International Law. Consistent with her multi-disciplinary approach, she has in recent years again focused her attention on Africanisation of legal education and epistemologies of the South. Given the breadth of her interests, she has published nationally and internationally in both scholarly journals and the popular media and delivered papers in many countries, institutions and fora, including the United Nations.

Emma Charlene Lubaale is an Associate Professor at the Faculty of Law of Rhodes University. She has previously taught law at the University of Venda. Prior to this, she taught and researched law in the capacity of a post-doctoral research fellow at the University of Pretoria's Institute of International and Comparative Law in Africa. She holds a doctorate and master's degree in law from the University of Pretoria; a bachelor's degree in law from Makerere University; and a post-graduate diploma in legal practice from Uganda's Law Development Center. She recently concluded her studies towards a post-graduate diploma in Higher Education at the University of Kwazulu Natal. Her current areas of interest are criminal law, international human rights law, women and children's rights and international criminal law. She is currently a member of the Organization of Women in Science for the Developing World, a member of the South African Young Academy of Science (SAYAS) and a rated researcher by the National Research Foundation (NRF) of South Africa. In January 2020, she was appointed by the NRF to serve on the NRF Standing Panel for the Humanities and Social Sciences (HSS) from 2020 to 2023. She has served as a law reviewer for publishers including Springer Nature, the Pretoria University Law Press, the South African Journal of Criminal Justice, the Journal of Sexual Aggression, Speculum Juris, De Jure, South African Crime Quarterly and Journal of Law, Society and Development.

Untalimile Crystal Mokoena is a lecturer at the University of Venda, South Africa. Her research interests are in human rights and social security law. As an emerging researcher, Crystal has written and co-authored various book chapters and journal articles. She is currently a doctoral student at the University of Pretoria and holds LLB and LLM degrees from the University of Venda. Her interest in women rights and social security law influenced her choice of doctoral topic which is on 'analysing widows' right to social assistance in South Africa'.

Cecilia Ngaiza is currently a Ph.D. Student in law at the University of Bayreuth. She holds a Master of Laws (LLM) and a Bachelor of Laws (Hons), both from the University of Dar es Salaam. She has a Post Graduate Diploma in Legal Practice from the Law School of Tanzania, an Advocate of the High Court of Tanzania and a member to the Tanganyika Law Society. She has worked with the community based human rights non-governmental organisation—Tanzania Women Lawyers' Association (TAWLA), before joining the University of Dar es Salaam, School of Law as an Assistant Lecturer.

Zahara Nampewo is a Ugandan lawyer and academic teaching at the School of Law at Makerere University. She also heads the Human Rights and Peace Centre (HURIPEC), a research and advocacy centre of the university. Dr. Nampewo received her Ph.D. from Emory University in the United States. Her areas of interest and expertise include human rights, health and gender justice. She has published on a range of subjects including disability, family law, sexuality, decentralisation and access to justice. Dr. Nampewo was winner of the 2019 5thWomen in Law Award for 'Female Lawyer Academic', awarded by the Uganda Law Society.

Asina A. Omari is a Lawyer with 15 years working experience as a legal officer, legal advisor, teaching and researching; specialising in women and children's issues. She holds a Bachelor of Laws (LLB), and an LLM from the University of Dar es Salaam where she currently teaches at the School of Law. Asina is currently serving as the Chairperson of the University Legal Aid Clinic. She is also serving as a Commissioner with the National Electoral Commission of Tanzania. She has been an active member of the Bar and the Tanzania Women Lawyers Association. And is currently a Doctoral Researcher at University of Bayreuth, Germany.

Raeesa Rajmohamed is Lecturer in Law, University of The Gambia. She recently spent a year as a Visiting Scholar and Lecturer in Law at the University of the Gambia through her work with the Bristol Human Rights Implementation Centre of the University of Bristol. She was the Public International Law Unit Coordinator, lectured Clinical Legal Education, ran the Gambia Law Review and was the Executive Director of the Gambia Law Clinic. Her research focuses principally on autonomy and human rights, often in a global health context. She has both a Master's of Law (LLM) in Health Law and Society and a Bachelors of Laws (LLB) from the University of Bristol.

Matadi M. Tholaine holds a bachelors degree in Law (LLM) from Université William Booth in Kinshasa in the Democratic Republic of Congo, a master's degree (LLM) and doctorate in Law (LLD) from the University of Zululand. As a Lecturer in the Law Department at the University of Zullans, Kwadlangezwa Campus in Kwazulu Natal, she has for many years lectured in the modules of Introduction to Law, Juridical interpretation, Legal research methods, Constitutional law and Fundamental Rights. Her research interests included children's rights, international law, health and the law. She has published in the field of fundamental rights and children's rights. She currently serves as a reviewer for children's rights paper submissions to various accredited and peer-reviewed journals.

Happy Mathew Tirivangasi has Master of Arts in Sociology from the University of Limpopo in South Africa as well as Master of Science in Governance and Development from University of Antwerp in Belgium. He is a skilled and well-published researcher in the field of political and environmental sociology. He has done research on governance issues, namely migration, elections, social movements, climate change and food security. Happy is currently a Research Associate in the Department of Research Administration and Development at the University of Limpopo.

Nelly Warega is a human rights lawyer based in Nairobi, Kenya. Her areas of expertise include: justice and accountability for survivors of sexual and gender-based violence crimes at national, regional and international levels; promotion of access to sexual and reproductive health rights for all women and girls; research and strategic litigation. She holds a Master of Laws degree (LLM) in Human Rights and Democratisation in Africa from the Centre for Human Rights, University of Pretoria, a post-graduate diploma in legal studies from the Kenya School of Law and a Bachelor's degree (LLB) in Law from the University of Nairobi.

Abbreviations and Acronyms

AC	African Commission
ÁCHPR	African Charter on Human and Peoples' Rights
AU	African Union
ACRWC	African Charter on the Rights and Welfare of the Child
AMTO	Assisted Medical Treatment Order
BEAM	Basic Education Assistance Module
BRADEA	Basic Rights and Duties Enforcement Act
CRC	Convention on the Rights of the Child
CEDAW	Convention on the Elimination of All Forms of Discrimination against Women
CRSV	Conflict-Related Sexual Violence
CRIN	Child Rights International Network
CDU	Child Development Unit
COPTIP	Coordination Office for Prevention of Trafficking in Persons
CRC	Constitutional Review Commission
DRC	Democratic Republic of Congo
DEVAW	Declaration on the Elimination of Violence Against Women
DVA	Domestic Violence Act

DPP	Director of Public Prosecutions
ECHR	European Court of Human Rights
EAC	East African Community
FGM	Female Genital Mutilation
GBV	Gender-based violence
GR	General Recommendation
GBVF	Presidential Summit on GBV and Femicide
HIV/ AIDS	Human Immunodeficiency Virus/Acquired Immunodeficiency Syndrome
HAWA	Haki za Wanawake
ICCPR	International Covenant on Civil and Political Rights
IPV	intimate partner violence
ICESCR	International Covenant on Economic, Social and Cultural Rights
ICGLR	International Conference in the Great Lakes Region
IMC	Inter-Ministerial Committee
ILO	International Labour Organisation
JOA	Juvenile Offenders Act
LHRC	Legal and Human Rights Centre
Maputo Protocol	Protocol to the African Charter on Human and Peoples' Rights on the Rights of Women in Africa
MONUSCO	United Nations Organisation Stabilisation Mission in the DRC
NDP	National Development Plan
NCRC	National Crime Research Centre
NSSA	National Social Security Authority
NGOs	Non-Government Organisations
OC	Ombudsperson for Children
OECD	Organisation for Economic Co-operation and Development
OHCHR	Office of the High Commissioner for Human Rights
PALERMO Protocol	Protocol to Prevent, Suppress and Punish Trafficking in Persons, Especially Women and Children, supplementing the United Nations Convention against Transnational Organised Crime
PACOTIPA	Prevention and Combating of Trafficking in Persons Act
PFVA	Prevention of Family Violence Act 133 of 1993
PFGM	Prohibition of the Female Genital Mutilation Act

PHR	Physicians for Human Rights
POA	Programme of Action
POBS	Pensions and Other Benefits Scheme
PRC	Post Rape Care
PTIPA	Prevention of Trafficking in Persons Act
PTSD	Post-Traumatic Stress Disorder
SA	South Africa
SADC	Southern African Development Community
SAPS	South African Police Service
SARS	Severe Acute Respiratory Syndrome
SDGs	Sustainable Development Goals
SRVAW	Special Rapporteur on Violence Against Women
SOA	Sexual Offences Act
SOSPA	Sexual Offence Special Provisions Act
SOP	Standard Operation Procedure
TAWLA	Tanzania Women Lawyer's Association
TAMWA	Tanganyika Law Society. Media organizations like the Tanzania Media Women
TRRC	Truth, Reconciliation and Reparations Commission
UN	United Nations
UNPF	United Nations Population Fund
UDHR	Universal Declaration of Human Rights
UNGA	United Nations General Assembly
UNICEF	United Nations Children's Fund
US AID	United States Agency for International Development
UNFPA	United Nations Population Fund
UNDP	United Nations Development Programme
UPR	Universal Periodic Review
UNODC	United Nations Office on Drugs and Abuse
USAID	United States Agency for International Development
VAW	Violence Against Women
VAWG	Violence Against Women and Girls
WLAC	Women Legal Aid Centre
WHO	World Health Organisation
RAINN	Rape, Abuse and Incest National Network
ZRP	Zimbabwe Republic Police
ZANU-PF	Zimbabwe African National Union-Patriotic Front

List of Figures

Chapter 5

Part I

Introduction

1

Introduction

Emma Charlene Lubaale and Ashwanee Budoo-Scholtz

The case of Buyisiwe, a survivor of gang rape in South Africa, exemplifies the plight of survivors of gender-based violence in their quest for justice.[1] Buyisiwe was gang raped on 2 October 2004. While four years after the rape, those accused of violence against her were convicted, her experience is far from praise-worthy. Buyisiwe's long walk to justice was an appalling

[1] Shadow Report of South Africa to the Committee on Elimination of Violence Against Women on criminal injustice: violence against women in South Africa (2010), https://tbinternet.ohchr.org/Treaties/CEDAW/Shared%20Documents/ZAF/INT_CEDAW_NGO_ZAF_48_10364_E.pdf.

E. C. Lubaale (✉)
Faculty of Law, Rhodes University, Grahamstown, South Africa
e-mail: e.lubaale@ru.ac.za

A. Budoo-Scholtz
Faculty of Law, University of Pretoria, Pretoria, South Africa
e-mail: ashwanee.budoo@up.ac.za

E. C. Lubaale and A. Budoo-Scholtz (eds.), *Violence Against Women and Criminal Justice in Africa: Volume I*, Sustainable Development Goals Series,
https://doi.org/10.1007/978-3-030-75949-0_1

one, with her experience being compounded by mishaps and secondary victimisation. In the course of the four years of her quest for justice, witness statements went missing. This led to the release of the accused persons and consequently, the striking off of the matter from the court roll. A year later, the matter was reinstated following protests from rights groups. Subsequent to this reinstatement, witness statements were re-taken because, as noted, the docket was missing. When the trial resumed, adjournments became the order of the day for reasons including non-appearance of defence witnesses in court. On two instances, the defence attorney failed to appear in court, only for the court to establish that he was not a registered legal practitioner. Securing a new defence attorney came with challenges including, requiring that Buyisiwe, who had already testified and been cross-examined, goes through the process of examination and cross-examination all over again. Hopes for a smooth trial after a new defence attorney took over the matter were shattered when the case was transferred to another court. Following this transfer, a new judicial officer had to be identified to preside over the case. Once again, this transfer came with glitches including, the non-availability of a judge to preside over the matter. After some time, a judge was identified to preside over the matter, proceedings continued and those accused were convicted. Four years later (on 4 September 2009), those accused of gang-raping Buyisiwe were sentenced. From the foregoing facts, it is undenaible that justice was served—but at what price for Buyisiwe?

Violence against women and girls remains one of the most alarming pandemics worldwide. Research reveals that one in every three women globally has experienced some form of violence in their lifetime.[2] Inevitably therefore, women are time and again interacting with the criminal justice system in seeking justice. However, what are these women's experiences in the justice system like? Are they even approaching the justice system to start with? Irrefutably, a few women are approaching the justice system. The question though is, are they accessing the much-desired justice they are seeking? For many survivors of gender-based violence in Africa, access to justice remains a myth. The

---

[2] World Health Organisation, Violence Against Women (November 29, 2017), https://www.who.int/news-room/fact-sheets/detail/violence-against-women#:~:text=A%202013%20analysis%20conduct%20by,partner%20or%20non%2Dpartner%20sexual.

case of Buyisiwe is the very tip of the iceberg of the hoops and hurdles that survivors of gender-based violence have to jump through to access justice. Fortunately for Buyisiwe, her story had a fairly good ending as a conviction was sustained. However, for many survivors, such endings remain a fairytale.

Needless to say, in light of Buyisiwe's experience, a decision to pursue justice for most women means consenting to the innumerable forms of victimisation that come with the rotten aspects of Africa's criminal justice systems. Ramadimetja et al. describe Buyisiwe's cross-examination experience as atrocious.[3] They consider the court environment she was subjected to as hostile and having no regard for the act of gang rape she went through.[4] Extremely disheartening was Buyisiwe's case timeline. Some dubbed her experience as a second form of rape[5]—the second time around by the criminal justice system which ought to have protected her but instead, 'raped', or, victimised her further. Especially disturbing is the fact that these flaws in the justice system rest comfortably alongside African states' international and national commitment to protecting women against violence. This causes one to take a step back to ponder whether there is real commitment to protect women. It does appear like commitment to international standards has become some form of window-dressing by African states. The questions for us as scholars then become: Where do we go from here in a bid to foster the much-needed change on the African continent? Could we perhaps add voice to the already loud voices on the rights of women? Conceivably, evidence-based scholarly research and publication could contribute towards the change we yearn for, hence, the timeliness of these two edited volumes.

The overriding objectives of the two edited volumes on *Violence against women and criminal justice in Africa* are as follows. First, the volumes stimulate scholarly discussions, interest and engagement with the challenge of violence against women. The volumes do so by presenting a

---

[3] Ramadimetja Mogale, Kathy Kovacs Burns and Solina Richter, 'Violence Against Women in South Africa: Policy Position and Recommendations' 18 *Violence Against Women* (2012): 580–594.

[4] *Ibid.*

[5] SangoNet Pulse, Buyisiwe Court Case - Raped Again! (2009), http://www.ngopulse.org/press-release/buyisiwe-court-case-raped-again.

comprehensive analysis of the latest research, thinking and practices of criminal justice systems on the African continent. Second, for the first time, they bring together high quality original and innovative material from diverse perspectives developed by legal practitioners, criminal justice experts and scholars from different criminal justice traditions operating on the African continent. Effectively, the volumes ensure that the African voice is heard on issues of justice for women. Third, in light of the fact that most African states share features such as geographical proximity, the colonial legacy, economic, social and cultural conditions, these volumes, in addition to individual country studies, adopt a comparative approach that highlights the gaps and good practices in a manner that provides a rich source of authoritative information for promoting an intra-African dialogue and cross-fertilisation of ideas across the different criminal justice traditions in Africa. Finally, the volumes act as a repository for generation of knowledge, expertise and experience on the continent on the subject of justice for women and girls. In so doing, they constitute an authoritative reference point for researchers, criminal justice practitioners, academics and policymakers. All four objectives have been advanced through scholarly contributions from emerging and internationally recognised African scholars, practitioners and experts in the fields of criminal justice, violence, gender studies and African legal studies. The majority of the contributors to both volumes are female.

The thematic focus of the book *Violence against women and criminal justice in Africa* is distinct. Despite the voluminous material on violence against women, this has long been a neglected topic in and on Africa. African scholarship and academia have largely been silent in this area of research, writing and teaching. The editors and contributors in the volume are Africans, based largely in Africa. The situations in all five of the main geopolitical blocks in Africa (West, East, Central, North and Southern Africa) are reviewed; while regional contributions are discussed, making this edited volume a comprehensive collection of African voices on the topic. The volumes invoke the use of case studies and doctrinal legal research approaches that espouse the current approaches and transformations in African criminal justice systems' approaches to violence against women. Given the dearth of research in the thematic focus of this volume and the unique African lens through which the volume is approached, there is no doubt that this volume makes a significant contribution to the existing body of knowledge on the subject of 'Violence against women and criminal justice in Africa'. The topical nature and rampancy of violence against women makes both volumes of the book extremely instructive not only for criminal justice practitioners but also women and girls, who, for lack of justice, are failing to realise their own potential and have for years failed to be free from violence and fear. Therefore, the central contribution that these volumes make is the uniquely African perspective through which national accountability for violence against women and girls is approached, understood and can be improved upon.

This first edited book volume, comprising of eleven chapters, focusses on two themes: *Criminal legislationand its implementation, and Limitation of criminal justice responses.* Subsequent to this introduction, Chapter 2 which is authored by Lubaale and Ashwanee provides an exposition of the book. With the two major themes running through the volume as a golden thread being *violence against women* and *criminal justice in Africa*, the authors locate accountability for violence against women within the broader framework of the sustainable development goal on elimination of violence against women and the African Union aspirations on achievement of gender equality. They provide meaningful content to the various expressions of gender-based violence and accordingly conceptualise freedom from violence as a right to be enjoyed by all women. They demonstrate that freedom from violence is a human right that comes with corresponding obligations, with these obligations deriving force from international, regional, sub-regional and national human rights standards. They underscore that these obligations mandate states to protect women from violence and to punish perpetrators when such violence occurs and one of the means to bringing perpetrators to justice is criminal prosecution.

The first theme of the volume deals with *Legislation and its implementation in addressing violence against women.* Notably, criminal laws are critical in responding to violence against women. They set norms and standards regarding acceptable conduct in societies and provide a basis for criminal justice practitioners to commence proceedings against perpetrators of violence against women. The United Nations reports that hundreds of countries have enacted laws on redress of violence against women.[6] It laments, however, that most of these laws are not implemented, let alone, in alignment with international standards.

In Chapter 3, Matadi and Calvino underscore the role of criminal law in addressing gender-based violence. Their comparative study of the Democratic Republic of Congo and South Africa, through the lens feminist legal theories, reveals that the poor implementation of legislation and the failure of the criminal justice system to protect survivors of violence impact negatively on their access to justice. They make recommendations for revision of the criminal justice frameworks of both countries at both the policy and legislative levels.

Mauritius remains the ideal travel destination for many, however, beneath the glamorous picture that the beautiful beaches of Mauritius paints are unaddressed gender-based violence issues including the child marriage problem. In Chapter 4, Georgijevic and Budoo tackle the issue of violence against girls in Mauritius. They examine the existing laws and the soon to be enacted Children's Bill with a view to assessing whether the country has enough safeguards to ensure that the girl child who is a survivor of violence has access to the justice system. They conclude that while the Children's Bill will bring a new child protection landscape, the country also needs to focus on non-legal measures to ensure a change in mindset, and to appraise the girl child of her rights.

The police system is the first port of entry for survivors of gender-based violence. Consequently, the manner in which the police system executes its tasks has a key bearing on whether or not women and girls have access to justice. In Chapter 5, Mothibi and Tirivangase highlight the role of police capacity building in dealing with domestic violence cases in South Africa. They proceed on the premise that police capacity-building in implementing the Domestic Violence Act of South Africa is an entry point for women to access justice. Their analysis reveals that the police system in South Africa is generally ill equipped and this is a barrier to women's access to justice. Against this backdrop, they propose Dr.

6 United Nations Office on Drugs and Crime, *The work of UNODC on violence against women* (2019) 3, https://www.unodc.org/documents/commissions/CCPCJ/CCPCJ_Sessions/CCPCJ_28/Brown-bag-lunches/Brown_bag_Swen_Pfeiffer.pdf.

Bengt-Ake Lindval's four knowledge taxonomy principles as an assessment tool to evaluate police domestic violence training procedures. They make recommendations on how to better equip the police system to effectively confront the scourge of gender-based violence.

It goes without saying that if cases of gender-based violence are not reported, access to justice remains in the rhetoric. In Chapter 6, Warega provides a socio-legal analysis of case reporting in Kenya. The author does this by focussing on access to justice for sexual violence against women. She demonstrates that while Kenya has made progress in terms of legislative reform, the law remains redundant because cases are hardly reported. The author submits that case-reporting is a prerequisite to access to justice for women. She subsequently interrogates the reporting structures and procedures in place, considers the socio-legal issues that arise and proffers possible solutions to combating these challenges.

The second theme of the volume focusses on the *Limitations of criminal justiceresponses to violence against women.* The theme comprises of five chapters and it is premised on the fact that criminal justice systems cannot operate in isolation, hence, the critical need for a coordinated approach to curbing gender-based violence. The theme commences with a chapter by Lansink and Nampewo who conceptualise human trafficking as a form of gender-based violence against women. Using South Africa and Uganda as case studies, the authors recognise the gendered nature of this crime. While underscoring the critical role of criminal prosecution in curbing the trafficking of women, they acknowledge the limitations of exclusive reliance on punitive responses. Against this backdrop, they recommend, among others, a multisectoral and victim-centred criminal justice approach.

In Chapter 8, Abourabi and Lubaale carry the theme of the section of limitation forward by engaging with the limits of legal reform in North Africa. While acknowledging the strides made and the critical role of legal reform in ensuring that women access justice in North Africa, the authors demonstrate that access to justice for women in North Africa will take more than legal reform. They accordingly provide enlightenment into the accountability gap of gender-based violence in two North African countries (Morocco and Egypt) by establishing the link between the deeply entrenched discriminatory social and religious attitudes on the one hand, and access to justice on the other. They recommend measures geared towards a change in social attitudes as well as interpretation of Muslim religious texts within their proper context. At the heart of this chapter is demonstration of the viewpoint that while various interpretations of the Quran by some Muslim societies in North Africa have justified acts of violence against women, there are alternative interpretations to these texts that are pro-women's rights and can be leveraged to fight against VAW in these countries.

There is no denying that issues of access to justice have an economic dimension to them. Notably, in instances where the perpetrator is a caregiver, most survivors have been hesitant to confront and report cases of violence, let alone pursue justice. In these circumstances, access to justice has been close to impossible because reporting has meant losing the much-needed financial support from the perpetrator. Cognisant of this complex issue, Mokoena's discussion in Chapter 9 highlights the need for discussions and actions on access to justice to go beyond mere implementation of criminal laws. She traverses the limits of exclusive reliance on prosecution by providing a link between the right to social security and access to justice for survivors of sexual violence in Zimbabwe. She concludes that social security is central to ensuring case-reporting and ultimately, access to justice for females suffering sexual abuses in Zimbabwe and Africa generally.

While governments are expected to be protectors of the rights of women, in Chapter 10, Rajmohamed brings an interesting perspective to the challenge of female genital mutilation in the Gambia and how the government of the Gambia has played a role in maintaining the practice. She revisits the roots of gender-based violence against women in the Gambia with focus on female genital mutilation as a form of gender-based violence. She demonstrates that the Gambia is yet to view female genital mutilation as a form of violence against women due to the internal suffering from pertinent and powerful 'resistors to change'. This, in the author's view, undermines legal enforcement. She concludes that lack of political will underpins female genital mutilation and prevents the criminal justice system from holding perpetrators to account. In her submission, all legal 'tools' opposing the practice including law reform and criminalisation have failed and will continue to fail due to deeply entrenched societal norms bleeding into higher powers. She takes a bold stance to the effect that the barriers to justice for women in the Gambia are found within the government itself and justice will only be achieved if the nation revaluates its stance on the matter and makes efforts to denounce the practice.

It is an indisputable fact that violence against women in Africa is a complex social problem rooted in gender inequality and deeply entrenched social and cultural norms. Many societies continue to normalise acts of violence against women and girls despite their devastating effects on the rights and lives of women and girls. Stereotypical societal norms to the detriment of women run deep, penetrating the criminal justice system to undermine women's access to justice. In Chapter 11, Ngaiza and Omari engage with this issue by providing a socio-legal perspective to violence against women in Tanzania. They demonstrate that the high incidence of violence against women in Tanzania is partly attributed to the historical socio-cultural practices which render the implementation of otherwise excellent laws illusory. Against this backdrop, they conclude that ensuring access to justice for victims of violence will take resolute efforts to change the socio-cultural challenges that go back in Tanzania's history.

In conclusion, all the chapters in this volume not only constitute uniquely contribute to literature but also call for action by relevant players in criminal justice structures including Africa's judiciaries, legislatures, executive arms of government and rights groups. They address key issues that are relevant to eliminating violence against women in Africa and in doing so, breathe life to the provisions of article 4 of the Maputo Protocol that requires States parties to hold perpetrators of violence to account and to eliminating all forms of violence against women and sustainable development goal 5 on elimination of all forms of violence against women and girls. The second volume of this book *Violence against women and criminal justicein Africa* carries the discussion further by engaging with two themes: *Sexual violence and vulnerability.*

References

Ramadimetja Mogale, Kathy Kovacs Burns and Solina Richter, 'Violence Against Women in South Africa: Policy Position and Recommendations' 18 *Violence Against Women* (2012): 580–594.

SangoNet Pulse, Buyisiwe Court case - Raped Again! (2009), http://www.ngopulse.org/press-release/buyisiwe-court-case-raped-again, December 7, 2020.

Shadow Report of South Africa to the Committee on Elimination of Violence Against Women on Criminal Injustice: Violence Against Women in South Africa (2010), https://tbinternet.ohchr.org/Treaties/CEDAW/Shared%20Documents/ZAF/INT_CEDAW_NGO_ZAF_48_10364_E.pdf, December 7, 2020.

United Nations Office on Drugs and Crime, The Work of UNODC on Violence Against Women (2019) 3, https://www.unodc.org/documents/commissions/CCPCJ/CCPCJ_Sessions/CCPCJ_28/Brown-bag-lunches/Brown_bag_Swen_Pfeiffer.pdf, December 7, 2020.

World Health Organisation, Violence Against Women (November 29, 2017), https://www.who.int/news-room/fact-sheets/detail/violence-against-women#:~:text=A%202013%20analysis%20conduct%20by,partner%20or%20non%2Dpartner%20sexual, December 7, 2020.

2

Violence Against Women in Africa: A Human Rights Violation Necessitating Criminal Accountability

Emma Charlene Lubaale and Ashwanee Budoo-Scholtz

1 Background

Violence against women, remarked the former United Nations Secretary General (Kofi Annan), 'knows no boundaries of geography, culture or wealth'.[1] 'It is perhaps the most shameful human rights violation', he added.[2] Decades after these thought-provoking remarks, gender-based

[1] United Nations, *Violence Against Women 'Most Shameful', Pervasive Human Rights Violation, Says Secretary-General in Remarks on International Women's Day* (March 9, 1999), https://www.un.org/press/en/1999/19990308.sgsm6919.html#:~:text=It%20knows%20no%20boundaries%20of,We%20have%20made%20some%20advances.

[2] *Ibid.*

E. C. Lubaale (✉)
Faculty of Law, Rhodes University, Grahamstown, South Africa
e-mail: e.lubaale@ru.ac.za

A. Budoo-Scholtz
Faculty of Law, University of Pretoria, Pretoria, South Africa

E. C. Lubaale and A. Budoo-Scholtz (eds.), *Violence Against Women and Criminal Justice in Africa: Volume I*, Sustainable Development Goals Series,
https://doi.org/10.1007/978-3-030-75949-0_2

violence continues to be widespread, with reports demonstrating a surge in numbers by the day.[3] It remains pervasive across settings be they public or private and cuts across ethnicity, race, geographical location, age, class, religion, education, social and economic status. The United Nations has in this regard observed that 'there is no region of the world, no country and no culture in which women's freedom from violence has been secured'.[4] At the regional level, the African Union has remarked that 'the persistent rates of violence against women and girls [have] impeded regional progress towards gender equality, sustainable development, peace and prosperity'.[5] But gender-based violence is not a new phenomenon. Historically, acts of violence against women were condoned and, in some cases, sanctioned legally. Notable are traditions and norms that gave men the right to chastise their wives.[6] In addition, women were considered property and treated as such.[7] The United Nations, in its Declaration on the Elimination of Violence Against Women, has affirmed that 'violence against women is a manifestation of historically unequal power relations between men and women, which have led to domination over and discrimination against women by men and to the prevention of the full advancement of women'.[8]

The United Nations defines violence against women as 'any act of gender-based violence that results in, or is likely to result in physical, sexual or psychological suffering to women, including threats such as coercion or arbitrary deprivation of liberty, whether occurring in public

[3] Human Rights Watch, *Submission to the UN Special Rapporteur on Violence Against Women* (May 22, 2020), https://www.hrw.org/news/2020/05/22/human-rights-watch-submission-un-special-rapporteur-violence-against-women., Office of the High Commissioner for Human Rights, *Violence Against Women*, https://www.ohchr.org/EN/Issues/Women/WRGS/Pages/VAW.aspx, Amnesty International, *South Africa: Gender-Based Violence and Femicide Offenders Must Face Justice* (September 6, 2019), https://www.amnesty.org/en/latest/news/2019/09/south-africa-gender-based-violence-and-femicide-offenders-must-face-justice/.

[4] United Nations, *Ending violence against women* (2006) 28.

[5] African Union, *A Multilateral Response to Eliminate All Forms of Violence Against Women & Girls* (May 7, 2020), https://au.int/en/pressreleases/20200507/multilateral-response-eliminate-all-forms-violence-against-women-girls.

[6] World Health Organisation, Changing cultural and social norms that support violence (2009) 1–18.

[7] *Ibid*.

[8] United Nations General Assembly, *Declaration on the Elimination of Violence against Women,* preamble (1993).

or private life'.[9] The foregoing definition refers to the notion 'gender-based violence'. The notions 'violence against women' and 'gender-based violence' are used interchangeably. This definition could be criticised in the light of the fact that the term 'gender' generally refers to both male and female. In addition, it is an undeniable fact that men have in many instances been victims of violence. It could therefore be argued that reducing the definition of gender-based violence to violence against women is problematic. However, the United Nations seems to have anticipated this concern and in this regard highlighted the fact that violence against women is rooted in the inequalities that exist between women and men, with most victims of violence being women.[10] This was further clarified in General Comment 35 of the Committee on the Convention on the Elimination of all forms of Discrimination Against Women (CEDAW Committee) that presents the term 'gender-based violence against women' as a more 'precise' term.[11]

At the African Union level, the Protocol to the African Charter on Human and Peoples' Rights on the Rights of Women in Africa (Maputo Protocol) adopts a more direct definition of violence against women as 'all acts perpetrated against women which cause or could cause them physical, sexual, psychological, and economic harm, including the threat to take such acts; or to undertake the imposition of arbitrary restrictions on or deprivation of fundamental freedoms in private or public life in peace time and during situations of armed conflicts or of war'.[12] Hence, it reflects the fact that women are more prone to violence than men. Moreover, the definition is more elaborate as it includes economic harm and mentions situations of armed conflicts and war. For the purposes of this book, reference is made to the notions violence against women and gender-based violence interchangeably while it adopts the definition of the Maputo Protocol. Furthermore, the book adopts the definition of 'women' as envisaged by the Maputo Protocol. In terms of this

[9] *Ibid.*, 1.

[10] *Ibid.*, Preamble.

[11] CEDAW Committee, *General Recommendation No. 35 on Gender-Based Violence Against Women, Updating General Recommendation No. 19* July 26, 2017 CEDAW/C/GC/35 paragraph 9.

[12] The Maputo Protocol, Article 1(j).

Protocol, 'women' refers to 'people of female gender, including girls'.[13] The Maputo Protocol does not explicitly resolve the issue of whether this definition includes individuals who self-identify as women such as transgender women. A purposive interpretation of this Protocol's definition, however, leads to the conclusion that individuals who self-identify as female are included in the definition. This conclusion can be gleaned from the fact that the Protocol categorically uses the term 'gender' rather than 'sex'. While sex and gender are often used interchangeably, they mean two different things. Sex refers to a set of biological attributes in human beings while gender entails an individual's socially constructed role, identity, behaviour and expression. For purposes of this book therefore, 'women' includes individuals who, despite not being of the female sex, self-identify as female.

Violence against women has taken different expressions including rape, domestic violence, stalking, trafficking of women, forced prostitution, sexual harassment, female genital mutilation, sexual slavery, femicide, child marriage, crimes against women in the name of honour, harmful cultural practices, gender-related killings, forced abortion, forced sterilisation, prevention of access to contraception and abortion services, online abuse, physical violence and psychological violence.[14] While all women are generally susceptible to violence, some women are more vulnerable than others. Notable are women in situations of armed conflict, migrant/displaced and refugee women, women from indigenous and minority communities, queer women, homeless women, older women, widows, women in remote or rural communities, those involved in commercial sex work, women in situations of detention, women living with HIV/ AIDS and women with disabilities.[15] In the context of Africa, the prevalence of these situations has meant that a considerable number of women are vulnerable and have in fact experienced and continue to experience violence in these circumstances.

The offensiveness of violence against women lies not just in the acts of violence against them, it is also in the devastating consequences it has on

---

[13] The Maputo Protocol, Article 1(k).

[14] United Nations, *International Day for the Elimination of Violence Against Women* (November 25, 2019), https://www.un.org/en/events/endviolenceday/.

[15] *Ibid.*

them and the society at large. The World Health Organisation reports that violence is the primary cause of death and injury of women in homes.[16] This Organisation considers it more lethal than cancer and road accidents.[17] It documents a number of health consequences of violence against women including physical injuries and disability, unwanted pregnancy and unsafe abortion, pregnancy and birth complications, sexually transmitted infections including HIV, traumatic gynaecological fistula, depression and anxiety, eating and sleep disorders, harmful drug and alcohol use, low self-esteem, post-traumatic stress disorder, self-harm, gastrointestinal disorders, chronic pain syndromes, chronic health problems, maternal mortality and other pregnancy-related consequences and increased use and cost of health services.[18] The burden that violence against women places on women and the health care systems cannot be over emphasised. For example, female genital mutilation, a form of violence pervasive in Africa, is known to cause bleeding and infection, urinary tract infections, challenges in childbirth and sometimes death.[19] Most of the women subjected to this procedure do not have the financial resources to address the health issues resulting from it and for many, death and chronic health challenges have been the result.[20]

In virtually all settings, women experience violence; however, in the context of Africa, there are a number of factors that make women more vulnerable. The prevalence of armed conflict and violence across the African continent has meant that a considerable number of women are likely to become victims of the violence that accompanies these situations such as rape as a weapon of warfare.[21] Equally notable is the fact that

---

[16] World Health Organisation, *Injuries and Violence: The Facts* (2014) 1–20, https://apps.who.int/iris/bitstream/handle/10665/149798/9789241508018_eng.pdf?sequence=1.

[17] *Ibid.*

[18] World Health Organisation, *Understanding and Addressing Violence Against Women: Health Consequences* (2012) 1–8.

[19] World Health Organisation, Understanding And Addressing Violence Against Women: Female Genital Mutilation (2012) 1–8.

[20] Masresha Andarge, *The Difficulties of Ending Female Genital Mutilation (FGM): Case of Afar Pastoralist Communities in Ethiopia* (2014) 32, https://www.ohchr.org/Documents/Issues/Women/WRGS/FGM/NGOs/ActionForIntegratedSustainableDevelopmentAssociation.pdf.

[21] Bakken I. Vik and Siri A. Rustad, *Conflict Trends in Africa 1989–2017* (2018), https://reliefweb.int/report/world/conflict-trends-africa-1989-2017.

the rights of sexual minorities remain largely undermined, with many of them constantly suffering violence.[22] For example, many African countries still maintain criminal codes that punish women on account of their sexual orientation.[23] The implication of this is that sexual minorities including lesbians and transgender women are at a higher risk of violence. Also unique to most African states are the archaic and dated applicable criminal laws. Most of the criminal codes in African states are a remnant of colonialism. These codes found their way into Africa's legal systems through the wave of colonialism. Upon attaining independence from the west, most African states retained these codes. Not many of them have been subjected to reform. For example, some of these codes still criminalise sodomy, homosexuality, adultery and sex work.[24] Many hardly have comprehensive provisions for protection and redress of violence against women. The consequence of this is that most African states do not have adequate legal and policy frameworks on protection of women.

Also unique to Africa are deeply entrenched cultural practices and social norms. Examples in this regard include widow inheritance, denying women the right to own or inherit property; female genital mutilation; and polygamy. These norms have created and maintained an environment for violence against women to thrive. It is also notable that Africa is considered to be the poorest continent globally.[25] Studies reveal that over 40% of Africa's population lives below the poverty line,

---

[22] Maguire Sebastian, 'The Human Rights of Sexual Minorities in Africa' 35 *California Western International Law Journal* (2004): 1–52; Muthien Bernedette, 'The Status of Sexual Minorities in Southern Africa' (2009): 1–29, https://www.oxfam.de/system/files/The_status_of_sexual_minorities_in_Southern_Africa_--_FINAL.pdf.

[23] See, e.g., the Penal Code Act of Uganda Chapter 120, Sect. 145 and the Malawian Penal Code Chapter 7, Sects. 156 & 157. These laws criminalise vague conduct such as unnatural sexual practices and indecent practices which have been vaguely interpreted to the detriment of women who engage in activities such as sex work. While these codes do not explicitly criminalise sexual orientation, they have been relied on to harass women on account of their sexual orientation. On this, see, e.g., Ugandan cases of *Victor Juliet Mukasa and Yvonne Oyo v The Attorney General of Uganda*, Misc. Cause No. 247 (2006).

[24] *Ibid.*

[25] World Bank, *Poverty in a Rising Africa: Africa Poverty Report* (2016) 5, http://documents.worldbank.org/curated/en/949241467996692059/pdf/103948-PUB-POVERTY-AFRICA-Box394870B-PUBLIC.pdf.

earning less than two dollars a day.[26] Women are on the extreme end of the vulnerability continuum in as far as poverty is concerned as many have limited access to resources including land and secure employment. For these poor women, the risk of experiencing violence is much higher because opportunities to either report, or flee from abuse are limited due to their dependence on perpetrators. Poor women are also more vulnerable to sexual exploitation including human trafficking.[27] In addition, the consequences of abuse against poor women are severe because poverty either deprives them of the resources to access health care, or the poor state of the health systems in most African countries renders access to the highest attainable standard of health care a myth. Reports, for example, suggest that most women subjected to female genital mutilation live in rural areas, with no access to health services.[28] Many cannot afford the necessary private health care services to address the health consequences resulting from female genital mutilation.[29] Quite a number therefore end up either dead or living with the disastrous consequences of this procedure. Moreover, with reports documenting a dramatic surge in cases of gender-based violence since the outbreak of the Covid-19 pandemic,[30] women in Africa are likely to suffer the brunt of such violence because of the vulnerable conditions they find themselves such as poverty.

With the pervasiveness of violence against women, it is less of a surprise that the statistics on violence against women have reached pandemic proportions. The United Nations estimates that globally, up to 35% of women worldwide have experienced some form of physical or

[26] *Ibid.*

[27] World Health Organisation, *Understanding and Addressing Violence Against Women: Human Trafficking* (2012) 1–8.

[28] Masresha Andarge, *The Difficulties of Ending Female Genital Mutilation* (2014) 32, https://www.ohchr.org/Documents/Issues/Women/WRGS/FGM/NGOs/ActionForIntegratedSustainableDevelopmentAssociation.pdf.

[29] *Ibid.*

[30] United Nations Population Fund, *Millions at Risk of Gender-Based Violence if COVID-19 Pandemic is Prolonged*, May 26, 2020, https://www.cfr.org/blog/millions-risk-gender-based-violence-if-covid-19-pandemic-prolonged.

sexual violence.[31] In the context of Africa, the United Nations Population Fund's study in Eastern and Sothern Africa has estimated that up to 20% of women between the ages of 15 and 24 reported experiencing some form of sexual violence.[32] These numbers are not just alarming but a cause for concern. Even more disquieting are reports documenting that a considerable number of cases of violence against women go unreported.[33] In some cases, the data relevant to paint a clear picture of the state of violence against women is not up to date. Effectively then, these percentages are the very tip of the iceberg in as far as violence against women is concerned.

But violence against women has not left women activist movements silent. There is greater visibility of activism in response to the heightened increase in the atrocities committed against women. These movements go back in history, with the first wave of such movements dating back to the latter part of the nineteenth century and the early years of the twentieth century.[34] This period saw feminist groups call for equal treatment of women in several aspects including the right to vote and access to work. The period between 1960 and 1970 saw another wave of feminist movements. This wave was mainly characterised by radical feminism.[35] Globalisation brought with it a third wave of feminist movements. This wave highlighted the intersectionality between discrimination against women and issues of class, race, age and gender.[36] In the 1970s, feminist movements began to slot discussions of violence against women in the overall feminist discourse.[37] This history set the pace for activist movements on issues of women. Over the years, several activist movements

---

31 United Nations, *Facts and Figures: Ending Violence Against Women* (2019), https://www.unwomen.org/en/what-we-do/ending-violence-against-women/facts-and-figures.

32 The United Nations Population Fund, Gender-Based Violence: What Do We Do (2020), https://esaro.unfpa.org/en/topics/gender-based-violence.

33 Muluken Dessalegn Muluneh, Virginia Stulz, Lyn Francis and Kingsley Agho, 'Gender Based Violence Against Women in Sub-Saharan Africa: A Systematic Review and Meta-Analysis of Cross-Sectional Studies' 17 *International Journal of Environmental Research and Public Health* (2020): 1–21.

34 History, *Feminism's Long History* (2019), https://www.history.com/topics/womens-history/feminism-womens-history.

35 *Ibid.*

36 *Ibid.*

37 *Ibid.*

have championed causes on elimination of violence against women. Many of the activist movements, be they local, national, regional or international, can be credited for reforms to laws, with the enactment of some national and international framework directly linked to their campaigns and activism.[38]

Progress has been made and this is evident in frameworks at national, regional and international levels. Examples in this regard include the enactment of a range of international regulatory frameworks specific to issues of women including the United Nations Convention on the Elimination of all forms of Discrimination Against Women,[39] the United Nations Declaration on Elimination of all forms of Violence Against Women,[40] the United Nations Resolution Strengthening crime prevention and criminal justice responses to violence against women[41] and the General Assembly Resolution on Taking Action Against Gender-Related Killing of Women and Girls.[42] At the regional level, mention can be made of the Protocol to the African Charter on Human and Peoples' Rights of Women in Africa commonly referred to as the Maputo Protocol.[43] Despite being similar to the CEDAW in some respects, this instrument addresses continent-specific issues including polygamy, child marriages, harmful cultural practices and violence in situations of armed conflict.

The pervasiveness of violence against women has also seen it secure a slot in development goals globally and regionally. Agenda 2063 of the African Union, adopted in 2015, is a 'shared framework for inclusive growth and sustainable development for Africa to be realised in the next 50 years'[44] and envisages an Africa where gender equality is achieved,

[38] Mahnaz Afkhami, Yakın Ertürk and Ann Elizabeth Mayer (eds) *Feminist Advocacy, Family Law and Violence Against Women* (2019) 1–259.

[39] United Nations Convention on the Elimination of all forms of Discrimination Against Women (1979).

[40] United Nations Declaration on Elimination of all forms of Violence Against Women (1993).

[41] United Nations General Assembly Resolution, Strengthening Crime Prevention And Criminal Justice Responses to Violence Against Women (2011).

[42] United Nations General Assembly Resolution, Taking Action Against Gender-Related Killing of Women and Girls (2014).

[43] Protocol to the African Charter on Human and Peoples' Rights of Women in Africa (2003).

[44] African Union Commission, *Agenda 2063: The Africa We Want* (2015) 2.

with no woman left behind.[45] Although it does not expressly mention violence against women, it includes its elimination since gender equality cannot be achieved if women are still being subjected to violence. Agenda 2040 adopted in 2016 emphasises protection of children (including girls) against violence, exploitation, neglect and abuse by 2040.[46] This Agenda was adopted by the African Committee of Experts on the Rights and Welfare of the Child. It focusses on fostering an Africa fit for children, making mention of some of the most pervasive forms of violence against in Africa including female genital mutilation and under-age marriages.[47] Adopted in the same year as Agenda 2063, Goal 5 of the United Nations Sustainable Development Goals (SDGs), which aims at achieving gender equality and empowering all women and girls by 2030,[48] specifically targets violence against women. Target 5.1 provides for the elimination of 'all forms of violence against all women and girls in the public and private spheres, including trafficking and sexual and other types of exploitation' while Target 5.2 mentions 'all harmful practices, such as child, early and forced marriage and female genital mutilation'. The fact that it has a separate target for harmful practices, which can also be considered as violence against women, demonstrates that the SDGs were adopted bearing in mind that some practices further exacerbate violence against women and they need to be individually targeted.

The target of elimination of all forms of violence against women by 2030 is incontestably commendable given the rifeness of this plague. This goal touches at the core of a challenge that has been around for generations. Suffice it to note that the SDGs came into effect in 2015 with 2030 being just ten years away. Bearing this in mind, it is critical to not only reflect on the progress made, but also the preparedness of the systems in Africa to deliver on this target. In this book, criminal accountability is considered a key strategy amongst the multiple strategies on elimination of violence against women. This chapter conceptualises freedom from violence as a human right that all women in Africa are

---

45 *Ibid.*, Aspirations 3 and 6.

46 African Committee of Experts on the Rights and Welfare of the Child, Agenda 2040: Fostering an Africa fit for children (2016), Aspiration 7.

47 *Ibid.*

48 United Nations, *Sustainable Development Goals* (2015).

entitled to. Being a right, it comes with corresponding obligations on the part of the state. These obligations include the mandate to establish effective structures to ensure that victims of violence access justice. Having conceptualised freedom from violence as a human right whose violation warrants criminal accountability, the chapter locates criminal accountability within the broader framework of a multi-sectoral approach. With violence against women being a problem that thrives where impunity is condoned, criminal accountability is conceptualised as vehicle through which impunity is addressed and women's right to access justice is realised.

2 Conceptualising Violence Against Women as a Violation of Human Rights

The adoption of the Universal Declaration of Human Rights (UDHR) in 1948 laid the 'foundation' for international human rights law.[49] Its first article states that '[a]ll human beings are born free and equal in dignity and rights'.[50] Article 2 further provides that the 'rights and freedoms' in the document is applicable to everyone, 'without distinction of any kind', including on the basis of sex. Although it does not have any specific provision relating to discrimination or violence against women, its articles 1 and 2 imply that women must be treated on an equal basis as men and not be subjected to violence on the basis of their sex. The UDHR gave birth to several documents,[51] the most relevant of which, in the context of violence against women, is the Convention on the Elimination of Discrimination Against Women (CEDAW) in 1979. The 16 substantive provisions of the CEDAW aim at eliminating discrimination against women in different spheres of life. However, apart from article

---

[49] Website of the United Nations, *The Foundation of International Human Rights Law* (2020), https://www.un.org/en/sections/universal-declaration/foundation-international-human-rights-law/index.html.

[50] Universal Declaration of Human Rights (1948), Article 1.

[51] The International Covenant on Civil and Political Rights and the International Covenant on Economic, Social and Cultural Rights adopted in 1966, together with the UDHR, are considered as the International Bill of Rights.

6 that makes reference to women trafficking and 'exploitation of prostitution of women', there is no other article that specifically provides for the elimination of violence against women. It instead provides a 'gender specific framework on the elimination of all forms of discrimination against women that encompasses violence against women'.[52]

This was rather disappointing given that there were several movements in the early 1980s that laid emphasis on violence against women as a human rights issue.[53] For instance, the 1980 Copenhagen World Conference of the UN Decade for Women called on states to enact and implement legislation to eliminate all forms of violence against women.[54] Additionally, the World Conference to Review and Appraise the Achievements of the UN Decade for Women held in Nairobi in 1985 recommended governments to, amongst others, take 'effective measures' to 'identify, prevent and eliminate all violence' against women.[55] Hence, around the same time the CEDAW was adopted, women's rights movements were engaging with the UN on violence against women as a human right issue, with the outcome documents requiring states to take steps to eliminate violence against women. It was therefore illogical for the UN to not expressly consider violence against women as a public matter while drafting the CEDAW.[56]

This lacuna of the CEDAW was filled by the CEDAW Committee, established under Part V of the document 'for the purpose of considering

---

52 Dubravka Šimonvić, 'Global and Regional Standards on Violence Against Women: The Evolution and Synergy of the CEDAW and Istanbul Conventions' 36 *Human Rights Quarterly* (2014): 590.

53 See generally Rashida Manjoo, 'Normative Developments on Violence Against Women in the United Nations System' in Rashida Manjoo and Jackie Jones (eds), *The Legal Protection of Women from Violence: Normative Gaps in International Law* (2018); Elizabeth Evatt, 'Finding a Voice for Women's Rights: The Early Days of CEDAW,' 32 *The George Washington International Law Review* (2002): 543; Jane Roberts Chapman 'Violence against women as a violation of human rights' 17 *Social Justice: Criminality, Imprisonment and Women's Rights in the 1990s* (1990): 54.

54 United Nations, *Report of the World Conference of the United Nations Decade for Women: Equality, Development and Peace,* Copenhagen A/CONF.94/35 (14 to 30 July 1980).

55 United Nations, *Report of the World Conference to Review and Appraise the Achievements of the United Nations Decade for Women: Equality, Development and Peace* Nairobi A/CONF.116/28/Rev.1 (July 15–26 1985) Paragraph 231.

56 Office of the High Commissioner for Human Rights, *Violence Against Women,* https://www.ohchr.org/EN/Issues/Women/WRGS/Pages/VAW.aspx.

the progress made in the implementation'. The CEDAW Committee, since its third session frequently started making reference to elimination of violence against women in its state reporting procedure.[57] Initially not making reference to specific articles of the CEDAW when discussing violence against women, it started linking the questions to the separate articles as from its sixth session.[58] The CEDAW Committee subsequently adopted General Recommendation 12 that requires states to report on the following concerning elimination violence against women: the existing legislation, other measures adopted, existence of support services and statistical data.[59] As a culmination of its efforts in framing violence against women as a human rights issue, the CEDAW Committee, with input from women's rights organisations, adopted General Recommendation 19 in 1992 during its 11th session.[60]

General Recommendation 19 presents gender-based violence 'as a form of discrimination that seriously inhibits women's ability to enjoy rights and freedoms on a basis of equality with men',[61] thus tying it to Article 1 of the CEDAW. It also states that gender-based violence is included in the definition of discrimination against women since it is violence that is 'directed against a woman because she is a woman' and affects her disproportionately.[62] An article does not necessarily need to have the term violence against women for it to be breached in such instances.[63] It further mentions that the provisions of the CEDAW cannot be fully implemented without states taking 'positive measures to eliminate all forms of violence against women'.[64] It emphasises that violence against women 'impairs or nullifies' the enjoyment of the following human rights by women under international human rights

[57] Elizabeth Evatt *supra* note 59, 544–545.

[58] *Ibid.*

[59] CEDAW Committee, *General Recommendation No 12: Violence Against Women* adopted during its eighth session 1989.

[60] CEDAW Committee, *General Recommendation No 19: Violence Against Women* adopted during its 11th session in 1992.

[61] *Ibid* paragraph 1.

[62] *Ibid* paragraph 6.

[63] *Ibid.*

[64] *Ibid* paragraph 4.

law[65]: (a) the right to life; (b) the right not to be subject to torture or to cruel, inhuman or degrading treatment or punishment; (c) the right to equal protection according to humanitarian norms in time of international or internal armed conflict; (d) the right to liberty and security of person; (e) the right to equal protection under the law; (f) the right to equality in the family; (g) the right to the highest standard attainable of physical and mental health; (h) the right to just and favourable conditions of work. In addition to elaborating on how violence against women affects the different human rights of women, General Recommendation 19 gives specific comments on the relationship of violence against women with the different articles of the CEDAW.[66] General Recommendation 19 also clarifies that violence against women is not limited to acts of governments but also of private actors, where government has to apply due diligence to prevent such acts.[67] Therefore, even if the CEDAW does not specify how violence against women is a human rights violation, General Recommendation 19 clarifies the same.

Following the adoption of General Comment 19 in 1992, there were several developments in reinforcing violence against women as a human rights issue. In June 1993, The Vienna Declaration and Programme of Action[68] considered gender-based violence as 'incompatible with the dignity and worth of the human person'[69] and called on General Assembly to speed up its efforts to adopt the draft Declaration in Elimination of Violence Against Women.[70] In the same year, the General Assembly of the UN adopted the Declaration on the Elimination of Violence Against Women.[71] This Declaration's objective was to 'strengthen and complement' the CEDAW in eliminating violence against women.[72] It echoes General Recommendation 19 of the

---

65 *Ibid* paragraph 7.

66 *Ibid* paragraphs 10 to 23.

67 *Ibid* paragraph 9.

68 Adopted by the World Conference on Human Rights in Vienna on June 25, 1993.

69 Vienna Declaration and Programme of Action Paragraph 18.

70 Vienna Declaration and Programme of Action Paragraph 38.

71 United Nations General Assembly, *Declaration on the Elimination of Violence against Women* (1993).

72 United Nations General Assembly, *Declaration on the Elimination of Violence against Women,* Preamble.

CEDAW Committee in that it presents violence against women as 'an obstacle to the achievement of equality' and as a violation of women's fundamental rights and freedoms.[73] It goes a step further than General Recommendation 19 of the CEDAW Committee and mentions that some groups of women are more prone to violence: 'women belonging to minority groups, indigenous women, refugee women, migrant women, women living in rural or remote communities, destitute women, women in institutions or in detention, female children, women with disabilities, elderly women and women in situations of armed conflict'.[74]

The Declaration on the Elimination of Violence Against Women was the first legal document to provide for a comprehensive definition of violence against women.[75] It adopted similar rights' violations listed in General Recommendation 19 of the CEDAW Committee except that it modified 'the right to equality in the family'[76] to 'the right to equality',[77] and replaces 'the right to equal protection according to humanitarian norms in time of international or internal armed conflict'[78] with 'the right to be free from all forms of discrimination'.[79] Hence, it was more liberal in that it did not restrict equality within the family. Moreover, the non-inclusion of equal protection of laws in time of international or internal armed conflict might be due to the fact that there is already a provision on right to equal protection under the law that applies in all situations. The addition of the right to be free from all forms of discrimination reinforces violence against women as limiting women's enjoyment of their rights and freedoms on an equal basis as men. In addition to the definition of violence against women and the rights being violated by the

---

73 United Nations General Assembly, *Declaration on the Elimination of Violence against Women,* Preamble.

74 *Ibid.*

75 United Nations General Assembly, *Declaration on the Elimination of Violence Against Women* Articles 1 and 2: see Sect. 1 above.

76 CEDAW Committee, *General Recommendation No 19: Violence Against Women* Paragraph 7(f).

77 United Nations General Assembly, *Declaration on the Elimination of Violence against Women* Article 3(b).

78 CEDAW Committee, *General Recommendation No 19: Violence Against Women* Paragraph 7(c).

79 United Nations General Assembly, *Declaration on the Elimination of Violence against Women* Article 3(e).

same, it imposes obligations on states to combat violence against women which are discussed in Sect. 3 below.

The years 1992 and 1993 can therefore be considered as milestone years in framing violence against women as a human rights issue. Since then, there have been several developments internationally to reinforce the protection of women against violence. For instance, in 1994, the UN Commission on Human Rights appointed a Special Rapporteur on Violence Against Women, including its causes and consequences.[80] In 1995, during the Fourth World Conference on Women, violence against women was considered as a critical area of concern for the realisation of women's rights and the Plan of Action elaborated on several steps that states must take to eliminate the same.[81]

More recently, in 2017, the CEDAW Committee adopted its General Recommendation 35[82] that updates the cornerstone General Recommendation 19. General Recommendation 35 was revolutionary in that it presents the prohibition of violence against women as a principle of customary international law.[83] It did so basing itself on the *opinio juris* and state practice since General Recommendation 19. General Recommendation 35, however, expressed concern that despite comprehensive international standards protecting women from violence, many states were still behind in the enactment and implementation of adequate laws that address violence against women.[84] This might be because they have the status of soft laws and are therefore only quasi-judicial and do not have the same force as a treaty. This acts as an obstacle in the protection of women from violence since they are not legally binding and can

[80] Office of the High Commissioner for Human Rights, *Question of integrating the rights of women into the human rights mechanisms of the United Nations and the elimination of violence against women*, 1994/1945 (1994) paragraph 6.

[81] Fourth World Conference on Women, *Beijing Declaration and Platform for Action* (September 4–15, 1995).

[82] CEDAW Committee *General Recommendation No. 35 on gender-based violence against women, updating General Recommendation No. 19* 26 July 2017 CEDAW/C/GC/35.

[83] CEDAW Committee *General Recommendation No. 35* paragraph 2.

[84] CEDAW Committee *General Recommendation No. 35* paragraph 7.

therefore give states an escape route.[85] There have been initiatives by civil society organisations, in collaboration with the UN Special Rapporteur on Violence Against Women, its Causes and Consequences to adopt a new protocol or a treaty on violence against women.[86] This will ensure that there is legally binding framework at the international level under which states can be held accountable.[87] Moreover, this new treaty could include new forms of violence that the digital age presents.[88] Nevertheless, such a protocol or treaty has not yet materialised due to several challenges such as fear of non-ratification, high cost implications,[89] lack of political/institutional will and duplication.[90] Thus, as it stands, standards relating to violence against women at the UN level emanate from soft laws, even if violence against women has been given the status of customary international law.

The UN standards apply to all its member countries. However, to bring the issue home, it is important to demonstrate how the African Union views violence against women.[91] The situation at the African Union level is different from that of the UN. The Organisation of African Unity (now the AU), following external pressure and democratisation in African countries,[92] formalised the African human rights system

[85] Richard B Bilder, 'Beyond Compliance: Helping Nations Cooperate' in Dinah Shelton (ed) *Commitment and Compliance: The Role of Non-Binding Norms in the International Legal System* (2000) 71–72.

[86] Human Rights Council, *Report of the Special Rapporteur on violence against women, its causes and consequences, Rashida Manjoo* May 28, 2014 (A/HRC/26/38) Paragraph 10.

[87] Ronagh McQuigg, 'Is it time for a UN Treaty on Violence Against Women?' 22 *International Journal of Human Rights* (2018): 305–324.

[88] Aisha K Gill, 'Introduction: Violence Against Women and the Need for International Law' in Rashida Manjoo and Jackie Jones (eds), *The Legal Protection of Women from Violence: Normative Gaps in International Law* (2018).

[89] Human Rights Council, *Report of the Special Rapporteur on Violence Against Women, Its Causes and Consequences, Rashida Manjoo* May 28, 2014 (A/HRC/26/38) Paragraph 10.

[90] Ronagh McQuigg, 'Is it Time for a UN Treaty on Violence Against Women?' *International Journal of Human Rights* 22, (2018): 319–322.

[91] See generally Nicholas Wasonga Orago and Maria Nassali, 'The African human rights system: Challenges and potential in Addressing Violence Against Women in Africa' in Rashida Manjoo and Jackie Jones (eds) *The Legal Protection of Women from Violence: Normative Gaps in International Law* (2018).

[92] Mutua Makau, 'The construction of the African human rights system: Prospects and pitfalls', in Power S and Allison G (eds) *Realising human rights: Moving from inspiration to impact* (2000) 143–166, 145.

by drafting and adopting the African Charter on Human and Peoples' Rights (African Charter)[93] of 1981 that entered into force in 1986. Article 2 of the African Charter provides for non-discrimination on the basis of, amongst others, sex, in the implementation of the rights and freedoms of the document. It uses a gender-neutral term for its articles which implies that the rights therein are applicable to both men and women. Moreover, Article 18(3) of the African Charter requires states to eliminate 'every discrimination against women and also ensure the protection of the rights of the woman and the child as stipulated in international declarations and conventions. This article therefore encompasses the soft law provisions of the UN concerning violence against women. The African Charter also establishes the African Commission on Human and Peoples' Rights (African Commission) 'to promote human and peoples' rights and ensure their protection in Africa'.[94] While implementing its duties, the African Commission can draw inspiration from 'international law on human and peoples' rights', including instruments adopted by the UN.[95] This implies that if there is a *lacuna* concerning violence against women at the regional level, the African Commission, while exercising its functions, can rely on standards of elimination of violence against women at the UN level.

This was confirmed in the case of *Egyptian Initiative for Personal Rights and Interights versus Arab Republic of Egypt* (Egyptian case).[96] The complainants in this case alleged that the state failed to prosecute perpetrators of sexual and physical violence on the ground that it was impossible to identify them despite the fact that the complainants could clearly identify them.[97] The complainants alleged violations of several articles of the African Charter, including Articles 2 and 18(3). In making their submissions under Article 18(3), the complainants stated that this case is an opportunity for the African Commission to 'confirm

---

93 Viljoen Frans, 'Africa's contribution to the development of international human rights and humanitarian law' *African Human Rights Law Journal* (2001):18–39.

94 African Charter, Article 30.

95 African Charter, Articles 60 and 61.

96 *Egyptian Initiative for Personal Rights and Interights versus Arab Republic of Egypt* African Commission December 16, 2011 Communication No. 323/2006.

97 Egyptian case, paragraphs 5–7, 9 11, 14, 17–18 and 22.

that violence against women can amount to discrimination under the African Charter'.[98] Therefore, states have the obligation to prosecute and punish perpetrators of violence against women. The African Commission combined Articles 2 and 18(3) of the African Charter together and stated that under these articles, states have to ensure that women are protected from discrimination.[99] It then proceeded to establish the relationship between discrimination and gender-based violence by making reference to the Maputo Protocol,[100] the CEDAW and General Recommendation 19 of the CEDAW Committee.[101] It came to the conclusion, amongst others, that the acts of violence were gender specific and discriminatory against women.[102] This case can be used to demonstrate that the African Charter encompasses violence against women.

However, to emphasise on the phenomenon, the Maputo Protocol, adopted as a supplement to the African Charter,[103] contains several provisions relating to the elimination of violence against women. The document was adopted to, amongst others, give effect to states' commitments 'to take concrete steps to give greater attention to the human rights of women in order to eliminate all forms of discrimination and of gender-based violence against women'.[104] The document is the first legally binding document at the AU level that provides definitions for discrimination against women[105] and violence against women.[106] Although most of the articles in the Maputo Protocol can be interpreted to include violence against women, it contains several provisions that expressly mention the same even if it omits some pertinent forms of violence against women such as marital rape and violence against

[98] Egyptian case, paragraph 87.

[99] Egyptian case paragraph 119.

[100] Egypt had not yet ratified the Maputo Protocol at the time of the facts.

[101] Egyptian case paragraphs 120–123.

[102] Egyptian case paragraphs 142–154.

[103] African Charter, Article 66.

[104] Maputo Protocol, Preamble.

[105] Maputo Protocol, Article 1(f): 'Discrimination against women' means any distinction, exclusion or restriction or any differential treatment based on sex and whose objectives or effects compromise or destroy the recognition, enjoyment or the exercise by women, regardless of their marital status, of human rights and fundamental freedoms in all spheres of life.'.

[106] See above.

queer women: Article 3(1) in the context of the right to dignity requires States Parties to adopt and implement measures to ensure that women are protected 'from all forms of violence, particularly sexual and verbal violence'; Article 4 that focuses on the rights to life, integrity and security of the person, contains several provisions on the steps that states are obligated to take to ensure the elimination of violence against women; Article 5 imposes an obligation states to protect 'women who are at risk of being subjected to harmful practices or all other forms of violence, abuse and intolerance', including female genital mutilation[107]; in the situations of armed conflicts, states have to ensure that 'asylum seeking women, refugees, returnees and internally displaced persons' are protected from 'all forms of violence, rape and other forms of sexual exploitation'[108]; and it requires states to ensure that vulnerable women such as elderly women and women with disabilities are protected from violence.[109] Unlike the CEDAW at the international level, the Preamble of the Maputo Protocol and its articles therefore ensure a regional legal framework for the protection of women from violence. In the case of the Maputo Protocol, there is no need for speculation as to whether violence against women is a human right protected by the document. This might be due to the fact that the document was drafted in the early 2000s, with its adoption in 2003, after clarification at the UN level that violence against women was indeed a human rights violation. It was only just for the Maputo Protocol to include violence against women in its provisions to ensure state accountability in the event States Parties are unable to ensure the protection of women from violence. In addition to the African Charter and the Maputo Protocol, there are other treaties at the African Union level that consider violence against women as a breach of their human rights. For instance, the African Charter on the Rights and Welfare of the Child (African Children's Charter),[110] without specifically

[107] Maputo Protocol, Article 5(d).

[108] Maputo Protocol, Article 11(3).

[109] Maputo Protocol, Articles 22 and 23.

[110] Adopted in 1990.

mentioning gender-based violence against the girl child,[111] puts the best interest of the child[112] in the forefront and protects the girl child from, amongst others, discrimination,[113] child abuse and torture, including sexual abuse,[114] discriminatory harmful social and cultural practices such as child marriage,[115] sexual exploitation,[116] and sale, trafficking and abduction.[117]

Two other documents relevant for the protection of women against women are the Protocol to the African Charter on the Rights of Older Persons in Africa (Older Persons' Protocol)[118] and the Protocol to the African Charter on the Rights of Persons with Disabilities in Africa (African Disability Protocol)[119] although they both do not yet have the minimum number of ratifications to enter into force. However, supplementing the provisions of the Maputo Protocol on these two categories of women, both of these documents will ensure a better protection from violence against women forming part of vulnerable groups once they come into force. On the one hand, the Older Persons' Protocol provides for the elimination of discrimination against older persons,[120] for their protection from abuse and harmful traditional practices,[121] and for the protection of 'the rights of [o]lder women from violence, sexual abuse and discrimination based on gender'.[122] On the other hand, the Preamble of the African Disability Protocol raises concern at 'the multiple forms of discrimination, ...and the great risk of violence, exploitation, neglect and abuse that women and girls with disabilities

---

111 African Children's Charter, Article 2: applies to 'every human being below the age of 18 years'; Article 3 provides for non-discrimination on the basis of sex in the implementation of the provisions of the African Children's Charter.

112 African Children's Charter, Article 4.

113 African Children's Charter. Articles 3 and 26.

114 African Children's Charter, Article 16.

115 African Children's Charter, Article 21.

116 African Children's Charter, Article 27.

117 African Children's Charter, Article 29.

118 Adopted in 2016.

119 Adopted in 2018.

120 Older Persons' Protocol, Article 3.

121 Older Persons' Protocol, Article 8.

122 Older Persons' Protocol, Article 9.

face'. While providing for non-discrimination and equality between men and women in its implementation,[123] the African Disability Protocol contains several provisions that protect persons with disabilities,[124] including the protection of women and girls with disabilities 'from sexual and gender-based violence'.[125]

Complementing the treaties and protocols of the AU, the African Commission and the African Committee of Experts on the Rights and Welfare of the Child have adopted soft laws that require states to eliminate violence against women to ensure that women enjoy their rights.[126] Hence, several treaties, protocols and soft laws at the African Union level expressly protect women from violence, including the girl child, women and girls with disabilities and older women. The legal protection of women from violence is more robust at the AU level since it presents violence against women as a human rights violation not only in soft laws, but in its legally binding documents. Nevertheless, as discussed in the introductory paragraph of this chapter, this legal protection at the regional level is not translating into protection at country levels since violence against women is a very rampant phenomenon in Africa. This implies that states are facing challenges in implementing their obligations to ensure that violence against women is eliminated. The section that follows elaborates on the obligations of African states to ensure accountability for violence against women under human rights law before zooming in on the book's theme of access to justice in cases of violence against women.

---

[123] African Disability Protocol, Article 3.

[124] African Disability Protocol, Articles 9, 10, 11, 28 and 30.

[125] African Disability Protocol, Article 27.

[126] African Commission *General Comments No.1 on Article 14(1)(d) and (e) of the Protocol to the African Charter on Human and Peoples' Rights on the Rights of Women in Africa* 2012, paras 3, 7, 11 and 29; African Commission *General Comment No.2 on Article 14.1 (a), (b), (c) and (f) and Article 14.2 (a) and (c) of the Protocol to the African Charter on Human and Peoples' Rights on the Rights of Women in Africa* 2014; African Commission *General Comment No.3 On the African Charter on Human and Peoples' Rights: The Right to Life (Article 4)* 2015 para 39; African Commission *General Comment No.4: The Right to Redress for Victims of Torture and Other Cruel, Inhuman or Degrading Punishment.*

or Treatment (Article 5) 2017 paras 18, 57–61, and 79(VII); Joint General Comment of the African Commission and African Children's Committee *Ending Child Marriage* 2017 paras 12, 32, 42 and 58; African Commission *Guidelines on Combatting Sexual Violence and Its Consequences in Africa* 2017.

3 The Obligation of States to Ensure Accountability for Violence Against Women

Given that violence against women is a human rights violation, several instruments at the international level impose obligations on states to ensure accountability for the same. Once violence against women was no longer considered as a private matter, in addition to being responsible for their own acts and omissions, states were also responsible for not applying due diligence to prevent acts and omissions of non-state actors.[127] Making reference to General Recommendations 19[128] and 28 of the CEDAW Committee,[129] General Recommendation 35 states that according to the obligation of due diligence, states have to 'adopt and implement diverse measures to tackle gender-based violence against women committed by non-State actors'.[130] Concerning violence against women, these measures include 'laws, institutions and a system in place to address' the same.[131] Hence, states will be in breach of their obligations to protect women from violence not only when they themselves inflict such violence but also if they are unable to prevent other persons, including companies,[132] from doing so.

Taking this into consideration, documents concerning elimination of violence against women adopted at the international level elaborate on different states' obligations to ensure accountability. Since this research focuses on the African continent, the Maputo Protocol is used as the baseline document to elaborate on the different steps that states are obligated to take to ensure that perpetrators of violence against

---

[127] CEDAW Committee, *General Recommendation 19* paragraph 9; Article 4 of the Declaration on the Elimination of Violence Against Women; CEDAW Committee *General Recommendation 35* paragraph 24(b); and Beijing Declaration and Platform for Action paragraph 124(b).

[128] General Recommendation 19 of the CEDAW Committee paragraph 9.

[129] CEDAW Committee, *General Recommendation No.28 on the Core Obligations of States Parties under Article 2 of the Convention on the Elimination of All forms of Discrimination Against Women* 2010 (CEDAW/C/GC/28) paragraph 13.

[130] General Recommendation 35 of the CEDAW Committee, paragraph 24(b).

[131] *Ibid.*

[132] *Ibid.*

women are held accountable. States have the general obligation to adopt 'legislative, institutional and other measures', including the inclusion of gender equality in their constitution, to combat discrimination against women.[133] In addition to Article 2 of the Maputo Protocol, these steps are mentioned in most of its other articles. The African Court has not hesitated to find a country in violation of the Maputo Protocol since its laws did not criminalise acts such as child marriage, discrimination and harmful cultural practices.[134]

States also have the obligation to 'modify the social and cultural patterns of conduct of women and men' through several initiatives and this includes eliminating gender stereotypes.[135] The most relevant article in the context of accountability for violence against women is Article 4 that protects the rights to life, integrity and security of the person. Its Article 4(2), in relation to accountability for violence against women, provides as follows:

> States Parties shall take appropriate and effective measures to:
>
> (a) enact and enforce laws to prohibit all forms of violence against women including unwanted or forced sex whether the violence takes place in private or public;
>
> (b) adopt such other legislative, administrative, social and economic measures as may be necessary to ensure the prevention, punishment and eradication of all forms of violence against women;...
>
> (e) punish the perpetrators of violence against women and implement programmes for the rehabilitation of women victims;
>
> (f) establish mechanisms and accessible services for effective information, rehabilitation and reparation for victims of violence against women;
>
> (g) prevent and condemn trafficking in women, prosecute the perpetrators of such trafficking and protect those women most at risk...

---

133 Maputo Protocol, Article 2.

134 African Court on Human and Peoples' Rights, *Association Pour le Progrès et la Défense des Droits des Femmes Maliennes (APDF) and The Institute for Human Rights and Development in Africa (IHRDA) v Republic of Mali* May 11, 2018: The African Court held that Mali was in violation of the Maputo Protocol and the CEDAW since the provisions of its Family Code violated their provisions concerning discrimination against women, child marriage, harmful practices and inheritance.

135 Maputo Protocol, Article 2(2).

> (i) provide adequate budgetary and other resources for the implementation and monitoring of actions aimed at preventing and eradicating violence against women....

Therefore, in addition to laws, states have to ensure that they have a functional system that ensures the prosecution and punishment of perpetrators of violence and facilitates victims' access to information to access the justice system, including legal aid.[136] Furthermore, states have to translate their commitments into reality by providing the financial resources[137] required to sustain a system that ensures accountability for violence against women.

From the above, it is clear that there are five main obligations on African states to ensure accountability for violence against women: (1) criminalising violence against women; (2) sensitising the population about violence against women, including stereotypes; (3) ensuring access to the criminal justice system, including the setting up of institutions and legal aid; (4) punishment for perpetrators of violence against women; and (5) allocation of budgetary resources to combat violence against women.

4 The Role and Place of Criminal Accountability in Cases of Violence Against Women

The preceding sections have highlighted the prevalence of violence against women; conceptualised violence against women as a human right; pointed out the various rights undermined when women suffer violence; underscored the obligation on states to ensure that victims of obtain redress; and demonstrated the nexus between criminal accountability and the human rights obligations entrenched in the various international and regional national human rights instruments. This section illustrates that criminal justice is a means to realising the right to access to justice and the right to a remedy. Worthy to note, in terms

[136] Maputo Protocol, Article 8.

[137] See also, Maputo Protocol, Article 26(2).

of international human rights law, before one seeks justice or a remedy, they must have suffered some form of harm. Effectively, they must be victims. The Basic Principles of Justice for Victims of Crimes and Abuse of Power define 'victims' as:

> persons who individually or collectively, have suffered harm, including physical or mental injury, emotional suffering, economic loss or substantial impairment of their fundamental rights, through acts or omissions that are in violation of criminal laws operative within Member States, including those laws proscribing criminal abuse of power.[138]

In the light of the above definition, it is irrefutable that women who experience violence suffer harm, thus, placing them squarely within the ambit of 'victims'. The Basic Principles do not stop at defining 'victims'; they also emphasise that access to justice is an entitlement for all victims of crimes. In this regard, these Principles implore states to ensure that victims of crime access mechanisms of justice and obtain redress promptly. States are also to ensure that 'proper assistance to victims seeking access to justice' is provided.

Access to justice is a fundamental right guaranteed under several international human rights instruments including the Protocol to the African Charter on Human and Peoples' Rights of Women in Africa.[139] The United Nations has further buttressed the critical nature of access to justice by listing it amongst the targets to be met by 2030.[140] Various national constitutions in Africa including the Constitution of the Republic of South Africa also guarantee this right in very strong terms.[141] To give force to this right, the CEDAW calls on states 'to establish legal protection of the rights of women on an equal basis with men and to ensure through competent national tribunals and other public institutions and the effective protection of women against any

[138] United Nations General Assembly Resolution, Declaration of Basic Principles of Justice for Victims of Crime and Abuse of Power (1985) paragraph 1.

[139] Article 8 of the Protocol to the African Charter on Human and Peoples' Rights of Women in Africa (2003).

[140] United Nations General Assembly, Transforming our world: The 2030 Agenda for Sustainable Development (2015) Target 16.

[141] The Constitution of the Republic of South Africa (1996), Sect. 34.

act of discrimination'.[142] In one of its General Recommendations, the Committee on the CEDAW has given meaningful content to the notion of access to justice by emphasising that states must ensure that women access affordable, timely and effective remedies when they approach judicial platforms to secure justice for the violations they experience.[143] At the judicial level, the Committee has pointed out that access to justice requires all judicial bodies 'to refrain from engaging in any act or practice of discrimination or gender-based violence against women'.[144] With the documented prevalence of violence against women, access to justice is an entitlement that all women who suffer violence should enjoy. As discussed in the preceding section, violence against women violates the full spectrum of guaranteed rights including dignity and equality. In this regard, access to justice constitutes a vehicle through which the harm caused by such violence is addressed.

The right to access to justice is inextricably linked to the right to a remedy. The latter derives force from treaties, customary international law and national laws.[145] The Principles on the Rights to Remedy give meaningful content to the obligations that come with this right by providing that:

> The obligation to respect, ensure respect for and implement international human rights law and international humanitarian law as provided for under the respective bodies of law, includes, inter alia, the duty to:
>
> (a) Take appropriate legislative and administrative and other appropriate measures to prevent violations;
>
> (b) Investigate violations effectively, promptly, thoroughly and impartially and, where appropriate, take action against those allegedly responsible in accordance with domestic and international law;

142 United Nations Convention on the Elimination of all forms of Discrimination Against Women (1979), Article 2.

143 Committee on the Elimination of Discrimination against Women, *General recommendation on women's access to justice* (2015).

144 Committee on the Elimination of Discrimination against Women, *General recommendation No. 35 on gender-based violence against women, updating general recommendation No. 19* (2017) paragraph 26.

145 United Nations General Assembly, *Resolution on Basic Principles and Guidelines on the Right to a Remedy and Reparation for Victims of Gross Violations of International Human Rights Law and Serious Violations of International Humanitarian Law* (2005) 1.

(c) Provide those who claim to be victims of a human rights or humanitarian law violation with equal and effective access to justice, as described below, irrespective of who may ultimately be the bearer of responsibility for the violation; and

(d) Provide effective remedies to victims, including reparation, as described below.[146]

In the light of the above conceptualisation, the crux of the obligations of states is accountability or remedial action for harm caused. Regarding remedial action, the Maputo Protocol emphasises that the remedies provided must be appropriate, timely and effective.[147] This obligation is in line with the well-established notion that a right without a remedy is illusory and absence of a remedy suggests that the entitlements labelled as rights are not a right at all.[148] With freedom from violence consistently conceptualised as a right, the right to a remedy and the right to freedom from violence are indivisibly tied to each other. There is therefore a reasonable expectation for states to establish mechanisms that ensure that justice is accessed and also, that effective remedies are obtained by women. The mechanisms established can either be civil or criminal in nature; however, this book focusses on the latter.

Criminal justice systems play an indispensable role in the dispensation of justice for women. They have the backing of the state and the authority they possess by virtue of such backing places them in good stead to positively wield authority with a view to protecting victims who are often vulnerable and powerless. The African Commission has in this regard resolved that African states should criminalise all forms of violence against women and having done that, take steps to establish effective structures within the justice system to ensure that victims

[146] *Ibid* paragraph 3.

[147] Maputo Protocol, Article 8.

[148] Ashley v White 1703 92 ER 126, 136. In this dictum, the Court ruled that 'it is a vain thing to imagine a right without a remedy.' The African Commission on Human and Peoples' Rights has also pronounced itself on the issue of the right to a remedy. See, e.g., African Charter on Human and Peoples' Rights, *General Comment No. 4 on the right to redress for victims of torture and other cruel, inhuman or degrading punishment or treatment* (2015).

obtain justice.[149] At the international level, international criminal law platforms such as the International Criminal Court are slowly but surely becoming vehicles through which gender-based crimes are prosecuted.[150] Crime detection, prosecution, conviction and sentencing are at the heart of criminal accountability. When these processes are effectively implemented, criminal justice ensures that those who commit atrocious acts against women are punished. Of course, in an ideal world, violence against women should not occur in the first place. In the unfortunate event that violence occurs, punishment of perpetrators can deter others from committing acts of violence against women. In this regard, criminal accountability sends out a message that acts of violence against women are not to be tolerated in society. Accordingly, failure to hold perpetrators to account not only condones impunity but also undermines the rule of law.

Suffice it to note that elimination of violence against women is a goal that cannot be achieved through exclusive reliance on criminal prosecution. Coordinated efforts across sectors including the justice, social, health and media are pivotal. The need for a multi-sectoral approach resonates with the reality that there are issues pertaining to violence against women that cannot be addressed solely by criminal prosecution. For example, cases abound on African states enacting women's rights-centred laws, yet violence against women remains pervasive in these states.[151] In addition, violence against women remains a complex social challenge embedded in discriminatory social norms and an unequal society. Many of these norms have normalised gender-based violence across African societies, thus limiting the effectiveness of criminal justice. Realities such as these affirm the view that over and above criminal

[149] African Commission on Human and Peoples' Rights, *111 Resolution on the Right to a Remedy and Reparation for Women and Girls Victims of Sexual Violence* (2007).

[150] Trial Chamber VI's judgement in the case of *The Prosecutor v Bosco Ntaganda*, issued 8 July 2019, in which the ICC convicted former Congolese rebel commander, Ntaganda Bosco, on counts of war crimes and crimes against humanity. Amongst the war crimes and crimes against humanity he was convicted of was sexual violence. While the conviction has been appealed, the fact that courts are now entertaining cases of gender-based violence is itself a milestone.

[151] For commentary on this in the context of South Africa, see Ramadimetja S. Mogale, Kathy K. Burns and Solina Richter, 'Violence Against Women in South Africa: Policy Position and Recommendations,' 18 *Violence Against Women* (2012): 580–594.

prosecution, a lot more needs to be done and multiple sectors need to be involved. For example, a change in attitude remains critical. In this regard, approaches such as awareness, education, media campaigns, community-based trainings and institution-based programmes can go a long way. Empowerment of women also remains pivotal in reducing their vulnerability to abuse and exploitation. With physical and emotional harm being an inevitable consequence of violence against women, the health sector becomes an indispensable player. In summary, viewed through a multi-sectoral lens, criminal accountability is one of the many invaluable pieces that complete the puzzle of elimination of violence against women. Criminal prosecution cannot be effective without approaches from the social, economic, educational and health dimensions and vice versa. Therefore, the role and limits of criminal justice in the broader multi-sectoral approach to elimination of gender-based violence are acknowledged. It is from this perspective that this edited volume views criminal accountability and the criminal justice systems in Africa generally.

5 Conclusion and the Unanswered Questions

Several points can be deduced from this chapter. The first is that violence is a pervasive problem globally with Africa being no exception. Secondly, freedom from violence is an entitlement that places an obligation on states to protect women from all forms of violence. Thirdly, there is an obligation on states to ensure that there are structures in place to address violence against women. Fourthly, criminal prosecution, when applied in coordination with other relevant responses, will play a key role in eliminating violence against women. From a human rights perspective, criminal prosecution constitutes a vehicle through which women's right to access to justice and the right to a remedy are enforced. Effectively, no perpetrator of violence against women must go unpunished. The question that remains unresolved, however, is whether African states are delivering on criminal accountability for violence against women.

As a starting point, criminal laws are critical in responding to violence against women. They set norms and standards regarding acceptable conduct in societies and provide a basis for criminal justice practitioners to commence proceedings against perpetrators of violence against women. The United Nations reports that hundreds of countries have enacted laws on redress of violence against women.[152] It laments, however, that most of these laws are not implemented, let alone in alignment with international standards.[153] Notable also, the laws of a significant number of African countries do not criminalise most acts of violence against women. Many of them are flawed and discriminatory. This begs the question, what is the state of the criminal laws in African countries and what implication does this have for women's access to justice.

Additionally, sexual violence in its various forms is perhaps the most prevalent of all forms of violence against women. The question arises: with freedom from violence conceptualised as a human right, has freedom from sexual violence been guaranteed for women in Africa? When sexual violence occurs, have states ensured that women access justice? Better still, do the laws of African states criminalise all acts of sexual violence to arm criminal justice practitioners with the relevant legal ammunition to prosecute sexual violence against women? What about women who experience sexual violence in appalling situations such as armed conflict? Do the national frameworks in African countries ensure that these exceptional circumstances are taken into account with a view to ensuring that these women obtain justice?

Furthermore, in one of the preceding sections above, it has been emphasised that criminal justice systems cannot operate in isolation, thus making a coordinated approach critical. What are some of the limitations of criminal accountability in Africa's criminal justice systems? Are there any relevant strategies in place to help give effect to a coordinated approach?

---

152 United Nations Office on Drugs and Crime, The work of UNODC on violence against women (2019) paragraph 3, https://www.unodc.org/documents/commissions/CCPCJ/CCPCJ_Sessions/CCPCJ_28/Brown-bag-lunches/Brown_bag_Swen_Pfeiffer.pdf.

153 *Ibid.*

It has been acknowledged that violence against women knows no boundaries. It is, however, indisputable that some women are more vulnerable to abuse than others. Who are some of the vulnerable women in the context of Africa and to what extent have the criminal justice systems in Africa ensured responsiveness to these women's vulnerability with a view to ensuring that they too access justice? Furthermore, it has been consistently noted in this chapter that violence against women in Africa is a complex social problem rooted in gender inequality and deeply entrenched social and cultural norms. How are these social norms playing out in Africa and what effect are they having on criminal accountability for violence against women? What strategies would need to be invoked to ensure that these norms are dismantled and that women who suffer violence can have access to justice? Elimination of violence against women requires these and many other questions to be answered and resolved, with scholarly research being one of the entry points to advancing this goal.

References

Aisha K Gill, 'Introduction: Violence Against Women and the Need for International Law' in Rashida Manjoo and Jackie Jones (eds), *The Legal Protection of Women from Violence: Normative Gaps in International Law* (2018).

Ashley v White 1703 92 ER 126, 136.

African Charter on Human and Peoples' Rights, *General Comment No. 4 on the right to redress for victims of torture and other cruel, inhuman or degrading punishment or treatment* (2015).

African Commission on Human and Peoples' Rights, *111 Resolution on the Right to a Remedy and Reparation for Women and Girls Victims of Sexual Violence* (2007).

African Commission General Comments No.1 on Article 14(1) (d) and (e) of the Protocol to the African Charter on Human and Peoples' Rights on the Rights of Women in Africa 2012.

African Commission General Comment No.2 on Article 14.1 (a), (b), (c) and (f) and Article 14.2 (a) and (c) of the Protocol to the African Charter on Human and Peoples' Rights on the Rights of Women in Africa 2014.

African Commission General Comment No.3 On the African Charter on Human and Peoples' Rights: The Right to Life (Article 4) 2015 para 39; African Commission General Comment No.4: The Right to Redress for Victims of Torture and Other Cruel, Inhuman or Degrading Punishment or Treatment (Article 5) 2017.

African Committee of Experts on the Rights and Welfare of the Child, *Agenda 2040: Fostering an Africa fit for children* (2016).

African Court on Human and Peoples' Rights, Association Pour le Progrès et la Défense des Droits des Femmes Maliennes (APDF) and The Institute for Human Rights and Development in Africa (IHRDA) v Republic of Mali May 11, 2018.

Amnesty International, South Africa: Gender-based violence and femicide offenders must face justice (September 6, 2019), https://www.amnesty.org/en/latest/news/2019/09/south-africa-gender-based-violence-and-femicide-offenders-must-face-justice/, June 24, 2020.

Bakken I. Vik and Siri Aas Rustad, *Conflict trends in Africa 1989–2017, 2018,* https://reliefweb.int/report/world/conflict-trends-africa-1989-2017, June 24, 2020.

Committee on the Elimination of Discrimination against Women, General Recommendation No.28 on the Core Obligations of States Parties under Article 2 of the Convention on the Elimination of All forms of Discrimination Against Women 2010 (CEDAW/C/GC/28).

Committee on the Elimination of Discrimination against Women, *General Recommendation on women's access to justice* (2015).

Committee on the Elimination of Discrimination against Women, *General Recommendation No.35 on gender-based violence against women, updating General Recommendation No. 19* (2017)

Committee on the Elimination of Discrimination against Women, *General Recommendation No 12: Violence Against Women adopted during its eighth session* 1989.

Committee on the Elimination of Discrimination against Women, *General Recommendation No 19: Violence Against Women*, adopted during its 11th session in 1992.

Constitution of the Republic of South Africa (1996). History, *Feminism's Long History*, (2019), https://www.history.com/topics/womens-history/feminism-womens-history, June 5, 2020.

Dubravka Šimonvić, 'Global and Regional Standards on Violence Against Women: The Evolution and Synergy of the CEDAW and Istanbul Conventions' 36 *Human Rights Quarterly* (2014).

Elizabeth Evatt, 'Finding a Voice for Women's Rights: The Early Days of CEDAW,' 32 *The George Washington International Law Review* (2002): 543.

Egyptian Initiative for Personal Rights and Interights v Arab Republic of Egypt, African Commission December 16, 2011 Communication No. 323/2006.

Fourth World Conference on Women, *Beijing Declaration and Platform for Action* (September 4–15, 1995).

Human Rights Council, Report of the Special Rapporteur on violence against women, its causes and consequences, Rashida Manjoo May 28, 2014 (A/HRC/26/38).

Human Rights Watch, Submission to the UN Special Rapporteur on Violence Against Women, May 22, 2020, https://www.hrw.org/news/2020/05/22/human-rights-watch-submission-un-special-rapporteur-violence-against-women, June 24, 2020.

Jane Roberts Chapman 'Violence against women as a violation of human rights' 17 *Social Justice: Criminality, Imprisonment and Women's Rights in the 1990s* (1990): 54.

Joint General Comment of the African Commission and African Children's Committee Ending Child Marriage 2017 paras 12, 32, 42 and 58; African Commission Guidelines on Combatting Sexual Violence and Its Consequences in Africa 2017.

Maguire Sebastian, 'The human rights of sexual minorities in Africa' *California Western International Law Journal* 35 (2004) 1–52.

Mahnaz Afkhami, Yakın Ertürk and Ann Elizabeth Mayer (eds) *Feminist Advocacy, Family Law and Violence Against Women* (2019).

Masresha Andarge, *The Difficulties of Ending Female Genital Mutilation (FGM): Case of Afar Pastoralist Communities in Ethiopia* (2014), https://www.ohchr.org/Documents/Issues/Women/WRGS/FGM/NGOs/ActionForIntegratedSustainableDevelopmentAssociation.pdf, June 5, 2020.

Muluken Dessalegn Muluneh, Virginia Stulz, Lyn Francis and Kingsley Agho, 'Gender Based Violence against Women in Sub-Saharan Africa: A Systematic Review and Meta-Analysis of Cross-Sectional Studies' 17 *International Journal of Environmental Research and Public Health* (2020):1–21

Muthien Bernedette, The Status of Sexual Minorities in Southern Africa (2009) 1–29, https://www.oxfam.de/system/files/The_status_of_sexual_minorities_in_Southern_Africa_--_FINAL.pdf.

Mutua Makau, 'The construction of the African human rights system: Prospects and pitfalls', in Power S and Allison G (eds) *Realising Human Rights: Moving from Inspiration to Impact* (2000) 143–166.

Nicholas Wasonga Orago and Maria Nassali, 'The African human rights system: Challenges and potential in Addressing Violence Against Women in Africa' in Rashida Manjoo and Jackie Jones (eds) *The Legal Protection of Women from Violence: Normative Gaps in International Law* (2018).

Office of the High Commissioner for Human Rights, Violence against women, https://www.ohchr.org/EN/Issues/Women/WRGS/Pages/VAW.aspx, June 24, 2020.

Office of the High Commissioner for Human Rights, Question of integrating the rights of women into the human rights mechanisms of the United Nations and the elimination of violence against women, 1994/1945 (1994).

Penal Code Act Chapter 7, Malawi.

Penal Code Act Chapter 120, Uganda.

Protocol to the African Charter on Human and Peoples' Rights of Women in Africa (2003).

Ramadimetja S. Mogale, Kathy K. Burns and Solina Richter, 'Violence Against Women in South Africa: Policy Position and Recommendations' (2012) 18 *Violence Against Women.*

Rashida Manjoo, 'Normative Developments on Violence Against Women in the United Nations System' in Rashida Manjoo and Jackie Jones (eds), *The Legal Protection of Women from Violence: Normative Gaps in International Law* (2018).

Richard B Bilder, 'Beyond Compliance: Helping Nations Cooperate' in Dinah Shelton (ed) *Commitment and Compliance: The Role of Non-Binding Norms in the International Legal System* (2000) 71–72.

Ronagh McQuigg, 'Is it time for a UN Treaty on Violence Against Women?' 22 *International Journal of Human Rights* (2018): 305–324.

The Prosecutor v Bosco Ntaganda, Trial Chamber VI's judgment issued 8 July 2019.

United Nations, *Facts and figures: Ending violence against women* (2019), https://www.unwomen.org/en/what-we-do/ending-violence-against-women/facts-and-figures, June 24, 2020.

United Nations Population Fund, *Gender-Based Violence: What Do We Do*? (2020), https://esaro.unfpa.org/en/topics/gender-based-violence, June 24, 2020.

United Nations Convention on the Elimination of all forms of Discrimination Against Women (1979).

United Nations Declaration on Elimination of all forms of Violence Against Women (1993).

United Nations General Assembly Resolution, *Basic Principles and Guidelines on the Right to a Remedy and Reparation for Victims of Gross Violations of International Human Rights Law and Serious Violations of International Humanitarian Law* (2005).

United Nations General Assembly Resolution, Declaration of Basic Principles of Justice for Victims of Crime and Abuse of Power (1985)

United Nations General Assembly Resolution, *Strengthening Crime Prevention and Criminal Justice Responses to Violence Against Women* (2011).

United Nations General Assembly Resolution, *Taking action against gender-related killing of women and girls* (2014).

United Nations General Assembly Resolution, *Transforming Our World: The 2030 Agenda for Sustainable Development* (2015).

United Nations, *International Day for the Elimination of Violence against Women* (November 20, 2019), https://www.un.org/en/events/endviolenceday/.

United Nations Office on Drugs and Crime, *The work of UNODC on violence against women* (2019), https://www.unodc.org/documents/commissions/CCPCJ/CCPCJ_Sessions/CCPCJ_28/Brown-bag-lunches/Brown_bag_Swen_Pfeiffer.pdf.

United Nations Population Fund, *Millions at Risk of Gender-Based Violence if COVID-19 Pandemic is Prolonged*, https://www.cfr.org/blog/millions-risk-gender-based-violence-if-covid-19-pandemic-prolonged, June 24, 2020.

United Nations, *Report of the World Conference of the United Nations Decade for Women: Equality, Development and Peace*, Copenhagen A/CONF.94/35 (14 to 30 July 1980).

United Nations, *Report of the World Conference to Review and Appraise the Achievements of the United Nations Decade for Women: Equality, Development and Peace Nairobi*, A/CONF.116/28/Rev.1 (July 15–26 1985).

United Nations, *Violence Against Women 'Most Shameful', Pervasive Human Rights Violation, Says Secretary-General in Remarks on International Women's Day* (1999), https://www.un.org/press/en/1999/19990308.sgsm6919.html#:~:text=It%20knows%20no%20boundaries%20of,We%20have%20made%20some%20advances, June 24, 2020.

Victor Juliet Mukasa and Yvonne Oyo v The Attorney General of Uganda, Misc. Cause No. 247 (2006).

Vienna Declaration and Programme of Action, adopted by the World Conference on Human Rights in Vienna on June 25, 1993.

Website of the United Nations, The Foundation of International Human Rights Law (2020), https://www.un.org/en/sections/universal-declaration/foundation-international-human-rights-law/index.html, June 24, 2020.

World Bank, *Poverty in a Rising Africa: Africa Poverty Report* (2016), http://documents.worldbank.org/curated/en/949241467996692059/pdf/103948-PUB-POVERTY-AFRICA-Box394870B-PUBLIC.pdf, June 24, 2020.

World Health Organisation, *Injuries and Violence: The Facts* (2014), 2020. https://apps.who.int/iris/bitstream/handle/10665/149798/9789241508018_eng.pdf?sequence=1, June 24, 2020.

World Health Organisation, *Changing Cultural and Social Norms That Support Violence* (2009).

World Health Organisation, *Understanding and Addressing Violence Against Women: Female Genital Mutilation* (2012).

World Health Organisation, *Understanding and Addressing Violence Against Women: Health Consequences* (2012).

World Health Organisation, *Understanding and Addressing Violence Against Women: Human Trafficking* (2012).

Part II

Legislation and its Implementation in Addressing Violence Against Women

3

Addressing Gender-Based Violence Epidemic Through Criminal Justice: A Case Study of South Africa and the DRC

Matadi M. Tholaine and Lizelle Ramaccio Calvino

1 Introduction

Gender-based violence (GBV) is not novel nor unique and as is the case for most epidemics, it does not discriminate.[1] People worldwide, regardless of their age, race or social standard, are exposed and fall victim to violent behaviour purely based on their gender.[2] Although both men and women can experience GBV, the root of the violence is often engrained

[1] Dartnall E and Jewkes R, 'Sexual Violence Against Women: The Scope of the Problem' 27 *Best Practice & Research Clinical Obstetrics & Gynaecology* (2012): 3–13.

[2] Nelson Mandela Foreword in World Report on Woman and Health (2002).

M. M. Tholaine (✉) · L. R. Calvino
University of Zululand, Richards Bay, South Africa
e-mail: matadit@unizulu.ac.za

L. R. Calvino
e-mail: calvinol@unizulu.ac.za

E. C. Lubaale and A. Budoo-Scholtz (eds.), *Violence Against Women and Criminal Justice in Africa: Volume I*, Sustainable Development Goals Series,
https://doi.org/10.1007/978-3-030-75949-0_3

in power inequalities between genders therefore resulting in the majority of victims being women and girls.[3] What makes this phenomenon even more disheartening is the fact that the perpetrator is often not an outsider but an intimate partner (IPV), parent or a person within the inner family circle.[4] GBV is an umbrella term that includes any form of harm that is caused against a person's free will and that is underpinned by power inequalities based on gender.[5]

Accordingly, the Declaration on the Elimination of Violence Against Women (DEVAW) defines violence against women as 'any act of GBV that results in, or is likely to result in, physical, sexual or psychological harm or suffering to women, including threats of such acts, coercion or arbitrary deprivations of liberty, whether occurring in public or private life.'[6] Despite GBV globally being viewed as a profound and pervasive violation of human rights and the United Nations (UN) including the elimination of all forms of violence against women and children as a goal in terms of their Substantial Development Goals 2030,[7] the reality is that GBV cases are still rampant.[8] This is particularly evident within the African context[9] where there are several cases that involve sexual violence.[10]

In terms of the United Nations Population Fund (UNPF), the East and Southern Africa region displays high rates of sexual violence.[11] Evidently, the UNPF indicates that about 20% of women aged between

---

[3] WHO, *Global and Regional Estimates of Violence Against Women,* (2013); *UNODC, Global Study on Homicide* (2019).

[4] Interpersonal Violence, *Global and Regional Estimates of Violence Against Women, WHO, 2013; Global Study on Homicide 2019, UNODC,* (2019).

[5] European Institute on Gender Equality.

[6] Article 1 of Declaration of elimination of violence Against Women (1993).

[7] The United Nations Sustainable Development Goals (SDGs) are 17 goals with 169 targets that all 191 UN Member States have agreed to try to achieve by the year 2030.

[8] Thirty-five percent of women worldwide have experienced either non-partner sexual violence or physical and/or sexual intimate partner violence (IPV) (WHO 2013), both manifestations of Gender-Based Violence (GBV).

[9] World bank, *Ending Violence Against Women and Children. Global and Regional Trends in Women's Legal Protection Against Domestic Violence and Sexual Harassment* (2018).

[10] UNICEF, *A Familiar Face: Violence in the lives of children and adolescent (*2017).

[11] The United Nations Population Fund, *Gender-Based Violence: What Do We Do* (2020), https://esaro.unfpa.org/en/topics/gender-based-violence.

15 and 24 years have reported that they have experienced sexual violence by an intimate partner.[12] Furthermore, it indicates that in conflict or post-conflict countries such as the DRC, Mozambique, Uganda and Zimbabwe there is higher rate of sexual violence of adolescent between the age of 15 years and below.[13] It should also be noted that persistence of harmful norms, alcohol abuse, a high level of poverty, violence in urban slum areas and conflict areas are factors that fuel the high rate of violence against women and girls in Africa.[14] Accordingly, there is a need to thoroughly address GBV in African countries specifically those in crisis whilst considering if that lack of commitment and/or political will, greed and corruption may influence such high statistics.[15] In some African countries despite the enactment and promulgation of national legislative framework on GBV, law enforcement and judiciary (that forms part of the criminal justice system) are unaware of women and girls' rights.[16]

For purposes of this chapter, South Africa and the DRC have been selected as case studies for three reasons. Firstly, both countries ratified international and regional (CEDAW and Maputo Protocol) instruments protecting women and girls against any forms of violence.[17] As State Parties, they are accordingly compelled to take necessary measures to end all forms of discrimination and violence against women and girls. Secondly, despite an available legislative framework and criminal justice system being in place in both South Africa and the DRC, high levels

12 *Ibid.*

13 *Ibid.*

14 *Ibid.*

15 Committee on the Elimination of Discrimination against Women, Concluding observations on the eighth periodic report of the Democratic Republic of the Congo, UN doc. CEDAW/C/COD/8 (9 July 2019).

16 The United Nations Population, *gender-based violence* (2020).

17 South Africa ratified CEDAW on December 15, 1995, and the Maputo Protocol on December 17, 2004, whereas DRC ratified CEDAW on October 17, 1986, and Maputo protocol on November 25, 2005.

of sexual violence still prevail.[18] In this regard, South Africa's progressive legislative framework to curtail GBV[19] will be compared to that of the DRC's.[20] It can be argued that the nature of sexual violence experienced in South Africa differs from that of the DRC given the fact that in the former, sexual violence is experienced in peacetime whereas in the latter, it is conflict-related sexual violence (CRSV).[21] CRSV is aggravated by ethnic, religious or ideological cleavages that intensify the level of hatred and brutality.[22] Furthermore, those exercising CRSV have several goals, namely to humiliate the entire community, to create terror and to spread the disease.[23] Thirdly, in both countries, unequal power relations and patriarchal continues to dominate and fuel gender-based violence resulting in GBV victims being reluctant to report and follow through with their complaints as often GBV is considered as a 'private affair.'[24]

The discussion in this chapter will therefore identify the causes and challenges South Africa[25] and the DRC[26] face in addressing GBV. Although many studies suggested the need to develop legislation that encourages the reporting of sexual violence and ensure prosecution of perpetrators,[27] few studies have explored the effectiveness of these

[18] SAHRC *research brief: Unpacking the gaps and challenges in addressing gender-based violence in South Africa* (April 2018)3. Home office, *Country Policy and information Note Democratic Republic of Congo (DRC): Gender Based Violence* Version 2, (September 2018).

[19] South Africa was ranked the highest country in Africa in progressing as far as gender equality and women's rights are concerned. Statistics South Africa, Gender Statistics in South Africa, 2011. http://www.statssa.gov.za. Law (Sexual Offences and Related Matters) Amendment Act 6 of 2012 was passed to provide for effective prosecution and conviction of offenders.

[20] World Bank Group, *Women, Business and the Law* (2018).

[21] Carlo Koos, 'Sexual Violence in Armed Conflicts: Research Progress and Remaining Gaps,' 38 *Third World Quarterly* (2017): 19–36.

[22] *Ibid.*

[23] Cohen, Dara Kay and Elisabeth Wood, *Is sexual violence during war exceptional- or a continuation of everyday violence?* ISQ online (2016), http://www.isanet.org/publications/ISQ/posts/id/5239/issexual-violence-during-war-exceptional-or-a-continuation-ot-everyday-violence.

[24] SAHRC *supra* note 18. See also Meyiwa and others, 'A Twenty-Year Review of Policy Landscape for Gender-Based Violence in South Africa' (2017) *Gender &behaviour*; Madre Sofepadi, *Gender based violence and discrimination against women and girls in the Democratic Republic of Congo: A report for CEDAW* (2018).

[25] *Ibid.*

[26] Madre Sofepadi *supra* note 24.

[27] Danjibo N and Akinkuotu A, 'Rape as a weapon of War against women and girls,' 19 *Gender & Behaviou*r (2019); Carlo Koos, 'Sexual violence in armed conflicts: research progress

national laws criminalising GBV and the manner in which survivors or victims of GBV obtain justice. It is against this backdrop that this chapter assesses the legislative measures taken by South Africa and the DRC to curb GBV in both countries and to evaluate the extent to which victims of GBV are protected. In addition, the effectiveness of the criminal justice system in both countries as well as possible challenges faced in terms of criminal accountability will be evaluated in arriving at recommendations for the effective implementation of GBV legislation.

To answer these questions, this study applies the doctrinal legal research which consists of rigorous analyses of legislative provisions in deriving at legal propositions through rational legal deductions.[28] Accordingly, the sources consulted for purposes of the research can be found in primary and secondary sources of law. Furthermore, the study is anchored within the feminist's legal theory. The feminist legal theory was developed in the 1960s.[29] According to this theory, law has always been used to subordinate women.[30] This theory alludes to the reality that men hold a socially and economically dominant position over women in all spheres of society.[31] It argues that although the law appears to be neutral on the surface, in reality it is biased in favour of men.[32] As a result, feminist legal theory seeks to change women's status through law reform, specifically customary laws. Given the fact that this chapter analyses the manner in which criminal justice endeavours to curb gender-based violence, it can be argued that this chapter is anchored in the female legal theory which places an emphasis on the dominance theory. The dominance theory unmasks the structural inequalities which tolerate

---

and Remaining Gaps,' 38 *Third World Quately* (2017): 19–36; Carolien Jacobs, 'Seeking justice, experiencing the state: the criminal justice and real legal uncertainty, in the Democratic Republic of Congo,' 50 *The Journal of Legal Pluralism and Unofficial Law* (2018): 280.

28 Kharel, Doctrinal Legal Research (February 26, 2018), https://ssrn.com/abstract=3130525 or http://dx.doi.org/10.2139/ssrn.3130525.

29 Meintjes and others *Introduction to South African Law: Fresh Perspectives* (2019).

30 *Ibid.*

31 Bowman GC, Schneider EM, 'Feminist Legal Theory, Feminist Lawmaking, and the Legal Profession,' 67 *Fordham Law Review* (1998): 249–271.

32 Meintjes *supra* note 29.

patriarchal structures of power in society.[33] In turn, the patriarchal structures of power condone the marginalisation of women and the resultant perpetuation of social violence against them.[34]

Ultimately, this chapter comprises six sections. Subsequent to the introduction, the second section unpacks the international legal framework for the protection of women and girls. The third section focuses on the overview of gender-based violence in South Africa and DRC. Thereafter, the legislative framework of both countries and access to justice are discussed in the fourth section followed by a discussion on the challenges that survivors of GBV face in accessing the criminal justice system from a South African and Congolese perspective. The chapter concludes with recommendations to strengthen the current legislative frameworks and the implementation thereof of the respective countries based on good practice.

2 International and Regional Legal Framework for the Protection of Women and Girls from GBV

One of the most profound declarations paving the way for gender equality is the 1948 Universal Declaration of Human Rights (UDHR). In terms of the UDHR, all humans are born free and equal; hence, every woman has a right to equal treatment and a right to dignity.[35] It begs noting that most of the UDHR provisions, including the equality and non-discrimination clause, have acquired the customary standard under international law, and as such, they are binding upon the states despite the fact that the UDHR (as a declaration) is not binding. In addition, the International Covenant on Civil and Political Rights (ICCPR) and the International Covenant on Economic, Social and Cultural Rights (ICESR) also guarantee women's rights. In this regard, the ICCPR requires that State Parties recognise the rights of 'all individuals' without

---

[33] Bowman and Schneider *supra* note 31.

[34] *Ibid.*

[35] UDHR, Article 1.

discrimination.[36] The use of the term 'all individuals' inevitably includes both men and women. Although the feminist approach would argue otherwise because such generalisation has always created avenues for vagueness in protection of women. Similarly, the ICESR requires State Parties to ensure equal rights for men and women when it comes to the enjoyment of their economic, social and cultural rights. South Africa and the DRC ratified the aforesaid covenants and must accordingly align themselves with the said human right treaties.[37]

Moreover, in 1967, the UN adopted the Declaration on the Elimination of Discrimination Against Women (DEVAW). This declaration, despite not having a binding effect, emphasised that discrimination against women should be considered as an offence against human dignity. Years after a proposal for a binding treaty was raised, the Convention on the Elimination of All Forms of Discrimination against Women (CEDAW) was adopted in 1979.[38] Essentially, the CEDAW defines violence against women as 'any act or gender-based violence that results in, or is likely to result in, physical, sexual or psychological harm or suffering.'[39] Despite extending women's rights,[40] the Convention did not specifically address GBV.[41] It was only in 1993 at the World Conference on Human Rights that violence against women was recognised as a human rights violation which ultimately leads to the appointment of a Special Rapporteur on Violence Against Women (SRVAW) in the Vienna Declaration and Programme of Action.[42] In order to strengthen and complement the provisions of CEDAW, the DEVAW was proclaimed by the UN General Assembly in 1993. Accordingly, the DEVAW became

---

36 ICCPR, Article 2.

37 South Africa ratified the ICCPR on December 10, 1998 and the ICESR on January 12, 2015 whilst the DRC ratified the ICCPR and the ICESR on November 1, 1976.

38 Convention on the Elimination of All Forms of Discrimination against Women Twentieth Anniversary 1979–1999, CEDAW Information Note 3. https://www.un.org/womenwatch/daw/cedaw/cedaw20/history.htm.

39 CEDAW, Article 1.

40 CEDAW, Article 3.

41 The General Recommendations 12–19 did, however, clarify that the Convention includes violence against women and makes detailed recommendations to States parties.

42 Resolution 1994/1945[9], *Global Norms and Standards: Ending Violence Against Women*, https://www.unwomen.org/en/what-we-do/ending-violence-against-women/global-norms-and-standards.

the first international instrument explicitly addressing violence against women that provided for a universal application of women rights with regard to 'equality, security, liberty, integrity and dignity of all human beings.'[43] The DEVAW specifically focussed on women and children as vulnerable groups to violence that requires protection.[44] The DEVAW reaffirms the definition of violence against women; however, it includes also 'threats such as acts, coercion, or arbitrary deprivation of liberty, whether occurring in the public and private sphere.'[45] It begs to note that the DEVAW, although it does not have a legal binding effect, remains an important source as far as international principles are concerned.[46] In addition, in identifying and extending the ambit of forms of violence, one of the most profound aims of the DEVAW was to change the stance of governments, in that GBV is not a private affair but an epidemic that requires urgent governmental intervention. In this regard, article 4 of the DEVAW requires that states should 'condemn violence against women and should not invoke any custom, tradition or religious consideration to avoid their obligations with respect to its elimination' as well as 'develop penal, civil, labour and administrative sanctions in domestic legislation to punish and redress the wrongs caused to women and girls who are subjected to violence.'[47]

At the same time, the 1999 Optional Protocol to the CEDAW encouraged victims to lodge their complaints directly with the CEDAW committee, which had a duty to investigate the violation of women's rights.[48] Similarly, in respect of the girl child, the 1989 Convention on the Rights of the Child (CRC) prohibits child discrimination on the basis of gender. It is noteworthy that in July 2017, the CEDAW Committee

[43] The resolution strengthens the work of the Convention on the Elimination of All Forms of Discrimination against Women and the Vienna Declaration and Programme of Action and provides a definition of violence against women that is widely used.

[44] DEVAW, Article 4.

[45] DEVAW, Article 1.

[46] Nicole Chalira and Leah Ndimurwino, 'Violence Against Women: A Comparative Analysis Between Malawi and South Africa,' 32 *Speculum Juris* (2018): 110.

[47] DEVAW, Article 4 (d).

[48] Optional Protocol of the CEDAW, Article 1.

updated the General Recommendation No. 19[49] with the adoption of the General Recommendation No. 35 (GR No. 35) on gender-based violence against women. In addition to extending the scope of GBV, GR No.35 intensified the state's responsibility and role in addressing GBV. In addition to giving a voice to causes of GBV and extending the ambit of GBV by listing different types of violence against women, GR No. 35 endorses particular methods that may be essential to address violence directed against women.[50]

In terms of the African Charter on Human and Peoples' Rights (African Charter) that was adopted in 1981 by the Organisation of African Unity, now the African Union (AU). Basically, this famous Charter prohibits discrimination on any ground including sex.[51] Furthermore, in 2003, a Protocol to the African Charter on Human and people's rights on the rights of women in Africa (Maputo Protocol) was adopted to supplement the provisions of the African Charter. The Maputo Protocol was adopted to supplement the provisions of the African Charter. Article 2 of the Maputo Protocol emphasises that State Parties should include in their national constitutions the 'principle of equality between men and women and ensure its effective implementation.'[52] In this regard, the Maputo Protocol makes specific reference to the elimination of discrimination against women,[53] a women's right to dignity[54] and integrity,[55] as well as a women's rights to access to justice

[49] General recommendation No.19 recognising gender-based violence as discrimination within Article 1 of the UN Convention on Elimination of All Forms of Discrimination against Women (the Convention). Committee on the Elimination of Discrimination against Women, CEDAW/C/GC/35.

[50] For an elaborate discussion on the General Recommendation No.35, see Chinkin C, CEDAW General Recommendation 35 on violence against women is a significant step forward (2017), https://blogs.lse.ac.uk/wps/2017/09/06/cedaw-general-recommendation-35-on-violence-against-women-is-a-significant-step-forward/.

[51] African Charter, Article 2.

[52] Maputo Protocol, Article 2 (a).

[53] Maputo Protocol, Article 2 stipulates that 'States Parties shall combat all forms of discrimination against women through appropriate legislative, institutional and other measures.'

[54] Maputo Protocol, Article 3.

[55] Maputo Protocol, Article 4 (2)(a) specifically provides that 'States Partiesshall take appropriate and effective measures to enact and enforce laws to prohibit all forms of violence against women including unwanted or forced sex whether the violence takes place in private or public.'

and equal protection before the law.[56] More so, the Maputo Protocol defines violence against women as 'all acts perpetrated against women which cause or could cause them physical, sexual, psychological, and economic harm, including the threat to take such acts, this definition extend to both private and public sphere and during both times of peace and war.'[57] In addition, the African Charter on the Welfare of the Child (ACRWC) provides that 'every child shall enjoy the rights and freedoms recognised by the Charter' without discrimination.[58] It should also be noted that the AU provided for judicial and quasi-judicial structures such as the African Commission (AC), the African Court and the African Committee of Experts on the Rights and the Welfare of the Child to manage the implementation of human rights.[59] In addition, to emphasise the importance of the fulfilment of women's rights, the African Commission created the mechanism of a Special Rapporteur on the Rights of Women in Africa with a specific mandate to promote and protect women's rights in the region.[60] Despite the aforesaid, the Special Rapporteur has an array of rights to focus on and it faces challenges in the form of accessibility.[61] Accordingly, the effectiveness of the Special Rapporteur as a mechanism to protect women's right faces challenges.

Consequently, it can be argued that at both the international and regional level, preventative structures have been established on respect, promotion and fulfilment of women and girls' rights. Nevertheless, despite all the international and regional mechanisms discussed, the violation of women and girls' rights remains a widespread challenge. For instance, the Special Rapporteur on violence against women indicates

[56] Maputo Protocol, Article 8 requires 'States Partiesto 'ensure effective access by women to judicial and legal services, including legal aid as well as support to local, national, regional and continental initiatives directed at providing women access to legal services, and to establish adequate educational and other appropriate structures with particular attention to women and to sensitise everyone to the rights of women.'

[57] Maputo Protocol, Article 1(J).

[58] ACWC, Article 3.

[59] Ashwanee Budoo, 'Analysing the Monitoring Mechanism of the African women's Protocol at the Level of the African Union,' 18 *African Human Rights Law Journal* (2018): 58–74.

[60] African Charter, Article 45(2).

[61] Budoo *supra* note 59, 74.

that failure of effective implementation of laws in South Africa facilitates violence against women and girls.[62] Similarly, a report prepared by Madree for CEDAW confirmed that conflict-related sexual violence and gender-based violence are still rampant in DRC.[63] The section below provides a brief overview of GBV in both countries.

3 Overview of Gender–Based Violence in South Africa and the Democratic Republic of the Congo

The forms of GBV experienced in South Africa and the DRC include *inter alia* sexual violence, emotional abuse, domestic violence, femicide and harmful practices.[64] As far as sexual violence is concerned, the World Health Organisation (WHO) defines it as 'any sexual act, attempt to obtain a sexual act, unwanted sexual comments or advances using coercion, threats of harm or physical force.'[65] Evidently, the United Nations Population Fund reported 5783 cases of sexual violence in 2017 in the eastern DRC.[66] Domestic violence is also prevalent in the DRC with most cases recorded within the family structure. The United Nations Population Fund indicated that 75% of females aged between 15 and 24 point out that wife beating is justified.[67] Similarly, despite South Africa having the Domestic Violence Act that identifies various forms of GBV and the Criminal Law (Sexual Offences and Related Matters) Amendment Act that prohibits sexual assault, the country is still experiencing high levels of sexual assault, rape and femicide.[68] What is especially

[62] United Nations Human Rights Council, *Report of the Special Rapporteur on Violence Against Women, its Causes and Consequences on Her Mission to South Africa,* A/HRC/32/42/Add2(2016) paragraph 19.

[63] Sofepadi *supra* note 24.

[64] SAHRC *supra* note 18, 1.

[65] WHO, *Report on Violence and Health* (2002).

[66] Sofepadi *supra* note 24.

[67] United Nations Population funds, Gender Based Violence: What Do We Do (2020) https://www.unfpa.org/gender-basedviolence.

[68] SAHRC *supra* note 18, 3.

disheartening is the fact that society does not always realise that certain acts constitute GBV as society generally condones these pervasive acts of violence and regards them as private matters that should be settled within the family structure.[69]

3.1 The South African Perspective

It is over two decades since South Africa became a democratic country. Although substantive advancements have been made in respect of legislation and policies, South Africa still faces high levels of gender-based violence as is evidenced from annual crime statistics.[70] In terms of South African Crime Statistics, GBV has a low reporting rate despite its high incidence. Accordingly, certain GBV crimes such as murder, assault (common and GBH) as well as sexual offences are only recorded under the 'contact crimes' category.[71] In this regard, the SAPS reported 53 293 sexual offence cases during the period April 2019 to March 2020[72] thereby increasing the total cases of sexual offences by 1.7% and sexual assault cases by 4.2%.[73] It is estimated that children constitute 46% of sexual abuse cases.[74] In addition to sexual offences, a study conducted in the Gauteng Province indicated that 37.7% of women have experienced physical and/or sexual intimate partner violence (IPV) and 46.2% reported economic or emotional abuse.[75] GBV is accordingly extremely prevalent in South Africa and ranked by the World Health Organisation

---

69 Ministry for the Advancement of Women and the Integration for Women in Development, *National Programme for the Promotion of Women's Leadership in Political and Public Life in the Republic of Congo* (2016), https://info.undp.org/docs/pdc/Documents/COG/Programme%20National%20Leadership%20féminin%20en%20politique%20en%20république%20du%20Congo.pdf.

70 Meyiwa *supra* note 24, 8607.

71 SAPS Annual Crime Statistics 2019/2020.

72 Crime Situation in RSA - (April to March 2019–20), https://static.pmg.org.za/april_to_march_2019_20_presentation.pdf. The case includes rape, sexual assault, attempted sexual assault and sexual assault.

73 SAPS Annual Crime Statistics 2019/2020.

74 *Ibid*.

75 Jewkes Penn-Kekana, Levin Ratsaka, and Schrieber, South Africa Demographic and Health Survey (2016).

(WHO) as a country with one of the highest rates of violence against women.[76]

As a signatory to various core international human right treaties,[77] in particular the DEVAW, South Africa is obliged to integrate international treaties into practice by way of promulgating domestic legislation.[78] In this regard, South Africa has been heralded for making significant strides in uplifting women in the country as well as having promulgated an 'arsenal of progressive laws and policies to deal with gender-based violence.'[79] The South African government has also identified GBV as a key concern and prioritised people's safety (especially women and children and those who are vulnerable) as a goal in terms of the South Africa's National Development Plan (NDP).[80] The impetus in the promulgation of legislation in an effort to curtail GBV can accordingly be found in the principles and values fundamental to the Constitution of the Republic of South Africa of 1996.[81]

---

[76] WHO, *South Africa*, http://www.unicef.org/south africa/hiv_aids_729.html.

[77] International Convention on the Elimination of All Forms of Racial Discrimination (1969); International Covenant on Civil and Political Rights (1966); Convention on the Elimination of All Forms of Discrimination Against Women (1979); Convention Against Torture and Other Cruel, Inhumane, or Degrading Treatment or Punishment (1987); Convention on the Rights of the Child (1989); Optional Protocol to the International Covenant on Economic, Social and Cultural Rights (2008); Optional Protocol to the International Covenant on Civil and Political Rights (1976); Optional Protocol to the Convention on the Rights of the Child on the involvement of children in armed conflict (2002).

[78] DEVAW, Article 4(a), requires State Parties to 'Develop penal, civil, labour and administrative sanctions in domestic legislation to punish and redress the wrongs caused to women who are subjected to violence.'

[79] Šimonovi´c Dubravka, *South Africa's Still Long Walk to Free Women from the Shackles of Violence: The UN special rapporteur on violence against women, during her visit to South Africa* (2015). The Domestic Violence Amendment Bill, The Criminal Law (Sexual Offences and Related Matters) Amendment Act Amendment Bill and The Criminal Matters Amendment Bill arrived at Cabinet in July 2020, took only 11 months as from executive drafting to tabling in the national legislatures.

[80] The Presidency of the Republic of South Africa: National Planning Commission National Development Plan 2030: Our future - make it work (2012) 43.

[81] Constitution of the Republic of South Africa, 1996 (hereinafter referred to as 'the Constitution').

3.2 The DRC Perspective

On the other hand, despite being a potentially rich country,[82] poverty and vulnerability largely characterise the DRC population,[83] with the average citizen earning less than two dollars a day.[84] A further result of the poverty-stricken DRC is the fact that women and girls become prostitutes to earn an income despite some men not remunerating them for their services.[85] The biggest factor impacting on the DRC's instability is the conflict which has been ongoing for the last forty years.[86] The main cause for the ongoing conflicts is 'local disputes over land and resources, the acquisitive goals of rebel groups and the predatory neighbouring states and ethnic and political grievances.'[87] As a result of the forty years of conflict, the DRC's economic growth has been stifled.[88]

In 2009, Carlsen portrayed the DRC as the home to the most horrific documented cases of sexual violence in the world.[89] Despite the war in the DRC officially ending in 2002,[90] women are still being raped, especially in the eastern part of the DRC which is limited to South Kivu, North Kivu, Maniema and Ituri. Accordingly, for purposes of this analysis, the focus will be on the above-mentioned four areas which constitute the eastern part of the DRC.[91] Arguably, sexual violence and

---

[82] Nice Nyemba, *The impact of poverty on Children's Rights in the Democratic Republic of Congo* (LLM thesis, University of Pretoria 2015).

[83] *Ibid.*, 22.

[84] Kandala Ngianga, Madungu Tumuaka, Emina James, Nzita KPD and Cappuccio Francesco, 'Malnutrition among children under the age of five in the Democratic Republic of Congo (DRC): Does geographic location matter?' *Public Health*, 11, (2011): 262.

[85] Sharan Burrow, 'Violence against women in Eastern Democratic Republic of Congo: whose responsibility? Whose complicity,' *International Trade Union Confederation,* (2011).

[86] Williams C, 'Explaining the Great War in Africa: How conflict in the Congo became a continental crisis,' 2 *The Fletcher Forum of World Affairs* (2013): 83.

[87] *Ibid.*, 81.

[88] Tholaine Matadi, *The Realisation of Children's Survival Rights in South Africa and the DRC: A Comparative Study* (Phd Thesis, University of Zululand 2018).

[89] Erika Carlsen, 'Rape and War in the Democratic Republic of the Congo,' 21 *Peace Review* (2009): 474.

[90] *Ibid.*

[91] United Nations, Office of the Special Representative of the Secretary General on sexual violence in conflict: Democratic Republic of the Congo, Report of the Secretary General to the Security Council (S/2020/487) June 2020.

GBV have a direct link to the exploitation of natural resources. For instance, the mining sector in the eastern DRC mostly appears artisanal and is often controlled by illegal armed groups and military units.[92] Recently, the United Nations Organisation Stabilisation Mission in the DRC (MONUSCO) documented 1,409 cases of CRSV which represents an increase of 34% since 2018.[93] Among these cases, 955 are perpetrated by the non-state armed groups, and with regard to state actors, the armed forces of the DRC were involved in 383 cases which represent 76% increase compared to previous year.[94] Moreover, it is important to note that, in as much as sexual violence in peace time might have similar roots as sexual violence in war time (that is to say gender inequality and socio-cultural opinions),[95] sexual violence in war time is aggravated by hatred and brutality on the part of perpetrators whose actions are ethnically motivated.[96]

In a study conducted by Banwell on sexual violence in the DRC, she noted that such violence encompasses rape, forced prostitution and sex-based discrimination.[97] Research conducted by Trenholm and others revealed that 'the plight of women is just the tip of the iceberg, beneath this lies an entire traumatised society, hidden agendas, and a clandestine corporate.'[98] As Carlsen points out, women and girls are prey to secondary victimisation of sexual violence due to the intimidation of perpetrators, high cost of prosecution, a collapse and ineffective judicial system.[99] With regard to children and infants, it is known that in rural areas, child abuse is frequent due to the traditional beliefs that harming children or sleeping with a virgin will bring wealth or preserve

---

92 Sharan Burrow, 'Violence Against Women in Eastern Democratic Republic of Congo: Whose Responsibility? Whose Complicity?' *International Trade Union Confederation* (2011).

93 United Nations *supra* note 62, 2.

94 *Ibid.*

95 Koos *supra* note 27, 1936.

96 *Ibid.*

97 Stacy Banwell, 'Rape and Sexual Violence in the Democratic Republic Of Congo: A Case Study of Gender-Based Violence,' 23 *Journal of Gender Studies* (2014): 45–58.

98 Trenholm JE, Olsson P and Ahlberg BM, 'Battles on women bodies: War, rape and traumatisation in Eastern Democratic Republic of Congo' 6 *International Maternal and Child Health* (2011): 152.

99 Carlsen *supra* note 89, 476.

combatants from dying in the battle field during armed conflict.[100] Banwell clearly confirms that the type of GBV experienced in the DRC is being 'perpetrated and facilitated at macro, meso and micro levels.'[101] Firstly, at the macro-level, there is a link between 'globalisation, hegemony masculinity, hyper capitalism and sexual violence committed in Congo,'[102] that is to say, transnational corporations from various countries all compete to take control and gain access to minerals in the eastern DRC.[103] Those corporations' control over the extraction, sale and illegal transport of Colton, gold, tin as well as other minerals.[104] Secondly, at the meso-level, aggressive heterosexual masculinity and violence are methods specifically designed to train soldiers that are able and willing to fight and kill.[105]

As a result, soldiers choose to engage in rape and other forms of violence during conflicts.[106] Thirdly, at the micro-level, rape and other forms of sexual violence are used by individual soldiers to prove their superiority and financial status over other men, whilst demeaning the women.[107] This is particularly evident in cases whereby the rapists are military personnel that use rape as a tactical weapon to destroy the victims' and the community security especially considering that women are the backbone of society.[108] Equally notable, in DRC, men are expected to have physical, economical as well as social power to protect their wives from other men.[109] However, cultural, ethnic and socio-economic constraints prevent them from fulfilling this aspiration.

---

100 Development Centre, *Democratic Republic of Congo* (2019).

101 Banwell *supra* note 97, 49.

102 *Ibid.*, 46.

103 Banwell *supra* note 97, 49.

104 Banwell *supra* note 97, 46. The UN Security council listed 100 companies involved in this global market some of them are African-based companies but a significant number of transnational corporations from countries such as Belgium, Canada, Germany, Israel, the Netherlands, Switzerland, the UK and the US. See United Nations Security Council, Report of the panel experts on the illegal exploitation of natural resources and other forms of wealth of the DRC. 2003.

105 Banwell *supra* note 97, 51.

106 *Ibid.*

107 Banwell *supra* note 97, 47.

108 Carlsen *supra* note 89, 479.

109 Banwell *supra* note 97, 53.

Consequently, this 'subordinate masculinity turns into hyper masculinity within the conflict zone to resolve conflict.'[110] The depiction of hyper-masculinity which encompasses aggression, excessive toughness and violence gives these marginalised men the opportunity during war to challenge their marginal position within gender hierarchy.[111] As a result, women are sexually abused. Ultimately, it should be noted that sexual violence has had a negative impact on victims as it has destroyed their physical bodies, their way of living and their mind set.[112]

Likewise, the CEDAW concluding observations on the eighth periodic report of the DRC[113] raised the following concerns:

> (a) The high prevalence of gender-based violence, including sexual violence and group rape, including of minors;
> (b) The limited access to justice and reparations by women and girls who are victims of gender-based violence and the lack of sanctions imposed on the perpetrators;
> (c) High rates of domestic violence owing to accepted social norms, the lack of cases of domestic violence, including marital rape, brought before courts owing to victims' fear of stigmatisation and the limited number of perpetrators who are punished;
> (d) The lack of criminalisation of domestic violence, including marital rape;
> (e) The lack of progress in adopting the draft law for the protection of vulnerable persons, which includes a framework for assistance for victims of sexual violence;
> (f) The lack of specific mechanisms for the protection of the victims of gender-based violence, including domestic and sexual violence, and the lack of shelters, counselling and rehabilitation services for them.

---

110 *Ibid.*

111 *Ibid.*

112 Bercky Zihindula, Jabulani Makhubele and Janet Muthuki, 'Challenges endured by women during the conflict related sexual violence in the Democratic Republic of the Congo,' 16 *Gender and Behaviour* (2018):1097.

113 CEDAW, concluding observations, *supra* note 15.

What can be gleaned from the above discussion is that in both countries, GBV is related to various factors including gender discrimination, outdated customs, hegemony masculinity, weak legal and judicial system, the culture of silence of the victims and the impunity of the perpetrators.[114]

The above said, the following section answers the question on measures taken so far in both countries to curb gender-based violence. It should be noted that South Africa and DRC enacted legislation to protect women against GBV.

4 Domestic Legal Frameworks: GBV and Access to Justice for survivors of GBV

This section discusses the legislative framework in South Africa and in the DRC protecting women against GBV. The available provisions in terms of access to justice will form part of this section.

4.1 South Africa

4.1.1 The Constitution of the Republic of South Africa, 1996

The Constitution of South Africa guarantees that every person under the South African jurisdiction has the right to be treated equally and not be discriminated against, and[115] has a right to life,[116] human dignity,[117] bodily and psychological integrity,[118] freedom and security[119] which

---

[114] Development Centre, *Democratic Republic of Congo* (2019).

[115] 2005 Constitution, section 9.

[116] 2005 Constitution, section 11.

[117] 2005 Constitution, section 10.

[118] 2005 Constitution, section 12(2).

[119] 2005 Constitution, section 12.

includes one's right to be free from all forms of violence.[120] In terms of section 7(2) of the Constitution, these rights must be respected, protected and promoted in accordance with the democratic values of the Constitution. Accordingly, all domestic laws must be consistent with the Constitution.

Although various post-constitutional laws have been promulgated[121] and policies adopted that touch on gender equality and GBV,[122] the most prominent legislation addressing GBV is analysed for purposes of this study. In particular, the Domestic Violence Act 118 of 1998 (DVA) that enables women to obtain protection against GBV by way of a protection order and the Criminal Law (Sexual Offences and Related Matters) Amendment Act 32 of 2007 (SOA) that provides the framework for protecting GBV victims that were sexually abused. It should further be noted that for purposes of this study the focus is placed on women and girls as the specific vulnerable groups at risk.

4.1.2 Domestic Violence Act of 1998[123]

Violence within the family structure was initially addressed in terms of the Prevention of Family Violence Act 133 of 1993 (PFVA). The provisions, as far as the scope and ambit of the Act was concerned, were, however, restrictive. In terms of section 1 of the PFVA, the Act was only applicable to 'parties to a marriage including a man and a woman who are or were married to each other according to any law or custom and also a man and a woman who ordinarily live or lived together as husband and wife, although not married to each other.' In addition, section 2 of the PFVA only made the provision that a respondent is not allowed to assault or threaten the applicant or a child, enter the matrimonial home or a part thereof, prevent the applicant or child to enter the matrimonial home or any other specified act.

---

[120] 2005 Constitution, section 12 (1) (c).

[121] The Promotion of Equality and Prevention of Unfair Discrimination Act 4 of 2000, that explicitly prohibits violence against woman; The Protection from Harassment Act 17 of 2011.

[122] The National Crime Prevention Strategy (NCPS) 1996 establishes crimes of violence against women and children as a national priority.

[123] Domestic Violence Act 118 of 1998.

The promulgation of the DVA broadened the definition of domestic violence to include *inter alia* 'intimidation, harassment, stalking, and damage to property as forms of domestic violence.'[124] In addition, the DVA extended the ambit of its predecessor by including same-sex relationships as well as extended families within the definition of a domestic relationship.[125] Further to extending the application of the DVA as far as violence was concerned, the DVA also provided for easier access to GBV protection by allowing a person of interest to apply for a domestic violence interdict on behalf of a victim.[126] In terms of the DVA, the scope of protection was correspondingly extended to include limiting contact with minor children that may be exposed to domestic violence,[127] providing monetary relief to a victim of violence,[128] and the removal of firearms from the care of a perpetrator.[129] A significant improvement from the PFVA was the inclusion of police duties and protocols in cases where a domestic violence interdict was contravened.[130] Accordingly, the DVA is the most prominent Act that provides protection for women and vulnerable groups against domestic violence and abuse.

4.1.3 The Criminal Law (Sexual Offences and Related Matters) Amendment Act, 2007

The promulgation of the SOA[131] and the repeal of the common law offence of rape resulted in a wider range of acts of sexual violation being included in terms of the SOA.[132] In addition, the SOA included special protection in respect of minors and disabled people as it is now

124 DVA, section 1.
125 DVA, section 1.
126 DVA, section 4(3).
127 DVA, section 7(6).
128 DVA, section 7(3) and (4).
129 DVA, section 7(2).
130 DVA, section 8.
131 The Criminal Law (Sexual Offences and Related Matters) Amendment Act, 2007 (Act No. 32 of 2007) also referred to as the Sexual Offences Act (hereinafter referred to as 'the SOA').
132 Chapter 2 of the SOA.

mandatory to report sexual offences in respect of the former vulnerable groups.[133] The provisions of the SOA improved the court process by changing the procedures applicable in cases of sexual offences. In addition, the SOA includes provisions enabling victims of sexual offences access to various supporting services.[134]

One of the most reflective improvements of the SOA is the establishment of a National Register for Sex Offenders that provides a record of all sex offenders and prevents them from working with vulnerable groups.[135] In addressing under-resourced courts and following a victim-centred approach by, among others, establishing sexual offences courts, victim support rooms and care centres, the SOA also provided for the adoption of a national policy framework regulating all matters in the SOA.[136] It is envisaged that the implementation of the Draft Regulations[137] will bring about the necessary mechanisms to establish, regulate and implement a more efficient judicial system and provide the inter-sectoral infrastructure conducive for victims of sexual offences.[138] The following section analyses the legislative framework in the DRC.

4.2 The Democratic Republic of Congo

The DRC signed and ratified the CEDAW and Maputo Protocol.[139] Being a monist state, once the DRC signs and ratifies an international convention, it automatically domesticates the provisions of the convention as national law.[140] As a result, there is no need for the enactment and promulgation of domestic law although international and regional

[133] Chapters 3 and 4 of the SOA.

[134] *Ibid,* Chapter 5.

[135] *Ibid,* Chapter 6.

[136] *Ibid,* Chapter 7.

[137] Draft Regulations Relating to Sexual Offences Courts: Criminal Law (Sexual Offences and Related Matters) Amendment Act, 32 of 2007.

[138] SAHRC *supra* note 18, 14.

[139] See status of ratification, *supra* note 17.

[140] Constitution of the Democratic Republic of the Congo, Article 215, 2006 (hereinafter referred to as the '2005 Constitution').

frameworks recommend that State Parties enact national legislation.[141] In as much as the DRC has ratified and signed several treaties, it should be noted that it has not signed and ratified the regional convention protecting children's rights (ACRWC).[142] Nonetheless, the government of the DRC has committed to taking appropriate measures to fulfil women and girls' rights as evident in the 2006 Constitution, the Child Protection Law and the Penal Code.

4.2.1 The Constitution of the DRC 2005

The 2005 Constitution is a result of several drafts and amendments.[143] It stresses compliance with several international treaties[144] and guarantees everyone's right to life and to physical integrity.[145] Furthermore, sexual violence including rape and sexual harassment is prohibited in terms of the 2005 Constitution and also considered a crime against humanity.[146] Article 14 guarantees protection and promotion of women's rights. The Constitution requires public authorities to eliminate all forms of discrimination against women.[147]

As far as a girl child is concerned, article 41 of the 2005 Constitution provides that a child has the right to family care and protection, and therefore, the state has a duty to protect its children against any form of maltreatment. In addition to the 2005 Constitution, the 2009 Child Protection Law extends protection to the child.

---

141 It should be noted that practice shows that the country needs to enact implementation law (*loi de mise en oeuvre).*

142 Treaties such as ICESCR ratified on November 1, 1976, ICCPR on November 1, 1976, ACHPR ratified on July 20, 1987 and signed on 23 July 1987.

143 Adopted by the National Assembly on May 13, 2005, and approved by the Congolese people by the referendum of December 18 and 19, 2005. For more details, see Gathii JT 'Popular authorship and constitution making: Comparing and contrasting the DRC and Kenya,' 49 William *& Mary Law Review* (2008): 1110.

144 See the preamble of 2005 Constitution.

145 2005 Constitution, Article 16.

146 2005 Constitution, Article 15.

147 2005 Constitution, Article 14.

4.2.2 Child Protection Law 09/001 of 2009

The Child Protection Law came into operation in January 2009 (the 2009 Child Law).[148] This piece of legislation divides the protection of the child into three sections, namely the social protection of the child,[149] the judicial protection of the child[150] and the criminal protection of the child.[151]

Social protection relates to *inter alia* parental rights and responsibilities, child work and the prohibition of the use of a child in armed conflict.[152] The Child Protection Law also guarantees child judicial protection in all institutions and organisations associated with the children's tribunal,[153] the competence of the children's tribunal,[154] the proceedings before the children's tribunal in conflict with the law[155] and mediation.[156] More so, criminal protection extends to the protection of the child before birth where the killing or injuring of a pregnant woman is specifically prohibited.[157] The intentional attack on the life and physical or mental integrity of a child is also prohibited in terms of the Child Protection Law.[158] Similarly, the Act also protects the child's honour and personal freedom.[159] Noteworthy is that the Act specifically provides for protection of the child from sexual assault.[160] In addition, a Congolese child cannot be endangered.[161] In the light of this discourse, it can be argued that the Congolese law adequately protects children from violence as it covers relevant aspects with regard to the child's life and integrity

[148] www.leganet.cd.

[149] Child Protection Law, Title II of the 2009.

[150] *Ibid*, Title III.

[151] *Ibid*, Title IV.

[152] Child Protection Law, Articles 71–73 2009.

[153] Child Protection Law, Arts 84–93.

[154] Child Protection Law, Articles 94–101.

[155] Child Protection Law, Articles 102–131.

[156] Child Protection Law, Articles 132–142.

[157] Child Protection Law, Articles 143–146.

[158] Child Protection Law, Articles 146–159.

[159] Child Protection Law, Articles 160–162.

[160] Child Protection Law, Articles 169–184.

[161] Child Protection Law, Articles 185–194.

without discriminating between boys and girls. Another law that guarantees women and children protection against violence is the Penal Code of 1940.

4.2.3 The Penal Code of 1940

The Penal Code was amended by the provisions of the Congolese law to protect victims of sexual violence.[162] This amendment was to align the definition of rape with international standards. The Penal Code provides that rape is punishable by five to twenty years of imprisonment.[163] Furthermore, when the victim is killed during the rape, the perpetrator's penalty is death or servitude in perpetuity.[164] Moreover, although the Congolese government has put in place a comprehensive strategy in curbing sexual violence, such strategy merely provides victims of sexual assault with medical and legal support[165] and is accordingly not sufficient.

As far as the child is concerned, the Penal Code punishes any attempt to indecently assault a child.[166] If the perpetrator assaults a child that is younger than fifteen years of age, the Penal Code provides that the sanction is between five to fifteen years of imprisonment.[167] In addition, the Code prescribes that a perpetrator that is found guilty of raping a child under the age of ten will be imprisoned for a minimum of twenty years.[168] In the light of the above, it can be argued that the government of the DRC has taken measures to protect women from violence against. However, whilst the laws are adopted, the major challenge is that they

---

[162] Law 06/018 of July 20, 2006 amending and completing the Decree of January 30, 1940, Congolese Penal Code.

[163] Penal Code, Article 170.

[164] Penal Code, Article 171.

[165] Development Centre, *Democratic Republic of Congo* 2019, Social Institution and Gender Index (2019), http://www.genderindex.org.

[166] Penal Code, Article 167.

[167] Penal Code, Article 168.

[168] Penal Code, Article 169.

are not implemented mainly because the government is not allocating sufficient financial resources to law enforcement.[169]

What transpires from the above discussion is that both countries have successfully signed and ratified international and regional conventions in respect of violence against women and girls as is evident from the above discussions.[170] Both countries have constitutions which give expression to the right to equality, human dignity, life and security of the person. It should, however, be noted that unlike South Africa, the DRC does not have a specific law that addresses GBV such as the Domestic Violence Act. Although the Penal Code of 1940 as amended by the law of 2006 contains mechanism to combat domestic violence, it is not adequate to protect women. Accordingly, the DRC should expedite the promulgation of GBV legislation as required by the CEDAW.[171] In addition, the DEVAW suggests that State Parties condemn violence against women.[172] Despite South Africa having a comprehensive legislative framework, there is still a need for government to commit to the implementation and enforcement of the legislation promulgated to protect women and girls from GBV violence.[173]

The tabling of the Domestic Violence Amendment Bill (that would *inter alia* provide for online applications for protection orders), the Criminal Law (Sexual Offences and Related Matters) Amendment Act Amendment Bill (that would provide for a new crime of sexual intimidation or the threat thereof) as well as the Criminal Matters Amendment Bill (providing for alternative modes of giving evidence through intermediaries and technology as well as stricter bail criteria) in August 2020 is reflective of the South Africa government's commitment to legislative reform to curtail GBV.

---

169 CEDAW, concluding observations, *supra* note 15.

170 See section 3 and section 4 of this chapter.

171 CEDAW, Article 2.

172 DEVAW, Article 4.

173 SAHRC *supra* note 18, 14.

5 Challenges for Survivors of GBV to Access the Criminal Justice System

Although criminal justice systems involve law enforcement, access to courts, prosecution, prison systems and probation agencies, the following section will focus on law enforcement as well as prosecution and access to justice.

5.1 South Africa

5.1.1 The Law, Jurisprudence and Policy

Article 34 of the Constitution provides that everyone has the right to access to courts. Furthermore, the state has a duty to promote, protect and fulfil the fundamental rights contained in the Bill of Rights.[174] South Africa has dealt with several GBV cases and in particular sexual violence.[175] In this regard, the case of *Carmichele v the Minister for Safety and Security*[176] is noteworthy. In this case, the victim was a woman who was brutally assaulted by a man who was previously charged with indecent assault. The court held that the state had a constitutional and international duty to protect and curb violence against women.[177] This decision in this case is a landmark decision for victims' rights and the battle to end violence against women. Ultimately, in respect of obstacles to justice, similar to the DRC, South Africa also encounters challenges which include lack of the implementation of the legislative framework

[174] 2005 Constitution, section 7(2).

[175] For example, *Van Eeden v Minister of Safety and Security* 2003 (1) SA 389 (SCA); *Rail Commuters'*.

Action Group v Transnet LTD and Others (2004); S v Chapman 1997 (3) SA 341(SCA).

[176] 2001 (4) SA 938 (CC).

[177] Mikateko Joyce Maluleke and Thuli Madonsela, 'women and the law in South Africa: gender equality jurisprudence in landmark court decisions.' *Department of Justice and Constitutional Development*, 5, (2004).

such as the establishment and support of sexual offences courts, inadequate resources resulting in inefficient court proceedings, shortage of prosecutors and court intermediaries and other court officials.[178]

Despite a progressive Constitution and solid legislation, such as the DVA and SOA, South Africa's GBV, cases remain alarmingly high,[179] with the economic and social impact of GBV being enormous.[180] The DVA is not sufficiently gender sensitive, thus disregarding the challenge of gender roles which is often perpetuated by police officials who are not committed to assisting victims of domestic disputes as they often regard GBV as a private matter.[181] In addition, studies have shown that inaccessibility to courts and police stations, especially in rural areas,[182] unfamiliarity with the court process and delays in processing domestic violence applications due to staff shortages and/or lack of interdepartmental cohesion discourage victims from obtaining the necessary protection provided for in terms of the DVA.[183]

Likewise consideration should be given to the history of South Africa, in particular how the apartheid era moulded and reinforced gender and race division within the diverse South African society.[184] By the same token, thought should also be given to the influence of socio-cultural factors (such as *Ukuthwala*, forced virginity testing and female genital mutilation) which have in one way or the other perpetuated the patriarchal system within which cultures of unequal gender power relations

---

178 SAHRC *supra* note 18, 14.

179 SAHRC *supra* note 18, 12.

180 It is estimated that the cost of GBV is between R24 and 42 billion annually. KPMG, 2015, too costly to ignore: The economic impact of gender-based violence in South Africa. See also South African Integrated Programme of Action Addressing Violence Against Women and Children (2013–2018): 16–20.

181 United Nations Human Rights Committee, *Report of the Special Rapporteur on violence against women, its causes and consequences on her mission to South Africa*, A/HRC/32/42/Add.2 (2016).

182 Vetten L, 'Violence against Women in South Africa,' in Buhlungu S, Daniel J, Southall R and Lutchman J (eds) *State of the Nation: South Africa* (2007); SAHRC *supra* note 18, 13.

183 Vetten L, 'Show Me the Money: A Review of Budgets Allocated towards the Implementation of South Africa's Domestic Violence Act' 32 *Politikon: South African Journal of Political Studies* (2005): 277–295; SAHRC *supra* note 18, 13.

184 UNHRC *supra* note 62, paragraph 7.

thrive.[185] The impact cultural beliefs have on reinforcing GBV is evident from statistical data that reveal that woman and girls are particularly reluctant to rapport GBV incidents due to perceptions that condone the practice of male control over women and violence against women.[186] This belief system accordingly contributes to abuse as many GBV incidents are not reported due to shame and the fear of being stigmatised by the community. A further contributing factor is that victims of GBV are often financially dependent on the male as the breadwinner.[187] Consequently, many GBV cases are unreported,[188] and if reported few perpetrators are eventually convicted.[189] It is noteworthy that according to her rapport, GBV cases were more recurrent in areas where socio-economic factors *inter alia* poverty, unemployment, alcohol and drug abuse were high.[190]

In addition to political, social, cultural and economic factors underpinning GBV cases, the lack of inter-sectoral departments to provide GBV victims with support (such as health care and accommodation)[191] as well as a centralised statistic system to differentiate between categories of violence committed against women and girls (other than the mere recording of sexual offences crimes under the SOA by the South African Police Service (SAPS)) provides inadequate data to effectively analyse and address GBV.[192] Moreover, it was found that as a result of a court system that is not victim-friendly, untrained SAPS and stereotyping judiciary members, many victims experience secondary traumatisation[193] which also contributes towards their distrust of the judicial system and

[185] UNHRC *supra* note 62, paragraphs 21–26.

[186] South African Integrated Programme of Action Addressing Violence Against Women and Children (2013–2018) 16–17; Crime against Women in South Africa: An in-depth analysis of the Victims of Crime Survey data (2018) 6.

[187] South African Integrated Programme of Action Addressing Violence Against Women and Children (2013–2018) 16–17.

[188] UNHRC *supra* note 62, paragraphs 17, 63.

[189] UNHRC *supra* note 62, paragraphs 41, 55.

[190] UNHRC *supra* note 62, paragraph 28.

[191] UNHRC *supra* note 62, paragraph 65.

[192] UNHRC *supra* note 62, paragraphs 7, 60–62; SAHRC *supra* note 18, 17.

[193] UNHRC *supra* note 62, paragraphs 69–80.

SAPS.[194] The aforesaid concerns were echoed by the UN Special Rapporteur, Dubravka Šimonović, in her 2016 rapport in acknowledging that in addressing GBV in South Africa, a multi-sectoral partnership and approach need to be adopted.[195]

For that reason, it was suggested that 'a National Strategic Plan on GBV with a set of clear strategic priorities and core measurable goals, should be adopted, disseminated and implement at provincial and district levels.'[196]

5.1.2 A National Drive to Eradicate GBV: The National Strategic Plan

The fundamental policies aimed at combatting GBV in South Africa are contained in the National Policy Framework on Child Justice and the National Policy Framework on the Management of Sexual Offences.[197] Even with this framework, the need to adopt an integrated programme of action to address violence against women and children has led to the establishment of a Cabinet-level Inter-Ministerial Committee (IMC) and a South African Integrated Programme of Action for 2013–2018 (POA).[198] Although the POA was cabinet approved and established a National Council Against Gender-Based Violence, the initiatives[199] introduced by the POA were not circulated at provincial or district level, lacked consultation with relevant stakeholders and had an insufficient budget allocation.[200] During the Presidential Summit on GBV

---

194 SAHRC *supra* note, 18.

195 UNHRC *supra* note 62 paragraph 82; South African Integrated Programme of Action *supra* note 186, 22.

196 UNHRC *supra* note 62, paragraph, 16.

197 South African Integrated Programme of Action *supra* note 186.

198 *Ibid*.

199 Including a range of existing and new measures aimed at complementing existing initiatives such as the Thuthuzela Care Centres, Sexual Offences Courts and other victim empowerment initiatives, the establishment of the Gender-Based Violence Command Centre by the Department of Social Development (DSD).

200 UNHRC *supra* note 62.

and Femicide (GBVF), an Interim GBVF Steering Committee was established in 2019 to develop a GBVF National Strategic Plan.[201]

The GBVF National Strategic Plan sets out to 'provide a multi-sectoral, coherent strategic policy and programming framework to strengthen a coordinated national response to the GBVF crisis.'[202] The Plan is underpinned by ten principle, *inter alia* a multi-sectoral approach to optimally harness the roles, responsibilities, resources and commitment across government departments and a meaningful participation by communities to ensure an inclusiveness, embracing diversity and intersectionality.[203]

The Plan has six outcomes, namely accountability, coordination and leadership; prevention and healing; law and policy; response, care and support; economic power and research and information systems.[204] As far as the first outcome is concerned, it is suggested that firm leadership and strengthened accountability by way of a multi-sectoral and resourced approach be implemented.[205] In this regard, a wider political commitment in addressing GBV is required to ensure effective coordination and collaboration among governmental departments.[206] The strategic approach therefore includes *inter alia* an educational platform.[207]

Outcome two entails proactive preventative and healing interventions by way of systemic and structural drivers of GBV. In this regard, the building of a social infrastructure that includes *inter alia* parenting programmes, alcohol abuse awareness campaigns and communication interventions is suggested to enable a societal shift around the use of violence overall and in particular changing the social acceptance of the propensity of male aggressive and dominant behaviour.[208] The Plan specifically acknowledges that for as long as gender-based discriminatory

201 National Strategic Plan on Gender-Based Violence Shadow Framework (2019).

202 Purpose of the National Strategic Plan on Gender-Based Violence.

203 The National Strategic Plan on Gender-Based Violence (2020–2030).

204 The National Strategic Plan on Gender-Based Violence (2020–2030).

205 The National Strategic Plan on Gender-Based Violence (2020–2030).

206 The National Strategic Plan on Gender-Based Violence (2020–2030) 42.

207 The National Strategic Plan on Gender-Based Violence (2020–2030) 43.

208 The National Strategic Plan on Gender-Based Violence (2020–2030) 51.

practices are condoned by society, woman's rights will fundamentally be compromised.[209]

As far as outcome three of the Plan is concerned, the strategy is to adopt transformative laws and to implement same and monitor effective enforcement.[210] During the presidential address, the need for progressive justice was highlighted amidst President Ramaphosa's plea for minimum sentencing in cases of gender-based violence.[211] Inter-sectoral victim-centred services and access to necessary resources is also fundamental to the Plan to ensure that service provision is coordinated, specifically in respect of accommodation, education and economic development.[212] Ultimately, in understanding GBV, vigorous monitoring of a multi-disciplinary information system is paramount to the effectiveness of the Plan.[213] For this to move from merely being an ambitious plan to a lasting solution to eradicate GBV in South Africa will require more than just funding but 'the involvement and support of our entire society.'[214] Although legislative amendment and proper implementation thereof is the first step to eradicate GBV, the bigger challenge is for South Africans to change their acceptance and condonation of GBV and to adopt a victim-centred approach to provide them with the required infrastructure and emotional support.

5.2 Drc

The Maputo Protocol requires that State Parties take appropriate measures to ensure that women have access to judicial and legal services.[215] In the DRC, article 12 of the 2005 Constitution guarantees equal access to justice for both men and women. Furthermore,

---

209 *Ibid,* 57.

210 *Ibid,* 56.

211 President Ramaphosa's address of the Nation, June 17, 2020.

212 The National Strategic Plan on Gender-Based Violence (2020–2030).

213 *Ibid.*

214 South African Government, *President Cyril Ramaphosa: South Africa's response to the COVID-19 Coronavirus Pandemic,* https://www.gov.za/speeches/president-cyril-ramaphosa-south-africa%E2%80%99s-response-covid-19-coronavirus-pandemic-17-jun-2020.

215 Maputo Protocol, Article 8.

article 19 guarantees everyone the right to be heard by the court, right to be assisted in all criminal procedures involving police or pre-trial investigation. These provisions are evidence that the Constitution guarantees access to court. However, in practice, women face challenges in approaching the court specifically in GBV cases.

Despite the landmark decision taken in South Kivu military court in the case of *The Government of the DRC v Frederick Batumike and other,*[216] it is clear that access to justice is not always possible in the DRC. This case concerned the rape of forty young girls. The cases were brought to court by the Task Force, a group of non-governmental organisations (NGO) who decided to fight impunity of perpetrators committing crimes against humanity.[217] Some of the constrains include high costs of legal proceedings, insufficient number of courts, corruption within the judicial system and the lack of sensitised judges and prosecutors.[218] Moreover, women lack basic knowledge of their rights, and they also experience fear of being rejected by the community if they approached the police with a rape case. Similarly, CEDAW concluding observations raised the following concern in respect of women access to justice[219]:

> (a) Women continue to face complex barriers to access to justice and remedies, such as the absence of courts, the limited number of judges in some provinces, the inability of the criminal justice system to locate perpetrators or collect evidence, the lack of sufficient financial resources among victims to pay the high costs of legal proceedings and the insecurity in conflict areas that limits travelling to distant judicial actors;
>
> (b) The adoption of the law on legal aid is still pending and there is no specific law to protect victims and witnesses;
>
> (c) Judicial facilities are inaccessible, especially in rural and conflict-affected areas, which prevents women, in particular vulnerable groups of women, from gaining access to justice and reparations;
>
> (d) Women are not sufficiently aware of existing laws, regulations and policies related to their rights and judges; prosecutors and law

---

[216] RP0105/2017. The final judgement in this case is available in French only at https://triali nternational.org/ wp-content/uploads/2017/12/Arr%C3%AAt-finalKavumuCM.pdf.

[217] See http://physiannsforhumanrights.org.

[218] Development Centre, *Democratic Republic of Congo* (2019).

[219] CEDAW, concluding observations, *supra* note 15.

> enforcement officials are not sufficiently and adequately trained on women's rights and the Convention on the Elimination of All Forms of Discrimination against Women;
>
> (e) Customary laws that discriminate against women continue to be enforced, including by traditional leaders and courts, in contravention of the statutory law, which prevails over customary law, according to the Constitution (art. 207).

Similarly, it can be argued that the DRC does not have specific mechanisms in place for the protection of survivors of GBV on their search for justice. What is commendable is that the government of the DRC also adopted a National Strategy in 2009 in response to violence against women and girls. Briefly, the strategy entails five components: '(i) fighting impunity, (ii) ensuring protection and prevention, (iii) undertaking security sector reforms, (iv) ensuring multi-sectoral assistance and (v) data and mapping.'[220] However, it has been indicated that 'The total appeal for the implementation of the Operational Plan between 2009 - 2011 is **US** $56million. To date actual (not pledged) donations within the STAREC funding Facility in support of this Plan are less than 20%.'[221]

In the light of the above exposition, it must be noted that despite comprehensive and progressive laws in place in especially South Africa to eradicate GBV, the implementation and enforcement of legislation are lacking. An obvious barrier to the effective implementation of legislation is financial constraints. Apart from the government's responsibilities to comply with conventions and protocols and provide protection to vulnerable groups exposed to GBV, one should also consider whether GBV is not a symptom of a wider challenge in society and therefore requiring a multi-sectoral or integrated approach.[222] The following section concludes this chapter and provides recommendations.

---

220 Development Centre *supra* note 218.

221 MONUSCO, *The Comprehensive Strategy on Combating Sexual Violence in the Democratic Republic of Congo,* https://monusco.unmissions.org/en/comprehensive-strategy.

222 Chalira and Ndimurwimo *supra* note 46.

6 Conclusion and Recommendations

The main question that this chapter sought to answer was whether legislative framework and the criminal justice system is effective to curb violence against women in South Africa and the DRC. In response, this chapter has identified the need for a multi-sectorial approach. In sum, this chapter firstly contextualised protection of women against GBV at international and regional level. Secondly, the overview of GBV in both South African and the DRC has been dealt with and to this end indicated that sexual violence as well domestic violence is prevalent in both countries. Thirdly, the legislative framework in respect of GBV and access to court has been discussed and it was emphasised that despite the provisions in place implementation remains a challenge. As indicated by the South African Human Rights Commission, there was also a lack of commitment on the part of government to apply several recommendations made at the domestic, regional and international level.[223] Fourthly, the chapter discussed the challenges that survivors face when seeking justice. It was revealed that the criminal system in both countries lacks adequate resources for effective enforcement. Having said this, the following are the recommendations:

- In both countries, GBV needs to be discouraged through addressing the root of the problem. Consequently, there is a need to deconstruct the patriarchal attitudes undermining the dignity of women and girls in society. Women must also be educated about their rights.
- In both counties, there is a need for training to sensitise law enforcement officials, as well as judicial authorities. This is to ensure a victim-centred approach. In this regard, there is a particular need for criminal justice reform in the DRC.
- There is a need for public awareness and community involvement. In this regard, men, including organisations and initiatives led by men, should drive the campaigns in preventing GBV.

[223] SAHRC *supra* note 18, 13.

- In addition, both governments should build a closer link and share information and exchange ideas with the local communities. As President Ramaphosa recently pointed out 'As a country we find ourselves in the midst of not one, but two, devastating epidemics which requires the involvement and support of our entire society.'[224] Local communities should therefore be made aware of the negative impact GBV have on women and society as a whole.

In conclusion, it is evident that a legislative framework in itself is not sufficient to curb GBV in South Africa nor in the DRC. Consequently, both countries should adapt an integrated approach which includes adequate resources, educational platforms to change societal perception on GBV, meaningful participation of all sectors of civil society as well as government commitment through strong leadership.

References

African Charter on Human and People's Rights (1981).

African Charter on the Rights and the Welfare of the Child (1990).

Banwell Stacy 'Rape and sexual violence in the Democratic Republic of Congo: A Case Study of Gender-Based Violence' 23 *Journal of Gender Studies* (2014): 45–58. https://doi.org/10.1080/09589236.2012.726603.

Budoo Ashwanee, 'Analysing the Monitoring Mechanism of the African Women's Protocol at the Level of the African Union' 18 *African Human Rights Law Journal* (2018): 58–74, https://doi.org/10.17159/1996-2096/2018/v18n1a3, June 20, 2020.

Burrow Sharan, 'Violence Against Women in Eastern Democratic Republic of Congo: Whose Responsibility? Whose Complicity' International Trade Union Confederation (November 2011).

Carlsen Erika, 'Rape and War in the Democratic Republic of the Congo' 21 *Peace Review* (2009): 474–483, https://doi.org/10.1080/1040265090332 3546.

[224] South African Government, President Ramaphosa address of the Nation June 17, 2020.

Carl Conradie and Shelly Whitman, *Our Work in the Democratic Republic of the Congo: 2009–2012* The Romeo Dallaire Childs soldiers initiative (2013), http://www.childsoldiers.org/publications/, June 20, 2020.

Carmichele v the Minister for safety and security 2001 4 SA 938 (CC).

Carolien Jacobs, 'Seeking Justice, Experiencing the State: The criminal Justice and Real Legal Uncertainty, in the Democratic Republic of Congo' 50. *The Journal of Legal Pluralism and Unofficial Law* (2018): 280–293.

Child Protection Law 09/001 of 2009 (DRC).

Chalira Nicole and Ndimurwimo Leah, 'Violence Against Women: A Comparative Analysis Between Malawi and South Africa' 32 *Speculum Juris* (2018): 107–122.

Cohen Dara Kay and Elisabeth Wood, *Is Sexual Violence During War Exceptional- or a Continuation of Everyday Violence?*' ISQ online (2016), http://www.isanet.org/publications/ISQ/posts/id/5239/issexual-violence-during-war-exceptional-or-a-continuation-ot-everyday-violence, June 20, 2020.

Committee on the Elimination of Discrimination against Women, Concluding observations on the eighth periodic report of the Democratic Republic of the Congo, C/COD/CO/8(2019).

Constitution of the Republic of South Africa (1996).

Constitution of the DRC (2006).

Convention on the Elimination of All forms of Discrimination against women (1979).

Criminal law (Sexual Offence and Related Matters) Amendment Act 32 of 2007.

Dartnall E and Jewkes R, 'Sexual Violence Against Women: The Scope of the Problem' 27 *Best Practice & Research Clinical Obstetrics & Gynaecology* (2012): 3–13.

Development Centre, *Democratic Republic of Congo* (2019), https://www.genderindex.org, June 20, 2020.

Domestic Violence Act 116 of 1998.

Draft Regulations Relating to Sexual Offences Courts: Criminal Law (Sexual Offences and Related Matters) Amendment Act, 32 of 2007.

Dubravka Šimonovi´c, *South Africa's Still Long Walk to Free Women from the Shackles of Violence,* The United Nations Special rapporteur on violence against women, during her visit to RSA (2015).

Gathii James Thuo, 'Popular Authorship and Constitution Making: Comparing and Contrasting the DRC and Kenya' 49 *William & Mary Law Review* (2008): 1110.

Gottschall Jonathan, 'Explaining Wartime rape' 41 *Journal of Sex Research* (2004): 129–136. https://doi.org/10.1080/00224490409552221, http://physiannsforhumanrights.org, June 20, 2020.
Home Office, 'Country Policy and Information Note Democratic Republic of Congo (DRC): Gender-Based Violence', September 2, 2018.
Kharel Amrit, *Doctrinal Legal Research* (February 26, 2018), https://ssrn.com/abstract=3130525 or https://doi.org/10.2139/ssrn.3130525, June 20, 2020.
Kandala Ngianga, Madungu Tumuaka, Emina, James Nzita and Cappuccio Francesco, 'Malnutrition Among Children Under the Age of Five in the Democratic Republic of Congo (DRC): Does Geographic Location Matter?' 11 *BMC Public Health* (2011), https://doi.org/10.1186/1471-2458-11-261.
Koos Carlo, 'Sexual Violence in Armed Conflicts: Research Progress and Remaining Gaps' 38 *Third World Quately* (2017): 1935–1951.
Law No 06/018 of 20 July 2006 modifying and completing the Decree of January 30, 1940 relating to the Congolese Penal Code (DRC).
MADRE, SOFEPADI, 'Gender-Based Violence and Discrimination Against Women and Girls in the Democratic Republic of Congo: A Report for CEDAW' (2018).
Maluleke Mikateko and Madonsela Thuli, 'Women and the Law in South Africa: Gender Equality Jurisprudence in Land Mark Court Decisions' (2004) *Department of Justice and Constitutional Development*.
Matadi Tholaine, *The Realisation of Children's Survival Rights in South Africa and the DRC: A Comparative Study* (PhD Thesis, University of Zululand 2018).
Meintjes-Van der Walt L, Singh P, Du Preez M, De Freitas SA, Chinnian K, Barratt A, Govindjee A, Iya P, De Bruin JH, Van Coller, *Introduction to South African Law: Fresh Perspectives* (2019).
Meyiwa T Williamson, Mased T and Ntabanyane Gladys-Magdeline, 'A Twenty-Year Review of Policy Landscape for Gender-Based Violence in South Africa' *Gender & Behaviour* (2017): 8607–8617.
Ministry for the Advancement of Women and the Integration for Women in Development, *National Programme for the Promotion of Women's Leadership in Political and Public Life in the Republic of Congo* (2016), https://info.undp.org/docs/pdc/Documents/COG/Programme%20National%20Leadership%20féminin%20en%20politique%20en%20république%20du%20Congo.pdf, June 20, 2020.
MONUSCO, *The Comprehensive Strategy on Combating Sexual Violence in the Democratic Republic of Congo*, https://monusco.unmissions.org/en/comprehensive-strategy, June 20, 2020.

Nyemba Nice Mpala, *The Impact of Poverty on Children's Rights in the Democratic Republic of Congo* (LLM Thesis, University of Pretoria 2015).

Ntlama Nomthandazo, 'The Role of Human Rights Activists in Exposing and Denouncing Human Rights Violations That Silence Women' 44 *Codicullus* (2003): 110–117.

Penal Code 06/018 of 2006.

Rail Commuters' Action Group v Transnet LTD and Others (2004).

S v Chapman 1997 (3) SA 341(SCA).

South African Human Rights Commission, *Research Brief: Unpacking the Gaps and Challenges in Addressing Gender-Based Violence in South Africa* (April 2018).

South African Integrated Programme of Action Addressing Violence Against Women and Children (2013–2018).

South African Government, *President Cyril Ramaphosa: South Africa's Response to the COVID-19 Coronavirus Pandemic*, (June 2020), https://www.gov.za/speeches/president-cyril-ramaphosa-south-africa%E2%80%99s-response-covid-19-coronavirus-pandemic-17-jun-2020, June 20, 2020.

The Government of the DRC v Frederick Batumike and Other RPO 105/2017.

The Presidency of the Republic of South Africa, *National Planning Commission National Development Plan 2030: Our Future - Make It Work* (2012).

Trenholm JE, Olsson P and Ahlberg BM, 'Battles on Women Bodies: War, Rape and Traumatisation in Eastern Democratic Republic of Congo' 6 *International Maternal and Child Health* (2011): 139–152.

United Nations Human Rights Council, *Report of the Special Rapporteur on Violence Against Women, its Causes and consequences on Her Mission to South Africa*, A/HRC/32/42/Add.2 (2016).

United Nations Children's Fund, *A Familiar Face: Violence in the Lives of children and adolescent* (2017).

United Nations Declaration on the Elimination of Violence against Women (1993).

United Nations Universal Declaration of Human Rights (1948), https://www.un.org/en/udhrbook/pdf/udhr_booklet_en_web.pdf, June 20, 2020.

UN General Assembly. *Transforming the World: The 2030 Agenda for Sustainable Development*, A/RES/70/1. (2015).

United Nations (1966). International Covenant on Civil and Political Rights, http://www2.Ohcr.org/English/law/ccpr.htm, June 20, 2020.

United Nations International Covenant on economic, social and Cultural Rights (1966), http://www2.Ohcr.org/English/law/cescr.htm, June 20, 2020.

United Nations Population Fund, *Gender Based Violence: What Do We Do* (2020) https://www.unfpa.org/gender-based-violence, June 20, 2020.

Van Eeden v Minister of Safety and Security 2003 (1) SA 389 (SCA).

Vetten L, 'Violence against Women in South Africa' in Buhlungu S, Daniel J, Southall R and Lutchman J (eds) *State of the Nation: South Africa* (2007).

Vetten L, 'Show Me the Money: A Review of Budgets Allocated towards the Implementation of South Africa's Domestic Violence Act' 32 *Politikon: South African Journal of Political Studies* (2003): 277–295.

Williams C, 'Explaining the Great War in Africa: How Conflict in the Congo Became a Continental Crisis' 37 *The Fletcher Forum of World Affairs* (2013): 81–100.

WHO, *Report on Violence and Health* (2002).

WH), *Global and Regional Estimates of Violence Against Women 2013: Global Study on Homicide* (2019).

Zihindula Bercky M, Makhubele Jabulani and Muthuki Janet, 'Challenges Endured by Women During the Conflict Related Sexual Violence in the Democratic Republic of the Congo' 16 *Gender and Behaviour* (2018), https://www.ajol.info/index.php/gab/cart/view/175287/164671, June 20, 2020.

Zongwe D, Butedi F and Mavungu P, *The Legal System and Research of the Democratic Republic of Congo (DRC): An Overview* http://www.nyulawglobal.org/globalex/DemocraticRepublicCongo1.htm, June 20, 2020.

4

Access to Justice for Survivors of Violence: A Case Study of the Girl Child in Mauritius

Shivani Georgijevic and Ashwanee Budoo-Scholtz

1 Introduction

Violence, it is generally agreed, is never a good thing. However, globally, cases abound of violence and children have not been spared. This seems to be a contradiction as different cultures around the world accept that

[1] 'Une mort atroce à deux ans: Pourquoi la mère d'Ayaan n'a rien fait?' *L'express.mu* (November 16, 2020), https://www.lexpress.mu/article/385149/une-mort-atroce-deux-ans-pourquoi-mere-dayaan-na-rien-fait.

S. Georgijevic
Faculty of Law and Management, University of Mauritius, Moka, Mauritius
e-mail: s.guness@uom.ac.mu

A. Budoo-Scholtz (✉)
Centre for Human Rights Faculty of Law, University of Pretoria, Pretoria, South Africa
e-mail: ashwanee.budoo@up.ac.za

E. C. Lubaale and A. Budoo-Scholtz (eds.), *Violence Against Women and Criminal Justice in Africa: Volume I*, Sustainable Development Goals Series,
https://doi.org/10.1007/978-3-030-75949-0_4

children are important. Mauritius is not an exception despite its seemingly peaceful society amidst the sandy beaches. Recently, in November 2020, the country was shaken by the death of a two-year-old boy who was killed by his stepfather.[1] This was the second incident of a child abused to death in 2020—another case involving a 10-year-old girl who was beaten to death by her mother and stepfather in March 2020.[2] These cases are extreme and unfortunately violence by parents against their children is rarely reported to the authorities until it is either extreme or too late.

Out of a population of about 1.3 million people, on 1 July 2019, there were about 156, 532 females who were under the age of 19 in Mauritius.[3] Although there are no official statistics by Statistics Mauritius on girls under the age of 18 (despite the Penal describing a child as 'an individual of each sex who is under the age of 18'),[4] the foregoing figures indicate that at least 10% of the population are girls under the age of 18. In patriarchal Mauritius,[5] many of the 10% face violence in the form of rape, incest, physical abuse, bullying, child trafficking

---

[2] 'Meutre d'une gamine de 10 ans: un bébé des parents déjà mort en janvier' *L'express.mu* (March 30, 2020), https://www.lexpress.mu/node/373708.

[3] Statistics Mauritius, *Population and Vital Statistics – 2019*, http://statsmauritius.govmu.org/English/Publications/Documents/2020/EI1505/Pop_Vital_Yr19.pdf.

[4] Mauritian laws, however, also strive to guarantee the child's protection by ensuring with special laws (*lex specialis*) that adequate protection is afforded according to the age of the minor. For instance, Sect. 9 of the Worker's Rights Act of 2019 addresses the issue of employment of young persons, i.e., minors of age between 16 and 18. In principle, those persons have the capacity required to enter a work agreement, but they benefit also from the special legal protection. The real minors, from the point of view of the Worker's Rights Act of 2019, are children under the age of 16. They do not have the necessary capacity to enter work agreements which are considered to be null and void. This rule is in line with Sect. 37 (2) of the Education Act of 1957 which stipulates that 'it shall be compulsory for every child to attend school up to the end of the academic year in the course of which he attains the age of 16'. In order to ensure the respect of the above mentioned rule, Sect. 37 (3) of the Education Act provides that 'any responsible party of a child under the age of 16 who, without reasonable cause, refuses or neglects to cause the child to attend school regularly in accordance with subsection (…) (2) shall commit an offence and shall, on conviction, be liable to a fine not exceeding 10,000 rupees and to a term of imprisonment not exceeding 2 years.'

[5] See generally Lindsey Collen *The Rape of Sita* (2004); Felicity Hand *The Subversion of Class and Gender Roles in the Novels of Lindsey Collen* (1948), *Mauritian Social Activist and Writer* (2010).

including sex work,[6] child marriage[7] and online child sexual exploitation.[8] The situation of vulnerability of a child is further exacerbated by abuse. The Child Rights International Network (CRIN) has ranked Mauritius 101th on the subject of the effectiveness of the country's legal system in guaranteeing children's right to access to justice.[9]

Statistics Mauritius has reported an increase from 2018 to 2019 of 9.5% per 100,000 female population in cases of sexual violence and sexual exploitation against women.[10] Additionally, amongst the 685 victims of these sexual offences, 92.6% were female. The vulnerability of minors is confirmed by the fact that 67% of the 685 victims of sexual offences were reported to be minors under 16 years of age. Furthermore, the majority (92.3%) of the juvenile victims of sexual violence and sexual exploitation were female.[11]

In respect of homicide in 2019, there were four juvenile victims of attempted intentional homicide and two juvenile victims, one female, of non-intentional homicide.[12] Moreover, the statistics for assault in the same year show that there were 813 juvenile victims amongst which 38.6% were girls.[13] The judiciary also provides insight into situations where minors, including girls, were involved in violence. Thus, in 2018,

[6] Jameela Jadoo for Defimedia.info, *Child abuse: The despicable side of our Paradise*, November 28, 2018 https://defimedia.info/child-abuse-despicable-side-our-paradise.

[7] A Budoo, *It's time Mauritius took decisive steps to outlaw child marriages*, The Conversation July 3, 2018 https://theconversation.com/its-time-mauritius-took-decisive-steps-to-outlaw-child-marriages-99226.

[8] Halley Movement and Pan-Mauritius Coalition and ECPAT International, *Sexual exploitation of Children in Mauritius' submitted to the 31st session of the Human Rights Council* (October–November 2018) on March 29, 2018 for the Universal Periodic Review of the human rights situation in Mauritius 3.

[9] https://archive.crin.org/en/access-justice-children-global-ranking.

[10] Statistics Mauritius, *Crime, Justice and Security Statistics 2019*, http://statsmauritius.govmu.org/English/Publications/Pages/CJS_Stats_Yr19.aspx.

[11] In respect of sexual violence and sexual exploitation, the following was further reported: 'From year 2018 to year 2019, victims of sexual violence and sexual exploitation increased by 17.1% from 475 to 556 mainly due to rises in 'Causing child to be sexually abused; accessing to a brothel; and engaging in prostitution' from 150 to 200 (+33.3%) and 'Sexual intercourse with minor under the age of 16' from 186 to 204 (+9.7%). There was one victim of 'Sexual harassment' in 2019 compared to 4 in 2018. It is to be noted that rape fell from 14 to 11 while sodomy rose from 17 in 2018 to 28 in 2019'. Statistics Mauritius *supra* note 10.

[12] Statistics Mauritius *supra* note 10.

[13] *Ibid.*

out of 1513 applications for Protection Orders (spouse/partner) made under the Protection from Domestic Violence Act 1997 at the District Courts, eight were made by females under the age of 18. Three orders were issued and one case was ordered to attend counselling sessions.[14]

The Ministry of Gender Equality and Family Welfare through the Child Development Unit (CDU) does not provide comprehensive data about the number and types of cases received. However, the 2017–2018 report of the Ombudsperson for Children (OC) states that from January to April 2018, the CDU received 1789 cases of child abuse, out of which 102 concerned child sexual abuse.[15] In 2017, 5105 cases were reported, with 260 on child sexual abuse.

It is undeniable that there is a problem of violence against the girl child in Mauritius. There are several laws in Mauritius that ensure that the girl child has access to justice in the event that she has been subjected to violence. To begin with, the Constitution of Mauritius provides for several civil and political rights and freedoms for each individual and these therefore extend to children.[16] In addition to the Constitution, other laws such as the Child Protection Act 1994, the Ombudsperson for Children's Act 2003 and the Penal Code contain provisions relating to the protection of the child and access to justice.[17] However, the international community through, for instance, the United Nations (UN) Committee on the Rights of the Child[18] and the African Commission on Human and Peoples' Rights (African Commission)[19] have time and again recommended that Mauritius adopts a comprehensive law on the rights of the child that gives effect to the provisions of international law. Hence, the draft Children's Bill, that will replace the Child Protection

---

[14] The Supreme Court of Mauritius, *Annual Report of the Judiciary* (2018), https://supremecourt.govmu.org/pubabout/Annual%20Report%20of%20the%20Judiciary%202018%20(1).pdf.

[15] Office of the Ombudsperson for Children Annual Report 2017–2018 262.

[16] Elaborated upon in part 3.1.1.

[17] These laws are further detailed below in Sect. 3.

[18] UN Committee on the Rights of the Child, *Concluding Observations to the combined third to fifth periodic reports of Mauritius*, CRC/C/MUS/CO/3–5, February 4, 2015 paragraph 8.

[19] African Commission 'Concluding Observations and Recommendations on the 6th to 8th Combined Report of the Republic of Mauritius on the Implementation of the African Charter on Human and Peoples' Rights' adopted at the 60th Ordinary Session of the African Commission from 8 to May 22, 2017 Section V paragraph xxvi.

Act, is an attempt to ensure a comprehensive protection for the rights of the child in line with international instruments. Therefore, in addition to studying the current framework, it is important to study the draft Children's Bill with the view of ascertaining whether it provides a holistic approach on access to justice for the girl child who is a survivor of violence.

This chapter analyses access to justice for the girl child who is a survivor of violence in Mauritius. It firstly introduces the topic. Second, while focusing on the global, regional and sub-regional level, it elaborates on Mauritius' international obligations to ensure that the girl child who is a survivor of violence has access to justice. Third, it does a situational analysis on access to justice for the girl child in cases of violence. Fourth, the draft Children's Bill is analysed with the view of assessing the extent to which, if any, the latter will change the landscape of access to justice for girls, survivors of violence. Fifth, the chapter studies the challenges that the girl child who is a survivor of violence faces in access justice in Mauritius. Finally, there is a conclusion and recommendations section.

2 Mauritius' International Obligations to Ensure that the Girl Child Who is a Survivor of Violence Has Access to Justice

2.1 United Nations and Access to Justice for the Girl Child

Several instruments at the UN level[20] provide for access to justice of the girl child who is a survivor of violence, the most important one here being the United Nations Convention of the Rights of the Child (UN CRC). It clearly sets out four general principles that every State Party needs to take into consideration for the rights of every child to be respected, protected and fulfilled. These principles include life, survival and development, non-discrimination, child participation and the best interests of the child. The right to life, survival and development is at the foundation of the necessity to ensure that violence against the girl child must be legally sanctioned as such violence goes against the right of the girl child to enjoy a life of quality with a healthy development.

[20] Convention on the Elimination of All Forms of Discrimination Against Women and General Recommendations 19 and 35 of the Committee on the Elimination of Discrimination Against Women; Para q of the Preamble of the Convention on the Rights of Persons with Disabilities (CRPD): 'Recognizing that women and girls with disabilities are often at greater risk, both within and outside the home, of violence, injury or abuse, neglect or negligent treatment, maltreatment or exploitation'; Article 16 of the CRPD: (1) States Parties shall take all appropriate legislative, administrative, social, educational and other measures to protect persons with disabilities, both within and outside the home, from all forms of exploitation, violence and abuse, including their gender-based aspects … (4) States Parties shall take all appropriate measures to promote the physical, cognitive and psychological recovery, rehabilitation and social reintegration of persons with disabilities who become victims of any form of exploitation, violence or abuse, including through the provision of protection services. Such recovery and reintegration shall take place in an environment that fosters the health, welfare, self-respect, dignity and autonomy of the person and takes into account gender- and age-specific needs … (5) States Parties shall put in place effective legislation and policies, including women- and child-focused legislation and policies, to ensure that instances of exploitation, violence and abuse against persons with disabilities are identified, investigated and, where appropriate, prosecuted and; Article 7 of the International Covenant on Civil and Political Rights: 'No one shall be subjected to torture or to cruel, inhuman or degrading treatment or punishment. In particular, no one shall be subjected without his free consent to medical or scientific experimentation.'

Moreover, article 39 of the CRC provides for the 'physical and psychological recovery and social reintegration of a child' who has been a victim of violence. Access to justice therefore can be argued to go beyond the punishment of the perpetrator of violence. The state has to ensure that, in line with the right to life, survival and development, measures are taken for the child to be given appropriate attention for her recovery and reintegration.

The non-discrimination principle reinforces the obligation to leave no child behind. Access to justice by every single child survivor of violence is primordial. Such access to justice is facilitated by ensuring that the girl child is able to participate in matters concerning herself. The UN Committee on the Rights of the Child (UN CRC Committee) has also emphasised on the right of the child to be heard as an important principle in the UN CRC and its relevance has been highlighted in the context of the criminal justice system to protect child victims.[21] This right has also been identified as being a useful tool in the family context to empower the child in the prevention of violence.[22] The Third Optional Protocol on communications procedure (OPIC) to the UN CRC is also in line with this principle.

Finally, the consideration of the best interests of the child requires acknowledging the vulnerability of the latter[23] and ensuring that all actions taken are compatible with the best interests of the child. Furthermore, the UN CRC Committee indicated that the notion of the best

[21] 'States parties must be aware of the potential negative consequences of an inconsiderate practice of this right [article 12], particularly in cases involving very young children, or in instances where the child has been a victim of a criminal offence, sexual abuse, violence, or other forms of mistreatment. States parties must undertake all necessary measures to ensure that the right to be heard is exercised ensuring full protection of the child.' Page 9, paragraph 21 in UN CRC Committee, General Comment No. 12 (2009), The right of the child to be heard, CRC/C/GC/12, July 20, 2009.

[22] An approach favouring the expression of views of the child 'serves to promote individual development, enhance family relations and support children's socialization and plays a preventive role against all forms of violence in the home and family', Page 21, paragraph 90 in UN CRC Committee, General Comment No. 12 (2009), The right of the child to be heard, CRC/C/GC/12, 20 July 2009.

[23] Para 75 UN CRC Committee General comment No. 14 (2013) on the right of the child to have his or her best interests taken as a primary consideration (art. 3, para. 1), May 2013 CRC/C/GC/14.

interest of the child, as stated by article 3 of the UN CRC, includes the right to be protected from all forms of violence and exploitation.[24]

Additionally, article 19 of the UN CRC specifically addresses the right to access to justice of the girl child who is a survivor of violence. It provides for the state's obligation to protect the child against violence 'while in the care of parent(s), legal guardian(s) or any other person who has the care of the child'.[25] This obligation calls for action at different levels, namely legislative, administrative, social and educational.[26] Article 19(2) of the UN CRC further requires states to set up mechanisms, including judicial involvement, to deal with instances of child maltreatment.

2.2 African Union and Access to Justice for the Girl Child

The three legal instruments at the African Union level that are relevant for this research are the African Charter on Human and Peoples' Rights (African Charter),[27] the Protocol to the African Charter on the Rights of Women in Africa (Maputo Protocol)[28] and the African Charter on the Rights and Welfare of the Child (African Children's Charter).[29] All three instruments are applicable to the girl child with the African Charter's non-discrimination clause,[30] the definition of a woman in the Maputo Protocol[31] and the definition of the child[32]

---

24 *Ibid.*, paragraph 73.

25 CRC, Article 19(1).

26 CRC, Article 19(1).

27 Mauritius ratified the African Charter in June 1992.

28 Mauritius ratified the Maputo Protocol in June 2017.

29 Mauritius ratified the African Children's Charter in February 1992.

30 African Charter, Article 2: 'Every individual shall be entitled to the enjoyment of the rights and freedoms recognized and guaranteed in the present Charter without distinction of any kind such as race, ethnic group, color, sex, language, religion, political or any other opinion, national and social origin, fortune, birth or other status.'

31 Maputo Protocol, Article 1(k): 'Women' means persons of female gender, including girls'.

32 African Children's Charter, Article 2: 'For the purposes of this Charter, a child means every human being below the age of 18 years.

and non-discrimination provision[33] in the African Children's Charter. The African Charter and the Maputo Protocol have specific provisions relating to access to justice,[34] with the Maputo Protocol having a specific provision requiring states to 'punish perpetrators of violence'.[35] Instead of a separate provision focusing on access to justice, the African Children's Charter includes such a right in most of its provisions when it requires states to take appropriate measures to ensure that the right of the child is not violated. This was confirmed by the African Committee on the Rights and Welfare of the Child's (African Children's Committee) General Comment 5 (General Comment 5) that expands on states' obligations under article 1 of the African Children's Charter and emphasises on the role of the a child-sensitive justice system in implementing its provisions.[36] Moreover, the Joint General Comment of the African Commission and the African Children's Committee on Ending Child Marriage (General Comment on Child Marriage) require States Parties to adopt institutional measures to promote access to justice for survivors of child marriage. As such, Mauritius has an obligation under the African Charter, the Maputo Protocol and the African Children's Charter to ensure that the girl child who is a survivor of violence has access to the justice system.

3 Current Framework on Access to Justice for the Girl Child in Cases of Violence

Access to justice has been defined as 'the system by which people may vindicate their rights and/or resolve disputes under the general auspices

[33] African Children's Charter,Article 3: 'Every child shall be entitled to the enjoyment of the rights and freedoms recognized and guaranteed in this Charter irrespective of the child's or his/her parents' or legal guardians' race, ethnic group, color, sex, language, religion, political or other opinion, national and social origin fortune, birth or other status.

[34] African Charter, Article 7; Maputo Protocol, Articles 1, 4 and 8.

[35] Maputo Protocol, Article 4(e).

[36] African Children's Committee General Comment No 5 'State party obligations under the African Charter on the Rights and Welfare of the Child (Article 1) and systems strengthening r child protection' (2018) 23.

of the state'.[37] Hence, the government has to adopt laws and set up systems to ensure that the rights of citizens are protected.[38] Taking this as a background, this section firstly studies the laws concerning access to justice and violence against the girl child. Second, it assesses the modalities through which the girl child can access the courts. Third, it expands on the policies and plans of actions that concern access to justice for the girl child in cases of violence. Fourth, it analyses how institutions can assist the girl child in accessing justice in cases of violence.

3.1 Legal Provisions on Violence Against the Girl Child and Access to Justice

3.1.1 The Constitution

The Constitution of Mauritius is the supreme law of the land[39] and its provisions apply to everyone irrespective of sex.[40] Although it does not expressly mention the girl child, the fact that it applies to everyone implies that it includes the girl child. The Constitution provides for several civil and political rights that can ensure that the girl is protected from violence. Some of these are the protection of the right to life,[41] protection of the right to personal liberty,[42] protection from slavery and forced labour,[43] protection from inhumane treatment,[44] protection of freedom of movement[45] and protection from discrimination.[46] However, the Constitution neither specifically mentions the protection of women

[37] Bryant G Garth and Mauro Cappelletti 'Access to justice: The Newest Wave in the Worldwide Movement to make Rights Effective' 27 *Buffalo Law Review* (1978): 182.

[38] Maria F Moscati *The Role of Transitional Justice and Access to Justice in Conflict Resolution and Democratic Advancement* (2015) 9–11.

[39] Constitution, Sect. 2.

[40] *Ibid*, Sect. 3.

[41] *Ibid*, Sect. 4.

[42] *Ibid*, Sect. 5.

[43] *Ibid*, Sect. 6.

[44] *Ibid*, Sect. 7.

[45] *Ibid*, Sect. 15.

[46] *Ibid*, Sect. 16.

from violence nor provides for the right to access courts despite providing for the right to fair trial. The girl child is legally protected from violence under Acts of Parliaments and the Penal Code.

3.1.2 The Penal Code

There are several provisions in the Mauritian Penal Code that criminalise different types of violence against the girl child. Concerning assault,[47] it specifically mentions assault on children under the age of 16 as an aggravating circumstance.[48] The Penal Code goes a step further and criminalises the written threat of violence.[49] It also criminalises rape and sexual intercourse with a minor under the age of 16.[50] Article 249(5) of the Penal Code further provides for indecent acts upon the stepchild, adopted child, child dependents and the child living under the same roof and article 250 criminalises sodomy and bestiality. Concerning child sex workers, there is a section on debauching youth, which includes exciting and facilitating debauchery or corruption and facilitating prostitution of the youth under 18,[51] and a section on procuring, enticing and exploiting prostitute.[52] Article 254 further provides for sexual harassment. The girl child who has been subjected to one of the above therefore has the means of redress since they are offences in the Penal Code.

3.1.3 The Sexual Offences Act

The Sexual Offences Act, adopted in 2007, defines 'specified persons' as including the following[53]:

(i) a stepchild or an adopted child, of whatever age, of the accused;

[47] Penal Code, Articles 228 to 232.
[48] Penal Code, Article 228(5)(a).
[49] Penal Code, Article 224.
[50] Penal Code, Sect. 249.
[51] Penal Code, Article 251.
[52] Penal Code, Article 253.
[53] Sexual Offences Act, Sect. 2(b.

(ii) a person under the age of 18 whose custody or guardianship has been entrusted to the accused by virtue of any other enactment or of an order of a Court;
(iii) a person under the age of 18, other than the spouse of, and living under the same roof as the accused;
(iv) the child of whatever age of the partner of the accused;
(v) a mentally handicapped person.

In terms of sexual offences, the Sexual Offences Act is more specific than the Penal Code in that it has specific provisions for rape of person under 16, sexual assault of person under 16 by penetration, sexual assaults on persons under 16 and under 12, causing a person under 16 to engage in sexual activity, engaging in sexual activity in the presence of a child and causing a child to watch a sexual act.[54] It specifies that sexual act with specified persons, even with consent, is an offence.[55]

3.1.4 The Child Protection Act

The Child Protection Act was adopted in 1994 and defines a child as 'any unmarried person under the age of 18'.[56] This implies that the provisions of this Act are not applicable to the girl child who has been emancipated by marriage and leave them in the same arena as adults who have been harmed. Harm, for the purposes of the Child Protection Act, is 'physical, sexual, psychological, emotional or moral injury, neglect, ill-treatment, impairment of health or development'.[57] The Child Protection Act mandates the Permanent Secretary of the Ministry of Gender Equality, Child Development and Family Welfare to enquire into a matter, including summoning a person to give evidence with or without the child, in the event he/she 'has reasonable cause to suspect that a child is being exposed to harm and is in need of assistance'.[58] It also provides

[54] *Ibid*, Sects. 11 to 16.
[55] *Ibid*, Sect. 18.
[56] *Ibid*, Sect. 2.
[57] *Ibid*.
[58] Child Protection Act, Sect. 3.

for emergency protection orders by a District Magistrate. In addition to the umbrella term harm, it has specific provisions and definitions for ill treatment, child trafficking, abandonment of child, abducting child, sexual offences, indecent photographs of children, licensed premises and mendicity.[59] The fact that the Act zooms on these terms and the punishment accompanying them indicates that the document is one that ensures that the child, including the girl child, has a remedy in the event she has been subjected to these acts of violence. The Children's Rights Bill that will replace the Child Protection Act is purported to strengthen the protection of the rights of the child, including the girl child when it comes to violence. This Bill will be discussed below.

3.2 The Girl Child and the Court

Once a girl has made a police complaint of acts of violence protected under the above laws, an enquiry will entail involving the Police and the Child Development Unit that will determine whether or not there will be prosecution. In Mauritius, the Director of Public Prosecutions (DPP) is mandated 'to institute and undertake criminal proceedings before any court of law'.[60] Hence, in a case of violence against the girl child, the prosecution will be instituted by the DPP. In the event the DPP refuses to prosecute the case, the aggrieved party may institute a private prosecution.

Once the case is before the Court, the girl who is a survivor of violence is allowed to be a witness. If she is less than nine years old, the Judge or Magistrate before whom the case is brought needs to be satisfied that she 'has sufficient intelligence to make a correct statement on the subject of the trial, although (s)he may not understand the nature of an oath or of a solemn affirmation'.[61] Such a child will make a promise to speak the truth in the presence of the Judge or Magistrate.[62] The Court has admitted such evidence in the cases of *Basenoo vs The Queen* 1983 MR

[59] *Ibid,* Sects. 13 to 17.

[60] Constitution, Sect. 72.

[61] Criminal Procedure Act of 1853, Sect. 109.

[62] *Ibid,* Sect. 110.

89, *Jeetah v the State* 2014 SCJ 337, *Pakeroo J v The State* 2014 SCJ 371 and *Cawder MR v. The State* 2016 SCJ 65.

In the case of *Jeetah v the State* 2014 SCJ 337, the Mauritian Supreme Court's Full Bench has clearly established the principles applicable to child witnesses, survivors of violence. The Court has founded its reasoning on Sects. 106 and 109 of the Criminal Procedure Act of 1853. This judicial decision is even more meaningful in the context of ensuring justice against violence in Mauritius as it disagrees with the case of *Basenoo v The Queen* 1983 MR 89, where the Supreme Court held that 'A person who is over the age of 9 is always competent to depone as a witness on oath or solemn affirmation'.[63] In the case of *Jeetah*, the Court held that minors aged between 9 and 14 have to undergo a competency test in order to establish whether or not the minor is competent to give evidence under oath or solemn affirmation. Finally, it has also been confirmed that a minor aged 14 or more is always competent to give evidence in cases of violence.[64]

The criminal justice system also provides for the protection of the privacy of the child. For instance, under Sect. 161A (b) of the Courts Act 1945, the Court may exclude persons under the age of 18 in proceedings in order to safeguard their welfare. Moreover, in cases of sexual offences, the victim or witness may depone through 'live video or live television link system'[65] although there is not yet any judgement by the Supreme Court pertaining to this situation. Hence, the girl child can access the Courts in the event she has been subjected to the acts of violence provided by the law.

---

[63] 'The first rule in Basenoo – the impugned dictum – was therefore wrongly formulated and should be reformulated to convey that any child who does not fall within the ambit of Sect. 109 [more than 9 years] of the Criminal Procedure Act can only be a competent witness giving evidence under oath or solemn affirmation under Sect. 106, if such competency is established following the holding of the appropriate test.'.

[64] The necessity of the right to be heard has been emphasised upon in respect to judicial and administrative proceedings. Page 9, paragraph 32 in UN CRC Committee, General Comment No. 12 (2009), The right of the child to be heard, CRC/C/GC/12, 20 July 2009.

[65] Courts Act, Sect. 161B (1).

3.3 Institutions

In addition to the Court, the state has set up institutions such as Child Development Unit (CDU) and the Ombudsperson for Children that focus specifically on children. These institutions ensure that the girl child who is a survivor of violence has access to justice.

3.3.1 The Child Development Unit

The CDU operates under the aegis of the Minister of Gender Equality and Family Welfare.[66] If a child is a survivor of violence, the CDU has the duty to intervene 'promptly' to ensure that the survivor has a comprehensive assistance. It enables access to justice of the girl child since it has the obligation to:

- provide for Protection Services to victims of violence, abuse and neglect on a 24 h 7 days basis;
- provide for hotline service with respect to reporting of a case and counselling as appropriate;
- provide victims with follow-up sessions to ensure recovery from trauma and thereafter their re-insertion in society;
- prepare and support children victims of violence for legal encounters;

  ...
- provide Alternative care to abused children, ranging from temporary removal to a shelter for children in distress, to foster caring and eventually, as a last resort, committal to a charitable institution;
- provide victims of Commercial Sexual Exploitation with curative, rehabilitative and reintegrative services;

  ...
- act as Central Authority in International Child Abduction cases;
- provide trained mentors to children seen to be in distress because of mild behavioural problems through a well-spelt child Mentoring Programme

[66] Website of the Minister of Gender Equality and Family Welfare, http://gender.govmu.org/English/Pages/Units/Child-Development-Unit.aspx.

The CDU therefore ensures that the girl child who is a survivor of violence is empowered to deal with the legal, psychological and rehabilitation procedures.

3.3.2 The Ombudsperson for Children

The Ombudsperson for Children's Act adopted in 2003 established the Office of Ombudsperson for Children, the objectives of which are to[67]:

(a) ensure that the rights, needs and interests of children are given full consideration by public bodies, private authorities, individuals and associations of individuals;
(b) promote the rights and best interests of children;
(c) promote compliance with the Convention.

In order to fulfil these objectives, the Ombudsperson for Children is mandated to, amongst others, investigate cases and complaints relating to violations of the rights of the child, including child labour.[68] Once the investigation is complete, the Ombudsperson for children can make a report to the authority that they consider appropriate.[69] It is to be noted that the Office of the Ombudsperson for Children is not allowed to investigate into a case that is pending before the Court although it 'may refer any child involved in such a case to the Ministry for advice, assistance or counselling'.[70]

Hence, if the girl child finds it daunting to go to Courts, she can approach the Office of the Ombudsperson for Children for redress and for support. However, it can be argued that the resources within the Office are insufficient with only five investigators constituting staff supporting the Ombudsperson for Children's work for the Mauritian territory, including outer islands.

[67] Ombudsperson for Children Act, Sect. 5.
[68] *Ibid*, Sect. 6.
[69] *Ibid*, Sect. 7(3).
[70] *Ibid*, Sect. 7(4).

3.3.3 The Judicial System

Currently, cases pertaining to children are heard under the same judicial system as that for adults. The Mauritian judicial system is made up of a Supreme Court with four divisions: civil, criminal, family and commercial divisions. Furthermore, there are subordinate courts being an Intermediate Court, an Industrial Court and thirteen District Courts. The latter are required to act as a juvenile court as per Sect. 3 of the Juvenile Offenders Act 1935 (JOA) and administer justice in cases involving juvenile offenders.

Regulations of judicial procedures are also sensitive to minors and complainants of sexual offences. In matters of evidence, any judge or magistrate may exclude from the proceedings persons other than those involved in the trial and their legal representatives in order to 'safeguard the welfare of persons under the age of 18'.[71] Furthermore, in respect of a complainant in a sexual offence case, the Court has discretion to allow the person to depone through live video or live television link system as may be approved in writing by the Chief Justice.[72]

The above judicial system is subject to reform as the Children's Bill proposes to introduce child-specific and child-friendly judicial institutions and procedures. This is in line with the Concluding Observations of the UN CRC Committee for Mauritius.[73] Sections 72 to 78 of the Bill provide for the creation of divisions within a specialised court for children, that is the Children's Court. Thus, there will be Protection Division of Children's Court as well as Criminal Division of the aforementioned Court. Those divisions will play an important role in ensuring access to justice in cases of violence against girls in Mauritius. They would undeniably also serve the purposes of prevention and repression of violence against children by standing as specialised judicial bodies adapted to children's needs.

---

[71] Courts Act, Sect. 161A.

[72] Courts Act, Sect. 161B.

[73] 2015 The Committee also requested the State to have 'designated specialized judges for children and ensure that such specialized judges receive appropriate education and training.'.

4 Provisions of the Draft Children's Rights Bill Relating to Access to Justice of the Girl Child in Cases of Violence

The Mauritian Children's Bill of 2020[74] constitutes has the potential to foster change in the Mauritian legal landscape for the protection of children, including girls. It will repeal the Child Protection Act 'and replace it with a more comprehensive and modern legislative framework' to better implement the provisions of the UN CRC and the African Children's Charter.[75]

There are several provisions in the Bill aimed at protecting minors, therefore including girls, against multiple forms of violence. One such form of violence as recognised by the Bill is child marriage.[76] The Children's Bill prohibits even religious marriages below the age of 18[77] and criminalises forcing or causing a child to be married, be it civilly or religiously.[78] This provision clearly aims at protecting minors in Mauritius, and girls in particular.

Harmful treatment of children has been rightly identified as a serious form of violence and such violence can be physical or moral in nature. Section 13 of the Bill stipulates that 'no person shall ill-treat a child or

---

[74] National Assembly of Mauritius, https://mauritiusassembly.govmu.org/Documents/Bills/intro/2020/bill172020.pdf.

[75] Paragraph 2 of the Explanatory Memorandum stipulates that the Bill 'makes provisions –

(a) for the better care, protection and assistance to children and their families;
(b) for the respect and the promotion of the rights and best interests of children;
(c) for the setting up of structures, services and means for promoting and monitoring the sound physical, psychological, intellectual, emotional and social development of children;
(d) for children under the age of 12 not to be held criminally responsible for any act or omission;
(e) for child witness and child victims under the age of 14 to be, under certain conditions, competent as witnesses without the need for them to take the oath or making solemn affirmation;
(f) for the setting up of a Children's Court, which shall consist of a Civil Division, a Protection Division and a Criminal Division; and
(g) for addressing the shortcomings in the Child Protection Act'.

[76] Children's Bill 2020, Sect. 2(e).

[77] *Ibid*, Sect. 13(2).

[78] *Ibid*, Sect. 12.

allow a child to be ill-treated so that the child suffers, or is likely to suffer, harm'. Sub-Sect. (3) of the Sect. 10 adds that the non-respect of the above-mentioned rule is a criminal offence sanctioned by a fine non-exceeding 200 000 rupees (US$5000) and by the imprisonment up to 5 years. The same idea is incorporated in Sect. 12 of the Bill that prohibits corporal or humiliating punishment on child. The punishment for this crime is similar to harmful treatment of the child. It is to be noted that very often the perpetrators of acts of corporal or humiliating punishment are parents or other persons under whose responsibility a child is.

The Children's Act further criminalises abandonment of children, abduction of children by parents, abduction of child by other persons, causing, inciting or allowing a child to be sexually abused, child prostitution and access to brothel, child pornography, child grooming and bullying, amongst others.

The Children's Bill, in its Sect. 11, also recognises the importance of protecting children against discrimination. It stipulates that 'no person shall discriminate against a child on the ground of the child's, or child's parents race, caste, place of origin, political opinion, colour, creed, sex, language, religion, property or disability'. It can be noted that the grounds of non-discrimination refer to either the child's description or that of the parents. Protection against discrimination ensures equal access to justice to all victims of criminal offences, including girls. However, sexual orientation as a ground for non-discrimination is missing, which is often a basis for violence against individuals where children, and girls specifically, are not spared.[79]

An adequate understanding of the Children's Bill cannot be achieved without an analysis of the Mauritian Civil Code. The latter indeed lays down rules which the Bill itself refers to, and consequently relies upon.[80] However, in one instance where it deems necessary, the Bill also increases

[79] UN Committee on the Rights of the Child, General comment No. 24 (2019) on children's rights in the child justice system, September 2019 CRC/C/GC/24 page 8 paragraph 40: 'Safeguards against discrimination are needed from the earliest contact with the criminal justice system and throughout the trial, and discrimination against any group of children requires active redress. In particular, gender-sensitive attention should be paid to girls and to children who are discriminated against on the basis of sexual orientation or gender identity.'

[80] Children's Bill, Sect. 3(2), refers to Articles 371 through Articles 387 of the Civil Code.

its protection of minors. The Mauritian Civil Code recognises the fact that there is a need to protect minors against violence which may be perpetrated by anyone, including legal guardians themselves. Hence, it provides for the deprivation or partial withdrawal of parental authority (guardianship rights) which contributes to combating violence against children. It is important to highlight that these mechanisms are not only repeated but reinforced in the Children's Bill.[81]

The loss of the guardianship rights is not an absolute one under the Mauritian Civil Code. Hence, according to article 380 of the Mauritian Civil Code, a parent who has been deprived, totally or partially, of guardianship rights may request the Supreme Court to restore his guardianship rights in whole or in part if there are new circumstances that justify such a decision. Moreover, article 380 of the Code stipulates that 'the request for reinstatement of rights can be made only one year at earliest after the decision declaring deprivation or partial withdrawal has become irrevocable'. When the request for reinstatement of rights has been rejected, a new one may be presented to the Supreme Court after one year.

The Children's Bill proposes a more severe approach through Sect. 30 which stipulates that 'any person who is convicted of an offence in respect of a child under this Part or under Sect. 249 section 249 or

[81] Mauritian Civil Code, Article 375. stipulates that 'a father and a mother who are convicted, either as perpetrators, co-perpetrators or accomplices of a crime or a misdemeanor committed against the person of their child, or as co-perpetrators or accomplices of a crime or a misdemeanor committed by their child, may be deprived of parental authority (guardianship rights)'. Moreover, according to article 376 of the Mauritian Civil Code 'apart from any criminal conviction, a father and a mother who, either by ill-treatment, or by pernicious examples of habitual drunkenness, notorious misconduct or delinquency, or by lack of care or lack of direction, clearly endanger the safety, health or morals of a child may be deprived of parental authority (guardianship *rights)* Article 376 of the Code adds that the action for deprivation of guardianship rights may be brought before the Supreme Court 'either by the Attorney General, or by the father, mother or another family member of the child or by his guardian'; Article 377 addresses the issue of scope of the deprivation of guardianship rights. Thus, the deprivation is sometimes total, and a parent is deprived of all components of the parental authority, save a different decision of the Court. On the other hand, there may be also partial withdrawal of parental authority (guardianship rights) (Article 378 of the Mauritian Civil Code); The Supreme Court of Mauritius will designate another parent or a third person who accepts the task, and the above-mentioned parent or third person will assume guardianship of a child. The Court will determine the extent of the powers of this person (Article 379 of the Mauritian Civil Code).

250 of the Mauritian Criminal Code, shall, notwithstanding any other enactment, be interdicted from any guardianship'. Such interdiction is for a period not exceeding 10 years when it concerns a parent and for a period not exceeding five years when it is not a parent. Thus, according to the Bill, when a father or a mother is convicted, either as perpetrator, co-perpetrator or accomplice of a crime or a misdemeanour committed against the person of their child, they will be allowed to ask for the reinstatement of their guardianship rights after a period going up to 10 years instead of a period of one year as is currently the situation. It can therefore be argued that the Bill identifies that a longer waiting period is needed and would seek to better protect children against violence.

The Children's Bill identifies the need for care and protection of minors and sub-parts I to III of Part IV lay down measures that are to be taken to protect any child in Mauritius in need of protection, including girl victims of violence. In case of violence against a girl, Sect. 32 of the Bill provides for a possibility for everyone to report such a violence to the Police. A supervising officer can also refer the matter to the police.[82] The supervising officer can also provide assistance to the child pending the report of an authorised person. Emergency protection orders and placement orders can also be applied at Protection Division of the Children's Court in certain cases. Placement orders are usually for three years but the supervising officer can motivate for long-term ones.[83]

5 Challenges in the Ensuring that the Girl Child Has Access to Justice in Cases of Violence

Mauritius has enacted or is in the process of enacting laws that ensure that the girl child has access to justice in cases of violence. However, there are still challenges in ensuring that the girl child has access to justice as is elaborated in the sub-sections below.

[82] Children's Bill, Sect. 32.

[83] *Ibid*, Sect. 37.

5.1 Delay in Enacting the Children's Bill

The Children's Bill, as demonstrated in Sect. 4 above, contains several provisions that ensure that the girl child who is a survivor of violence has access to justice, including specialised children's courts and a reinforced protection for children. However, this Bill has been debated for years[84] and it was revised in 2020. This delay in finalising and enacting the Children's Bill creates a legal gap to ensure access to justice for the girl child.

5.2 Non-Criminalisation of Some Types of violence

5.2.1 Child Marriage

The proposed Children's Bill has many provisions in line with the CRC and the African Children's Charter, including the prohibition of child marriage. The Mauritian Civil Code allows, under certain conditions, marriages of children of the age 16 and 17. Article 145 of the Civil Code stipulates that 'minors who are less than 18 years but more than 16 years may enter into marriage with the consent of their father and mother or of the one of them who exercise exclusively parental authority'. The consent of one of the parents will suffice, when the other has already deceased or when it is impossible for the other parent to express his will. Sub-Sect. 2 of article 145 provides that 'in the absence of a father and mother or of one of them who exercises parental authority, the Judge in Chambers may grant an exemption of age to the minor if it is in the latter's interest'. Hence, child marriage is still allowed in Mauritius in certain cases.

The Mauritian legislator has considered that parents who exercise the guardianship rights over their minor child are the most appropriate persons to decide whether the marriage of their child is in the best

[84] 'The Children's Bill' *Mauritius Times* September 30, 2019 http://www.mauritiustimes.com/mt/the-childrens-bill/.

interest of the latter or not. However, similar to international law,[85] there is an opinion, voiced out by the local non-governmental organisations, that child marriage should be prohibited in Mauritian Law, because a child, including a girl, does not possess the necessary degree of maturity to take the responsibility generated by matrimonial life.[86] The stand arguing for a complete ban of child marriage is well supported by the following reasoning: child marriage goes against the childhood needs of minors thereby depriving them of their fundamental human rights, enhances vulnerability in respect of sexually transmissible diseases and increases the risk of poverty.[87]

5.2.2 Marital Rape

Although rape is criminalised in Mauritius,[88] marital rape is a topic that is not addressed by the laws since it is considered as a private matter. However, General Recommendation 24 of the Committee on the Elimination of Discrimination Against Women (CEDAW Committee) on Women and Health clearly presents marital rape as a harmful traditional

---

85 African Children's Charter, Article 21(2); Maputo Protocol Article 6(b) and Joint General Comment on Ending Child Marriage by the African Commission and the African Children's Committee.

86 https://www.lexpress.mu/article/334035/mariage-mineurs-ce-que-dit-loi; There has been a vibrant and unequivocal call for a ban of child marriage through the shadow report presented by Gender Links (GL) Mauritius where inputs were gathered from GL Mauritius, Media Watch Organisation, SOS Femmes and Young Queer Alliance. It is important to note that this is the first time that a Mauritian non-governmental organisation (NGO) presented a shadow report at the United Nations, CEDAW Committee. https://genderlinks.org.za/casestudies/gl-mauritius-takes-child-marriages-to-cedaw/. The UN CEDAW Committee which recommends the following '[r]epeal or amend Sect. 145 of the Civil Code to completely preclude consent by parents or guardians as a sufficient requirement to allow marriage of those under the age of 18 and to allow court approval only under exceptional circumstances for marriages of those between the ages of 16 and 18, ensure that the planned children's bill reflects this provision'. Page 15, paragraphs 38(c) Concluding observations on the eighth periodic report of Mauritius CEDAW/C/MUS/CO/8, November 14, 2018.

87 Marriage of minors - #ChildNotBride: A priority issue for the country, https://www.lexpress.mu/node/361994.

88 Mauritian Penal Code, Sect. 249.

practice.[89] Since the girl child does get married in Mauritius,[90] she is at risk of marital rape. Since marital is not criminalised, the girl child survivor of this type of violence does not have a remedy.

5.3 Absence of Public Interest Litigation

The Constitution of Mauritius, as noted in Sect. 3.1.1 above, contains some provisions that can be interpreted to include the protection of the girl child from violence. Hence, for violence such as child marriage,[91] civil society organisations who have voiced out concerns about the issue as noted in Sect. 5.2.1 could have approached the Supreme Court to decide that child marriage as provided for by the Mauritian Civil Code is a form of violence against the girl child and the laws providing the same should be unconstitutional. The same holds true for marital rape which is not criminalised in Mauritius.

Nevertheless, according to Sect. 17 of the Constitution,[92] only an aggrieved person can apply to the Supreme Court for redress. This is a challenge since it is daunting for a girl child to confront her family and agree to be the face of a constitutional judicial action.

---

[89] CEDAW Committee, *General Recommendation No. 25 on Article 12 of the Convention (Women and Health* A/54/38/Rev.1 1999, paragraph 18.

[90] Ahmad Macky, *Child Marriage: 803 children including 705 girls from 15 to 19 years married between 2015–2017*, Sunday Times, https://www.sundaytimesmauritius.com/child-marriage-803-children-including-705-girls-from-15-to-19-years-married-between-2015-2017/.

[91] Girls Not Brides, *Child marriage: A form of violence against the Child* (2019).

[92] Constitution, Sect. 17(1): 'Where any person alleges that any of Sects. 3 to 16 has been, is being likely to be contravened in relation to him, then, without prejudice to any other action with respect to the same matter that is lawfully available, that person may apply to the Supreme Court for redress.'.

5.4 Insufficient Collaboration Between Relevant Stakeholders

The Office of the Ombudsperson for Children in Mauritius has identified '*insufficient collaboration and consultation among important stakeholders*' in the context of child sexual abuse.[93] This can be extended to all forms of violence against the girl child since there are several stakeholders working with survivors at different levels. We can argue here that an ideal stakeholder partnership would include state agencies, civil society organisations, private institutions and children organisations. Including the latter would enable children to participate in matters concerning them and would allow truly adapted measures to be taken.

5.5 Patriarchy

Mauritius is still a patriarchal society[94] where most women are expected to be homely and take care of the household irrespective of their educational background.[95] Saving their marriage is more important than saving their lives in most cases.[96] Reporting cases of domestic violence or sexual violence is, in many instances, a matter of shame.[97] This patriarchy also influences the cultural practices of the country. For instance, in the context of child marriage, in most cases, the girl child will get married before 18 because the father of the girl so decides. The reasons for such marriages are often to avoid embarrassment within the family because the girl is dating someone, she is not performing well in school, she is pregnant or to prevent her from dating someone. Patriarchy also affects the discussions around marital rape since once someone is

---

93 Office of the Ombudsperson for Children, 'Annual Report' (2017–2018) 257.

94 Verena Tandrayen-Ragoobur 'Gendering governance: The case of Mauritius' 33 *Equality, Diversity and Inclusion: An International Journal* (2014): 554.

95 Ramola Ramtohul 'Women's Political Representation in Small Island Developing States: A comparative analysis of Mauritius and Seychelles 3 *Small States and Territories* (2020): 91.

96 Defimedia.info, *Domestic violence: The silent epidemic,* June 5, 2016, https://defimedia.info/domestic-violence-silent-epidemic.

97 *Ibid.*

married, it is assumed that she has given her consent to have sexual intercourse with her husband for life or until they are divorced. Moreover, most legislators, as a reflection of the patriarchal society, are men and this under-representation of women in politics affects 'their ability to represent women's interest'.[98]

5.6 Insufficient Data on the Girl Child

Mauritius has adopted several initiatives for gender-sensitive data collection such as Domestic Violence Information System.[99] However, the country is still lacking in collecting gender-sensitive data when it comes to the girl child. The fact that Statistics Mauritius collects data for those who are between 15 and 19[100] shows that data collection is not child sensitive. Moreover, there is insufficient gender-disaggregated data concerning education, reproductive rights, poverty, women forming part of vulnerable groups, child marriages and child sexual abuse.[101] The revised 2020–2021 budget proposed the setting up of Gender-Based Violence Observatory[102] that might provide for more accurate statistics on violence against the girl child. This would respond adequately to one of the concerns of the CEDAW Committee.[103] However, this is yet to be done. Having adequate and sufficient data would enable the state to identify problems and evaluate results.

---

[98] Mi Yung Yoon and Sheila Bunwaree '*Is a Minority Truly Powerless? Female Legislators in Mauritius*' 24 *Asian Women* (2008): 83–102.

[99] Website of the Republic of Mauritius http://www.govmu.org/English/News/Pages/Domestic-violence-hotline-139-becomes-toll-free.aspx

[100] Section 1 above.

[101] See generally CEDAW Committee *Concluding Observations on the Eighth Periodic Report of Mauritius* November 9, 2018 CEDAW/C/MUS/CO/8.

[102] Minister of Finance, Economic Planning and Development Budget Speech 2020–2021, *Our new Normal: The economy of Life*, paragraph 321 http://budget.mof.govmu.org/budget2020-21/2020_21budgetspeechEng.pdf.

[103] 'There is a lack of comprehensive data, disaggregated by sex, age, disability, ethnicity, location and socioeconomic status, on the numbers of child marriages, unregistered religious marriages and polygamous marriages.' Page 14, paragraph 37(e) Concluding observations on the eighth periodic report of Mauritius CEDAW/C/MUS/CO/8, November 14, 2018.

6 Recommendations and Conclusions

In a nutshell, the girl child in Mauritius finds herself in many situations that amount to violence. The Mauritian legislators have adopted laws and mechanisms to ensure that survivors of such violence have access to the criminal justice system. Furthermore, there have been proposals to reform the current legal framework. Nevertheless, as demonstrated in Sect. 5 above, there are still several challenges in ensuring the right of the girl child to access the justice system. The following recommendations, if implemented, can minimise these challenges:

The enactment of the Children's Bill without any further delay to give legal effect to its provisions is a necessary step in improving the gaps in the Mauritian framework. For girl victims of violence, counselling is primordial and they should be ensured access to such services without any barrier, including age.[104]

Laying emphasis on non-legal measures is as important as legal ones to ensure effectiveness of the latter. Hence raising awareness campaigns to change patriarchy and 'cultural attitudes'[105] is a relevant measure in ensuring access to justice. The creation of a one-stop shop for all services related to violence against the girl child would help respond to the lack of collaboration between different stakeholders: in so doing, the involvement of both public and private institutions should be contemplated.[106] The adoption of a comprehensive child-friendly and gender budgeting

[104] 'The right to counselling and advice is distinct from the right to give medical consent and should not be subject to any age limit.' UN CRC Committee, General Comment No. 12 (2009), The right of the child to be heard, CRC/C/GC/12, 20 July 2009, page 23 paragraph 101.

[105] https://genderlinks.org.za/casestudies/gl-mauritius-takes-child-marriages-to-cedaw/ and also a recommendation of the UN CEDAW Committee Page 15, paragraph 38(f) Concluding observations on the eighth periodic report of Mauritius CEDAW/C/MUS/CO/8, November 14, 2018.

[106] 'Private social welfare institutions include private sector organizations – either for-profit or non-profit – which play a role in the provision of services that are critical to children's enjoyment of their rights, and which act on behalf of or alongside Government services as an alternative.' Para 2 (2) page 8 of UN CRC General comment No. 14 (2013) on the right of the child to have his or her best interests taken as a primary consideration (art. 3, para. 1), May 2013 CRC/C/GC/14.

would furthermore ensure that the necessary resources are made available. Finally, the development of prevention strategies which include children in the process by ensuring that they are consulted[107] would further help to create an environment conducive to dialogue.

The girl child in Mauritius can be presumed to have all the protection she needs in a country which stands as an example on the African continent in many respects. However, it is unfortunately not the case. As much as the achievements can be glorified, the unfinished battles must not be forgotten.

References

A Budoo, *It's Time Mauritius Took Decisive Steps to Outlaw Child Marriages*, The Conversation (July 3, 2018), https://theconversation.com/its-time-mauritius-took-decisive-steps-to-outlaw-child-marriages-99226, December 12, 2020.

African Children's Committee General Comment No 5 'State party obligations under the African Charter on the Rights and Welfare of the Child (Article 1) and systems strengthening child protection' 2018.

African Commission 'Concluding Observations and Recommendations on the 6th to 8th Combined Report of the Republic of Mauritius on the Implementation of the African Charter on Human and Peoples' Rights' adopted at the 60th Ordinary Session of the African Commission from 8 to May 22, 2017.

Ahmad Macky, *Child Marriage: 803 Children Including 705 Girls from 15 to 19 Years Married Between 2015–2017,* Sunday Times, https://www.sunday

[107] 'The Committee notes that the voices of children have increasingly become a powerful force in the prevention of child rights violations. Good practice examples are available, inter alia, in the fields of violence prevention in schools, combating child exploitation through hazardous and extensive labour, providing health services and education to street children, and in the juvenile justice system. Children should be consulted in the formulation of legislation and policy related to these and other problem areas and involved in the drafting, development and implementation of related plans and programmes.' UN CRC Committee, General Comment No. 12 (2009), The right of the child to be heard, CRC/C/GC/12, July 20, 2009, page 27 paragraph 122.

timesmauritius.com/child-marriage-803-children-including-705-girls-from-15-to-19-years-married-between-2015-2017/, December 12, 2020.

Bryant G Garth and Mauro Cappelletti, 'Access to justice: The Newest Wave in the Worldwide Movement to make Rights Effective' 27 *Buffalo Law Review* 1978.

CEDAW Committee Concluding observations on the eighth periodic report of Mauritius CEDAW/C/MUS/CO/8, November 14, 2018.

CEDAW Committee, General Recommendation No. 35 on gender-based violence against women, updating general recommendation No. 19 (2017).

CEDAW Committee, *General Recommendation No. 35 on gender-based violence against women, updating General Recommendation No. 19* 26 July 2017 CEDAW/C/GC/35.

CEDAW Committee, *General Recommendation No. 25 on Article 12 of the Convention Women and Health* A/54/38/Rev.1 1999.

CEDAW Committee *Concluding Observations on the Eighth Periodic Report of Mauritius* November 9, 2018 CEDAW/C/MUS/CO/8.

Defimedia.info *Domestic Violence: The Silent Epidemic* (June 5, 2016), https://defimedia.info/domestic-violence-silent-epidemic, December 12, 2020.

Felicity Hand *The Subversion of Class and Gender Roles in the Novels of Lindsey Collen (1948), Mauritian Social Activist and Writer* (2010).

Girls Not Brides, *Child marriage: A form of violence against the Child* (2019).

Halley Movement and Pan-Mauritius Coalition and ECPAT International 'Sexual exploitation of Children in Mauritius' submitted to the 31st session of the Human Rights Council (October-November 2018) on March 29, 2018 for the Universal Periodic Review of the human rights situation in Mauritius.

Jameela Jadoo for Defimedia.info, *Child abuse: The despicable side of our Paradise* (November 18, 2018), https://defimedia.info/child-abuse-despicable-side-our-paradise, December 12, 2020.

L'express.mu, *Meutre d'une gamine de 10 ans: un bébé des parents déjà mort en janvier* (March 30, 2020), https://www.lexpress.mu/node/373708, December 12, 2020.

L'express.mu, *Une mort atroce à deux ans : Pourquoi la mère d'Ayaan n'a rien fait?* (November 16, 2020), https://www.lexpress.mu/article/385149/une-mort-atroce-deux-ans-pourquoi-mere-dayaan-na-rien-fait, December 12, 2020.

L'express.mu https://www.lexpress.mu/article/334035/mariage-mineurs-ce-que-dit-loi.

Lindsey Collen, *The Rape of Sita (*2004).

Maria F Moscati, *The Role of Transitional Justice and Access to Justice in Conflict Resolution and Democratic Advancement* (2015).

Mi Yung Yoon and Sheila Bunwaree, 'Is a Minority Truly Powerless? Female Legislators in Mauritius' 24 *Asian Women* (2008): 83–102.

Minister of Finance, Economic Planning and Development Budget Speech 2020–2021, *Our new Normal: The Economy of Life*, http://budget.mof.govmu.org/budget2020-21/2020_21budgetspeechEng.pdf, December 12, 2020.

Office of the Ombudsperson for Children, *'Annual Report'* 2017–2018 257.

Ramola Ramtohul 'Women's Political Representation in Small Island Developing States: A comparative analysis of Mauritius and Seychelles' 3 *Small States and Territories* (2020): 83–98.

Statistics Mauritius 'Population and Vital Statistics – 2019.'

UN Committee on the Rights of the Child 'Concluding Observations to the combined third to fifth periodic reports of Mauritius' CRC/C/MUS/CO/3–5, February 4, 2015.

UN Committee on the Rights of the Child, General comment No. 24 (2019) on children's right in the child justice system, September 2019 CRC/C/GC/24.

UN CRC Committee General comment No. 14 (2013) on the right of the child to have his or her best interests taken as a primary consideration (article 3, paragraph 1) May 2013 CRC/C/GC/14.

UN CRC Committee, General Comment No. 12 (2009), The right of the child to be heard, CRC/C/GC/12, 20 July 2009.

Verena Tandrayen-Ragoobur 'Gendering governance: The case of Mauritius' 33 *Equality, Diversity and Inclusion: An International Journal* (2014): 535–563.

5

Police Capacity Building in Dealing with Domestic Violence Cases in South Africa: An Entry Point to Women's Access to Justice

Mothibi A. Kholofelo and Happy Mathew Tirivangasi

1 Introduction

As already alluded to in the abstract, domestic violence remains rife in many African societies, South Africa included.[1] Laws on redress of domestic violence are critical in responding to gender-based violence in the light of the fact that women remain the major victims of this

[1] Institute of Security Services, *Domestic Violence in South Africa* (2014), https://www.safers paces.org.za/uploads/files/PolBrief71.pdf.

M. A. Kholofelo (✉)
Department of Safety and Security Management, Tshwane University of Technology, Pretoria, South Africa

H. M. Tirivangasi
Department of Research Administration and Development, University of Limpopo, Polokwane, South Africa
e-mail: happy.tirivangasi@ul.ac.za

E. C. Lubaale and A. Budoo-Scholtz (eds.), *Violence Against Women and Criminal Justice in Africa: Volume I*, Sustainable Development Goals Series,
https://doi.org/10.1007/978-3-030-75949-0_5

scourge.[2] Moreover, with the police being the first point of contact in criminal justice processes,[3] their ability to interpret and apply relevant laws is critical in fostering access to justice for women.

This chapter investigates the need for police capacity building in dealing with domestic violence in South Africa. The need for continuous research on domestic violence is explained by the increase in domestic violence in South Africa. There is a high rate of both reported and unreported cases of domestic violence.·[4] This chapter proceeds on the premise that there is a need for police capacity building in dealing with domestic violence cases.

Domestic violence was widely identified as a social problem as far back as the 1970s.[5] Stone and Lopes[6] find that this is a problem that has continued to trouble societies, the medical service sector, social workers, policy makers, criminologist and the police service sector. Domestic violence cases have been on the rise in South Africa since 1994.[7] Despite the existence of legal protection and statutory instruments that prohibit domestic violence such as the Domestic Violence Act 116 of 1998, the Victims Charter 2004, Prevention of Family Violence Act 133 of 1999, among others, there continues to be violence in the context of families. Domestic violence and partner abuse are among the least likely

---

[2] United Nations Women, *Violence Against Women and Girls: The Shadow Pandemic* (April 6, 2020), https://www.unwomen.org/en/news/stories/2020/4/statement-ed-phumzile-violence-against-women-during-pandemic.

[3] Retief Rita and Green Sulina, 'Some Challenges of Policing Domestic Violence,' *Journal of Social Work* (2015): 135–147.

[4] Folami, Olakunle Michael, 'Survey of Unreported Cases of Domestic Violence in Two Heterogeneous Communities in Nigeria' 4 *International Review of Law* (2013): 4; Huecker Martin and Smock William, *Domestic Violence* (2019), http://www.ncbi.nlm.nih.gov books/NBK 499,891/.

[5] Vetten Lisa, 'The Ghost of Families Past: Domestic Violence Legislation and Policy in Post-Apartheid South Africa,' 28 *Journal of the Contemporary Women for Gender Equity* (2014): 48–57.

[6] Stone Kelly and Claudia Lopes, *Policing Responses to Domestic Violence: Exploring Reactions by the Police to Women in Need of Shelter* (2018), https://za.boell.org/sites/default/files/hbf_saps_research_paper_web_1.pdf.

[7] Merten Marianne, *Statistics SA: One in Five SA Women Experience Physical Violence, Young Women Hard-Hit by HIV/Aids*, Daily Maevrick, May 15, 2017, https://www.dailymaverick.co.za/article/2017-05-15-statistics-sa-one-in-five-sa-women-experience-physical-violence-young-women-hard-hit-by-hivaids/.

cases to be reported to the police.[8] MacLeod and others[9] corroborate the findings by UNODC[10] on this reality by establishing that only one in five victims of violence report abuse to police following incidences of domestic violence. This study[11] also revealed that in contrast to other violent crimes, around two in five victims of violent domestic crimes report their cases to the police.

A study by Artz[12] reveals that policing domestic violence itself is a complicated task as domestic violence has a very long list of abuses which include: sexual, emotional, verbal, psychological, economic abuse harassment, damaging property, stalking, entrance into the plaintiff's property without his or her consent where she or he is not living with the defendant (abuser), and lastly, behaviour that may cause immediate harm to the complainant. A study by Buzawa[13] advances the view that police officials need to be trained to be able to take advantage of the opportunities to collect evidence such as photographs and documentation of the nature violence, the location of violence, extent of injuries; defensive injuries; weapons used and to gather all relevant evidence.

Understanding what a domestic relationship entails is equally critical in responding to domestic violence cases. Failure to understand the notion of domestic relationships may undermine one's interpretation of domestic violence as well as the enforcement of the law

[8] Macqueen Sarah and Norris Paul, 'Police Awareness and Involvement in Cases of Domestic and Partner Abuse,' *Policing and Society* (2016): 1–22.

[9] Macleod Pat, Kinver Andrea, Page Leon, Iliasov Aibek and Williams Rachel, *2008–09 Scottish Crime and Justice Survey Partner Abuse* (2009), https://www2.gov.scot/resource/doc/296149/0092065.pdf.

[10] United Nations Office on Drugs and Abuse, South Africa: Are We Doing Enough to End Violence Against Women? (2020), https://www.unodc.org/southernafrica/en/vaw/index.html.

[11] *Ibid.*

[12] Artz Lillian, 'Policing the Domestic Violence Act: Teething Troubles or System Failure,' 16 *Journal Agenda: Empowering Women for Gender Equity* (2001): 1–13.

[13] Buzawa Eve, 'Intimate Partner Violence,' 32 *Journal of Policy Analysis and Management* (2012): 139–141. See also Emma Charlene Lubaale, *Bridging the justice gap in the prosecution of acquaintance child sexual abuse: a case of South Africa and Uganda* (PhD Thesis, University of Pretoria 2015) 1–351 on the evidentiary challenges of prosecuting offences involving intimate partners.

applicable to domestic violence. Artz[14] offers insight into the definition of 'domestic relationship'. She notes that it 'involves people who are married, divorced, cohabiting, same-sex partners (whether they live together or not), customary relationship, including an actual or perceived romantic relationship; intimate or sexual relationships of any duration; people who share custody of a child or the parents of a child'. Interpretation and gaining understanding of domestic violence may require substantive training. Other researchers also note that interventions in domestic violence are very complex processes as victims may require attention which transcends the usual police work.[15] In a study by Eigenberg et al.,[16] the scholars note that police need to be trained about the diversity of domestic violence acts, victims and offenders. This can be advanced by ensuring an understanding of the evolving nature of domestic relationships as well as the types of abuses that are categorised as domestic violence.

There are innumerable constraints to dealing with domestic violence. A study by Robinson et al.[17] in America and the United Kingdom reveals difficulties in policing domestic violence as these scholars show that domestic violence goes beyond physical abuse as often understood by victims. Despite the fact that police officers are aware that domestic violence goes beyond physical violence, they often don't urgently attend to non-violent cases of domestic violence. Guthrie and Kunkel[18] demonstrate how police conceptualisation of domestic violence affects victims and how the law enforcement agencies respond to it. In this case, the disregard for non-violent cases may result in such cases not being

---

[14] *Ibid.*

[15] Corcoran Jacquelin, Stephenson Margaret, Watkins Derrelyn Perryman and Shannon Allen, 'Perceptions and Utilisation of a Police- Social Work Crisis: Intervention Approach to Domestic Violence,' 82 *Families in Society: The Journal of Contemporary Human Services* (2001): 393–398.

[16] Eigenberg Helen, Kappeler Victor and McGuffee Karen, 'Confronting the Complexities of Domestic Violence: A Social Prescription for Rethinking Police Training,' 12 *Journal of Police Crisis Negotiations* (2012): 122–145.

[17] Robinson Amanda, Gillian Pinchevsky and Guthrie Jennifer, 'Under the Radar Policing Non-Violent Domestic Abuse in the US and UK,' 40 *International Journal of Comparative and Applied Criminal Justice* (2016): 195– 208.

[18] Guthrie Jennifer and Adrianne Kunkel, 'Problematising the Uniform Application of the Formula Story: Advocacy for Survivors in a Domestic Violence Support Group,' 38 *Women & Language* (2015): 43–62.

taken seriously and consequently, few cases being reported or pursued. Tuerkheimer[19] argues that when it comes to forms of violence that are not physical, often the arm of criminal law has been too short to reach them. Furthermore, a study by Bourlet[20] reveals that the police has only been quick to intervene when serious injury has occurred, or, is imminent. This undermines and restrains the police from dealing with domestic violent cases effectively. Moreover, Guthrie and Kunkel[21] write that victims feel obliged to report cases when they have visible injuries which is quite problematic in light of the devastating effects of injury-free violence. Buzawa[22] argues that police need to be trained on the current legislation, officer safety and intervention mechanisms to ensure that the cases of domestic violence are properly addressed.

Recently, Rolle et al.[23] found that a multifaceted definition of domestic violence has emerged which includes all forms of violence—both physical and non-physical. Given the myriad of issues associated with domestic violence, this research identifies the need to find out how the police should engage in capacity building in relation to domestic violence and its various forms of manifestations. The police are the gate keepers of criminal justice[24] hence the critical need to get their perceptions or views on whether there is a need to engage in capacity building with a view to ensuring effective policing.

Moreover, police capacitation is in line with fulfilment of the United Nations Sustainable Development Goal (SDG) 16 which seeks to 'promote peaceful and inclusive societies for sustainable development, provide access to justice for all and build effective, accountable and inclusive institutions at all levels'. Furthermore, achieving SDG 16 would also result in the achievement of Goal 11 Africa Union Agenda 2067

---

[19] Tuerkheimer Deborah, 'Recognising and Remedy the Harm of Battering; A Call to Criminalise Domestic Violence,' 94 *The Journal of Criminal Law and Criminology* (2014): 959–1024.

[20] Bourlet Allan, *Police Intervention in Marital Violence* (1990).

[21] *Ibid.*

[22] *Ibid.*

[23] Rollè Luca, Shulamit Ramon and Piera Brustia, 'New Perspectives on Domestic Violence: From Research to Intervention' 10 *Frontiers in psychology* (2019): 641.

[24] Retief Rita and Green Sulina, 'Some Challenges of Policing Domestic Violence,' 51 *Journal of Social Work* (2015).

which seeks to advance 'democratic values, practices, universal principles of human rights, justice and the rule of law entrenched'. These two goals at the continental level establish priority areas which are similar—democracy and good governance being the first and human rights, rule of law and justice being the second. One can attest to the fact that capacitating the police to effectively deal with domestic violence cases would result in the upholding of the rule of law and human rights in South Africa. This makes this research timely as the South African government is striving to achieve both AU Agenda 2067 and the UN SDG 16. With the police being key enforcement agents, boosting their capacity would ensure that those most affected by domestic violence (women) are able to access justice.

In South Africa, police capacity building is the mandate of the Department of Community Safety as provided for by the Constitution of the Republic of South Africa.[25] The department monitors the SAPS' Compliance with various pieces of legislations including the DVA as promulgated in 1999.[26] The department noted in 2019 that it has been twenty years since the enactment of the DVA. However, the SAPS has been lagging behind in terms of compliance due to inadequate capacity, and this is posing challenges such as trauma and untimely deaths.[27] The Constitution of South Africa, in terms of Section 18 (4)a, provides that failure by members of the SAPS to handle or implement laws (including the DVA) is a punishable offence which can result in dismissal or suspension from work.[28] The department of Community Safety has also pointed out that training and workshops for SAPS members can be a solution to the problem of non-responsiveness and lack of skill on the part of police officers in dealing with domestic violence cases in South Africa.[29] Reports on the shortcomings of the SAPS in dealing with domestic violence are worrisome especially in light of aspirations to attain SDG 16 in 2030 and goal 11 of the African Union Agenda in 2067.

---

[25] South African Department of Community Safety, Concept Document on the Work Sessions of South African Police Service (2019).

[26] *Ibid.*

[27] *Ibid.*

[28] *Ibid.*

[29] *Ibid.*

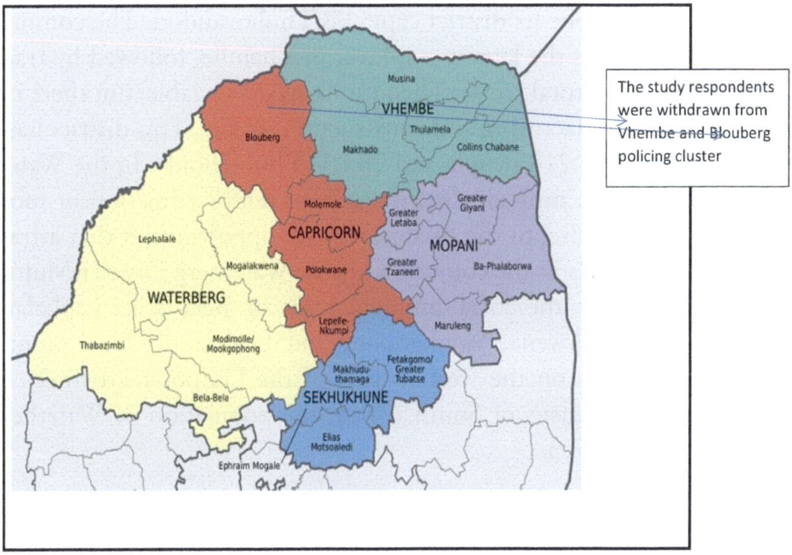

Fig. 1 The Map of Limpopo province in South Africa (*Source* Department of Cooperative Governance and Traditional Affairs. *Vhembe District Municipality Profile*, Retrieved on 30 October 2019, from www.cogta.gov.za)

Therefore, through our proposed Dr. Bengt-Ake Lindval's[30] four knowledge taxonomy principles (Know-What; Know-how; Know-why; Know-who)—as an assessment tool to evaluate domestic violence training procedure—the study will be able to provide a clear analysis and workable strategy for SAPS' response to domestic violence cases in South Africa.

1.1 Study Area

Extending over 21 349 square kilometres, the Vhembe District Municipality is situated in the northern part of Limpopo Province (Fig. 1). The Kruger National Park lies to the east of this Municipality. To the north and north-west, it shares international borders with Zimbabwe and

[30] Lundvall Bengt-Ake, *Knowledge Management in the Learning Economy* (2000), http://www3.druid.dk/wp/20060006.pdf.

Botswana, respectively. Its district capital is Thohoyandou. The community services sector is the largest employer in Vhembe, followed by trade and then the agricultural sector. The mining sector is stable, but there is a decline in the manufacturing and construction sectors. This district has a population of 1,232,218 people and 285,375 households. In the Waterberg District of this municipality, there is currently a fraction of more males than females due to the presence of job opportunities that attract men from other areas in the country. Outside Waterberg District Municipality (WDM) are the local municipalities of Bela-Bela, Lephalale, Modimolle, Mogalakwena, Mookgopong and Thabazimbi local municipalities and that lie on the western part of the Limpopo Province. As per the last 2011 census of South Africa, the population of Waterberg District was 67933613.

1.2 Methods

In addition to empirical data, in this study, we also used secondary literature to complement the quantitative data. The authors systematically reviewed literature indexed in the Web of Science, ScienceDirect, university institutional repository and South African National Portal on domestic violence. The strategy employed on ScienceDirect included free text and grammatical phrases for instance 'Domestic Violence' (Topic/Abstract), 'Domestic violence in South Africa' (Topic/Abstract), 'Domestic violence and policing' (Topic/Abstract), 'Domestic violence and SAPS training', 'Police training on Domestic violence' (Topic/Abstract), 'Police strategies to tackle domestic violence in South Africa' (Topic/Abstract), 'Police training and domestic violence in Africa' (Topic/Abstract) and ' culture and policing domestic violence' (Topic/Abstract). The search process is illustrated below (Fig. 2):

This strategy was effective and was also applied on the Web of Science. At the time of this publication, although the search is still ongoing for final analysis, a total of 220 hits were made, and we screened by title and abstracts. Approximately, a combined total of 42 were eliminated for duplication. We did not impose a time limit on the articles selected. Articles that speak to domestic violence were selected. Articles written

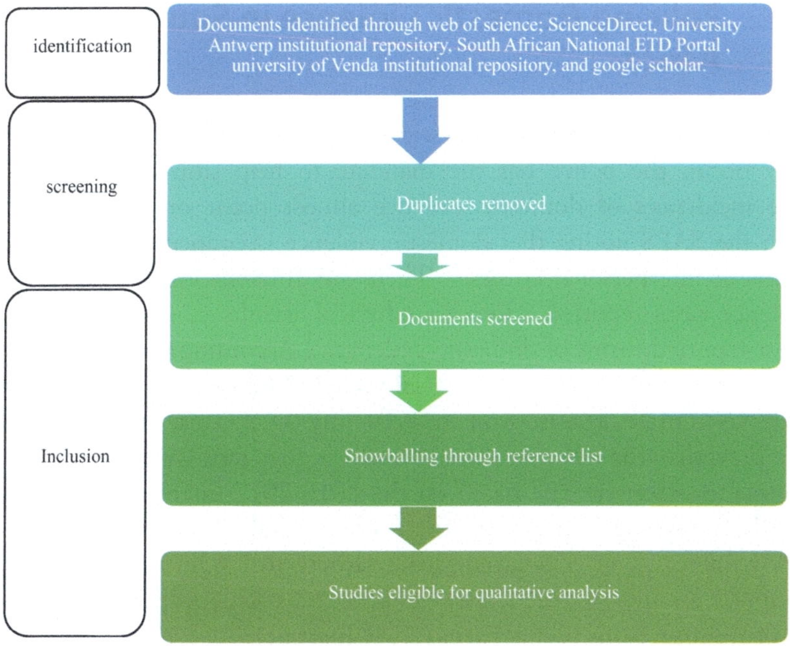

Fig. 2 Search strategies (*Source* Authors)

in English were mainly utilised and those which were in other languages removed (n = 4). Articles with no domestic violence and police terms were also removed (n = 10). Articles related to domestic violence in South Africa (n = 12) were included. Equally included were articles on theoretical frameworks (n = 8); articles on domestic violence and Africa (n = 35); articles on domestic violence and police training (n = 6); and articles on domestic violence by province in South Africa.

To improve the literature search strategy, we also used the list of references of key authors to identify new sources. This was effective in identifying the authorities on the subject both in South Africa and internationally. During the analysis, articles were grouped based on similarities and differences in topic.

2 Policing Domestic violence in South Africa

There are growing cases of domestic violence in South Africa, and when they occur, the police has the mandate to help stop such crimes.[31] The incidences of domestic violence almost occur on a daily basis, with the SAPS noting that domestic violence is connected to all other forms of interpersonal crimes.[32] There are different forms of domestic violence cases reported. However, physical assaults continue to be the most reported forms of domestic violence.[33] According to official crime statistics for the 2017/2018 financial year, 177 620 social contact crimes were committed against women, reflecting an increase of 2.4% from the previous year. Of particular concern is that most types of violence appear to be on the rise based on the 2016/2017 financial year. Based on the foregoing year report, there was a total of 2 930 of murders (11% increase), 3 554 attempted murders (6.7% increase), 81 142 common assaults (3.9% increase) and 53 263 assaults with the intention to commit grievous bodily harm (2.5% increase).[34]

In a provincial report by the Western Cape by the SAPS, it was indicated that most assaults occur on Fridays or Saturdays in homes where police would not know if not notified.[35] In spite of the fact that the arm of the law is long, many cases go unreported because the traditional policing strategies have hardly been adapted to address violence

[31] Mpani Patience and Nsibande Nondumiso, *Understanding Gender Policy and Gender-Based Violence in South Africa; A Literature Review* (2015); Soul City Institute for Justice: Safer Spaces, https://www.saferspaces.org.za/resources/entry/understanding-gender-policy-and-gender-based-violence-in-south-africa.

[32] Stone Kelly and Claudia Lopes, *Policing Responses to Domestic Violence: Exploring Reactions by the Police to Women in Need of Shelter* (2018), https://za.boell.org/sites/default/files/hbf_saps_research_paper_web_1.pdf.

[33] Bishop Charlotte, 'Domestic Violence: The Limitations of a Legal Response' in Sarah Hilder and Vanessa Bettinson (eds) *Domestic Violence* (2016) 59–79.

[34] *Ibid.*

[35] *Ibid.*

in people's private spaces.[36] Stones and Lopes[37] have added that during weekends, alcohol and drug abuse are prevalent in most communities and this exacerbates domestic violence occurrences. This means that most of the domestic violence crimes are motivated by the high prevalence of alcohol and drug abuse.[38]

The Commission for Gender Equality reported in 2016 that domestic violence is common in communities that do not report cases as there seems to be no deterrent structure in place.[39] It is also noted that in such communities, community members do not trust the police because their cases have not been handled well.[40] It is such bad experiences that deter people from reporting domestic violence cases. In a study by Richards,[41] it was found that the average number of domestic incidents reported per shift ranges from 5 to 12 depending on the geographical area of the police station in South Africa.[42] Richards[43] found that even though actual figures are difficult to obtain, South Africa still has more reported cases of domestic violence than any other country in Africa. Moreover, there is a difference in the number of cases reported and solved in urban and rural areas because of geo-location and access to resources.[44]

Moosa[45] also notes that the police, as the protectors of the community, are the first port of call for the victims of violence, hence, whoever is affected usually reports at the police station. In South Africa, according

36 Mazars Celine, *What Works to Prevent Violence Against Women and Girls*, Evidence Review UK Aid, SaferSpaces (2015) 1–65, https://www.whatworks.co.za/documents/publications/35-global-evidence-reviews-paper-2-interventions-to-prevent-violence-against-women-and-girls-sep-2015/file.

37 *Ibid.*

38 *Ibid.*

39 Commission for Gender Equality, Annual report 2016–2017, https://nationalgovernment.co.za/entity_annual/1170/2017-commission-for-gender-equality-(cge)-annual-report.pdf.

40 *Ibid.*

41 Richards Laura, *Getting Away With It; A Profile of the Domestic Violence Sexual Assault and 'Serious' Incident Analysis* (2004), https://paladinservice.co.uk/wp-content/uploads/2013/07/Getting-Away-with-It.pdf.

42 *Ibid.*

43 *Ibid.*

44 Mpani and Nsibande *supra* note 32.

45 Moosa Zohra, *A Theory of Change for Tacking Violence Against Women and Girls* (2012), https://www.actionaid.org.uk/sites/default/files/doc_lib/theory_of_change_on_vawg.pdf.

to the provisions of the laws, police should assist survivors to apply for protection orders as provided for by the DVA. It is further expected that forensic detectives should take and document a detailed statement of crimes, collect forensic evidence and maintain the chain of evidence ensuring non-contamination. The police also have a duty to safeguard the survivor, remove weapons and arrest perpetrators where needed. With poor skills, all these remain far-reaching goals.

Be that as it may, in all these instances, the police are guided by the DVA. The main purpose of the DVA is to provide the highest form of protection from domestic violence. This law tasks the police (in its capacity as an arm of the state) to ensure that survivors of domestic violence are able to apply for protection orders to prevent abusers from entering a mutual home or the survivor's home or place of work.[46] In 2012, Tshwaranang's study focused on reviewing the implementation of the DVA and it was found that a substantial percentage of police officers had limited knowledge of the provisions of this Act, let alone their responsibilities with regard to this Act.[47] According to Vetten,[48] domestic violence matters are classified as social crimes in the SAPS and the lack of clarity on what social crimes means compounds the problem of not viewing this act as a serious matter.

3 Challenges of policing Domestic violence

In a study carried out by Mogstad[49] in the South African township of Khayelitsha, it was revealed that it was not the inability of police to assist victims of domestic violence, the institutional failures or the lack of training that caused challenges in the reporting of domestic violence cases. Rather, most victims did not report cases due to the norms and

---

[46] Vetten *supra* note 5.

[47] Mpani and Nsibande *supra* note 32.

[48] *Ibid.*

[49] Mogstad Heidi, Dominique Dryding and Olivia Fiorotto, 'Policing the Private Social Barriers to the Effective Policing of Domestic Violence,' 56 *South African crime quarterly* (2016): 5–17.

values held by the community members. Whereas the authors were not quick to dismiss the need for training, knowledge and resources by the police staff were needed. Mogstad[50] recognised that policing domestic violence is not without stereotypical challenges. Similarly, Retief and Green's[51] study revealed that according to some police practitioners, the domestic household space is a space where privacy existed and what happens between the couple ought to be resolved by them. The study revealed that even community members would prefer to have the couples resolve their issues without external interferences. The study by Mogstad et al.[52] concurs with Retief and Green[53] in noting that whenever domestic violence occurs, the police is not the first port of call as community members think issues can be resolved between couples and their relatives without interferences by the police. Lopes[54] takes the view that this system of mediation favours the perpetrator (the husband), with the woman's views rarely considered. Reporting the violence is often not an option for women as women are made to think that this would result to a breakdown of familial bonds, ridicule and a disappointment to the societal expectations.

A study by Retief and Green[55] made an important contribution to literature by articulating the ways to ensure that policing of domestic violence is effective and dealt with when such social and patriarchal challenges arise. As the first port of call for the victims of domestic violence, the authors recommended annual refresher training courses in dealing with domestic violence and cultural awareness training to assist them in their investigative roles. The researchers argued that refresher courses would help the police officers to be tactical and make good decisions on how to maintain optimal performances when faced with difficult

[50] *Ibid.*

[51] Retief and Green *supra* note 3.

[52] Mogstad et al. *supra* note 50.

[53] Retief and Green *supra* note 3.

[54] Lopes Massawe, and Mangwiro M, 'Criminal Justice Responses: Assessing Implementation of the Domestic Violence Act in Gauteng' *Cape Town: Heinrich Böll Foundation and Tshwaranang Legal Advocacy Centre to End Violence Against Women*, (2013).

[55] Retief and Green *supra* note 3.

cases. Further,[56] advanced the notion that each police station should have trained personnel to deal with domestic violence effectively. The authors encouraged the sharing of information between the SAPS departments in different provinces to respond to domestic violence effectively. The authors further recommended a need for the police to conduct community awareness and to establish partnerships with community members so that they respond with more sensitivity to the respective expectations of the different cultural groups during each police encounter.

4 Social Interactionist Perspective on Domestic violence

Theories greatly assist in providing clarity on domestic violence issues. This study applied theoretical explanations of domestic violence from the field of sociology in order to try to get an understanding of why police fails to adequately respond to domestic violence cases. We also understand that it may not be accurate to attribute failure in policing to institutional failures only; hence, there is a need to look at other factors.

To engage with this complicated phenomenon of domestic violence, we employed symbolic interactionism perspective on domestic violence. The symbolic interaction theory was originally coined by Blumer[57] to explain the ideas of Mead.[58] The main point of departure in the symbolic interactionist is on interactions and how individuals interpret self, interpret their environment and how they interpret others. This theory provides that people interact with other people based on the actions or meanings that are derived from their everyday interactions.,[59,6061] Literature articulates that the notion of 'self' is a reflexive process where individuals see themselves as both subjects and objects. In the broadest

[56] *Ibid.*

[57] Blumer Herbert, *Symbolic Interactionism: Perspective and Method* (1969).

[58] Mead Herbert, *Mind, Self and Society* (1934).

[59] Howard Judith and Hollander Jocelyn, *Gender Situations, Gendered Selves* (2000).

[60] Buzawa *supra* note 13.

[61] Vetten *supra* note 5.

sense, the self involves the process of observing and conversing with oneself and then responding to oneself as one imagines others would. The symbolic interactionist helps us to understand what goes on in the mind of the victim of domestic violence. A woman or child who has been abused in a household setting does engage in a reflective process. This is a process of thinking where one positions him or herself in a household and looks at how the other members of the household see him or her. In a patriarchal society, a woman knows her place as one of submitting to a man. She would see herself as deserving of punishment when she has done something wrong. This reflection is based on the societal meanings created from the norms that govern interactions between a man and a woman. The chances of a woman reporting abuse to the police would be slim as one would look at the expected social action for a person in their position.

As noted, the symbolic interactionist focuses on interactions and meaning—with emphasis on how individuals view themselves, others and their environment (situations). In the light of this, one would also note that the interactions between the police and the victim may also be determined by the preconceived views held in societies where crimes occur. The police in some societies would not consider domestic violence a crime as it is often regarded as a personal issue.[62] These ideas are based on the interactions and constructions of meaning within the society as to what the society would label deviant conduct.[63] The symbolic interactionist would make us question if the police officer attending to a case is trained or not. The 'self' develops via communication with others on a symbolic level through the ability to see one's self imaginatively from the standpoint of the other.[64] In that case, our argument is that if domestic violence is grossly imbedded within the African societal stereotypes on gender roles, with men often exercising this right to exercise dominion over women, then it may also pose problems for the male police officer taking on a case of domestic violence without proper training to address the case beyond such stereotypes on the status of men

---

[62] Summers Randal and Allan Michael Hoffman (eds) *Domestic Violence: A Global View* (2002).

[63] Goode Erich, *Deviant Behaviour* (2015).

[64] Mead Herbert, *Mind, Self and Society* (1934).

and women in society. The assumption, like Mead[65] has noted, is that a person presented with a case would self-reflect and see themselves in the mirror. Such perceptions do not just inform police decisions, they also inform the response and perceptions of victims. Take an example of a battered woman in which case such woman perceive herself as deserving of abuse. Women in such situations often have feelings of guilt, shame and confusion. Subsequently, they don't report abuse police because societies normalise the abuse.

5 Results and Discussion

In this section, results are presented and discussed based on the responses given during the survey research conducted.

5.1 Profile of Participants

In presenting the results, we begin by profiling the participants so that the readers have insight into the participants we engaged with and the probable implications that arise from this. In this study, 61% of the respondents were male officers, with most holding the position of a captain. Most female officers were ranked as sergeants (19.2%) whilst the majority (55.8%) occupied other ranks. No female officers interviewed were less than 25 years of age or less (10%). None of these female officers had attained the age of at least 55 years. On the other hand, the ages for male officers were skewed to the right with more than 70% of the respondents being 45 years and above. This age revealed that most of the respondents who participated in the study already had years of experience on the job and were mature enough to understand the subject of domestic violence.

In terms of education, Figure 3 below shows the education levels attained by the sampled individuals within the SAPS. More than 60% of the responding officers had attained at least a metric qualification whilst

65 *Ibid.*

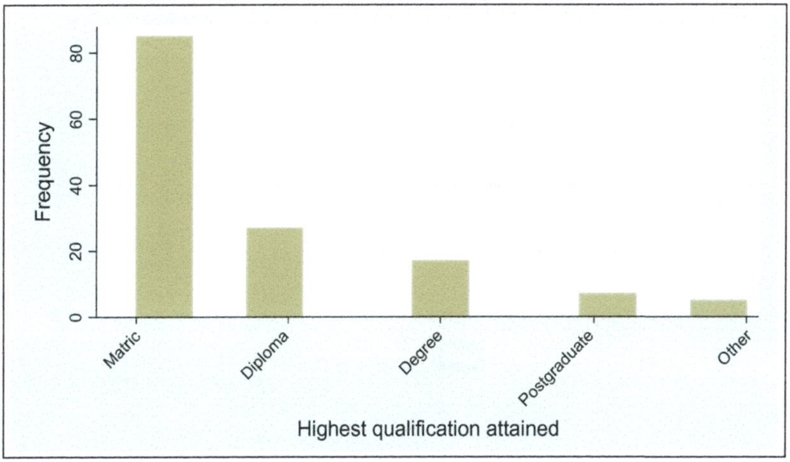

Fig. 3 Highest qualification of SAPS officers (*Source* Authors)

less than 5% had advanced level degrees. In a study by Retief and Green[66] titled 'Educating and training the future police office', the researchers noted that it has always been the vision of the countries to have college-educated police officers. However, this vision remains unrealised and in light of our current study among the SAPS officials, the education levels remain low. From the study by Retief and Green,[67] the reasons for low education were attributable to the fact that mainstream education offers a path that is often divergent from policing aspirations.

The minimum educational backgrounds of the SAPS officers and its effect on enforcement of the law indicate the need for rigorous training on how to handle cases of domestic violence.

Our next question sought to find out if the SAPS officers were trained with skills relevant to handle the victims of domestic violence. Figure 4 below highlights the positions held by the respondents within the DVA sector. The results show that on average (58%), these respondents were police officers whilst a small percentage (10%) were victim empowerment officers. These positions can reveal that within the SAPS, very few

---

66 Retief and Green *supra* note 3.

67 *Ibid.*

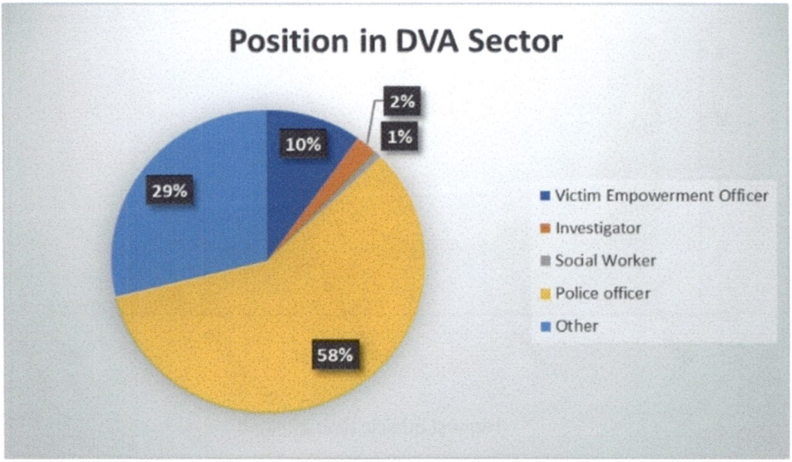

Fig. 4 Positions held in the DVA sector (*Source* Authors)

officers are trained into specialised positions that deal with domestic violence cases. This points to the need to improve the education of police officers as most officers have limited education and trained on mainstream policing.

5.2 Need for Police capacitation

In this study, 85.9% of the respondents indicated their familiarity with the Domestic Violence Act 116 of 1998 although 60% of the female officers were not aware of the Act. The results showed that there was a close association between gender of the respondent and their familiarity with DVA 116 of 1998 as shown by a significant chi square value of 6.18% at 5% level. Furthermore, 71.0% of those familiar with DVA had received training as far back as 1990. Those who did not receive training highlighted that they were not informed of the Act. For example, one officer highlighted that 'I was not aware of the training program and where to be trained…' The results further show that more than 95% (65.4% strongly agree and 31.6% agree) of the respondents support the view that DVA training is necessary to capacitate SAPS to better handle domestic violence cases. On another note, 29.9% of the responses strongly disagree that police stations have enough resources and capacity to deal with domestic violence especially in Vhembe district whilst 22.6% agree that they are capacitated.

The views on the need for police capacitation were also noted by other scholars in the field. Eigenberg et al.[68] reveal that family violence calls may cause safety threats to police officers responding to such calls. The scholars allude that police officers responding to domestic violence disputes will be at risk. Given the high incidence of violence in South Africa, appropriate training will be required to handle domestic violence cases. In the aftermath of such training, the police will be able to more effectively respond and help victims of domestic violence. Also, statistics have proved that officers are murdered more in responding to domestic violence incidents than any other type of police incident.[69] This further buttresses the need for training to ensure that police officers respond in an effective manner while at the same ensuring that they are safe.

5.3 How to Capacitate the police

The research results revealed that at least 42,8% of the respondents support the idea that stations can better handle domestic violence cases through frequent personnel training, whereas 34.8% requested for additional resources to support the police services. In addition, some respondents advocated for a swift response (15.2%) to cases dealing with domestic violence. These responses are presented in Fig. 5.

5.3.1 Training of police on Domestic violence

To successfully implement domestic violence training, we put forward the model used by Dr. Bengt-Ake Lindval's four knowledge taxonomy principles (Know-What; Know-how; Know-why; Know-who) as an assessment tool to evaluate family violence. In using this assessment tool,

---

[68] Eigenberg Helen, Kappeler Victor and McGuffee Karen, 'Confronting the Complexities of Domestic Violence: A Social Prescription for Rethinking Police Training,' 12 *Journal of Police Crisis Negotiations* (2012): 122–145.

[69] *Ibid.*

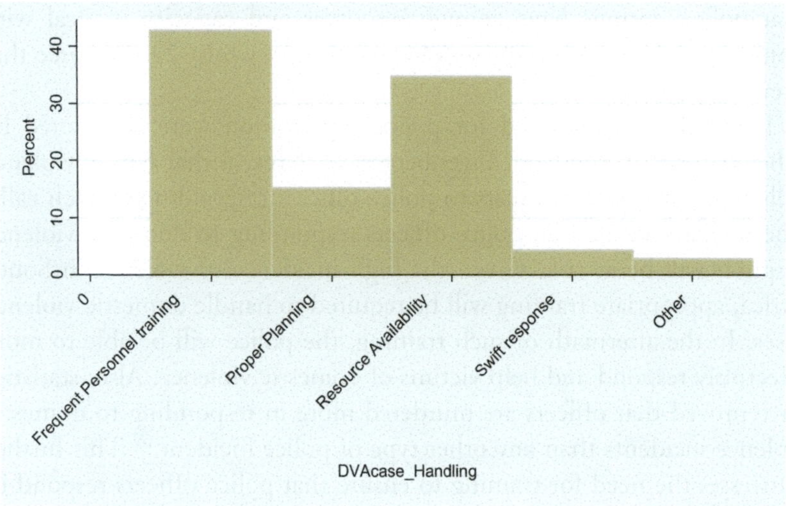

Fig. 5 DVA case handling (*Source* Authors)

the implementors can start by looking at *know-what*. In this instance, one should know whether the police officers are aware of the national laws and other laws such as the DVA that govern domestic violence. This would involve passing the knowledge on what the law entails in this regard.

The history of the efforts against domestic violence by activists as well as health organisations should be taught to the police. This knowledge should also include discussions on how husbands have used 'physical chastisement' to abuse women and children.[70] This can further be explained by providing trainings and studies on patriarchy and its link to domestic violence. Other scholars[71] are of the opinion that 'trainers should use history to define domestic violence, family violence, intimate partner violence, victim, offender, and other frequent terms found in legal language. Trainers should provide facts on how the creation

[70] Stalnaker Sylvia, and Patricia Shields, 'Perspectives of Violence by Attorneys, Police and Women's Shelter Directors: Divisive Differences and Significant Similarities,' 10 *Journal of Police and Criminal Psychology* (1994): 29–36.

[71] McDaniel Jasmine, *Police Training on Domestic Violence: Bengt-Ake Lundvall's Taxonomy of Knowledge Principles* (2017).

of shelters, hotlines, centers, local organisations have helped the need'. The history of domestic violence under the Police Domestic Violence Training *Know-what* can easily inform or provide insight to police on how domestic violence cases were historically viewed as personal issues. This information on *know-what* police training helps to change the attitude of the police detectives towards domestic violence cases.

The second principle under the Police Domestic Violence Training *Know-how*. This tenet involves the actual practise of policing domestic violence, where the police officers learn and practise the skills of dealing with domestic violence.[72] *Knowing how* is stored knowledge and used to accomplish complex tasks (Lundvall, p. 6). In this case, the police should understand the procedure and know how to put it into practice. McKean and Hendricks[73] argue that this skill is required especially in cases that involve intimate relationships. Our observation also extends to training police officers to deal with non-traditional families such as same-sex relationships. The skills required under the *Know-how* technique include skill sets of skills including analytical skills, communication skills, authority skills and conflict management skills.

The third technique under the Police Domestic Violence Training suggested is *Know-why*. In this case, police officers need to be aware of why they need to rely on training to solve domestic violence issues. Training should educate officers on why they need to handle domestic violence calls in a specific manner.[74] Police officers should also be cognisant of the need to protect their personal safety.[75] Training is important because it helps promote officer safety when responding to domestic violence cases.

The last technique under the Police Domestic Violence Training is the *Know-who*. Lundvall's *know-who* knowledge refers to knowledge of

---

72 Schmidtchen David, 'The Rise of the Strategic Private: Technology, Control and Change in a Network-Enabled Military,' *The Australian Army* (2006): 146–160.

73 McKean Jerome and Hendricks James, 'The Role of Crisis Intervention in the Police Response to Domestic Disturbances,' 8 *Criminal Justice Policy Review* (1997): 269–294.

74 Blaney Elizabeth, 'Victims of Intimate Partner violence assaults' 33 *An International Journal* (2010): 354- 375.

75 *Ibid.*

others' abilities and resource. *Know-who* knowledge involves collaborating with others to achieve the desired results.[76] The training should provide a platform for police officers to be aware of whom to contact (experts) when cases are reported, or, when they are approached by victims. Furthermore, the police should be trained to know who the actors or perpetrators are in domestic violence cases.

In one of the successful case studies on police training on domestic violence carried in Dallas in the USA,[77] the police training on family violence usually goes on for one month and it could be extended until police officers are competent enough to handle domestic violence cases. This training can be hosted in various settings and during these trainings, police officers gain practical experience in handling complex investigations related to family violence. Furthermore, senior officers are also given refresher training on protocols to follow when dealing with domestic violence cases. Detectives are also refreshed on protocols and procedures to use to respond to domestic violence disputes. Usually, new detectives will be paired with experienced detectives for training, and once they have demonstrated that they can perform as qualified family violence detectives, they become independent detectives. The new detective will be promoted based on the recommendation from the senior detective.

6 Conclusion

Women constitute the major victims of domestic violence. The nature of response that they receive from the police is particularly critical as it determines whether they access justice or not. The study in this chapter has revealed gaps in training and skills by members of the SAPS. It is against this backdrop that a conclusion is drawn that the SAPS should equip its members with skills and tools to deal with cases of domestic violence. Police capacitation can impact on the rate at which

[76] *Ibid.*

[77] McDaniel *supra* note 71.

victims report cases. It is also helpful in ensuring that police understand all the dynamics involved in dealing with domestic violence. Dr. Bengt-Ake Lindval's four knowledge taxonomy principles (Know-What; Know-how; Know-why; Know-who) has been advanced in this study as an assessment tool to evaluate family violence. It is a tool that finds relevance in the South African context. Knowledge taxonomy principles assist the police to have better knowledge of what domestic violence is.

References

Artz Lillian, 'Policing the Domestic Violence Act: Teething Troubles or System Failure' *Journal Agenda: Empowering Women for Gender Equity* 16 (2001): 1–13.

Bishop Charlotte, 'Domestic Violence: The Limitations of a Legal Response' in Sarah Hilder and Vanessa Bettinson (eds) *Domestic Violence* (2016) 59–79.

Blaney Elizabeth, 'Victims of Intimate Partner violence assaults' 33 *An International Journal* (2010): 354- 375.

Blumer Herbert, *Symbolic Interactionism; Perspective and method* (1969).

Bourlet Allan, *Police Intervention in Marital Violence* (1990).

Buzawa Eve, 'Intimate Partner Violence' 32 *Journal of policy Analysis and Management* (2012): 139–141.

Carney Michelle Mohr and John Barner, 'Prevalence of Partner Abuse: Rates of Emotional Abuse and Control' 3 *Partner Abuse* (2012): 286–335.

Commission for Gender Equality, Annual report 2016–2017, https://nationalgovernment.co.za/entity_annual/1170/2017-commission-for-gender-equality-(cge)-annual-report.pdf, October 12, 2020.

Corcoran Jacquelin, Stephenson Margaret, Watkins Derrelyn Perryman and Shannon Allen, 'Perceptions and Utilisation of a Police- Social Work Crisis: Intervention Approach to Domestic Violence' 82 *Families in Society: The Journal of Contemporary Human Services* (2001): 393–398.

Eigenberg Helen, Kappeler Victor and McGuffee Karen, 'Confronting the Complexities of Domestic Violence: A Social Prescription for Rethinking Police Training' 12 *Journal of Police Crisis Negotiations* (2012): 122–145.

Folami Olakunle Michael, 'Survey of Unreported Cases of Domestic Violence in Two Heterogeneous Communities in Nigeria' 4 *International review of law* (2013): 1–19.

Goode Erich, *Deviant Behavior* (2015).

Guthrie Jennifer A and Adrianne Kunkel, 'Problematising the Uniform Application of the Formula Story: Advocacy for Survivors in a Domestic Violence Support Group' 38 *Women & Language* (2015): 43–62.

Howard Judith and Hollander Jocelyn, *Gender Situations, Gendered Selves* (2000).

Huecker Martin and Smock William, *Domestic Violence* (2019), http://www.ncbi.nlm.nih.govbooks/NBK499891/, June 20, 2020.

Kunkel Andrianne and Guthrie Jennifer, 'Survivor: Women's Stories of Navigation and Tensions in a Domestic Violence Shelter' *Western Journal of Communication* (2015): 100–120.

Lubaale Emma Charlene, *Bridging the justice gap in the prosecution of acquaintance child sexual abuse: a case of South Africa and Uganda* (PhD Thesis, University of Pretoria 2015).

Lundvall Bengt-Ake, *Knowledge Management in the Learning Economy* (2000), http://www3.druid.dk/wp/20060006.pdf, June 20, 2020.

Macleod Pat, Kinver Andrea, Page Leon, Iliasov Aibek and Williams Rachel, *Partner Abuse.* (2009).

Macqueen Sarah and Norris Paul, 'Police Awareness and Involvement in Cases of Domestic and Partner Abuse' 10 *Policing and Society* (2016): 1–22.

Mazars Celine, What Works to Prevent Violence Against Women and Girls, Evidence Review UK Aid, Safer Spaces (2015) 1–65, https://www.whatworks.co.za/documents/publications/35-global-evidence-reviews-paper-2-interventions-to-prevent-violence-against-women-and-girls-sep-2015/file, June 20, 2020.

McDaniel Jasmine, *Police Training on Domestic Violence: Bengt-Ake Lundvall's Taxonomy of Knowledge Principles* (2017).

McKean Jerome and Hendricks James, 'The Role of Crisis Intervention in the Police Response to Domestic Disturbances' 8 *Criminal Justice Policy Review* (1997): 269–294.

Mead Herbert, *Mind, Self and Society* (1934).

Merten Marianne, *Statistics SA: One in Five SA Women Experience Physical Violence, Young Women Hard-Hit by HIV/Aids*, Daily Maevrick, May 15, 2017, https://www.dailymaverick.co.za/article/2017-05-15-statistics-sa-one-in-five-sa-women-experience-physical-violence-young-women-hard-hit-by-hivaids/, June 20, 2020.

Moosa Zohra, *A Theory of Change for Tacking Violence Against Women and Girls* (2012), https://www.actionaid.org.uk/sites/default/files/doc_lib/theory_of_change_on_vawg.pdf, June 20, 2020.

Mpani Patience and Nsibande Nondumiso, *Understanding Gender Policy and Gender-Based Violence in South Africa; A Literature Review* (2015) https://www.saferspaces.org.za/resources/entry/understanding-gender-policy-and-gender-based-violence-in-south-africa, June 20, 2020.

Oehme Karen and Martin Annelise, 'A Practical Plan for Prevention and Intervention: Florida's New Model Policy on Officer-Involved Domestic Violence' 24 *Criminal Justice Studies* (2011): 395–408.

Retief Rita and Green Sulina, 'Some Challenges of Policing Domestic Violence' 51 *Journal of Social Work* (2015): 135–147.

Richards Laura, *Getting Away With It; A profile of the Domestic Violence Sexual Assault and 'Serious' Incident Analysis* (2004), https://paladinservice.co.uk/wp-content/uploads/2013/07/Getting-Away-with-It.pdf, June 20, 2020.

Robinson Amanda, Gillian Pinchevsky and Guthrie Jennifer, 'Under the Radar Policing Non-Violent Domestic Abuse in the US and UK' 40 *International Journal of Comparative and Applied Criminal Justice* (2016): 195–208.

Rollè Luca, Shulamit Ramon and Piera Brustia, 'New Perspectives on Domestic Violence: From Research to Intervention' 10 *Frontiers in Psychology* (2019): 641.

Schmidtchen David, 'The Rise of the Strategic Private: Technology, Control and Change in a Network-Enabled Military' *The Australian Army* (2006): 146–160.

South African Department of Community Safety, *Concept Document On The Work Sessions Of South African Police Service* (2019).

Stone Kelly and Claudia Lopes, *Policing Responses to Domestic Violence: Exploring Reactions by the Police to Women in Need of Shelter* (2018), https://za.boell.org/sites/default/files/hbf_saps_research_paper_web_1.pdf, June 20, 2020.

Tuerkheimer Deborah, 'Recognising and Remedy the Harm of Battering; A Cll to Criminalise Domestic Violence' 94 *The Journal of Criminal Law and Criminology* (2004): 959–1024.

United Nations Office on Drugs and Abuse, South Africa: Are We Doing Enough to End Violence Against Women? (2020), https://www.unodc.org/southernafrica/en/vaw/index.html, June 20, 2020.

Vetten Lisa, 'The Ghost of Families Past; Domestic Violence Legislation and Policy in Post-Apartheid South Africa' 28 *Journal of the Contemporary Women for Gender Equity* (2014): 48–57.

6

Access to Justice for Sexual Violence Against Women: A Socio-Legal Analysis of Case Reporting in Kenya

Nelly Warega

1 Introduction

According to the United Nations, the most widespread form of abuse experienced in the world is violence against women.[1]This includes physical, sexual or mental harm suffered by women either in public or in private spaces. In 2013, the World Health Organization (WHO) conducted a study which revealed that one in three women have experienced physical and/or sexual violence at a point in their life.[2]

[1] 'In depth study on all forms of violence against women, UN Secretary-General Report,' July, 2006, http://www.un.org/womenwatch/daw/vaw/violenceagainstwomenstudydoc.pdf.

[2] World Health Organisation, *Global and Regional Estimates of Violence Against Women: Prevalence and Health Effects of Intimate Partner Violence and Non-Partner Sexual Violence* (2013).

[3] Lori L. Heise, 'Violence Against Women: An Integrated Ecological Framework,' 3 *Violence Against Women* (1998): 262–290.

N. Warega (✉)
Utu Wetu Trust, Nairobi, Kenya

E. C. Lubaale and A. Budoo-Scholtz (eds.), *Violence Against Women and Criminal Justice in Africa: Volume I*, Sustainable Development Goals Series,
https://doi.org/10.1007/978-3-030-75949-0_6

The World Report on Violence and Health defines sexual violence as[3]:

> ...any sexual act, attempt to obtain a sexual act, unwanted sexual comments or advances, or acts to traffic, or otherwise directed against a person's sexuality using coercion, by any person regardless of their relationship to the victim, in any setting including but not limited to home and work.

Basile et al. explain that sexual violence also includes the unwanted touching of a person's body parts like buttocks, breasts, penis and inner thighs. They also emphasise that other non-contact actions may also amount to sexual violence due to the impact they have on survivors. Such actions include forceful or unwilling exposure to pornographic material to both adults and children.[4]

Much literature has been developed over the years on access to justice for survivors of sexual violence.[5] This literature mainly focuses on state responsibility to prevent these crimes, investigations and prosecutions where these crimes have occurred, and provision of reparation for survivors of such crimes.[6] These four factors contribute to access to the justice value chain especially for survivors of sexual violence. However,

---

[4] Basile KC, Smith SG, Breiding MJ, Black MC and Mahendra RR, 'Sexual Violence Surveillance: Uniform Definitions and Recommended Data Elements,' Atlanta (GA): National Center for Injury Prevention and Control, Centers for Disease Control and Prevention (2014).

[5] *Ibid*. 3; Bruce Baker, 'Justice for Survivors of Sexual Violence in Kitgum, Uganda,' 29 *Journal of Contemporary African Studies* (2011): 245–262; International Commission of Jurists, *Women's Access to Justice for Gender Based Violence: A Practitioner's Guide* (2016); Nduku Kilonzo et al., 'Sexual Violence Legislation in Sub-Saharan Africa: The Need for Strengthened Medico-Legal Linkages,' 13 *Reproductive Health Matters Journal* (2009); Julie Freccero et al., 'Responding to Sexual Violence: Community Approaches,' Sexual Violence & Accountability Project, Working Paper Series, Human Rights Centre, University of California Berkeley (2011); Yakin Erturk, 'Integration of the Human Rights of Women and the Gender Perspective: Violence Against Women,' U.N. Doc. E/CN.4/2006/61, pp. 17 https://www.refworld.org/pdfid/45377afb0.pdf; Action Aid, 'A Theory of Change for Tackling Violence Against Women and Girls' (2012); OHCHR, UN Women and PHR, *Breaking Cycles of Violence: Gaps in Prevention of and Response to Electoral Related Sexual Violence* (2019): 10–15, https://www.ohchr.org/Documents/Countries/KE/OHCHRPHRUNWOMENKenyaGapAnalysisDec20191.pdf.

[6] General Recommendation No. 28 on the Core Obligations of State Parties under Art 2 of CEDAW, December 16, 2010, CEDAW/C/GC/28, https://undocs.org/en/CEDAW/C/GC/28; Guidelines on Combating Sexual Violence and its Consequences in Africa (Niamey Guidelines), https://www.achpr.org/public/Document/file/English/achpr_eng_guidelines_on_combating_sexual_violence_and_its_consequences.pdf.

within these four factors are other equally critical conversations that are essential for the success of the four. Such is the issue of reporting which is one of the most important steps in gaining meaningful access to justice. Reporting, as relevant literature reveals, has not been given adequate attention. The author notes that while an entirely different conversation is required to discuss state obligations during conflict or emergency situations, where investigations can be done without reporting,[7] the decision to report a case to the authorities lies entirely with survivors. The discussion is aimed at creating an atmosphere of justice which promotes reporting of cases to aid in curbing the menace of sexual violence in Kenya while also supporting autonomy in such decision-making.

In carrying out this research, this chapter considers available literature on reporting by victims of sexual violence in Kenya. This includes reports, academic research and various sources of law. In applying this literature, the chapter assesses reporting as an important aspect of access to justice for victims of sexual violence in Kenya and is divided into seven main parts. The first part introduces the chapter while the second part examines the available literature on reporting of sexual violence in Kenya. The third part discusses the normative framework on sexual violence and state obligations in responding to such violence. It further analyses the latter's roles in ensuring effective mechanisms for response to violence and promotion of access to justice for women and girls in Kenya. The fourth part examines reporting of sexual violence in practice in Kenya while the fifth part considers the societal and institutional response to sexual violence in Kenya. This part conceptualises the context within which survivors are denied access to justice in Kenya. The sixth part makes recommendations on how to resolve the issues highlighted in the paper and concludes in the last part.

---

[7] OHCHR, UN Women and PHR, 'Breaking Cycles of Violence: Gaps in Prevention of and Response to Electoral Related Sexual Violence' (2019): 10–15.

2 Contextualising Reporting for victims of Sexual Violence

According to Rape, Abuse and Incest National Network (RAINN), three out of four cases in the United States of America of sexual assault cases go unreported.[8] In 2006, the WHO conducted a study in 10 selected countries which revealed that 55% of women who experience sexual violence and other forms of gender-based violence do not report the violation to any persons in authority.[9] Similarly, in a report published by the United Nations in 2015, it was reported that less than 40% of women who experience violence globally seek any form of assistance afterwards.[10] In Kenya, 14% of women between the ages of 15 and 49 experience sexual violence at least once in their lifetime.[11] The National Crime Research Centre (NCRC) in 2014, however, recorded only up to 15.2% of sexual violence reports by female respondents.[12]

The first stage is providing any form of redress for survivors of sexual violence is through reporting of the crime—either at a health facility or to law enforcement agents. However, as we can see in the paragraph above, this is often not the case as reporting rates are often much lower than actual incidences of sexual violence. Other forms of reporting include confiding in family and trusted friends for emotional support. When survivors visit health facilities, they receive treatment for physical and/or internal injuries, potential sexually transmitted diseases including

---

[8] RAINN, *The Criminal Justice System: Statistics*, https://www.rainn.org/statistics/criminal-justice-system#:~:text=The%20Majority%20of%20Sexual%20Assaults,out%20of%204%20go%20unreported.&text=Members%20of%20the%20military%3A%2043,10%25%20of%20male%20victims%20reported.

[9] World Health Organization, *Prevalence of Intimate Partner Violence: Findings from the WHO Multi Country Study on Women's Health and Domestic Violence* (2006).

[10] United Nations, *The World's Women 2015: Trends and Statistics*, https://unstats.un.org/unsd/gender/downloads/WorldsWomen2015_report.pdf.

[11] Kenya National Bureau of Statistics, Ministry of Health/Kenya, National AIDS Control Council/Kenya, Kenya Medical Research Institute and National Council for Population and Development/Kenya, *Kenya Demographic and Health Survey* (2014): 297–299, http://dhsprogram.com/pubs/pdf/FR308/FR308.pdf.

[12] National Crime Research Centre, *Gender Based Violence in Kenya* (2014): 59, http://crimeresearch.go.ke/wp-content/uploads/2018/02/wwwroot_publications_Gender-Based-Violence-in-Kenya.pdf.

HIV and necessary care for prevention of unwanted pregnancies. Psychological support which is equally important is often also administered at this point. This process is useful for collection of forensic evidence for survivors who wish to pursue legal action against their perpetrators. The evidence collected is used by the police in their investigation of the crime and prosecution of the alleged perpetrator. It is therefore imperative that the two institutions work together to ensure proper management of the survivor's needs and evidence collected to ensure proper redress for harm suffered.[13]

Unfortunately, the nature of sexual violence crimes often makes it difficult for survivors to report the crime. The physical and emotional effects of the violations leave survivors with feelings of shame, and sometimes even blame, which often leads to silence for fear of not receiving the support deserved.[14] Survivors' responses may also mirror those of the reporting and justice mechanisms. For example, those who have witnessed timely, confidential and highly professional response by the authorities for crimes reported and especially gender-based violence cases are more likely to report than those who have witnessed a lack of care by the authorities and subsequently zero accountability for other victims.[15] Furthermore, survivors may choose not to report cases because they are unaware of the importance of reporting, how to do it or what to expect when they do so. Others who may wish to report such cases may experience difficulties such as lack of access to reporting mechanisms including law enforcement agencies and health facilities. This is further demonstrable in physical accessibility such as distance to police stations or reporting facilities and economic accessibility such as transport costs required to get to such facilities.

While the disparity between the personal experiences and actual reported cases may be common in most jurisdictions due to the nature of sexual violence crimes as discussed above, much more can be done to reduce this gap by providing an environment that encourages survivors

---

[13] University of California Berkeley, *The Investigation and Prosecution of Sexual Violence*, https://www.usip.org/sites/default/files/missing-peace/seelinger-the-investigation.pdf.

[14] MCASA, *Reporting Sexual Assault: Why Survivors Often Don't*, https://ocrsm.umd.edu/files/Why-Is-Sexual-Assault-Under-Reported.pdf.

[15] *Ibid*.

to report cases to the authorities. Therefore, it is important to consider the various responsibilities of these authorities under the law.

3 An Assessment of Kenya's Normative Framework on Access to Justice for Victims of Sexual Violence under International Human Rights law

International human rights standards recognise sexual violence as a human rights violation with adverse long-term effects on victims[16] and direct negative impact on other human rights and freedoms such as the right to life, the right to equality and non-discrimination, right to dignity, freedom of liberty and the right to good health amongst other rights.[17] Other international human rights instruments that prohibit all forms of violence against women include the Convention Against Torture and Other Cruel Inhuman or Degrading Treatment or Punishment, the Convention on the Elimination of all Forms of Discrimination Against Women and the Convention on the Rights of the Child.[18]

Regionally, Kenya is a party to the African Charter on Human and Peoples' Rights (African Charter).[19] Article 1 of the Charter provides

---

[16] *Ibid*, 6.

[17] The right to life, equality and non-discrimination, right to dignity and freedom of liberty are recognized by the UN International Covenant on Civil and Political Rights (ICCPR) arts 6, 3, 10 and 9, respectively. The right to good health is provided by UN International Covenant on Economic, Social and Cultural Rights (ICESCR) article 12.

[18] UN General Assembly, *Convention Against Torture and Other Cruel, Inhuman or Degrading Treatment or Punishment*, December 10, 1984, United Nations, Treaty Series, https://www.ohchr.org/en/professionalinterest/pages/cat.aspx; UN General Assembly, *Convention on the Elimination of All Forms of Discrimination Against Women*, December 18, 1979, United Nations, Treaty Series, https://www.un.org/womenwatch/daw/cedaw/text/econvention.htm; UN General Assembly, *Convention on the Rights of the Child*, November 20, 1989, United Nations, Treaty Series, https://www.ohchr.org/Documents/ProfessionalInterest/crc.pdf.

[19] African Charter on Human and Peoples' Rights ('Banjul Charter'), 27 June 1981, CAB/LEG/67/3 rev. 5, 21 I.L.M. 58 (1982), https://au.int/sites/default/files/treaties/36390-treaty-0011_-_african_charter_on_human_and_peoples_rights_e.pdf; African Union, *Protocol to the African Charter on Human and People's Rights on the Rights of Women in Africa,* July 11, 2003, https://au.int/sites/default/files/treaties/37077-treaty-0027_-_protocol_to_the_african_charter_on_human_and_peoples_rights_on_the_rights_of_women_in_africa_e.pdf.

that '...member states shall recognize the rights, duties and freedoms enshrined in the Charter'. These rights include the right to life and integrity of the person, the right to security of person, right to equal protection of the law, right to freedom of movement and the right to the highest attainable standard of both physical and mental health.[20] Further, the African Charter provides for the elimination of all forms of discrimination against women with an obligation placed on states to ensure such protection for women, children including the aged and persons with disabilities.[21] The 2016 African Commission Guidelines for Combating Sexual Violence in Africa provide measures that must be implemented by states to promote reporting of sexual violence cases.[22] These measures include the creation of toll free numbers, effective referral systems to ensure survivors receive all the support they require, the use of one stop centres where possible to bring all these services together for easy reporting and reduced revictimisation and the provision of counselling and shelters services.[23]

Similarly, the Protocol to African Charter on the Rights of Women in Africa (Maputo Protocol) which Kenya ratified in 2010 provides for the protection of rights for all women in Africa by eliminating all forms of discrimination against women recognised by international conventions and declarations.[24] Another relevant regional instrument that Kenya has ratified is the African Charter on the Rights and Welfare of the Child (ACRWC) which provides for the protection of the rights of all children including protection from sexual violence and torture.[25]

---

[20] *Ibid*, Art 3,4,5,6 and 12.

[21] *Ibid*, Art 18(3)(4).

[22] Principle 6, Guidelines on Combating Sexual Violence and its Consequences in Africa (Niamey Guidelines), African Commission on Human and Peoples' Rights, https://www.achpr.org/public/Document/file/English/achpr_eng_guidelines_on_combating_sexual_violence_and_its_consequences.pdf.

[23] *Ibid*.

[24] African Union, Protocol to the African Charter on Human and People's Rights on the Rights of Women in Africa, 11 July 2003, https://au.int/sites/default/files/treaties/37077-treaty-0027_-_protocol_to_the_african_charter_on_human_and_peoples_rights_on_the_rights_of_women_in_africa_e.pdf.

[25] *Ibid*, Art 16.

Chapter four of the Constitution of Kenya contains the Bill of Rights which mirrors international human rights standards and provides for the respect and protection of rights for all persons regardless of gender, race, tribe, age and all other factors used to unfairly discriminate against others.[26] The right to life, right to equality and non-discrimination, right to dignity, freedom and security of the person and access to justice are all provided by the Constitution.[27] It particularly places the duty on the state to ensure protection of vulnerable groups of people such as women, persons with disabilities, children and older persons.[28] Because victims and survivors of sexual violence experience a violation of these rights, the Constitution provides that they have the right to access justice and seek compensation for the harm suffered from local courts.[29]

The Sexual Offences Act of Kenya (SOA) is another piece of national legislation which was enacted to specifically provide guidance on prosecution of sexual offences.[30] The SOA was established at a time when cases of rape and defilement were rampant in the country but due to a lack of legislation, were either wrongly charged and prosecuted as assault under the Penal Code[31] or were not prosecuted at all. While the SOA does a good job at defining various forms of sexual violence, it does not provide guidance on other important procedures such as reporting, effective and timely investigations, the role of security agents and the protection of survivors from their perpetrators during the investigation and prosecution process.[32] To bridge this gap, the Ministry of Health, Kenya, in 2009, developed National Guidelines on the Management of Sexual Violence in Kenya to address the medical, legal and psycho-social needs of survivors of sexual violence.[33]

---

[26] Constitution of Kenya, Article 27 (2010).

[27] Constitution of Kenya, Articles 26,27,28, 29 and 48.

[28] Constitution of Kenya, Article 21(3).

[29] Constitution of Kenya, Articles 48 and 23(3).

[30] Sexual Offences Act of Kenya, No. 3 of 2006.

[31] Chapter 63, Laws of Kenya.

[32] Nelly Warega, *Sexual Violence in Kenya: Understanding the Legal and Socio-Cultural Contexts* (Masters degree thesis, University of Pretoria 2018): 24–26.

[33] Ministry of Public Health and Sanitation & Ministry of Medical Services, *National Guidelines on the Management of Sexual Violence in Kenya* 2nd Edition (2009), http://www.endvawnow.org/uploads/browser/files/national_guidelines.pdf.

The Constitution of Kenya provides that general rules of international law and all treaties and conventions ratified by the country form part of Kenyan law.[34] Therefore, the country is bound by the provisions in international and regional instruments that it has signed and ratified. The state therefore has an obligation to protect Kenyan women and girls from discrimination and all forms of violence. Where violence occurs, the state has a duty to conduct proper investigations and prosecutions and provide effective remedies for survivors.[35] The state has several obligations when it concerns sexual violence as discussed below.

i. The *obligation to prevent* sexual violence requires that the State must put all necessary measures in place that contribute towards prevention of such violence. This requires a multi-faceted approach which involves access to information on sexual violence, its impact on individuals and what measures are to be taken by survivors and other stakeholders such as law enforcement agents, health care workers and legislators to ensure effective response.[36] Information dissemination must be done through means that are accessible to all women and girls including those living in rural and urban areas and those with no access to internet services. It must also be simplified for all to understand, educated or not and in languages understood by the various communities.[37] Beyond provision of information, it also requires that a system be put in place to prevent occurrence of sexual violence and where it occurs those in authority such as police officers understand their role in minimising the impact on survivors. Measures taken by states must also take into consideration emergency situations such as the COVID-19 pandemic period which has seen a number of states respond to the virus at the expense of such duties. In Kenya, for example, the pronouncement of curfew orders did not take into consideration survivors of gender-based violence who often require open channels within which they can seek support. Initial

[34] Art 2(5)(6) Constitution of Kenya 2010.

[35] *Ibid*, 2.

[36] *Ibid*, 18.

[37] *Ibid*.

guidelines issued by the Ministry of Health[38] did not provide for survivors who may need to seek services at any time of day and night. Focus shifted to COVID-19 patients leading to a lack of awareness on where survivors of sexual violence and gender-based violence in general could seek help due to the closure of smaller health facilities or small departments in big hospitals and police stations such as gender desks.[39]

ii. The *obligation of the state to protect* citizens from sexual violence requires the state to adopt legislations and policies that act as a deterrent to perpetrators. Kenya has the SOA which was enacted into law to provide for the prosecution of sexual offences. The Act further provides for strict punishments for perpetrators found guilty of committing sexual offences. Other ways in which states fulfil this obligation is by minimising the impact of sexual violence on its citizens. This means adoption of measures to ensure that survivors of sexual violence receive comprehensive care from reporting of cases to police who have the skills and capacity to handle cases with the sensitivity they deserve, to medical service providers who are well trained in collection and storage of forensic evidence, to accessing psychosocial care, and lastly where necessary, economic support is provided for those in need. For example, those in need of free legal aid services.

iii. The third obligation requires that when survivors report cases to the police, they must be *investigated and prosecuted*. It is the duty of the police to conduct, investigate crimes, arrest suspects where there is evidence pointing to such and present them to the state prosecutors for trial in a court of law. During this process, it is important that the needs of the survivor continue to be prioritised. For example, provision of protection or security where evidence given compromises the

[38] Kenya COVID-19 RMNH Guidelines: A Kenya Practical Guide for Continuity of Reproductive, Maternal, New Born and Family Planning Care and Services in the Background of COVID-19 Pandemic, Ministry of Health, Kenya, April 2020, https://www.health.go.ke/wp-content/uploads/2020/04/KENYA-COVID19-RMNH.pdf.pdf.pdf.

[39] 'African Women in Law, *Uphold the Rights of SGBV Victims in the COVID-19 Response in Kenya* (2020), https://www.africanwomeninlaw.com/post/uphold-the-rights-of-sgbv-victims-in-the-covid-19-response-in-kenya.

security of the survivor/witness, timely and impartial investigations and prosecution of cases.[40]

iv. Lastly, the *obligation to provide reparations* for survivors of sexual violence means that adequate remedies must be given to survivors for the harm suffered. These can be awarded either through judicial systems such as court decisions or through other administrative means that seek to alleviate the suffering of survivors who may choose not to go to court but who deserve to be compensation due to the violations of sexual violence. Reparations must be timely and appropriate to the harm suffered.[41]

The subsequent section engages with one of the components of access to justice which is reporting of cases of sexual violence; the focus is on two obligations: the obligations to protect, investigate and prosecute cases. It is, however, important to understand that for any state to effectively respond to and address issues of sexual violence all four obligations must be met. Effective implementation of all four obligations also means adopting a survivor-centred approach which ensures that the needs of survivors are all met.

4 Reporting in Practice: Examining the Current Status of Reporting of Sexual Violence in Kenya

According to a study conducted by the National Crime Research Centre in Kenya, only 15.2% of female respondents who had ever been sexually violated reported the crime or had someone report the crime on their behalf.[42] The study also showed that women are more likely to report sexual violence perpetrated by a non-intimate partner rather than

[40] *Ibid,* 18.

[41] *Ibid*; *Egyptian Initiative for Personal Rights and Interights v Egypt* (2011) AHRLR 90 (ACHPR 2011).

[42] *Supra* note 12.

that by their partners.[43] Only 13.5% of women reported incidences by their intimate partners as compared to 33.3% women who reported cases perpetrated by non-intimate partners.[44] Men on the other hand were found to be more reserved than women and so whether the sexual violence was perpetrated by an intimate or non-intimate partner, the levels of reporting remained low.[45]

The study also found that a majority of the cases reported are reported to the police and to local provincial administrations with very few cases reported to mothers and fathers. Out of the cases reported to the police, 56.5% were by male while only 32.4% were reported by women. Much can be inferred from this, one of which can be that men may be more comfortable with reporting cases to the police than women are. In a society where women are more likely to experience sexual violence than men,[46] one can only imagine the many number of women who choose silence, for various reasons, when they experience such kind of violence.

With regard to action taken after reporting of cases, the study reported that 29.1% of female and 29.4% of men recorded a lack of action by the authorities. 11.8% of men and 8.9% of female had completely no idea whether action was taken or not as they never heard back from them.[47] The low levels of response and feedback to survivors, particularly women, can be inferred to be the reason why survivors of sexual violence in Kenya prefer not to file cases. The inaction by trusted persons in authority has over time created a lack of confidence in the very same institutions tasked with the responsibility to protect and respond to incidences of sexual violence and other forms of gender-based violence.[48] The police interviewed during the study reported that the biggest challenge they

[43] *Supra* note 12, 60.

[44] *Supra* note 12, 59.

[45] *Supra* note 12.

[46] Kenya National Bureau of Statistics, Ministry of Health/Kenya, National AIDS Control Council/Kenya, Kenya Medical Research Institute and National Council for Population and Development/Kenya, *Kenya Demographic and Health Survey* (2014): 297–299, http://dhsprogram.com/pubs/pdf/FR308/FR308.pdf; Cynthia Wangamati, *Why Attitudes Towards Sexual Violence in Kenya Need a Major Refresh*, The Conversation, July 22, 2018, https://theconversation.com/why-attitudes-towards-sexual-violence-in-kenya-need-a-major-refresh-100033.

[47] *Supra* note 12.

[48] *Ibid*.

experience in their response to gender-based violence as a whole is the lack of reporting of cases and the lack of cooperation by persons who witness the crimes.[49]

In 2015, a survey conducted by Ipsos Synovate reported that only 49% of victims of crime in Kenya report the crimes to the police. Those who report recorded unsatisfactory response with a majority complaining about lack of follow up investigations and corruption as the main issues they experienced. Other challenges included slow or no response from the police.[50] Although this data refers to a lack of reporting of general crimes, it emphasises the fact that Kenyans generally do not believe that the police and the institutional response as a whole can sufficiently respond to these crimes and especially incidences of sexual violence.

To understand this further, this chapter studies the context in which sexual violence occurs and how it is viewed in Kenya. It elaborates on the societal response and the institutional response to the crime as these two aspects play an important role in curbing such cases.

5 Social and Institutional Response to Sexual Violence in Kenya

Kenya is a highly patriarchal society in which men are still regarded as the superior gender and thus hold the power to dominate in all aspects of life.[51] From a very young age, boys are taught to be strong and aggressive to prove their masculinity while girls are taught to be quiet, obedient and submissive.[52] This system of power is nurtured from a very young age, creating an environment in which young men and women's understanding of masculinity and femininity is dictated by misinformed

[49] *Supra* note 12, 65.

[50] Ramadhan Rajab, *Kenyans Don't Report Crime, Says Survey*, The Star, September 4, 2015 https://www.the-star.co.ke/news/2015-09-04-kenyans-dont-report-crime-says-survey/.

[51] Cynthia Khamala Wangamati, Johanne Sundby and Ruth Jane Prince 'Communities' Perceptions of Factors Contributing to Child Sexual Abuse Vulnerability in Kenya: A Qualitative Study'12 *Culture, Health and Sexuality* (2018):1394–1408, https://www.tandfonline.com/doi/abs/10.1080/13691058.2018.1438666.

[52] *Ibid.*

community standards. These are standards that expect women to always submit to men as higher authority and on the other hand expects men to lead by dominating and exercising their power over women.

This culture of dominance is also seen in the way men and women relate sexually. The society teaches girls that sex is mainly to be initiated and enjoyed by men and that the role of women is to satisfy men sexually and to procreate.[53] Similarly, conversations around sex are considered to be private family affairs that are held behind closed doors between married couples which in most cases means it is the man passing down his decisions on sexuality, sexual intimacy and on the woman's reproductive health. This culture makes women more vulnerable and susceptible to violence and other forms of discrimination such as sexual harassment, sexual violence, assault and economic abuse.[54] When violence happens, because women have been taught that the men are superior and have a right to punish women when these gender norms are not met, many women struggle to understand this as abuse and those who do are hesitant to report the cases for fear of being ostracised by family and community at large for going against culture and traditions. The silence around sex also means that women who experience sexual violence, either in the home or outside, may be too embarrassed to discuss issues considered private and confidential.[55] This also means that many who seek medical care do not disclose to the health care providers that they are victims of sexual violence to allow for proper medical examinations and required protocols.

---

[53] Kramarae C, 'The Condition of Patriarchy' in C Kramarae & D Spender (eds) *The Knowledge Explosion: Generation of Feminist Scholarship* (1992); Lerner G *The Creation of Patriarchy* (1986).

[54] Cynthia Wangamati, *Why Attitudes Towards Sexual Violence in Kenya Need a Major Refresh*, The Conversation, July 22, 2018, https://theconversation.com/why-attitudes-towards-sexual-violence-in-kenya-need-a-major-refresh-100033.

[55] Crystal Corman 'Violence Against Women and Girls in Kenya: Roles of Religion and Response of Faith Actors,' *Policy Brief Berkley Centre for Religion Peace and World Affairs* (2016): 1–3, https://s3.amazonaws.com/berkleycenter/160829BCWFDDViolenceAgainstWomenGirlsKenyaRolesReligionResponseFaithActorsPolicyBrief.pdf.

5.1 Social Responses to Sexual Violence in Kenya

In some communities, sex before marriage is seen to devalue women and so when looking for wives, men often go for women who are considered 'pure'.[56] This makes it extremely difficult for women, who experience sexual violence, especially those who are still single, to report their cases to anyone because of the likely negative implications. In considering the social responses to sexual violence in Kenya, the next aspect of the chapter considers stigma and victim blaming, and lack of information on available treatments or remedies for victims of sexual violence.

5.1.1 Stigma and Victim Blaming

Sexual violence is a violent crime which violates a person's physical integrity and dignity. It is embarrassing and more often than not victims choose silence because they are worried that no one will believe them.[57] More often than not, there are no witnesses due to the nature of the crime which is often committed in private spaces.

When W.A, as she is referred to in her court case, opened up on twitter about her rape ordeal in the hands of two famous rugby boys in Kenya, Kenyans on twitter resorted to blaming her for making false accusations and trying to destroy the dreams of the young talented sportsmen who were considered 'role models' to many other young people.[58] This victim blaming culture faced by W.A is not new as everyday survivors of sexual violence in Kenya encounter great hurdles for their voices to be heard.[59] The society contributes to the blame game causing shame and stigma. Women are blamed for walking alone at night, for wearing the wrong clothes, for leading men on, for angering their perpetrators

---

[56] Stella Okoronkwo, *Facts about Sex for Youth* (2005): 35.

[57] Dee Smythe, *Rape Unresolved: Policing Sexual Offences in South Africa* (2015).

[58] Rono II @ rono Alphas, *There is Nowhere a Single Sided Story Can be Shoved Down Anyone's Throat. Accuse and Prove. No Need to Look for Sympathy Online. False Allegations Are as Risky as the Accusation Itself*, June 16, 2020, https://twitter.com/RonoAlphas/status/1272837221373095938.

[59] Faith Oneya, *No Matter How Famous One Is, Rape Is Inexcusable*, Daily Nation, August, 2019, https://www.nation.co.ke/kenya/blogs-opinion/opinion/no-matter-how-famous-one-is-rape-is-inexcusable-195456.

and for drinking alcohol, amongst others.[60] In February 2020, a top university in Nairobi was called out for blaming female students who were victims of rape for being reckless.[61] The memo which was drafted by the head of security at the university went as far as advising girls to be careful in social gatherings and to walk in groups in order to avoid getting raped. In another incident in 2018, a young woman was raped in Nairobi's central business district as a crowd which had gathered nearby cheered. The woman who was raped by a street urchin was blamed for her behaviour and interaction with the street urchins, with many people arguing that the two knew each other well.[62]

In June 2020, when a survey by the Kenya Health Information System reported about 4000 teenage pregnancies in Machakos County in Kenya between the months of January and May, it did not take long before the blame shifted to the girls for being reckless and engaging in sex with their fellow teenage boys and with men much older than them, and to parents for failing to look after their daughters. At no point were the perpetrators, who prey on underage girls who legally cannot consent to sex, called out.[63] The culture of shame, stigma and victim blaming contributes to the lack of reporting of sexual violence cases and creates an environment in which survivors would rather keep their violations to themselves than report to trusted persons, the police or persons in authority and be subjected to even more violations.

---

[60] Cynthia Wangamati, *Why Attitudes Towards Sexual Violence in Kenya Need a Major Refresh*, The Conversation, July 22, 2018, https://theconversation.com/why-attitudes-towards-sexual-violence-in-kenya-need-a-major-refresh-100033.

[61] 'Kenya University's Rape Memo Sparks Anger,' *BBC News*, April 26, 2020, https://www.bbc.com/news/world-africa-51644876.

[62] Ureport, *Fear Strikes Nairobi CBD After Video of Woman Being Raped by Street Boy Surfaces Online*, Standard Media, April 26, 2018, https://www.standardmedia.co.ke/ureport/story/2001278270/fear-strikes-nairobi-cbd-after-video-of-woman-being-raped-by-street-boy-surfaces-online.

[63] Scheaffor Okore (@scheafferoo), *4 Thousand Girls in Machakos County Have Been Raped and Ended Up Pregnant in the Past 4 Months, Meaning One Thousand Girls Were Raped in a Span of 30 Days but Somehow in This Tragedy Parents Are Being Blamed Instead of the Actual Rapists! Do Leaders Understand Rape Culture?* June 17, 2020, https://twitter.com/scheafferoo/status/1273198822735446021.

5.1.2 Lack of Information

While many women and girls do not report cases of sexual violence due to socio-cultural reasons and the accompanying shame and stigma that accompany, for many others it is because of a lack of understanding of sexual violence and its impact, lack of information on reporting procedures and the support available for victims.

A survey conducted in 2018 revealed that there was a general lack of awareness and understanding of sexual violence in Nakuru and Kiambu counties in Kenya. Survivors who visited the Naivasha Referral Hospital and the Thika Level 5 hospital did not have information on available services or where to go find such information. This was attributed to the stigma that surrounds sexual violence and the cultural norms which contribute to the silence around the crime.[64]

It is therefore important that community awareness programmes are implemented in order to ensure Kenyans have comprehensive information on sexual violence in order to reduce stigma and increase reporting rates. Information will also enable community members to detect sexual violence when they or persons they know experience the violation and to seek medical, legal and psychosocial support.[65] The trainings should also target those in service provision such as health care workers and police officers to ensure that they respond in a timely and sufficient manner when cases are reported to them.[66]

5.2 Institutional Response to Sexual Violence

Neither the SOA of Kenya nor the National Guidelines on the Management of Sexual Violence in Kenya provides reporting guidelines for survivors of sexual violence. They further do not elaborate on guidelines to service providers to ensure comprehensive support to survivors. For

---

[64] Gatuguta et al., 'Missed Treatment Opportunities and Barriers to Comprehensive Treatment for Sexual Violence Survivors in Kenya: A Mixed Methods Study,' 18 *BMC Public Health* (2018): 769, https://bmcpublichealth.biomedcentral.com/track/pdf/10.1186/s12889-018-5681-5.

[65] *Ibid.*

[66] *Ibid*, 3.

this reason, in 2013, the Ministry of Health through collaborative efforts with other stakeholders came up with the Multi-Sectoral Standard Operating Procedures on Prevention and Response to Sexual Violence (SoPs) aimed at operationalising the National Guidelines.[67]

The SoPs provide minimum standards for health care workers and other sectors that offer legal and psycho-social care. They show the linkages between the sectors, and a clear-cut referral pathway between the police, medical doctors, counsellors and other support facilities like shelters. Unfortunately to this day, these SoPs are yet to be operationalised.[68] This means that survivors do not have a reference point on the type of services they should receive at police stations and health care centres. This makes accountability difficult and potentially exposes survivors to more harm by service providers who lack the knowledge and capacity to handle cases of sexual violence.

5.2.1 Response by Health Care Workers

For most survivors, the first point of reporting is often to a health facility followed by a visit to the police station. This is crucial for a survivor to receive medical treatment including prevention of pregnancy and sexually transmitted diseases as well as initial psycho-social support. It is at this stage that forensic and other types of evidence should be preserved and recorded in the event the survivor chooses to pursue legal redress against the perpetrator.[69] This evidence should be recorded in two documents, a P3 form[70] and a Post Rape Care (PRC) form.[71] The challenge, however, is that P3 forms are police documents used for recording cases of assault including sexual violence. Therefore, survivors who start with

[67] Ministry of Health, *Multi-Sectoral Standard Operating Procedures on Prevention and Response to Sexual Violence* (2013) https://www.law.berkeley.edu/wp-content/uploads/2015/10/Kenya_National-Health-Sector-SOPs-on-Mgmt-of-SV-in-Kenya_2014.pdf.

[68] *Ibid*, 33.

[69] *Ibid*.

[70] Kenya Police Service, *P3 Form*, http://www.kenyapolice.go.ke/downloads/category/4-police-forms.html.

[71] Legal Notice 133 of 2012 SOA (Medical Treatment Regulations), https://www.law.berkeley.edu/wp-content/uploads/2015/10/Kenya_National-Health-Sector-SOPs-on-Mgmt-of-SV-in-Kenya_2014.pdf.

the health facility as their first point of reporting often have to go to the police station and then return to the health facility for the health worker to fill in the medical report section. The National Guidelines provide that any registered nurse or clinical officer can fill in this section of the P3 form. Nevertheless, police officers always insist on having this done by the government police doctor. These are false directives that complicate reporting and make survivors give up on the legal process.[72] Another challenge is that PRC forms are not always available in health facilities meaning that in places where these are missing, survivors do not receive the right documentation required to be submitted in court as evidence. Most health facilities also charge a fee for these documents which are supposed to be free, making them inaccessible to those who cannot afford to pay for them.[73]

5.2.2 Response by Law Enforcement Agents

After presenting at health facilities and receiving the care needed, survivors are referred to police stations to report the crime to allow police officers to investigate the crime. According to the study conducted by the National Crime Research Centre, one of the main reasons why survivors in Kenya do not report cases of sexual violence is due to ineffective response by the police.[74] This ranges from humiliation of survivors reporting cases, lack of privacy and confidentiality, attitude of the police, lack of follow up on cases and corruption.

To address these challenges, gender desks were established in local police stations. These desks were to be manned by officers trained on how to handle sexual violence cases and to protect the survivors from having to report their cases at the front desk where everyone can hear.[75] As it is currently, these gender desks are not available all over the country,

---

[72] *Ibid.*

[73] Nduku Kilonzo, *Post Rape Services in Kenya: A Situation Analysis*, (December 2003) 48 https://svri.org/sites/default/files/attachments/2016-07-18/postrapeserviceskenya_0.pdf.

[74] *Ibid.*

[75] Institute of Economic Affairs, 'Status of Gender Desks at Police Stations in Kenya,' *IEA Research Series*, (September 2009), https://www.ieakenya.or.ke/publications/research-papers/status-of-gender-desks-at-police-stations-in-kenya.

and where they exist, they are rarely manned by trained officers.[76] In fact, in some instances, they have been found to be manned by men making it difficult for women, who make up the majority of survivors, to report their cases.[77]

The attitude presented by police officers is another challenge. Their views on sex and sexual violence are informed by what I discussed earlier to be a highly patriarchal approach. These personal beliefs are unfortunately carried into the professional workspace. The impact of this is seen in the way they handle sexual violence and other forms of gender-based violence cases. Complaints have been recorded of police officers sending away victims to go and resolve cases with the perpetrator, especially where they are relatives.[78] Survivors have also complained about victim blaming from police officers stationed at gender desks who when recording cases have asked inappropriate questions such as 'What were you wearing?' or made comments such as 'You should not have been walking alone at night'.[79]

Police officers have also been reported to be ignorant of the law. This is seen in the way charges are recorded in charge sheets. For instance, some do not know the difference between rape, defilement and sexual assault. Such mistakes have serious impact on any victim's case. Another example is where police officers turn away victims who do not have any witnesses to support their allegations. They do not understand the role of the P3 and PRC forms which, when filled in properly, are sufficient evidence that sexual violence was committed. Many are also ignorant of the fact that PRC forms alone are sufficient to prosecute perpetrators of sexual violence.[80]

Lastly, there have been cases of police misconduct where police officers are engaged in corrupt behaviour such as taking bribes from perpetrators

---

[76] Albert Ndungu Wanjohi, *The Effectiveness of Police Gender Desks in Addressing Gender Based Violence: A Case of Nyandarua County -Kenya* (Masters thesis, Kenyatta University 2016): 30–58.

[77] *Ibid.*

[78] *Ibid*, 56.

[79] Cynthia Khamala Wangamati et al., 'Post Rape Care Services to Minors in Kenya: Are the Services Healing or Hurting Survivors,' 8 *International Journal of Women's Health* (2016): 249–259 https://www.ncbi.nlm.nih.gov/pmc/articles/PMC4938142/.

[80] National Police Service Standing Orders, National Police Service, http://www.nationalpolice.go.ke/downloads/category/5-acts.html.

or their families in order to drop cases, distort potentially incriminating evidence, frustrate the case by not showing up in court to give evidence or purposefully filing wrong charge sheets so that the case is thrown out of court. One such case is that of police officer George Otieno of Kinyach police station who was covering up for officer Elias Kinyua who allegedly defiled a minor.[81]

The challenges listed above contribute greatly to the failure of the police to investigate cases of sexual violence and prosecution by the courts. The lack of timely and thorough investigations means the system aids perpetrators in getting away with these crimes and confirms that studies such as the ones conducted by Ipsos and National Crime Research Centre are really a true reflection of the despair and lack of faith in Kenya's reporting and justice system.

5.2.3 Other Institutional Gaps

There are many instances in which survivors do not report cases for fear of reprisals. Furthermore, safety measures are not made available to survivors who need to be protected from their perpetrators. This poses challenges in instances where the perpetrators have been granted bail by the courts or are relatives of the complainant. There are very few state run shelters in the country and the few private ones are always full to capacity leaving victims with very few options.[82] The Witness Protection Agency is also greatly underfunded thus limiting the support the institution can offer Kenyans.[83] The study conducted by the Office of the High Commissioner for Human Rights (OHCHR), United Nations Women (UN Women) and Physicians for Human Rights (PHR) revealed that

[81] Boniface Mwangi @bonifacemwangi, *Poice Officer Elias Kinyua alias Kijana Mdogo Allegedly Defiled a Minor, a Class Seven Pupil. The Officer Commanding Kinyach Police Station George Otieno Is Said to be Covering Up*, June 20, 2020, https://twitter.com/bonifacemwangi/status/1274433430676221952.

[82] Edith Kimani, *Kenyan Safe Houses Overwhelmed During Coronavirus Pandemic*, DW News, July, 17, 2020, https://www.dw.com/en/kenyan-safe-houses-overwhelmed-during-coronavirus-pandemic/av-54223703.

[83] The Platform, *Legal Tenets and Structural Confines of Witness protection in the Kenyan Judicial System*, https://www.theplatform.co.ke/legal-tenets-and-structural-confines-of-witness-protection-in-the-kenyan-judicial-system/.

nine out of the 44 police officers interviewed in the course of the study did not know about the Witness Protection Agency and the protective measures it offers to witnesses.[84]

6 Towards an Effective Reporting System for Victims of Sexual Violence in Kenya

Firstly, young boys and girls need to be educated on gender equality. It is important that this education begins in the early stages of their lives before they develop false gender norms and negative attitudes. A study which was conducted in Nairobi in 2015 as a gender-based violence prevention programme found that boys who participated in the 'Your Moment of Truth' programme developed positive attitudes towards women amounting to non-tolerance of gender-based violence.[85]

Secondly, there is a need for awareness raising campaigns targeting all the different stakeholders in the community on human rights and sexual violence as a rights violation. Through this campaign comprehensive information can be shared on the various types of sexual violence, what to do when one is a victim including evidence collection and reporting, and what support measures exist for survivors. The Human Immunodeficiency Virus/Acquired Immunodeficiency Syndrome (HIV/AIDS) awareness raising campaign in the 90's is an example of a successful campaign which educated Kenyans on the disease. The campaign which had a long-term strategy focused on disseminating as much information on the disease to prevent rates of infection and better management of positive cases.[86]

Thirdly, to promote reporting of sexual violence cases, the current institutions should go through a reform process to:

---

[84] OHCHR, UN Women and PHR, *Breaking Cycles of Violence: Gaps in Prevention of and Response to Electoral Related Sexual Violence* (2019): 10–15.

[85] Jennifer Keller et al., 'A 6-Week School Curriculum Improves Boys' Attitudes and Behaviours Related to Gender-Based Violence in Kenya,' 4 *Journal of Interpersonal Violence* (2015):32, https://doi-org.uplib.idm.oclc.org/10.1177/0886260515586367.

[86] Avert, *HIV and AIDS in Kenya*, https://www.avert.org/professionals/hiv-around-world/sub-saharan-africa/kenya.

a) Integrate legal, medical and psycho-social support services into a one stop shop to avoid the current complicated reporting procedures; this will encourage reporting of cases because it will reduce the number of times survivors have to share their ordeal with service providers.
b) Conduct an open, public and transparent police audit to weed out those who lack ethics and integrity;
c) Ensure only police officers with knowledge and capacity to handle sexual violence cases are assigned to gender desks;
d) Undertake disciplinary measures for police officers found guilty of frustrating investigations of sexual violence cases or engaging in any forms of corruption;
e) Strengthen capacity of police officers for proper documentation of cases and effective investigation of the same;
f) Establish safe houses that offer protection to survivors/witnesses who are at risk.

Fourth, the government needs to operationalise and implement the Multi-Sectoral Standard Operating Procedures on Prevention and Response to Sexual Violence (SoPs).

7 Conclusion

This chapter sought to discuss reporting as an important component of access to justice for survivors of sexual violence. This has been done by discussing literature on reporting of sexual violence globally and in Kenya, the normative framework and state obligations in prevention, protection, investigation and prosecution of sexual violence as well as the responsibility to provide reparations for harm suffered. The chapter further analysed the status of reporting of sexual violence cases in Kenya and the context within which reporting or lack of it occurs by looking at the societal and institutional challenges. The chapter finds that while reporting rates of sexual violence cases are generally low globally, those in Kenya can greatly be improved if efforts are put towards education and awareness creation on sexual violence, its causes and the impact on survivors and society at large. This knowledge will address the incidences of victim blaming and shaming faced by survivors which, if reduced, will encourage even more survivors to report their cases and pursue justice. The chapter also finds that survivor's needs must always be at the centre of any response mechanisms if they are to be embraced by survivors. Therefore, proposals such as establishing one stop centres which take into consideration the physical and mental torture of having to narrate one's violation are likely to contribute to an increase in reporting. Lastly, the chapter finds that well-trained and committed law enforcement agents and health workers greatly influence the number of survivors who report cases as they are the first point of interaction with survivors. It is therefore imperative that those who are employed in these two institutions understand the important role they play in justice delivery.

Finally, it is important to note that in order to eradicate sexual violence in any society, states must be willing to fulfil their obligations to adopt measures that effectively protect citizens from such violations. This protection cannot be achieved if perpetrators are not held accountable for their actions. Furthermore, where accountability processes are not timely, effective and accessible to all, this responsibility is not met. This chapter has mainly focused on one component of this—the reporting process and its challenges. It is, however, important to acknowledge that to effect change, reforms must be implemented across board. A system that is supportive of survivors is one which instils measures to prevent violence and offers comprehensive support to those who suffer violations. This includes medical care, psychosocial support, legal support and reparations for harm suffered.

References

Action Aid, *A Theory of Change for Tackling Violence Against Women and Girls* (2012) https://www.actionaid.org.uk/sites/default/files/doc_lib/theory_of_change_on_vawg.pdf, July 14, 2020.

African Charter on Human and Peoples' Rights ('Banjul Charter'), June 27, 1981, CAB/LEG/67/3 rev. 5, 21 I.L.M. 58 (1982), https://au.int/sites/def

ault/files/treaties/36390-treaty-0011_-_african_charter_on_human_and_peoples_rights_e.pdf, June 18, 2020.

African Union, Protocol to the African Charter on Human and People's Rights on the Rights of Women in Africa (2003), https://au.int/sites/default/files/treaties/37077-treaty-0027__protocol_to_the_african_charter_on_human_and_peoples_rights_on_the_rights_of_women_in_africa_e.pdf

Avert, *HIV and AIDS in Kenya*, https://www.avert.org/professionals/hiv-around-world/sub-saharan-africa/kenya

BBC News, *Kenya University's Rape Memo Sparks Anger*, April 26, 2020, https://www.bbc.com/news/world-africa-51644876, July 14, 2020.

Boniface Mwangi @bonifacemwangi, *Poice Officer Elias Kinyua alias Kijana Mdogo Allegedly Defiled a Minor, a Class Seven Pupil. The Officer Commanding Kinyach Police Station George Otieno is Said to be Covering Up*, https://twitter.com/bonifacemwangi/status/1274433430676221952, July 14, 2020.

Bruce Baker, 'Justice for Survivors of Sexual Violence in Kitgum, Uganda,' 29 *Journal of Contemporary African Studies* (2011): 245–262.

Corman, Crystal, 'Violence against Women and Girls in Kenya: Roles of Religion and Response of Faith Actors,' *Policy Brief Berkley Centre for Religion Peace and World Affairs* (2016): 1–3, https://s3.amazonaws.com/berkley-

Gatuguta Anne, Merrill Katherine G, Colombini Manuela, Soremekun Seyi, Seeley1 Janet, Mwanzo Isaac and Karen Devries, 'Missed Treatment Opportunities and Barriers to Comprehensive Treatment for Sexual Violence Survivors in Kenya: A Mixed Methods Study,' 18 *BMC Public Health* (2018): 769, https://bmcpublichealth.biomedcentral.com/track/pdf/https://doi.org/10.1186/s12889-018-5681-5, July 14, 2020.

General Recommendation No. 28 on the Core Obligations of State Parties under Art 2 of CEDAW, December 16, 2010, CEDAW/C/GC/28 https://undocs.org/en/CEDAW/C/GC/28

Guidelines on Combating Sexual Violence and its Consequences in Africa (Niamey Guidelines), https://www.achpr.org/public/Document/file/English/achpr_eng_guidelines_on_combating_sexual_violence_and_its_consequences.pdf, June 18, 2020.

Institute Of Economic Affairs, *Status of Gender Desks at Police Stations in Kenya*, IEA Research Series (September 2009), https://www.ieakenya.or.ke/publications/research-papers/status-of-gender-desks-at-police-stations-in-kenya, July 14, 2020.

International Commission of Jurists, *Women's Access to Justice for Gender Based Violence: A Practitioner's Guide* (2016).

Julie Freccero, Lauren Harris, Melissa Carnay and Cole Taylor. *'Responding to Sexual Violence: Community Approaches' Sexual Violence & Accountability Project* (Working Paper Series). Human Rights Centre, University of California Berkeley (2011).

Keller Jennifer, Benjamin O. Mboya, Jake Sinclair, Oscar W. Githua, Munyae Mulinge, Lou Bergholz, Lee Paiva, Neville H. Golden and Cynthia Kapphahn, 'A 6-Week School Curriculum Improves Boys' Attitudes and Behaviours Related to Gender-Based Violence in Kenya,' 4 *Journal of Interpersonal Violence* (2015): 32, https://doi-org.uplib.idm.oclc.org/https://doi.org/10.1177/0886260515586367.

Kenya National Bureau of Statistics, Ministry of Health/Kenya, National AIDS Control Council/Kenya, Kenya Medical Research Institute and National Council for Population and Development/Kenya, *Kenya Demographic and Health Survey* (2014) http://dhsprogram.com/pubs/pdf/FR308/FR308.pdf, July 14, 2020.

Kenya Police Service, *P3 Form*, http://www.kenyapolice.go.ke/downloads/category/4-police-forms.html, July 14, 2020.

Kimani Edith, *Kenyan Safe Houses Overwhelmed During Coronavirus Pandemic,* DW News, July 17, 2020, https://www.dw.com/en/kenyan-safe-houses-overwhelmed-during-coronavirus-pandemic/av-54223703, July 17, 2020.

Kimuyu, Hillary, *Author flees Kenya After Court Rules Her in Smitta's Sexual Assault Case,* Nairobi News, August 30, 2019, https://nairobinews.nation.co.ke/life/author-flees-kenya-after-court-rules-against-her-in-smittas-sexual-assault-case, July 14, 2020.

Kramarae C, 'The Condition of Patriarchy' in C Kramarae & D Spender (eds) *The Knowledge Explosion: Generation of Feminist Scholarship Edited by* (1992).

Legal Notice 133 of 2012 SOA (Medical Treatment Regulations), https://www.law.berkeley.edu/wp-content/uploads/2015/10/Kenya_National-Health-Sector-SOPs-on-Mgmt-of-SV-in-Kenya_2014.pdf, July 14, 2020.

Lerner, G, *The Creation of Patriarchy* (1986).

Lori L. Heise, 'Violence Against Women: An Integrated Ecological Framework,' 3 *Violence Against Women* (1998): 262–290.

Ministry of Health, *Multi-Sectoral Standard Operating Procedures on Prevention and Response to Sexual Violence* (2013), https://www.law.berkeley.edu/wp-content/uploads/2015/10/Kenya_National-Health-Sector-SOPs-on-Mgmt-of-SV-in-Kenya_2014.pdf, July 14, 2020.

Ministry of Public Health and Sanitation & Ministry of Medical Services 2nd Edition, *National Guidelines on the Management of Sexual Violence in*

Kenya (2009), http://www.endvawnow.org/uploads/browser/files/national_guidelines.pdf, June 18, 2020

National Crime Research Centre, *Gender Based Violence in Kenya* (2014), http://crimeresearch.go.ke/wp-content/uploads/2018/02/wwwroot_publications_Gender-Based-Violence-in-Kenya.pdf, July 14, 2020.

National Police Service, *National Police Service Standing Orders*, http://www.nationalpolice.go.ke/downloads/category/5-acts.html, July 14, 2020.

Nduku Kilonzo, Njoki Ndung'u, Nerida Nthamburi, Caroline Ajema, Miriam Taegtmeyer, Sally Theobald and Rachel Tolhurst, 'Sexual Violence Legislation in Sub-Saharan Africa: The Need for Strengthened Medico-Legal Linkages,' 17 *Reproductive Health Matters* (2009): 10–19.

OHCHR, UN Women and PHR, *Breaking Cycles of Violence: Gaps in Prevention of and Response to Electoral Related Sexual Violence* (2019): 10–15, https://www.ohchr.org/Documents/Countries/KE/OHCHRPHRUNWOMENKenyaGapAnalysisDec20191.pdf, July 14, 2020.

Okoronkwo Stella, *Facts about Sex for Youth* (2005).

Oneya Faith, *No Matter How Famous One is, Rape is Inexcusable*, Daily Nation, August, 2019, https://www.nation.co.ke/kenya/blogs-opinion/opinion/no-matter-how-famous-one-is-rape-is-inexcusable-195456, July 14, 2020.

Rajab Ramadhan, *Kenyans Don't Report Crime, Says Survey*, The Star, September 4, 2015, https://www.the-star.co.ke/news/2015-09-04-kenyans-dont-report-crime-says-survey/, July 14, 2020.

Rono II @ronoAlphas, *There Is Nowhere a Single Sided Story Can Be Shoved Down Anyone's Throat. Accuse and Prove. No Need to Look for Sympathy Online. False Allegations Are as Risky as the Accusation Itself*, June 16, 2020, https://twitter.com/RonoAlphas/status/1272837221373095938, July 14, 2020.

Scheaffor Okore @scheafferoo, *4 Thousand Girls in Machakos County Have Been Raped and Ended Up Pregnant in the Past 4 Months, Meaning One Thousand Girls Were Raped in a Span of 30 Days but Somehow in this Tragedy Parents Are Being Blamed Instead of the Actual Rapists! Do Leaders Understand Rape Culture?* June 17, 2020, https://twitter.com/scheafferoo/status/1273198822735446021, July 14, 2020.

Smythe Dee, *Rape Unresolved: Policing Sexual Offences in South Africa* (2015).

The Conversation, Gender Based Violence in Kenya: Why Attitudes Towards Sexual Violence in Kenya Need a Major Refresh, July 22, 2018, https://theconversation.com/why-attitudes-towards-sexual-violence-in-kenya-need-a-major-refresh-100033, July 14, 2020.

The Platform, *Legal Tenets and Structural Confines of Witness protection in the Kenyan Judicial System*, https://www.theplatform.co.ke/legal-tenets-and-structural-confines-of-witness-protection-in-the-kenyan-judicial-system/, July 14, 2020.

UN General Assembly, *Convention Against Torture and Other Cruel, Inhuman or Degrading Treatment or Punishment*, December 10, 1984, United Nations, Treaty Series, https://www.ohchr.org/en/professionalinterest/pages/cat.aspx, June 18, 2020.

UN General Assembly, *Convention on the Elimination of All Forms of Discrimination Against Women*, December 18, 1979, United Nations, Treaty Series, https://www.un.org/womenwatch/daw/cedaw/text/econvention.htm, June 18, 2020.

UN General Assembly, *Convention on the Rights of the Child*, November 20, 1989, United Nations, Treaty Series, https://www.ohchr.org/Documents/ProfessionalInterest/crc.pdf, June 18, 2020.

Ureport, *Fear Strikes Nairobi CBD After Video of Woman Being Raped by Street Boy Surfaces Online,* Standard Media, April 26, 2018, https://www.standardmedia.co.ke/ureport/story/2001278270/fear-strikes-nairobi-cbd-after-video-of-woman-being-raped-by-street-boy-surfaces-online, July 14, 2020.

Wangamati Cynthia Khamala, Sundby Johanne and Ruth Jane Prince, 'Communities' Perceptions of Factors Contributing to Child Sexual Abuse Vulnerability in Kenya: A Qualitative Study,' 20 *Culture, Health and Sexuality* (2018): 1394–1408, https://www.tandfonline.com/doi/abs/https://doi.org/10.1080/13691058.2018.1438666, July 14, 2020.

Wangamati Cynthia Khamala, Thorsen Viva Combs, Gele Abdi Ali and Johanne Sundby, 'Post Rape Care Services to Minors in Kenya: Are the Services Healing or Hurting Survivors,' 8 *International Journal of Women's Health* (2016): 249–259.

Wanjohi Albert Ndungu, *The Effectiveness of Police Gender Desks in Addressing Gender Based Violence: A Case of Nyandarua County-Kenya* (Masters thesis, Kenyatta University 2016).

Warega Nelly, *Sexual Violence in Kenya: Understanding the Legal and Socio-Cultural Contexts* (Masters thesis, University of Pretoria 2018).

Yakin Erturk, *Integration of the Human Rights of Women and the Gender Perspective: Violence Against Women,* U.N. Doc. E/CN.4/2006/61, https://www.refworld.org/pdfid/45377afb0.pdf, October 4, 2020.

Part III

Limitations of Criminal Justice Responses to Violence Against Women

7

Sex Trafficking as a Form of Gender-Based Violence Against Women: Lessons from South Africa and Uganda

Annette Lansink and Zahara Nampewo

1 Introduction

Trafficking in women is a complex crime and societal phenomenon that continues unabated in Africa and globally. It is also a form of gender-based violence against women (GBV).[1] Among others, the Beijing Declaration and Platform for Action, General Recommendation No 38 (2020) of the Committee on the Elimination of Discrimination

[1] United Nations Beijing Declaration and Platform for Action, *Fourth World Conference on Women* (1995), https://www.un.org/en/development/desa/population/migration/generalassembly/docs/globalcompact/A_CONF.177_20.pdf. The elimination of trafficking and assistance to victims of violence due to prostitution and trafficking is one of the three Strategic Objectives in the Beijing Declaration and Platform of Action. See also Jennifer Sorensen, Sara Piazzano, Olga DiPretoro and Carolyn O'Donnell, *Addressing Inter-Linkages Between Gender-Based Violence and Trafficking in Persons to Prevent Reinforcement of Inequalities* (2012), https://www.winrock.org/wp-content/uploads/2016/03/Addressing-inter-linkages.pdf.

A. Lansink (✉)
School of Law, University of Venda, Thohoyandou, South Africa
e-mail: Annette.lansink@univen.ac.za

E. C. Lubaale and A. Budoo-Scholtz (eds.), *Violence Against Women and Criminal Justice in Africa: Volume I*, Sustainable Development Goals Series,
https://doi.org/10.1007/978-3-030-75949-0_7

against Women (CEDAW) and some regional treaties have identified trafficking in women as a form of violence against women (VAW).[2] The complexity of trafficking in women for purposes of sexual exploitation calls for multidisciplinary and multisectoral responses that require the involvement of specialist law enforcement agencies, social services and preventive and educational strategies. This chapter focuses on the criminal justice responses to combating trafficking in women as a form of violence against women in two countries in Africa—South Africa and Uganda. It identifies shortcomings and draws upon the experiences of these two countries to make recommendations.

Since the adoption of the Protocol to Prevent, Suppress and Punish Trafficking in Persons, Especially Women and Children, supplementing the United Nations Convention against Transnational Organised Crime (Palermo Protocol), and the subsequent ratification of the treaties by almost all States,[3] considerable legal strides have been made to address this crime. The Palermo Protocol forms the basis of legislation in many states in Africa and beyond. It defines trafficking in persons as:

> the recruitment, transportation, transfer, harbouring or receipt of persons, by means of the threat or use of force or other forms of coercion, of abduction, of fraud, or deception, of the abuse of power or of a position of vulnerability or of the giving or receiving of payments or benefits to achieve the consent of a person having control over another person, for the purposes of exploitation. Exploitation shall include, at a minimum, the exploitation of the prostitution of other or other forms of sexual

---

Z. Nampewo
School of Law, Makerere University, Kampala, Uganda
e-mail: zahara.nampewo@mak.ac.ug

[2] Committee on the Elimination of Discrimination against Women General Recommendation No. 38 (2020) on Trafficking in women and girls in the context of global migration. CEDAW/C/GC/38, 6 November 2020. Article 2(b) of the Inter-American Convention on Violence against Women.

[3] Protocol to Prevent, Suppress and Punish Trafficking in Persons, Especially Women and Children, supplementing the United Nations Convention against Transnational Organised Crime, 2000, adopted by resolution A/RES/55/25 on 15 November 2000 in Palermo, Italy and entered into force on 25 December 2003. As of 28 June 2020, there are 177 States Parties to the Trafficking Protocol and 190 States Parties to the Convention. See UN Treaty collection at www.

exploitation, forced labour or services, slavery or practices similar to slavery, servitude of the removal of organs.[4]

Unlike earlier treaties, the Palermo Protocol is a comprehensive treaty that requires the criminalisation of all forms of trafficking such as trafficking for purposes of forced labour, exploitative labour in factories, domestic work under slavery-like conditions or forced marriage. However, the emphasis of this chapter is on sex trafficking of women for its manifest gender dimensions as a form of violence against women. The Protocol to the African Charter on Human and Peoples' Rights on the Rights of Women (Maputo Protocol) imposes an obligation on State parties to take appropriate and effective measures to prevent and condemn trafficking in women, prosecute the perpetrators of such trafficking and protect women most at risk.[5] At the African level, the Ougadougou Action Plan to Combat Trafficking in Human Beings, especially Women and Children, was adopted in 2006, and is purposed to scale up efforts in the fight against human trafficking.[6]

In 2009, the Africa Union (AU) Commission adopted an anti-trafficking initiative aimed at 'galvanising activities' towards coordinated action to combat trafficking in persons in Africa and implementation

treaties.un.org. The other Protocols supplementing the United Nations Convention against Transnational Organised Crime are the Protocol against Smuggling of Migrants by Land, Sea and Air and, the Protocol against the Illicit Manufacturing and Trafficking of Firearms, their Parts and Components and Ammunition of 31 May 2001.

[4] Article 5 of the UN Trafficking Protocol (henceforth Palermo Protocol) requires States to criminalise trafficking, attempting to commit trafficking, participating as an accomplice, and organising or directing other persons to commit the criminal offence.

[5] Protocol to the African Charter on Human and Peoples' Rights on the Rights of Women (2003) Article 4(2)(g), https://au.int/en/treaties/protocol-african-charter-human-and-peoples-rights-rights-women-africa. See also Convention on Elimination of all forms of Discrimination Against Women (1979) and General Recommendation No 35 (2017) updating General Recommendation No 19 (1992) on Violence against Women.

[6] The Action Plan has been adopted by the Ministerial Conference on Migration and Development, Tripoli, in 2006 and is a joint international Framework for Action between the African

of the Ougadougou Action Plan.[7] In the Southern African context, the SADC Protocol on Gender and Development aims to eliminate gender-based violence, which includes targets to combat trafficking in persons.[8] In the East African region, the Protocol on the Prevention and Suppression of Sexual Violence against Women and Children of the International Conference in the Great Lakes Region (ICGLR)[9] and the

---

Union and the Europe Union for the prevention, suppression and punishment of trafficking in persons, in particular women and children, https://africa-eu-partnership.org/sites/default/files/documents/doc_au_commit_ouagadougou_ap_en_0.pdf.

[7] African Union Commission, *AU.COMMIT Campaign: When the Fight Against Trafficking Becomes a Priority for Africa*, https://au.int/en/newsevents/28064/au-commission-initiative-against-trafficking-aucommit-campaign; https://africa-eu-partnership.org/en/success-stories/aucommit-campaign-when-fight-against-trafficking-becomes-priority-africa.

[8] The Southern African Development Community (SADC), *Protocol on Gender and Development* (2008) as amended in 2016 to align it with the SDGs, Beijing + 20 and the goals of the African Union 2063 Agenda, https://www.sadc.int/issues/gender/gender-based-violence.

[9] International Conference on the Great Lakes Region, Protocol on the Prevention and Suppression of Sexual Violence against Women and Children (2006).

Goma Declaration on Eradicating Sexual Violence and Ending Impunity in the Great Lakes Region[10] provide similar guidance.

Many African States adopted legislative and other measures to combat human trafficking.[11] There are successes in terms of increased awareness and the adoption of legal and policy frameworks, but many challenges remain. Most African countries are not doing well in terms of complying with the minimum standards to combat trafficking in persons.[12] For instance, out of 34 countries globally listed on Tier 1 only one African country, Namibia, is represented.[13] The rest are all on Tier 2 and 3. Both Uganda and South Africa appear on Tier 2 although Uganda fares worse as it appears on the Tier 2 Watch List. On the legislative front, it should be noted that state practice varies in this regard in Africa. Human trafficking attracts between five to ten years' imprisonment in

The Protocol is aimed at establishing a legal framework for the prosecution and punishment of crimes of sexual violence in relation to trafficking, genocide, crimes against humanity and war crimes. https://www.peaceau.org/uploads/final-protocol.sexual-violence-rev-en-2.pdf.

[10] International Conference on the Great Lakes Region, Improving Access to Justice and Ending Impunity for SGBV in the ICGLR Member States, https://www.icglr-rtf.org/publication/view/improving-access-to-justice- and-ending-impunity-for-sgbv-in-the-icglr-member-states-rtf-sgbv-study/.

[11] See the United States Department of State, Trafficking in Persons (TIP) Report, June 2020 generally and specifically Tom Obokata, 'Human Trafficking in Africa Opportunities and Challenges for the African Court of Justice and Human Rights' in Charles C Jalloh (ed) *The African Court of Justice and Human and Peoples' Rights in Context Development and Challenges* (2019): 529–552, https://doi.org/10.1017/9781108525343.020.

[12] Minimum standards as determined by the United States Department of State (2020), https://www.state.gov/wp-content/uploads/2020/06/2020-TIP-Report-Complete-062420-FINAL.pdf.

[13] Namibia was upgraded to a Tier 1 country by the US State Department in its 2020 TIP Report, June 2020. https://na.usembassy.gov/tag/trafficking-in-persons-tip-report.

Burkina Faso,[14] the Central African Republic,[15] Equatorial Guinea,[16] whereas the punishment is much higher in Gabon,[17] Kenya[18] and South Africa.[19] Although these variations are understandable, a major problem from the point of view of law enforcement is that these discrepancies can lead to concentration of human trafficking in states where punishment is weak. It is for this reason that identification of the shortcomings in the implementation process of the legal frameworks, ranging from prevention, prosecution, protection and partnership strategies to increased accountability within criminal justice systems, is pivotal.

This chapter analyses the measures implemented by South Africa and Uganda to combat the scourge of trafficking in women and girls as a form of gender-based violence. Since trafficking is a multifaceted phenomenon, multiple interventions are necessary to improve the criminal justice responses to this crime, the protection of victims and address the root causes of trafficking and violence against women. The chapter argues that a multidisciplinary, multisectoral and gender sensitive approach with high-level accountability and monitoring is required to address the shortcomings in the criminal justice systems. Beyond the criminal justice system, government institutions and civil society, through raising awareness and education, must address violence against women and the demand side for sexual services and exploitative labour to prevent trafficking in women.

The United Nations envisages a world free of violence and fear which is reflected in its efforts to combat transnational organised crime and many of its human rights treaties, declarations and Sustainable Development Goals (SDGs). Its vision to end violence, poverty, discrimination and promote human rights, gender equality, the rule of law and justice

---

[14] Law No. 029–2008/AN on the Fight against Trafficking in Persons and Similar Practices of Burkina Faso.

[15] Penal Code of the Central African Republic, art. 151.

[16] Law No. 1/2004 on the Smuggling of Migrants and Trafficking in Persons of Equatorial Guinea.

[17] Law 09/04 Concerning the Prevention and the Fight Against the Trafficking of Children in the Gabonese Republic.

[18] Counter-Trafficking in Persons Act 2010 of Kenya.

[19] Section 13 of the Prevention and Combating of Trafficking in Human Beings Act 7 of 2013 of South Africa makes provision for the imposition of life sentences.

underpins the SDGs.[20] Similarly, human trafficking is part of the 2030 Agenda. Trafficking in women broadly falls within SDGs 5, 8 and 16 gender on equality, decent work and economic growth, and the need for strong institutions, all of which need to operate together to adequately respond to this heinous crime.[21] As a result of the obligations of reporting under human rights treaties and the SDGs, an increasing number of countries are reporting exact numbers of identified trafficking victims which leads to a better understanding of the volume and types of trafficking although the full scale of the clandestine operations remains hidden from sight.

The examination of the various responses throws light on the effectiveness or deficiencies in the criminal justice responses to trafficking in women in South Africa and Uganda with a view to making recommendations for strengthening not only the in-country systems but the existing regional mechanisms as well. Uganda and South Africa are selected for the study for several reasons, one being that both countries are source, transit and destination countries for men, women, and children subjected to sex trafficking. Ugandan victims have been identified in neighbouring countries, including Kenya, South Sudan and the DRC. Young women remain the most vulnerable to transnational trafficking,

---

[20] The United Nations, Sustainable Development Goals set in 2015 by the United Nations General Assembly and intended to be achieved by the year 2030, https://sustainabledevelopment.un.org/post2015/transformingourworld.

Goal 1 aims at ending poverty in all its forms everywhere. Poverty is a clear factor exacerbating the vulnerability of women and girls.

[21] Under Goal 8 of the Sustainable Development Goals, target 8.7 urges states to take immediate efforts against forced labour, modern slavery and human trafficking while Goal 5 aims at achieving gender equality and ending all forms of discrimination against all women and girls everywhere and eliminating 'all forms of violence against all women and girls in the public and private spheres, including trafficking and sexual and other types of exploitation'. Goal 16 includes access to justice and target 16.2 specifically aims 'to end abuse, exploitation, trafficking and all forms of violence and torture against children'. The United Nations Office on Drugs and Crime (UNODC) has been tasked to monitor the implementation of Goal 16.2

mostly attributed to the high levels of school drop-out rate for females.[22] For a while now, the media in Uganda has been dominated by testimonies of both the returnee girls and some who were still held captive. They decried not only the deplorable conditions of work in host countries in the Middle East but also reported of sexual abuse. For example, in November 2014, two undercover journalists revealed that 'for years, Ugandan girls have been trafficked to different countries under the guise of finding them employment but they end up in sex slavery, some are tortured while others end up in prison'.[23] In fact, the matter of sexual exploitation of Ugandan female workers in the Middle East became so intense that it attracted a parliamentary plenary session at which one of the legislators while describing what he saw in Saudi Arabia during a visit there stated 'what we are actually calling 'domestic workers' are 'sex slaves' that side'.[24]

South Africa provides a slightly different picture. The country serves as a destination, source and transit country.[25] Because of its large economy, it is a magnet that attracts migration flows from other African countries. Victims have been trafficked to South Africa intra-regionally and

as the global reporting agency on the 'number of victims of human trafficking per 100,000 population, by sex, age and form of exploitation'.

[22] Samuel Kamugisha, *Over 5 Million Pupils Drop out of Primary School*, The Observer Newspaper, February 27, 2017, https://observer.ug/education/51488-over-5-million-pupils-drop-out-of-primary-school.html. According to Samuel Kamugisha who undertook an analysis of figures from the Uganda National Examinations Board and Education and Sports Sector Annual Performance Reports (ESSAPRs), there are more girls than boys who drop out of school annually.

[23] Joyce Namutebi and Moses Walubiri, *Uganda Told to Ban Export of Domestic Workers, The New Vision,* November 27, 2014, http://www.newvision.co.ug/new_vision/news/1316069/uganda-told-ban-export-domestic-workers.

[24] Bernard Atiku, *Export of Domestic Workers Is Slavery Dressed Up as Greener Pastures*, Daily Monitor April 10, 2017.

[25] United Nations Office on Drugs and Crime, *Trafficking in Person in the SADC Region: A Statistical Report*, (2014–2016) 57. https://www.unodc.org/documents/southernafrica/Stories//EN_-_TIP_Statistical_Report.pdf.

from as far afield as Asia and Eastern Europe.[26] Within South Africa, women and children are recruited and transported from rural areas to cities for exploitation.[27] Although there has been increasing awareness of human trafficking in South Africa during the last twenty years,[28] the lack of exact data contributes to contestations around the phenomenon and denialism.[29] However, as pointed out by Kruger and van der Watt, trafficking is a reality, the reported cases and jurisprudence tell a different

[26] *Ibid*.

[27] Thozama Mandisa Lutya, *Human Trafficking of Young Women and Girls for Sexual Exploitation in South Africa* (2012), http://dx.doi.org/10.5772/39202.

[28] The Cape Town based non-governmental organisation Molo Songolo released a report on trafficking in women in 2000. The International Organisation for Migration (IOM) in Pretoria, *Seduction, Sale and Slavery: Trafficking in Women and Children for Sexual Exploitation in Southern Africa* (2003), https://www.unhcr.org/4d523c689.pdf; The South African Law Reform Commission Report on Trafficking in Person (2008), https://www.justice.gov.za/Salrc/reports/r_pr131_trafficking_2008.pdf.

[29] Naledi Mashishi, Lerato Kganyago's Claims About Child Trafficking in South Africa, Eyewitness News, September 23, 2020, https://ewn.co.za/2020/09/23/fact-check-lerato-kganyago-s-claims-about-child-trafficking-in-south-africa.

story.[30] Given the hidden nature of the crime, there is likely more underreporting than overreporting of trafficking.

This chapter contributes to the discourse by linking trafficking in women for purposes of sexual exploitation and GBV to the criminal justice responses in the two African countries, and by its comprehensive list of recommendations. These recommendations include advocacy of an African Convention on GBV, strengthening monitoring, and an emphasis on international accountability of States, which is increasingly being recognised, as a consequence of the positive obligations on States to investigate, prosecute and punish trafficking. Thus, States are liable in terms of international human rights obligations for failure to effectively combat trafficking in women.

The chapter is divided into five sections, starting with an introduction and then outlining how trafficking in women manifests as violence against women. The third and fourth section discuss the various response mechanisms in both Uganda and South Africa. The chapter concludes by recommending that African states adopt a victim-centred approach that integrates human rights and a gender perspective into the criminal justice response to trafficking in women as a form of gender-based violence, and further complement this through strengthening law enforcement and other multidisciplinary and multisectoral approaches. It also emphasises the need for intra-African cooperation to share best practices in order to ensure effective prosecution of the perpetrators and the right of access to justice for trafficked victims.

Centre for Child Law, Child Trafficking: Exploring the Myths and Realities (2020), http://centreforchildlaw.co.za/wp-content/uploads/2020/08/WEB-CFCL-Child_Trafficking-Report.pdf; Marcel van der Watt, 'Response to the Centre for Child Law Trafficking (in South Africa): Report Presentation, August 2020. https://doi.org/10.13140/RG.2.2.21790.15687; Beatri Kruger and Marcel van der Watt 'What Do We Know About Child Trafficking Prevalence in South Africa', Presentation September 2020. https://doi.org/10.13140/RG.2.2.24306.73920.

[30] van der Watt and Kruger *supra* note 29.

2 Trafficking as a Form of Violence Against Women

Believed to be a very lucrative criminal activity, trafficking in persons is a serious crime and a grave violation of human rights. In 2019, 42,517 victims of trafficking were identified in sub-Saharan Africa.[31] Victims are often duped with promises of a better life in the city or another country and coerced into forced labour, domestic servitude or sexual slavery. There are both push and pull factors that contribute to the existence of human trafficking. The lack of employment opportunities, poverty, gender and ethnic discrimination, political instability, armed conflict and economic imbalances among regions of the world contribute to the push factors. In contrast, the pull factors include demand for workers and possibilities of higher standards of living in cities or outside Africa.[32] Trafficking has gender connotations not only because a disproportionate number of women are being trafficked, but also because of the exploitation of the vulnerability of women and girls, feminised poverty and pervasive discrimination in society.

Trafficking in women is a form of violence against women. Article 6 of the Convention on the Elimination of all Forms of Discrimination against Women (CEDAW) compels States to take 'all appropriate measures, including legislation, to suppress all forms of trafficking in women and the exploitation of prostitution of women'. Moreover, already in 1992, the Committee on the Elimination of Discrimination against Women (CEDAW Committee), in general recommendation No 19, proclaimed that discrimination against women includes gender-based violence, which is a form of discrimination that seriously inhibits women's ability to enjoy rights and freedoms on a basis of equality with men.[33] In 1993, the Declaration on the Elimination of all Forms of

---

[31] United States Department of State, Trafficking in Persons (2020): 56, https://www.state.gov/wp-content/uploads/2020/06/2020-TIP-Report-Complete-062420-FINAL.pdf;

[32] Louise Shelley, *Human Trafficking: A Global Perspective* (2010): 37.

[33] CEDAW, Article 1 defines discrimination against women as 'any distinction, exclusion or restriction made on the basis of sex which has the effect or purpose of impairing or nullifying the recognition, enjoyment or exercise by women, irrespective of their marital status, on a basis of equality of men and women, of human rights and fundamental freedoms in the political,

Violence against Women affirmed violence against women as 'any act of gender-based violence that results in, or is likely to result in, physical, sexual or psychological harm or suffering to women, including threats of such acts, coercion or arbitrary deprivation of liberty, whether occurring in public or in private life'.[34] The Declaration recognises that violence against women is:

> a manifestation of historically unequal power relations between men and women, which have led to domination over and discrimination against women by men and to the prevention of the full advancement of women, and that violence against women is one of the crucial social mechanisms by which women are forced into a subordinate position compared with men.[35]

The Declaration identifies several forms of violence against women (VAW), including trafficking and forced prostitution.[36] CEDAW general recommendation No 35 of 2017, updating general recommendation No 19, uses the 'more precise term' of gender-based violence against women, which is violence 'directed against a woman because she is a woman or that affects women disproportionately'.[37] The term GBV against women makes explicit 'the gendered causes and impact of the violence' and includes 'acts or omissions intended or likely to cause or result in death or physical, sexual, psychological or economic harm or suffering to women, threats of such acts, harassment, coercion and arbitrary deprivation of liberty'.[38] Routinely, traffickers use not only one but many of the above

---

economic, social, cultural, civil or any other field.' CEDAW general recommendation No.19 paragraph 1 asserts GBV as a form of discrimination.

[34] Article 1 of the Declaration on the Elimination on all Forms of Violence against Women, UNGA A/RES/48/104 of December 20, 1993, https://www.refworld.org/docid/3b00f25d2c.html.

[35] *Ibid.* Preamble of the Declaration.

[36] *Ibid.* Article 6 of the Declaration.

[37] CEDAW General Recommendation No. 35 (2017) on gender-based violence against women, updating general recommendation No 19 (1992), CEDAW/C/GC/35, paragraph 19.

[38] *Ibid.* CEDAW No. 35 (2017), paragraph 9 and paragraph 14. Gender based violence may breach specific provisions of CEDAW, 'regardless of whether those provisions expressly mention violence'.

acts causing physical, sexual and psychological harm, using threats and coercion and by depriving victims of the freedom to move.

Sex trafficking is rooted in gender-related factors such as the 'ideology of men's entitlement and privilege over women, the need to assert male control or power, and enforces gender roles'.[39] Notably, the CEDAW Committee argues that, the prohibition of violence against women has become a rule of customary international law having met the requirements of *opinion iuris* and State practice.[40] This entails that the prohibition on violence against women is binding on all States even those which have not ratified relevant human rights treaties.

Significantly, in the case of the *Egyptian Initiative for Personal Rights v Egypt*, the African Commission, held that the female complainants had been subjected to gender-based violence as the sexual abuse was gender-specific and amounted to discrimination on the grounds of sex.[41] According to the Commission, the victims who were all women, were not protected by the State against the perpetrators and other unidentified actors, and the violations were perpetrated because the victims were women.[42] The African Commission held that the verbal attacks were gender-specific and aimed at degrading the complainants. Notably, the specific acts of touching the body, harassment and physical violence during the demonstrations were gender-specific, and the threats were gender-specific.[43] It was further decided that the acts of sexual molestation amounted to inhuman and degrading treatment and, as a result, Egypt was found to have violated, *inter alia*, Article 5 of the African Charter on Human and Peoples' Rights.[44] In this case, the African Commission confirmed that States have a duty to exercise 'due diligence to prevent, investigate and, in accordance with national legislation,

[39] CEDAW No 35, paragraph 19.

[40] CEDAW No. 35, paragraph 2.

[41] *Egyptian Initiative for Personal Rights v Egypt*, African Commission, Decision, Comm. No. 323/2006, ACmHPR, Dec. 2011, paragraphs 140–142.

[42] *Ibid*, paragraph137.

[43] *Ibid*, paragraph143–157.

[44] *Ibid*, paragraph 202. The African Commission decided that Egypt was in violation of Articles 1, 2, 3, 5, 9(2), 16(1), 18(3) and 26 of the African Charter. Paragraph 275.

punish acts of violence against women, whether those acts are perpetrated by the State or by private persons'.[45]

While the above case does not deal with trafficking in women, the reasoning and principles relied upon by the Commission regarding gender-based violence against women are consistent with those expressed in instruments such as CEDAW's general recommendations and the United Nations General Assembly (UNGA) Declaration on Violence against Women and therefore have a bearing on trafficking in women. The African Commission affirmed an important legal principle regarding the liability of States for failure to exercise due diligence in the protection of women against gender-based violence.

This can effortlessly be applied to trafficking. Thus, States will incur liability for failure to prevent, investigate, prosecute and punish perpetrators of gender-based violence within the context of trafficking against women. In other words, a State may be held accountable for violating the African Charter on Human and Peoples' Rights or the Maputo Protocol for failure to protect the human rights of the victim against acts committed by its own agents or by non-state actors. States parties to the Maputo Protocol, like State parties to CEDAW, are under a legal duty to take appropriate and effective measures to prevent and condemn trafficking in women, prosecute the perpetrators of such trafficking and protect women most at risk.[46]

Similarly, in *Rantsev v Cyprus and Russia,* the European Court of Human Rights (ECHR) found that trafficking itself falls within the scope of Article 4 of the European Convention on Human Rights and Fundamental Freedoms, without finding it necessary to identify whether trafficking was slavery or servitude *or* forced labour.

> trafficking in human beings, by its very nature and aim of exploitation, is based on the exercise of powers attaching to the right of ownership. It treats human beings as commodities to be bought and sold and put to

---

[45] Declaration on Violence Against Women, Article 4(c). Paragraphs 163 and 204 of the decision by the African Commission.

[46] Maputo Protocol, Article 4(2)(g) https://au.int/en/treaties/protocol-african-charter-human-and-peoples-rights-rights-women-africa. See also CEDAW and General Recommendation No 35 (2017) updating General Recommendation No 19 (1992) on Violence against Women.

> forced labour, often for little or no payment, usually in the sex industry but also elsewhere.... It implies close surveillance of the activities of victims, whose movements are often circumscribed. It involves the use of violence and threats against victims, who live and work under poor conditions...[47]

The Court held that Cyprus had failed to conduct a proper investigation and had failed to protect the deceased Russian national against trafficking and exploitation, whereas Russia was found liable by failing to investigate the alleged trafficking.[48] Article 5 of the African Charter contains a similar prohibition.

The Inter-American Court on Human Rights delivered its first judgement on slavery and human trafficking in the case of *Hacienda Brasil Verde Workers v. Brazil*.[49] The court distinguished between slavery, servitude, trafficking and forced labour and expanded on the due diligence duty to prevent these crimes. The Court held Brazil responsible for violations of the prohibition on slavery and trafficking.[50]

The gendered nature of trafficking is apparent in the numbers. Trafficking for forced commercial sexual exploitation affects women and girls disproportionately as the latest statistics from the United Nations Office on Drugs and Crime (UNODC) confirm that: among identified women

---

47 *Rantsev v Cyprus and Russia*, ECHR, paragraph 281, https://ec.europa.eu/anti-trafficking/sites/antitrafficking/files/rantsev_vs_russia_cyprus_en_4.pdf

48 *Rantsev v Cyprus and Russia*, ECHR, the court held that Cyprus was in violation of Articles 2 (procedural obligation), 4 and 5; it further held that Russia violated a positive procedural obligation to investigate trafficking in terms of Article 4.

49 *Hacienda Brasil Verde Workers v. Brazil* Inter-American Court of Human Rights, Case of the Preliminary Objections, Merits, Reparations and Costs. Judgment of October 20, 2016. Series C No. 318. https://www.corteidh.or.cr/cf/Jurisprudencia2/overview.cfm?doc=1728&lang=en.

50 *Ibid*.

victims, 83% have been trafficked for purposes of sexual exploitation,[51] and 72% of identified girl victims have been trafficked for this purpose.[52]

When all different forms of trafficking are considered, women and girls are still disproportionally affected as they together make up 72% of *all* identified trafficking victims globally.[53] There are, however, substantial regional differences. In sub-Saharan Africa, the majority of the identified trafficking victims are girls and boys in more or less equal numbers, whereas in Europe and the Americas, the majority of detected victims are women, including women from Africa who have been trafficked to other continents.[54]

Trafficking generally results in gross human rights violations and crimes such as forced labour, slavery, servitude and ill treatment. In the context of female victims, this often extends to sexual exploitation, forced marriage, forced prostitution and the exploitation of prostitution. Trafficking is a violation of the right to dignity, the right to freedom and security of the person, the right not to be subjected to slavery, servitude and forced labour. Trafficking restricts freedom of movement of women, the right to access health care services and in general the right to fair labour practices.

Trafficking not only results in human rights violations, but is also often a consequence of human rights violations. In patriarchal societies, the fault-lines of unequal power relations and sexism are deeply entrenched, depriving women of equal educational and employment opportunities.

---

51 United Nations Office on Drugs and Crime, *Global Report on Trafficking in Persons* (2018): 28, https://www.unodc.org/documents/data-and-analysis/glotip/2018/GLOTiP_2018_BOOK_web_small.pdf. The United Nations Office on Drugs and Crime uses the word 'detected' instead of identified. The opposite was found among men who are predominantly trafficked for purposes of forced labour whereas only 13% of women were trafficked for purposes of forced labour.

52 *Ibid.*, 25 and 28. Globally, 72% of detected girls were trafficked for purposes of sexual exploitation, 21% for forced labour whereas a quarter of detected boys were trafficked for sexual exploitation (which is considerably higher than the percentage of men). Fifty percent of boys were trafficked for purposes of forced labour and 23% for other forms of exploitation (begging, as child soldiers and forced criminal activities).

53 *Ibid.* The statistics are estimates based on information received from 110 countries. Adult men account for 21%, almost half of the total number of identified trafficking victims globally are adult women (49%), girls for 23% and boys for 7%.

54 *Ibid.*, 29 and 30. In 2016, in Southern Africa, East and West Africa, and the Middle East the number of detected victims trafficked for purposes of forced labour was higher than the

Violence against women, gender inequality and other human rights violations are among the causes of trafficking that render women without access to opportunities more vulnerable to exploitation and becoming victims of trafficking.

Notwithstanding, South Africa's progressive Constitution and the government's best intentions to address inequality and violence against women, the gap between constitutional aspirations and lived reality is wide. Violence against women in particular has become a 'pandemic' in South Africa.[55] This environment becomes a push factor and the increased vulnerability is conducive to deceiving women and girls with false promises of better social and economic opportunities.

Remarkably though, female offenders are also engaged in trafficking of girls and fellow women,[56] it is documented that women are considered to be more effective in entrapping victims of the same gender by gaining their trust.[57] This presents astonishing gendered connotations often unexpected because women would be the least expected to prey on fellow women. Consequently, human trafficking is the only area of transnational crime in which women are significantly represented—as victims and perpetrators.[58] Although in South Africa women traffickers are a small minority,[59] it still raises the question whether the social image of women as perennial disempowered victims is accurate or whether a more complex picture is needed to match the current reality of trafficking.

In some instances, victims of trafficking are labelled and identified as prostitutes without proper investigation as to whether they have been

recorded number of victims of other forms of trafficking—contrary to the patterns in the rest of the world.

55 South African President Cyril Ramaphosa, Speech to the nation, June 2020, 6–9. http://www.dirco.gov.za/docs/speeches/2020/cram0617.pdf. See also Report of the Special Rapporteur on violence against women, its causes and consequences on her mission to South Africa in 2015, https://www.ohchr.org/EN/NewsEvents/Pages/DisplayNews.aspx?NewsID=16877&LangID=E.

56 Office of the High Commissioner for Human Rights, *Human Rights and Human Trafficking Fact Sheet No.36* (2014), https://www.ohchr.org/Documents/Publications/FS36_en.pdf.

57 *Ibid*.

58 Louise Shelley *supra* note 32.

59 United Nations Office on Drugs and Crime '*Trafficking in Person in the SADC Region: A Statistical Report* (2014–2016): 55.

trafficked.[60] This labelling is often based on the assumption that they knowingly entered into the transaction from the onset and should therefore deal with the consequences of their actions. So, rather than be handled with leniency as victims, they are confronted by a biased and harsh legal system. Sadly, this negativity deters efforts to seek justice.

Another obfuscating factor is that trafficking in women covers a broad range of situations and takes on different forms. It includes abduction and selling of women as sex slaves or mail-order brides by criminal syndicates but also situations in which the physical or psychological abuse of vulnerability and exploitation is subtle and not immediately evident. A sex worker may have initially agreed to engage in commercial sex work but not to the working conditions and the ensuing exploitation. Thus, a sex worker who is being held in debt bondage, or who has her passport confiscated, and is without control over her earnings or coerced into receiving more clients than agreed, is no longer consenting to the work she is engaged in, whatever the initial agreement might have been. In such circumstances, the initial consent is dissipated, and she has become a victim of trafficking.

Although the question whether a woman ever really voluntary consents to prostitution or sex work has kept feminists divided, the Palermo Protocol found a way around it by making a distinction between trafficking and prostitution or sex work. Not all prostitution is the result of trafficking, but prostitution within the context of trafficking is always unacceptable because it is done by nonconsensual means and for exploitative purposes. Regulation or (de)criminalisation of prostitution was therefore left to individual states and falls outside the ambit of the Protocol.[61] Exploitation includes the exploitation of prostitution and

[60] Madeleine Rees, *The Gendered Dimensions of Sex Trafficking* (2012), http://www.cddrl.fsi.standford.edu/sites/deefault/files/Rees_06_19_12pdf.

[61] Annette Lansink 'Human Rights Focus on Trafficked Women: An International Law and Feminist Perspective' 20 *International Feminist Journal* (2006): 45–56. The Palermo Protocol does not define 'sexual exploitation', although a substantial number of human rights and feminist groups non-governmental organisations (NGOs) ('abolitionists') would have wanted all prostitution, which is held to be degrading, dehumanising, exploitative and a form of violence against women, to be included in the definition of trafficking. However, an equally substantial number of human rights and feminist NGOs did not want to conflate trafficking and prostitution.

other forms of sexual exploitation, and forced labour or services, slavery or practices similar to slavery and servitude. Trafficking for the purposes of sexual exploitation when it involves forced prostitution is forced labour and, possibly, depending on whether the necessary elements are present in a given case, qualifies as slavery or a practice similar to slavery. Trafficking may also amount to torture, inhuman or degrading treatment or international crimes, in particular, crimes against humanity or war crimes in cases of sexual slavery, rape and forced prostitution in armed conflicts.

Criminal justice practitioners who apply a gendered lens to the discourse understand that no monolithic category of women exists, that women make choices and have agency and that not all sex workers want to be 'rescued and rehabilitated' but that consent must be meaningful and informed. There is no consent if a trafficker abuses the vulnerability of a person by making the victim believe that she or he has no real option or reasonable alternative but to submit to the exploitation.[62] While one needs to guard against constructing women as perpetual minors, one also needs to guard against denialism.

The reality is, as shown in selected cases below, that traffickers exploit their victims. They prey upon vulnerable women and girls, in particular those who are vulnerable as a result of drug dependency, childhood abuse and dysfunctional family background, and manipulate their lives to such an extent that some of the victims suffer from trauma bonding ('Stockholm syndrome').[63] In these instances, there is physical, emotional and psychological dependency on the trafficker. In terms of the South African Prevention and Combating of Trafficking in Persons Act 7 of 2013 (PACOTIP), it is not a defence if an adult person who is a victim of trafficking has consented to the intended exploitation. If one or more of the means listed in section4(1) (a) to (j) such as coercion, fraud, deception,

[62] South African PACOTIP Act, section 1.

[63] United States Trafficking in Persons Report (2020) 20. Trauma bonding may occur when victims are isolated and depend on the trafficker psychologically as a result of trauma exposure or as a result of drug addiction; the traffickers make them believe there is no escape possible and the victims become numb and disconnected from other sources of support with the result that they become attached to their 'tormentors' in order to survive.

abuse of power or vulnerability have been used,[64] then consent ceases to be a defence. This is in line with the Palermo Protocol that adopts a definition of trafficking requiring an '*act*' (recruitment, transportation, transfer, harbouring or receipt), *means* (coercion, deception and other) and *purpose* (exploitation) and states that consent to the intended exploitation is irrelevant if any of the listed means have been used.[65] Despite that consent is not an element of the crime if one of the means has been proven, the issue is often central in court proceedings as a result of the line of defence put forward by the accused. It is incumbent on the courts to look at the totality of evidence, the manipulation and the psychological and gradual erosion of the independence of the victims.[66]

3 Beyond the Rhetoric: Prosecution and Punishment

Uganda and South Africa, like many other countries, are battling the scourge of human trafficking as source, transit and destination countries. The phenomenon of trafficking in South Africa and Uganda is both national and transnational. In these two countries, the national trafficking involves trafficking of men, women and children from rural or poor communities to the cities and transnational trafficking denotes trafficking to and from countries—in the case of Uganda mostly to the Middle East.[67] In Uganda, the majority of identified trafficking victims in sub-Saharan Africa are nationals, or, originate from neighbouring

[64] Section 11(1) of the PACOTIP Act. In line with Article 3(c) of the Palermo Protocol, this section in the South African legislation also provides that in the case of a child, consent is no defence to a charge even if none of the listed means are used.

[65] Palermo Protocol, Article 3(b).

[66] See also United Nations Office on Drugs and Crime Evidential Issues in Trafficking in Persons Cases, CASE DIGEST, United Nations, Vienna (2017) 20, 68–69, 132–137, https://www.unodc.org/documents/human-trafficking/2017/Case_Digest_Evidential_Issues_in_Trafficking.pdf.

[67] The Government of Uganda Annual Report on the trend of trafficking in Persons in Uganda (2013) lists the destination countries for registered victims of transnational trafficking to include (in the order of largest intake), Kuwait, the Democratic Republic of Congo, Malaysia, India, United Arab Emirates, Turkey, Kenya, Qatar, South Sudan, etc.

countries within the sub-region.[68] Intercontinental trafficking flows in Southern Africa are mostly to Europe, while trafficking victims from East and South Asia have also been detected in Southern Africa.[69]

In both South Africa and Uganda, factors such as inadequate employment opportunities, quality education and social welfare structures, prevalence of violence against children and rape contribute to the departure of mostly young people seeking better opportunities for themselves.[70] Although trafficking is often associated with movement from a familiar place to another place, trafficking does not necessarily mean movement across or within national borders; there is no requirement that the victim must have been transported from one place to another for the crime to have taken place. Trafficking includes 'harbouring' or 'receipt of a person' by illicit means for purposes of exploitation.[71]

As the main subjects of international law, states have the primary obligation to combat human trafficking.[72] This occurs both through legal and extra-legal strategies. Courts are particularly important and can play a central role in combating trafficking in women through legal means. Beyond deciding upon the guilt or innocence of alleged perpetrators and sentencing considerations, judges also elaborate upon the nature and the extent of relevant obligations of the state and make key decisions on the interpretation of trafficking laws and the evidence required to establish the crime. Their decisions also affect victim identification criteria, impact upon assessments of victim credibility and may involve protection steps on behalf of victims. All these decisions are critical to the overall success of anti-trafficking efforts. Depending on the jurisdiction, judges may also provide guidance to law enforcement agencies and/or actively participate

---

[68] United Nations Office on Drugs and Crime, *Global Report on Trafficking in Persons* (2018): 43–44.

[69] *Ibid.*, 83.

[70] The Violence Against Children Survey (2018) that was released by the Ministry of Gender in Uganda documented widespread incidences of sexual violence in the country but concluded that only a few cases are reported to the authorities which impacts on children's access to justice. Trafficking flows in women for sexual exploitation from Southern Africa are mostly to Europe, South Africa is also a country of destination for women trafficked from Mozambique and the East. US Department of State TIP, June 2020.

[71] Palermo Protocol, Article 3 (a) and PACOTIP Act, section 4(1).

[72] See Obokata *supra* note 11.

in the investigation phase. Furthermore, judges may be called upon to cooperate and exchange information with judicial officials from various countries, especially in the light of the transnational nature of the crime.

3.1 Uganda

The government of Uganda has taken some steps to purge the act of trafficking in women, the most prominent being the enactment in 2009 of the anti-trafficking legislation, the Prevention of Trafficking in Persons Act (PTIP) and Regulations to implement the same ten years later.[73] This law adopts the definition of human trafficking of the Palermo Protocol. It criminalises sex trafficking and labour trafficking, and prescribes punishments of up to 15 years' imprisonment for offences involving adult victims and up to life imprisonment for those involving child victims. It also applies to offences committed outside Uganda, giving the courts extra-territorial jurisdiction to try offences to do with human trafficking.[74] These penalties are sufficiently stringent and, with respect to sex trafficking, commensurate with those prescribed for other serious crimes, such as kidnapping. At the same time, Uganda uses the 4Ps framework in its legal policy framework for anti-trafficking, that is: Prevention, Prosecution, Protection and Partnership.[75] In line with this, the PTIP Act creates the Coordination Office for Prevention of Trafficking in Persons (COPTIP) to coordinate counter-trafficking efforts between the government and civil society organisations.[76] Since the creation of this office, the Ugandan government has made considerable progress in counter-trafficking such as the development and implementation of a National Action Plan for the Prevention of Trafficking in Persons.

[73] The passing of this law confirms with the obligation expressed in Art 5(1) of the Palermo Protocol to adopt legislative measures to establish trafficking as a criminal offence.

[74] Section 19 of the Prevention of Trafficking in Persons Act (2009).

[75] Kyla Johnson, *Supplying Slaves: The Disguise of Greener Pastures: An Exploratory Study of Human Trafficking in Uganda* (2019): 13, https://digitalcollections.sit.edu/isp_collection/3052.

[76] Section 21 Prevention of Trafficking in Persons Act (2009).

Similarly, this legal framework is enhanced by the establishment of a trafficking-specific desk in the Directorate of Public Prosecutions (DPP) for prosecuting trafficking crimes.[77] Through this initiative, a specialised prosecutor was designated to oversee all human trafficking cases around the country. There is also a specialised Human Trafficking Department in the Ugandan police force to support investigations in cases involving trafficking.[78] As a result, there have been some success in regard to litigating cases of trafficking, resulting into some cases being channelled through the criminal justice system. In 2018, the government reported investigating 286 cases of suspected traffickers, prosecuting 63 cases under the anti-trafficking act and 34 for fraudulent recruitment, and convicting six traffickers under the PTIP and four for fraudulent recruitment.[79]

However, there are still challenges in attracting appropriate sentences through the courts. For instance, of the six cases litigated under the anti-trafficking law in 2019 in Uganda, the courts sentenced two traffickers to two years' imprisonment, one to 14 months imprisonment, two to community service and one to a fine. In regard to traffickers convicted of fraudulent recruitment, one received three years' imprisonment, another received one year and two received warnings. The majority of convicted traffickers did not receive sentences that would be considered adequate to deter this crime.[80] A case in point is that of *Uganda v Umutoni Annet*[81] where the accused, though charged with two serious trafficking offences—one involving aggravated child trafficking, the judge gave a lenient sentence, especially considering that the victim, aged only 14 years at the time was trafficked and had been forced into sexual intercourse and infected with a sexually transmitted disease. Furthermore, she looked malnourished at the time she was recovered from the convict's home. While the PTIP provides for a maximum sentence of life imprisonment, the accused was sentenced to a prison term of eight years which is not deterrent enough.

---

[77] US Department of State Report, *Trafficking in Persons Report: Uganda* (2019), https://www.ecoi.net/en/document/2010927.html.

[78] Human Trafficking Institute, https://www.traffickinginstitute.org/uganda/.

[79] United States of America, Department of State Report (2019) *supra* note 75.

[80] *Ibid*.

[81] *Uganda v Umutoni Annet* HCT- 00- ICD-CR-SC- No. 003 of 2014.

Additionally, successful prosecution of trafficking cases has been hindered by the reluctance of courts to apply international law in domestic courts, thus, restricting the application of relevant standards such as those in the Palermo Protocol. Such reluctance was evident in the case of *Paul Ssemogerere & others v Attorney General*[82] where the Constitutional Court stated:

> The International human rights conventions mentioned in the petition are not part of the Constitution of the Republic of Uganda. Therefore, a provision of an Act of Parliament cannot be interpreted against them.

This regressive trend has however slowly been eroded with the courts becoming more accepting of international law.[83]

3.2 South Africa

By contrast, the South African Constitution unmistakably recognises the place of international law and its jurisprudence bears testimony to the importance attached to international law, and reference is made to the Palermo Protocol and international human rights law treaties in trafficking cases. South African law enforcement agencies have been recognised for 'increased efforts to investigate, prosecute and convict traffickers, including within organised criminal networks that facilitate the crime'.[84] In 2019, the Directorate of Priority Crime Investigations (the *Hawks)* investigated 24 potential trafficking cases, for sex trafficking and forced labour. The National Prosecuting Authority prosecuted 71 cases of trafficking in the same year and there were eight convictions.[85] The PACOTIP Act, 2013 came into operation in 2015 and largely follows

[82] *Paul Ssemogerere & 5 Ors v The Attorney General*, Constitutional Petition No.5/2002 (Unreported).

[83] See decision in *Susan Kigula & 417 Others v The Attorney General*, Constitutional Appeal No.2/2000 where the Supreme Court invoked international human rights law in arriving at its decision regarding the death penalty.

[84] United States Department of State Trafficking in Persons Report, June 2020, https://www.state.gov/wp-content/uploads/2020/06/2020-TIP-Report-Complete-062420-FINAL.pdf

[85] *Ibid.*, 454.

the broad definition of trafficking in the Palermo Protocol. Its objectives include Prevention, Prosecution, Protection and Partnerships (the 4Ps).[86] PACOTIP also includes two sections for compensation; a court may order a convicted person to make payment to the victim and the state.[87] The provision of compensation is an important mechanism for victims to obtain justice. Both domestic and transnational trafficking have been criminalised, and the Act also provides for extra-territorial jurisdiction.[88]

South Africa has made tremendous progress in prosecuting cases of trafficking against women which has contributed to a growing jurisprudence on protection of women's rights generally. The gender aspects of trafficking are sharply brought to the fore in *S v Jezile.*[89] The appellant in this case intended to conclude a customary marriage with a fourteen-year-old school girl who, according to his wishes, should have been a virgin and younger than 18 years.[90] The negotiations with the girl's uncles about the proposed marriage and the '*lobola*' were concluded over the course of a day, after which the complainant was informed about the intended marriage. The appellant tried to rely on the traditional Xhosa practice of *ukuthwala*[91] but the court held that he could not rely on the 'aberrant form' of the customary practice as a justification against charges of trafficking and rape. Central to the perpetrator's defence was his assertion that the girl had consented to the customary marriage and sexual intercourse. The fact that the girl had twice ran away was dismissed by him as 'a normal thing' for a newlywed.[92] But the High Court agreed with the trial court's conviction for trafficking and rape of a minor;

---

[86] PACOTIP Act, section 3.

[87] PACOTIP Act, sections 29 and 30. In terms of section 30, the court may make an order for the payment by the convicted person to the Criminal Assets Recovery Account in addition to payment to the victim. Compare the United Nations Voluntary Trust Fund for Victims of Trafficking in Persons, Especially Women and Children was established in 2010 as part of the Global Action Plan. https://www.unodc.org/unodc/human-trafficking-fund.html

[88] PACOTIP Act, section 12.

[89] S v Jezile, 2016 (2) SA 62 (WC), High Court of South Africa, Western Cape Division.

[90] *Ibid.*, paragraph 5.

[91] *Ukuthwala* means 'to carry' away for purposes of marriage and is, according to the Women's Legal Centre Trust, a 'harmful traditional practice' (see footnote 10 in *S v Jezile*).

[92] *S v Jezile,* paragraphs 38 and 86.

the sentence imposed was an effective 22 years direct imprisonment.[93] Several of the *amici curiae* admitted in this case described the 'aberrant form' of the customary practice as sexual slavery under the guise of a customary practice.[94] In terms of both the Palermo Protocol and the South African PACOTIP Act, consent may not be invoked as a defence against a charge of trafficking of a minor.[95] This case is notable because it provides a nexus between unequal power relations, sexism and other harmful discriminatory beliefs and practices, GBV and trafficking.[96]

Another significant court case that highlights relevant parts of criminal procedure and the operation of an international network is the case of *Aldina dos Santos v S*.[97] The trafficker was a 28-year-old female Mozambican national who was sentenced to life imprisonment after being convicted of trafficking for the purpose of sexual exploitation. According to the court, the victims who had been recruited under false promises from Mozambique to work in the appellant's hair salon in Pretoria were forced to have sexual intercourse with many men, were living in constant fear, prevented to leave the house, given little food, no money and were subjected to inhuman treatment.[98] The court agreed with the conclusion of the Regional Magistrate that an illicit infrastructure existed to transport the complainants and other young females between Mozambique and South Africa and that this could not have been done without the involvement of corrupt government officials.[99] Corruption is a serious obstacle in anti-trafficking activities in South Africa, but is receiving

---

[93] *Ibid.*, paragraph 96. Life imprisonment was not considered by the trial court due to the failure of the state to reflect the minimum sentence in the charge sheet, paragraph101.

[94] *Ibid.*, paragraph 78 with reference to three of the *amici* listed in paragraph 55; *amicus curiae* (friends of the court) are permitted to give advice to the court on a specific matter in the case. The court and several of the *amici* agreed that the 'traditional form' of the customary practice was not before the court.

[95] Palermo Protocol, Article 3 (c) and s11(1)(a) PACOTIP.

[96] United Nations Special Rapporteur on Violence Against Women – visit to South Africa (2015. She indicates 'widespread use of drug and alcohol, high unemployment rate and the continuing stereotypical portrayal of women in the media'.

[97] *Aldina dos Santos v S*, High Court of South Africa (Gauteng Division, Pretoria), Case No: A2612014.

[98] *Ibid.*, paragraph 9.

[99] *Ibid.*, paragraph 11.

attention in that a few complicit law enforcement officials have been prosecuted in recent years.[100]

Detailed evidence collected by police officers is essential as the case of *S v Eze*[101] shows, in which the warrant officers observations corroborated the testimony of the complainants and assisted the court in rejecting the accused's version that he had no hand in the prostitution of the two women, who were addicted to drugs. The court considered the question 'whether this vicious circle was of the complainants' free and voluntary doing or whether the accused exploited their addiction to the extent that he was in effective control of their lives'.[102] Expert witnesses testified that drug addiction helps traffickers to keep prostitutes virtually enslaved and in the 'expansive grip of psychological control' beyond the mere physical control which explains why women repeatedly return to their captors.[103] In this case, the accused was found guilty of rape of one of the complainants and trafficking on both counts. The latter on the basis that he kept the complainants 'in an altered state of consciousness, by employing fear and the threat of harm and by exploiting their addiction gave the accused the power over their vulnerability, to the extent that the complainants were inhibited from indicating their unwillingness or resistance to being trafficked, or unwillingness to participate in such an act'.[104]

In recent years, the South African courts have imposed hefty sentences fitting the crimes. For example, in the case of *S v Obi,*[105] several life sentences were imposed by the High Court judge for both trafficking and for rape of the three trafficked children, of the three counts, in addition, several maximum sentences were imposed on related counts, including an additional 15 years for using the services of trafficking victims. Judges seem to be very aware of the serious impact of the crimes committed

100 US Department of State TIP Report, June 2020, 454.

101 UNDOC No. ZAF015 *S v Eze* paragraph 54. See also the Regional Magistrate in *S v Veeran Palan and Edwina Norris*, Case no: RCD 13/14. Regional Court of KwaZulu-Natal, Port Shepstone, 12 June 2015.

102 *S v Eze* paragraphs 52 and 68.

103 *Ibid.,* paragraph 65.

104 *Ibid.,* paragraph 68.

105 S *v Obi & four Others,* Case no CC40/2018, Sentencing by the High Court of South Africa, Gauteng Division on September 18, 2019.

against the victims and make use of expert witnesses on the operation of trafficking networks and psychological impact on the victims.[106]

South African government departments, often with the assistance of the United Nations Office on Drugs and Crime (UNODC), have been rolling out training to government officials. Increased professionalism of warrant officers assist the National Prosecutors to secure convictions such as in the case of *S v Eze* above. In this case, the warrant officers were part of the *Hawks* unit and specially trained to work in the field of human trafficking. Another successful investigation in an intelligence driven joint operation by the Hawks supported by various teams and departments, including Home affairs, metro police and Forensic Science Laboratory, led to the convictions of two brothers in *S v Benjamin Obioma Abba & Another.*[107]

However, in *SL & Another v Minister of Home Affairs & Another,* the police failed to identify as potential victims of trafficking, women who had been arrested in a raid in a hotel in Johannesburg and were about to be deported to Thailand.[108] The judge found it 'astonishing' that the police and the department of Home Affairs undertook such a large operation to disrupt trafficking but then did not handle the matter in accordance with the PACOTIP Act to protect the victims.[109] Although the victims who did not speak English had 'agreed' to be deported, the court ordered that their status should first be established and that they were entitled to protection in terms of the legislation such as protective custody or a safe house.

Foreign victims also have the right to remain for a period of recovery and reflection in South Africa to decide whether they are willing to cooperate as witnesses in the case against the traffickers, however, three of the relevant sections of the PACOTIP Act are not yet in force as the accompanying immigration regulations for the visitor's visa have not

---

[106] *Ibid.*

[107] Media statement by the Hawks and the Police on September 19, 2018, https://www.saps.gov.za/newsroom/msspeechdetail.php?nid=17462.

[108] *SL, TH, CD and CK v The Minister of Home Affairs & Another*, High Court of South Africa, Gauteng Local Division, Johannesburg Case No: 2016/01352. *Amicus curiae:* Commission for Gender Equality.

[109] *Ibid.*, Modiba J at paragraph 26.

been issued yet.[110] Victims are not always willing or able to cooperate with law enforcement agencies in the investigation and prosecution of the traffickers for several reasons such as lack of trust of the police, fear of retaliation or threats to them or their family, and therefore, the period of recovery and reflection should not be made dependent on the willingness to cooperate with the investigation. It will only be after this period of recovery and reflection that a foreign victim may be repatriated but this must be done with due regard for the safety of the victim.

As van der Watt points out, the crime of human trafficking for sexual exploitation is 'steeped in hiddenness, deception and multiple truths' that hampers criminal investigations, is a constant battle between organised criminals and law enforcement and other different stakeholders (such health, welfare, shelters) and requires a multidisciplinary response with special skills as it involves multiple abuses and abusers.[111] The complexity of the crime and scale of the operations requires specialised units.[112] Trafficking is a much more complicated crime to solve than other serious crimes and investigations require time, commitment, energy and resources; it may take many years to complete an investigation.[113] Trafficking remains a low-risk and high-profit crime as the number of cases detected and the rate of convictions for trafficking in sub-Saharan Africa is low.[114]

In *S v Palan and Norris*,[115] the magistrate of the regional court held that the two unemployed complainants had been deceived into believing that they would work in regular employment at a hotel, instead they were forced to engage in prostitution to pay back the travel expenses

---

[110] Sections 15, 16 and 31(2)(b)(ii) PACOTIP Act are not yet in force. These are very relevant provisions for foreign victims of trafficking in line with international standards. It is therefore recommended that the South African government makes these sections operational.

[111] Marcel van der Watt, *Investigating Human Trafficking for Sexual Exploitation: From 'Lived Experiences' Towards a Complex Systems Understanding* (2018): 22 and 48.

[112] *Ibid*, 230.

[113] Van der Watt's interviews with participants, 223 and 230.

[114] United Nations Office on Drugs and Crime, *Global Report on Trafficking in Persons* (2018), https://www.unodc.org/documents/data-and-analysis/glotip/2018/GLOTiP_2018_BOOK_web_small.pdf.

[115] *S v Palan and Norris*, Case No RCD 13/14, Regional Court of KwaZulu-Natal, Port Shepstone, 12 June 2015.

incurred by the accused. In this case, it was also found that although the complainants may have had opportunities to escape the situation, this should be evaluated with regard to:

> the vulnerability of the two in a strange place where they did not know anyone who could help them, where they were scared of the pimp and held in debt bondage, where their appeals for assistance to the customers did not help them much; where the one person they knew and trusted, accused 2, also applied pressure on them…[116]

Finally, with the adoption of the National Policy Framework on the Management of Trafficking in Persons (NPF) in 2019, South Africa has added a critical strategic planning tool to its legislative and policy framework to combat trafficking. Based on the principles of a human rights and victim-centred approach, the NPF aims, *inter alia*, to coordinate the responses of relevant government departments and civil society, raise awareness, secure resources, reduce vulnerability to trafficking and improve responses.[117]

As the jurisprudence shows, South Africa has made more progress aimed at protecting female victims of trafficking, and Uganda has some lessons to learn from her sister country.

4 Access to Justice for Trafficked victims

In terms of international human rights law, states are under an international obligation to respect, protect, promote and fulfil human rights of those under its jurisdiction. Under international law, states are responsible for their own acts and are increasingly held responsible under the 'due diligence' standard for their failure to prevent private persons or

[116] *Ibid*.

[117] The National Policy Framework on the Management of Trafficking in Persons, adopted in April 2019, adds to the legislation, regulations and directives of the Department of Justice and Correctional Services aimed at combating trafficking in persons, https://www.unodc.org/unodc/en/human-trafficking/glo-act/south-africa-launches-prevention-and-combating-of-trafficking-in-persons-national-policy-framework.html.

non-state actors from interfering with the ability of individuals to exercise their rights, and the failure to investigate or punish private violations of human rights. This principle was established in international law in the *Velasquez Rodriguez* case in the context of human rights violations, whereby the Inter-American Court specifically mentioned the duty upon the state to prevent violations, conduct a serious investigation and identify those responsible, to impose appropriate punishment and ensure compensation to the victim.[118] More recently, the same Court elaborated on the principle in the context of positive obligations upon States to prevent slavery and human trafficking.[119]

The principle was affirmed by the African Commission on Human and Peoples' Rights in *SERAC and CESR v Nigeria*[120] and *Egyptian Initiative for Personal Rights v Egypt*.[121] Supportive persuasive evidence is to be found in the European Court of Human Rights' decision to affirm State accountability on the basis of the 'due diligence' principle in several cases, including *MC v Bulgaria* in which the Court found that the investigators and prosecutors 'fell short of the requirement inherent in the states' positive obligations—viewed in the light of the relevant modern standards in comparative and international law—to establish and apply effectively a criminal law system punishing all forms of rape and sexual abuse'.[122] In a case on trafficking, France was held to have violated Art 4 of the European Convention on Human Rights and Fundamental Freedoms in *Siliadin v France*,[123] by failing to provide effective protection

[118] *Velasquez Rodriguez v Honduras*, Inter-American Court of Human Rights, Judgment of July 21, 1989 paragrahs 172–174. See also Recommended Principles and Guidelines on Human Rights and Trafficking, Office of the UN High Commissioner for Human Rights (2010): 77–80.

[119] *Hacienda Brasil Verde Workers v Brazil supra* note 49.

[120] *SERAC and CESR v Nigeria* Ref: ACHPR/COMM/A044/1 May 27, 2002, https://www.escr-net.org/sites/default/files/serac.pdf and https://www.achpr.org/public/Document/file/English/achpr30_155_96_eng.pdf

[121] *Egyptian Initiative for Personal Rights v Egypt, Decision, Comm. No. 323/2006 (ACmHPR, December 2011)*; African Commission on Human and Peoples' Rights, Communication No. 323/2006, December 16, 2011, https://africanlii.org/afu/judgment/african-commission-human-and-peoples-rights/2011/85.

[122] *MC v Bulgaria* 15 Butterworths Human Rights Cases 627.

[123] *Siliadin v France*, July 26, 2005 ECHR 73,316/01.

to a young victim of trafficking from Togo in the form of criminal law legislation against debt bondage and servitude.

In *Rantsev v Cyprus and Russia*,[124] the ECHR held that there was a positive obligation on the States to investigate trafficking by private individuals. This also includes the procedural obligation to investigate the possibility that individuals or networks operating in a State's territory were involved in trafficking.[125] While the European Convention does not specifically mention trafficking, evolving human rights standards allowed the court to bring trafficking within the scope of the prohibition on slavery, servitude and forced labour.[126] The 'due diligence' standard is relied upon specifically in the context of acts of gender-based violence and has been reinforced by CEDAW. Accordingly, states which continue to fail in their duty to prevent, investigate, prosecute, punish the crimes of trafficking and violence against women are liable for human rights violations against the victims.

The blueprint above forms a normative basis from international human rights law to which states are expected to adhere in protecting individuals within their jurisdiction against trafficking and points to lessons from Africa and other continents. It sets the scene for a discussion on the performance of the countries under study in this chapter.[127] With regard to access to justice, the Palermo Protocol which is specific to the crime of trafficking requires a comprehensive approach that includes protection, prevention, prosecution and partnership. Beyond merely having a law in place, the Protocol mandates states to avail information on relevant court and administrative proceedings so that victims can seek justice. While the Palermo Protocol is primarily a law-enforcement instrument, concern for protection and assistance to victims with full

---

124 *Rantsev v Cyprus and Russia,* https://ec.europa.eu/anti-trafficking/sites/antitrafficking/files/rantsev_vs_russia_cyprus_en_4.pdf

125 *Rantsev v Cyprus and Russia,* paragraph 307.

126 *Ibid.,* paragraph 277.

127 In the landmark decision of *Carmichele v Minister of Safety and Security* 2001 (4) SA 938 (CC); 2001 (10) BCLR 995 (CC) (August 16, 2001), the South African Constitutional Court developed the common law delictual duty to act and established that failure by the police and prosecutors to protect members of the public in general and women and children in particular against the invasion of their fundamental rights by violent crime may lead to delictual liability and a claim for damages. Paragraphs.4 and 62.

respect for their human rights is one of the three objectives of the Trafficking Protocol.

The sections relating to protection and assistance are not mandatory. According to article 6 of the Palermo Protocol, each state 'shall consider' implementing measures to provide for the physical, psychological and social recovery of trafficking persons, including, in appropriate cases, in cooperation with non-governmental organisations, other relevant organisations, and other elements of civil society, in particular, the provision of appropriate housing; counselling and information, in particular, as regards their legal rights, in a language that the victims of trafficking can understand; medical, psychological and material assistance; employment, educational and training opportunities. The Council of Europe Convention on Action Against Trafficking in Human Beings goes beyond the Palermo Protocol by foregrounding human rights and gender equality in the protection of trafficked victims.[128]

The incorporation of a non-punishment provision for illicit activities by the victims of trafficking as a direct consequence of 'their situation as victims' can be viewed as an extension of the principle to protect and assist victims.[129] The South African PACOTIP Act may guide other African states in this regard as the Act makes provision for the withdrawal of the criminal prosecution or the discharge of the victim if the prosecutor is satisfied that 'the offence was committed as a direct result of person's position as a victim of trafficking'.[130]

The South African government makes considerable efforts to protect and assist victims of gender-based violence and trafficking. It has established a large number of Thuthuzela Care Centres for victims of rape and sexual violence, including for victims of trafficking, it also provided partial funding to accredited shelters run by NGOs and funding to

[128] Council of Europe Convention on Action Against Trafficking in Human Beings (COE) (2005), see articles 10–17 on protection to victims and article (1)(1)(a), 5(3), 6(d) on gender equality. See Annette Lansink, Report of the International Law Association's Committee on Feminism and International Law, on Women and Migration, Toronto (2006), 602, 637–640.

[129] Report of the Special Rapporteur on trafficking in persons, especially women and children, Maria Grazia Giammarinaro, to the UNGA, A/75/169, 17 July 2020, paragraphs 28 and 70.

[130] Section 22(3) PACOTIP Act.

several semi-accredited shelters for short stays for victims. The government departments and NGOs identified 112 potential victims in sex trafficking (the majority of victims identified were found in forced labour), and many of the victims were referred to shelters across the country and provided with protective services.[131] The organisations that aid will only be accredited when they meet norms and standards (regarding safety, access to health services, separate facilities for women and men, hygiene) as set out in the Act. While accredited organisations must offer the required services relating to accommodation and counselling, the sections on rehabilitation and therapeutic services to victims are not couched in a mandatory language as these programmes 'may' be offered.[132]

In general, the South African Department of Justice and Correctional Services has adopted a victim-centred approach to gender-based violence and trafficking.[133] An increase in protective services, a victim-centred approach and trained professionals led to a substantial number of victims assisting law enforcement officials as witnesses. Victims also received medical and psycho-social support, and the Department of Social Development assisted with providing rehabilitation programmes and provided financial support for victims to overcome drug addiction.[134] Whereas the protection and assistance services are shaping up, South Africa has not done much with regard to prevention strategies besides awareness raising and has not addressed the demand for sex trafficking or other forms of exploitative labour or services.[135] Prevention strategies are expected to address the socio-economic circumstances leading to vulnerability to trafficking and include training programmes.

The efforts of the government of Uganda have mostly focused on capacity building of responsible officers through training on the laws but

---

[131] United States State Department Trafficking in Persons (2020) 453.

[132] Sections 25 and 26 PACOTIP Act.

[133] See for example, https://www.unodc.org/southernafrica/en/vaw/index.html. See also the Department of Justice Directive, *Victims Charter*, https://www.justice.gov.za/legislation/acts/2013-007-Directives.pdf.

[134] United States State Department Trafficking in Persons (2020): 454.

[135] See in this regard also the recommendation of the Special Rapporteur on trafficking in persons, especially women and children in her Report to the Human Rights Council, April 2020, A/HRC/44/45, paragraph 65.

without provision of adequate funding for the implementation of the victim protection provisions in the law. For instance, the government remained without a national formal mechanism used by all front-line officials to systematically identify and refer trafficking victims to appropriate care.[136] The COPTIP reported receiving an insufficient budget, and this affected government's ability to conduct thorough investigations and provide protection to trafficking victims. Thus, the government continued to rely on NGOs and international organisations to provide the vast majority of victim services via referrals to NGO-operated shelters, which provided psychological counselling, medical treatment, family tracing, resettlement support and vocational education without contributing in-kind or financial support.

Additionally, the government did not adequately assist Ugandan victims identified abroad. It generally provided replacement travel documents to facilitate the repatriation of its citizens, while NGOs provided funding for return travel; however, the lack of embassies in many destination countries hindered repatriation efforts.[137] Where embassies existed, they lacked the capacity to provide adequate assistance for Ugandan nationals abroad. Also, the Ugandan government has still not established the Joint Implementation Committees needed to implement many of the stipulations and migrant protections within bilateral agreements between Uganda and receiving countries. However, the government reported securing a temporary shelter in the UAE and an emergency fund in Saudi Arabia for distressed Ugandan nationals, which was used by trafficking victims prior to their repatriation.[138]

On the criminal justice front, while the prosecution of offenders has continued to gain ground with the enactment of the PTIP and in fact judicial officers often encouraged trafficking victims to participate in the investigation and prosecution of their traffickers to prevent the victimisation of others, there is limited capacity in law enforcement to undertake thorough investigations which inevitably affected the outcome of such

136 United States State Department Trafficking in Persons (2020): 454.

137 *Ibid.*

138 *Ibid.*

cases. For instance, in the case of *Uganda v Orwothwun Martin,*[139] where the accused was charged with two counts of Aggravated Trafficking in Children, the accused was acquitted due to a failure by the prosecution to prove any of the essential elements of the offence beyond reasonable doubt. The accused was found not guilty and consequently acquitted. The outcome of this case was largely attributed to the poor prosecution techniques invoked by the police and prosecution.

The poor record of investigation and case success, coupled with the absence of victim-witness protection legislation, hinders many victims from seeking justice especially since testimonies from some of them pointed to the fact that perpetrators threaten and blackmail them to discourage their participation in trials. Sadly, ten years after the passing of the PTIP, there is still no formal policy to provide cooperating victims and witnesses with assistance, support or safety in a systematic way. And while the law permits victims to keep their identities anonymous by using voice distortion and video link facilities, this practice is yet to be implemented in the courts. This causes further prejudice to victims, more so those of GBV. Thus, while justice mechanisms exist in Uganda against trafficking, their implementation is not effective enough to snare the majority of perpetrators, and this leaves victims with little recourse for justice.

Another dilemma in enforcing justice for victims of trafficking in Uganda is the lack of technical knowledge on trafficking-based evidence. A considerable number of public officials are still unaware of the PTIP Act which is a fairly new law and often confuse trafficking with other offences. For example, cases of child trafficking have often been reported as defilement, kidnapping or child stealing under the Penal Code Act rather than the PTIP Act.[140] For domestic sex trafficking, cases are reported as rape. In the same regard, in view of the fact that there is a lot of trafficking across Uganda's borders, is not likely that the border patrol officers are well versed in the distinction between illegal migration and human trafficking, and this ends up prejudicing the victims twice

[139] *Uganda v Orwothwun Martin* HCCS Case No. 0052 of 2017.

[140] Tanima Kishore, The Human Trafficking Institute, www.unodc.org/documents/data-and-analysis/glotip/2018/GLOTiP_2018

since victims of trafficking once captured, are often treated as criminals or illegal immigrants and either arrested or deported.[141] Furthermore, since trafficking victims are usually not in their country of origin, there is often a language barrier between enforcement officers and the victims making evidence gathering problematic.

It should be kept in mind that trafficking is frequently a crime of a transnational nature, transcending national borders and jurisdictions. Law enforcement efforts are often confounded by the need to conduct investigations or pursue criminals across international borders, and requiring huge amounts of resources which are not always available.[142] Louise Shelley argues that the traffickers are rarely prosecuted because of their ability to neutralise law enforcement through bribes and intimidation.[143] These perpetrators also often operate in transnational groups, and yet the legal controls are state based. Through their flexibility and because of their networks, they avoid cumbersome legal procedures which prevents law enforcement from striking effectively at their structures that cross regions and continents.[144] Even when captured, it is never the real kingpins of trafficking that are netted, but rather the smaller frontrunners, agents or pawns. As such, even where African countries have established systems in place against trafficking, enforcement is still a big challenge leaving justice for trafficked victims more of an illusion than a reality.

5 Conclusion

Trafficking in women is a form of violence against women and a violation of human right and has been recognised as such in both international and regional human rights instruments. Both Uganda and South Africa are battling this scourge as source, transit and destination countries. From the discussions above, it is clear that South Africa and Uganda have

---

[141] *Ibid*.

[142] RTE: How Uganda has dealt with Human Trafficking, https://www.rte.ie/brainstorm/2020/0220/1116471-how-uganda-has-dealt-with-human-trafficking/.

[143] Shelley, Louise, *Human Trafficking: A Global Perspective* (2010).

[144] *Ibid*.

stepped up efforts to combat trafficking, mostly involving the legislative initiative of enacting anti-trafficking laws. However, the problem of effective implementation of these laws remains a challenge in both countries. It is evident that legislation alone is not enough for the substantial fight against human trafficking.

Access to justice especially for victims of GBV is still a far thought. Gathering of adequate evidence to prosecute such cases is still challenging especially the inadequate facilitation of the agencies involving, the technical incapacities of the officers involved and the intricate and complex nature of trafficking as a transnational crime. Furthermore, criminal justice systems need to be supported by aspects from all the 4Ps—Protection, Prevention, Prosecution and Partnership.

States need to strengthen their implementation of the provisions of the Palermo Protocol by enforcing a human rights-based approach to access justice for trafficked victims at two levels. The first level entails internal measures aimed at addressing the direct needs of the victims especially through provision of counselling and information, medical, psychological and material assistance as well as employment, education and training.[145] States should further consider providing translation and interpretation services where necessary and assistance to the victims so that their rights be presented during the criminal proceedings.[146] Any assistance offered, including a reflection and recovery period, should not be made conditional on the willingness of the victim to cooperate in the investigation of the crime. Support should also come with resources for investigation and prosecution of cases targeting both state and non-state agencies working with victims of trafficking as well as training of law enforcement personnel. At the second level, states should employ a comprehensive international approach within Africa by undertaking measures to prevent and punish trafficking and protecting victims. This should entail better management and sharing of data as well as tracking

145 Palermo Protocol, Article 6. See also sections 18(7), 19(7) and 21 of the South African PACOTIP Act.

146 See Art 12 of the COE (2005), http://www.coe.int/trafficking.

and coordination of victims and perpetrators. This enhanced intra-African cooperation in the fight against trafficking and sharing of best practices will improve the criminal justice response in many countries.

Also, technological advancement offers opportunities to tackle trafficking. Criminals use the Internet to advertise trafficked women for sexual services and women are often contacted by clients using mobile phones. In order to match the gravity of the pandemic of trafficking, this would require a technologically advanced response by criminal justice systems and the necessary resources to follow the trails using information technologies platforms.[147] There is also often a close link with the illicit drug trade. Investigations into associated crimes, in particular corruption and the illegal drugs trade, illicit financial flows and money-laundering should be coordinated. Such a broad approach is crucial because, for instance, traffickers create or abuse the drug dependency of women in order to exploit their prostitution. The complexity of the crimes involved in trafficking means that the criminal justice response must be multidisciplinary and specialised with coordination between different facets of criminal law.

Similarly, the development and adoption of an African Protocol on Gender-based Violence or an African Charter for Victims of Crimes[148] would focus the political will of African governments on the GBV pandemic by providing an additional tool to address the GBV pandemic. This instrument would aid in intra-African cooperation and could be executed possibly through organs of the African Union. Manjoo and Nekara have also expressed support for an African Convention against VAW, which would 'strengthen the human rights system' by focusing on the development of normative standards with its own monitoring body.[149] Alternatively, a United Nations Convention on GBV could fill the gap.

---

[147] See also the Organisation for Security and Cooperation in Europe (OSCE) 2018/2019, https://www.osce.org/files/f/documents/2/8/439712_1.pdf.

[148] The proposed Protocol could be added, like the Women's Protocol (Maputo Protocol), to the African Charter on Human and Peoples' Rights. An African Charter for Victims of Crimes would provide a regional update to the existing but outdated UN Declaration of Basic Principles of Justice for Victims of Crime and Abuse of Power (1985).

[149] Rashida Manjoo and Ruth Nekara, 'Does Africa Need a Regional Treaty on Violence Against Women? A Comparative Analysis of Normative Standards in Three Regional Human Rights

It is further proposed that each African State should consider appointing either an independent national rapporteur on trafficking or an independent group of experts to advice and evaluate the measures adopted to prevent trafficking, protect victims, prosecute and punish traffickers in its country. Experience in other countries with independent monitoring or evaluation has proven successful.[150] An independent national monitoring body is an essential instrument in assessing the implementation of counter-trafficking legislative measures, strategies and the criminal justice system. In addition, the voice of victims in the development of anti-trafficking strategies should be heard. It is recommended that African government departments consider recognising women, who were victims of trafficking, as experience experts. These experience experts may be consulted, on a purely voluntary basis, as their insights in the operation of trafficking will be valuable in the development of policies or investigation strategies. If implemented, the efforts outlined here would assist in combating trafficking in women as one of the worst forms of GBV.

References

African Union Commission, https://au.int/en/newsevents/28064/au-commission-initiative-against-trafficking-aucommit-campaign, November 4, 2020.

African Union, Action Plan, Tripoli, 2006, https://africa-eu-partnership.org/sites/default/files/documents/doc_au_commit_ouagadougou_ap_en_0.pdf, November 4, 2020.

Systems' *Acta Juridica,* 197 (202): 221, 226. Rashida Manjoo is a former United Nations Special Rapporteur on violence against women, its causes and consequences (2009–2015).

150 Directive on Trafficking 2011/36/EU of the European Parliament and of the Council of the European Union of 5 April 2011 on preventing and combating trafficking in human beings and protecting its victims, and replacing Council Framework Decision 2002/629/JHA. Article 19 of the Directive requires States to establish national rapporteurs to carry out assessments of trends, measuring results of anti-trafficking action, including statistics in close cooperation with civil society. The COE Trafficking Convention's monitoring body 'GRETA' consist of between 10 and 15 independent and highly qualified experts who evaluate the States Parties to the Convention and prepares a report to the Committee of the Parties.

Carmichele v Minister of Safety and Security 2001 (4) SA 938 (CC); 2001 (10) BCLR 995 (CC) (August 16, 2001).

Centre for Child Law (2020), *Child Trafficking: Exploring the Myths and Realities*, http://centreforchildlaw.co.za/wp-content/uploads/2020/08/WEB-CFCL-Child_Trafficking-Report.pdf., November 4, 2020.

Committee on Elimination of Discrimination Against Women General Recommendation No. 35 (2017), General recommendation No 19 (1992), CEDAW/C/GC/35.

Council of Europe Convention on Action Against Trafficking in Human Beings (COE) (2005) Counter-Trafficking in Persons Act 2010 of Kenya.

Declaration on the Elimination on all Forms of Violence against Women, UNGA A/RES/48/104, December 20, 1993, https://www.refworld.org/docid/3b00f25d2c.html, November 4, 2020.

Department of Justice and Correctional Services, *National Policy Framework on the Management of Trafficking in Persons* (2019), https://www.unodc.org/unodc/en/human-trafficking/glo-act/south-africa-launches-prevention-and-combating-of-trafficking-in-persons-national-policy-framework.html, November 4, 2020.

Egyptian Initiative for Personal Rights v Egypt, Decision, Comm. No. 323/2006 (ACmHPR, December 2011), African Commission on Human and Peoples' Rights, Communication No. 323/2006, December 16, 2011, https://africanlii.org/afu/judgment/african-commission-human-and-peoples-rights/2011/85, November 4, 2020.

General Recommendation No. 38 (2020), CEDAW/C/GC/38.

Goma Declaration on Eradicating Sexual Violence and Ending Impunity in the Great Lakes Region, https://www.icglr-rtf.org/publication/view/improving-access-to-justice-and-ending-impunity-for-sgbv-in-the-icglr-member-states-rtf-sgbv-study/, November 4, 2020.

Government of Uganda, Ministry of Gender, Labour and Social Development. Preliminary Report of the Committee on Gender, Labour and Social Development, www.gov.ug, November 4, 2020.

Hacienda Brasil Verde Workers v Brazil Inter-American Court of Human Rights, Case of the Preliminary Objections, Merits, Reparations and Costs. Judgment of October 20, 2016. Series C No. 318, https://www.corteidh.or.cr/cf/Jurisprudencia2/overview.cfm?doc=1728&lang=en, November 4, 2020.

Inter-American Convention on Violence against Women, Organisation of American States, affirms trafficking as a form of violence against women, https://www.oas.org/en/mesecvi/docs/BelemDoPara-ENGLISH.pdf and https://www.state.gov/wp-content/uploads/2020/06/2020-TIP-Report-Complete-062420-FINAL.pdf, November 4, 2020.

International Organisation for Migration (IOM) in Pretoria, *Seduction, Sale and Slavery: Trafficking in Women and Children for Sexual Exploitation in Southern Africa*, May 3, 2003, 3rd edition.

Johnson Kyla, 'Supplying Slaves: The Disguise of Greener Pastures: An Exploratory Study of Human Trafficking in Uganda' *Independent Study Project (ISP) Collection* 3052 (2019), https://digitalcollections.sit.edu/isp_collection/3052, November 4, 2020.

Kishore Tanima, *The Human Trafficking Institute* (2018), www.unodc.org/documents/data-and-analysis/glotip/2018/GLOTiP_2018, November 4, 2020.

Kruger Beatri and van der Watt Marcel, *What Do We Know About Child Trafficking Prevalence in South Africa*, presentation September 2020. DOI: https://doi.org/10.13140/RG.2.2.24306.73920.

Lansink Annette, 'Human Rights Focus on Trafficked Women: An International Law and Feminist Perspective' 70, *Agenda: International Feminist Journal* (2006): 45–56.

Lansink Annette (with Justice Manohar Sujata and Chuang Janie), 'Women and Migration' Third Report of the ILA Committee on Feminism and International Law, Report of the 72nd Conference of the International Law Association, Toronto (2006), published by the International Law Association, Charles Clore House, London, 602–643 ISSN 0074 6738.

Law No. 029–2008/AN on the Fight Against Trafficking in Persons and Similar Practices of Burkina Faso.

Law No. 1/2004 on the Smuggling of Migrants and Trafficking in Persons of Equatorial Guinea.

Law 09/04 Concerning the Prevention and the Fight Against the Trafficking of Children in the Gabonese Republic.

Manjoo Rashida and Nekara Ruth, 'Does Africa Need a Regional Treaty on Violence Against Women? A Comparative Analysis of Normative Standards in Three Regional Human Rights Systems' *Acta Juridica* (2020): 221.

Mashishi Naledi, *Lerato Kganyago's Claims About Child Trafficking in South Africa*, Eyewitness News, September 23, 2020, https://ewn.co.za/2020/09/23/fact-check-lerato-kganyago-s-claims-about-child-trafficking-in-south-africa, November 4, 2020.

MC v Bulgaria 15 Butterworths Human Rights Cases 627 (2003).

Obokata Tom, 'Human Trafficking in Africa Opportunities and Challenges for the African Court of Justice and Human Rights' in Charles C Jalloh

(ed) *The African Court of Justice and Human and Peoples' Rights in Context Development and Challenges* (2019).
Office of the United Nations High Commissioner for Human Rights, *Recommended Principles and Guidelines on Human Rights and Trafficking* (2010), https://www.ohchr.org/documents/publications/commentary_Human_Trafficking_en.pdf, November 4, 2020.
Organisation for Security and Cooperation in Europe, Report of the OSCE Special Representative and Co-ordinator for Combating Trafficking in Human Beings: New Challenges and New Opportunities OSCE, https://www.osce.org/files/f/documents/2/8/439712_1.pdf, November 4, 2020.
Paul Ssemogerere & 5 Ors v The Attorney General, Constitutional Petition No.5/2002 (Unreported).
Penal Code of the Central African Republic (2010).
Prevention and Combating of Trafficking in Human Beings Act 7 of 2013 of South Africa.
Prevention of Trafficking in Persons Act of Uganda (2009).
Protocol on the Prevention and Suppression of Sexual Violence against Women and Children of the International Conference on the Great Lakes Region (ICGLR), (2020, November 30). https://www.peaceau.org/uploads/final-protocol.sexual-violence-en-rev-2.pdf.
Protocol to Prevent, Suppress and Punish Trafficking in Persons, Especially Women and Children, supplementing the United Nations Convention against Transnational Organised Crime, 2000, A/RES/55/25, November 15, 2000.
Protocol to the African Charter on Human and Peoples' Rights on the Rights of Women (2003), https://au.int/en/treaties/protocol-african-charter-human-and-peoples-rights-rights-women-africa, November 4, 2020.
Rantsev v Cyprus and Russia, https://ec.europa.eu/anti-trafficking/sites/antitrafficking/files/rantsev_vs_russia_cyprus_en_4.pdf, November 4, 2020.
Rees Madeleine, *The Gendered Dimensions of Sex Trafficking* (2012), http://www.cddrl.fsi.standford.edu/sites/deefault/files/Rees_06_19_12pdf, November 4, 2020.
S v Eze UNDOC No. ZAF015.
S v Jezile, 2016 (2) SA 62 (WC), High Court of South Africa, Western Cape Division.
S v Veeran Palan and Edwina Norris, Case no: RCD 13/14. Regional Court of KwaZulu-Natal, Port Shepstone, June 12, 2015.
SERAC and CESR v Nigeria Ref: ACHPR/COMM/A044/1 May 27, 2002, https://www.escr-net.org/sites/default/files/serac.pdf and https://www.achpr.

org/public/Document/file/English/achpr30_155_96_eng.pdf, November 4, 2020.

Shelley Louise, *Human Trafficking: A Global Perspective* (2010).

Siliadin v France, 26 July 2005 ECHR 73316/01.

SL, TH, CD and CK v The Minister of Home Affairs & Another, High Court of South Africa, Gauteng Local Division, Johannesburg Case No: 2016/01352. *Amicus curiae:* Commission for Gender Equality.

Sorensen Jennifer, Sara Piazzano, Olga DiPretoro and Carolyn O'Donnell, Addressing Inter-Linkages Between Gender Based Violence and Trafficking in Persons to Prevent Reinforcement of Inequalities, Winrock International, October 2012, https://www.winrock.org/wp-content/uploads/2016/03/Addressing-inter-linkages.pdf, 4 November 2020.

South African Law Reform Commission Report on Trafficking in Person (2008), https://www.justice.gov.za/Salrc/reports/r_pr131_trafficking_2008.pdf, November 4, 2020.

South African President Cyril Ramaphosa, Speech to the Nation, June 17, 2020, http://www.dirco.gov.za/docs/speeches/2020/cram0617.pdf, November 4, 2020.

Southern Africa Development Cooperation (SADC), Protocol on Gender and Development (2008), https://www.sadc.int/issues/gender/gender-based-violence, 4 November 2020.

South African Department of Justice Directive: Victims Charter, https://www.justice.gov.za/legislation/acts/2013-007-Directives.pdf, November 4, 2020.

Susan Kigula & 417 Others v The Attorney General, Constitutional Appeal No.2/2000.

Thozama Mandisa Lutya, *Human Trafficking of Young Women and Girls for Sexual Exploitation in South Africa*, http://dx.doi.org/https://doi.org/10.5772/39202, November 4, 2020.

Uganda v Orwothwun Martin HCCS Case No. 0052 of 2017.

Uganda v Umutoni Annet HCT- 00- ICD-CR-SC- No. 003 of 2014.

United Nations Beijing Declaration and Platform for Action, Fourth World Conference on Omen, United Nations General Assembly (1995), https://www.un.org/en/development/desa/population/migration/generalassembly/docs/globalcompact/A_CONF.177_20.pdf, 4 November 2020.

United Nations Human Rights Office of the High Commissioner, Human Rights and Human Trafficking: Fact Sheet No.36. New York and Geneva: Office of the High Commissioner for Human Rights (2014).

United Nations Office on Drugs and Crime, Evidential Issues in Trafficking in Persons Cases, CASE DIGEST, United Nations, Vienna, 2017.

United Nations Office on Drugs and Crime, Global Report on Trafficking in Persons 2018, 28, https://www.unodc.org/documents/data-and-analysis/glotip/2018/G.LOTiP_2018_BOOK_web_small.pdf, 4 November 2020.
United Nations Office on Drugs and Crime, UNODC-DNR, Research brief (2016), https://www.unodc.org/documents/research/UNODC-DNR_research_brief.pdf, November 4, 2020.
United Nations Special Rapporteur on Trafficking in Persons, Especially Women and Children, Maria Grazia Giammarinaro, Reports A/75/169 and A/HRC/44/45.
United Nations Special Rapporteur on Violence Against Women, Its Causes and Consequences Report of the Special Rapporteur, Dubravka Šimonović, on her Mission to South Africa 2015, A/HRC/32/42/Add.2.
United States Department of State Report (2020) Trafficking in Persons Report, https://www.state.gov/wp-content/uploads/2020/06/2020-TIP-Report-Complete-062420-FINAL.pdf.s, November 4, 2020.
United States Department of State, Report on Trafficking in Persons (2019).
Van der Watt Marcel, *Investigating Human Trafficking for Sexual Exploitation: From 'Lived Experiences' Towards a Complex Systems Understanding* (2018), http://uir.unisa.ac.za/bitstream/handle/10500/24803/thesis_Vander Watt_M.pdf?isAllowed=y&sequence=1, 4 November 2020.
Van der Watt, Marcel, 'Response to the Centre for Child Law Trafficking (in South Africa) Report. Presentation, August 2020. DOI: https://doi.org/10.13140/RG.2.2.21790.15687, November 4, 2020.
Velasquez Rodriguez v Honduras, Inter-American Court of Human Rights, Judgment of 21 July 1989.

8

Criminal Accountability for Gender-Based Violence in North Africa: Beyond Legal Reforms

Yousra Abourabi and Emma Charlene Lubaale

1 Introduction

Gender-based violence is one of the most widespread forms of human rights violations worldwide.[1] It is a major social challenge that affects all societies regardless of sociocultural specificities. It is generally defined

Emma Charlene Lubaale would like to acknowledge funding from the National Research Foundation (Funding Grant to EC Lubaale-Grant no: 127504) towards the funding of research retreats that informed the development and conceptualisation of this edited book idea and the writing and revisions to all the chapter contributions in this edited volume as well as those in Volume II of this book. The funding and support of the Directorate of Research of Rhodes University is also acknowledged.

[1] UN, MONUSCO, *Gender and Violence* (2016), https://monusco.unmissions.org/genre-et-violence.

Y. Abourabi
Universite Intenationale de Rabat, Rabat, Morocco
e-mail: yousra.abourabi@uir.ac.ma

E. C. Lubaale (✉)
Faculty of Law, Rhodes University, Makhanda, South Africa

E. C. Lubaale and A. Budoo-Scholtz (eds.), *Violence Against Women and Criminal Justice in Africa: Volume I*, Sustainable Development Goals Series,
https://doi.org/10.1007/978-3-030-75949-0_8

as any violent act perpetrated against a person on the basis of socially ascribed gender differences[2] resulting from historically unequal power relations and often materialised by male domination.[3] The foregoing definition is gender neutral; however, some definitions have offered a gender exclusive definition that narrows gender-based violence down to violence against women. For example, the 1993 United Nations Declaration on Elimination of all forms of Violence Against Women defines violence against women as 'any act of gender-based violence that results in, or is likely to result in, physical, sexual or psychological harm or suffering, including threats of such acts, coercion or arbitrary deprivation of liberty, whether occurring in public or in private life.'[4] From the foregoing definition, violence against women is synonymous with gender-based violence. This gender exclusive definition finds support in the indisputable reality that most of the victims of violence are women.[5] Generally, gender-based violence constitutes a major obstacle to the advancement of equality, development and social peace.[6] It also constitutes a major barrier to the attainment of the United Nations Sustainable Development Goals which envisage, among others, that by 2030 all forms of violence against women in both the private and public sector will have been eliminated. The African Union Agenda 2063 and Agenda for Children 2040 which underscore gender equality and elimination of violence against children, respectively, would also be crippled with the continued pervasiveness of gender-based violence on the African continent.[7]

---

[2] Inter-Agency Standing Committee (IASC), *Directives en vue d'interventions contre la violence basée* September 6, 2005, https://interagencystandingcommittee.org/system/files/legacy_files/GBV%20Guidelines%20French.pdf.

[3] UN, MONUSCO, *Gender and Violence*, https://monusco.unmissions.org/genre-et-violence.

[4] United Nations Déclaration on Elimination of all Forms of Violence against Women (1993).

[5] World Health Organisation, *Violence against women*, November 29, 2017, https://www.who.int/news-room/fact-sheets/detail/violence-against-women.

[6] Office of the United Nations High Commissioner for Human Rights, *Declaration on the Elimination of Violence against Women* (1993), https://www.ohchr.org/FR/ProfessionalInterest/Pages/ViolenceAgainstWomen.aspx.

[7] African Committee of Experts on the Rights and Welfare of the Child, *Agenda 2040: Fostering an Africa fit for children* (2016) Aspiration 7; African Union Commission, *Agenda 2063: The Africa We Want* (2015) 2.

In North Africa, violence against women is so pervasive that the society has normalised it. According to the World Bank, the Middle East and North African regions are some of the most hostile environments for women.[8] These regions also record the lowest levels of equality between genders.[9] Despite the existence of universally accepted standards on women's rights, their effective integration in most North African countries varies greatly from society to society on account of the difference in norms and social attitudes. As Eléonore notes: 'the boundaries of violence also include their social dimensions, which make certain acts socially acceptable in some contexts and reprehensible in others.'[10] In this regard, Morocco's Permanent Representative to the United Nations, Mohamed Bennouna, stressed at a meeting of the Committee on Elimination of Discrimination against Women that 'the implementation of the Convention on the Elimination of All Forms of Discrimination against Women is not a problem of religion or of law, but of mentality.'[11] Bennouna is spot on as there is indeed strong resistance both within the administrative apparatus of countries such as Morocco and among those responsible for enforcing the law. Even with established norms on women's rights, many deliberately refuse to accord due regard to women's rights. Thus, while law reform plays a critical role, improving the situation of women in North Africa will rest heavily on the extent to which social attitudes and norms are addressed. This is the case because gender inequality is primarily entrenched in stereotypical sociocultural attitudes and habits.[12]

---

[8] General Recommendations Adopted by the Committee on the Elimination of Discrimination against Women, Eleventh session (1992), General Recommendation No. 19: Violence against Women, https://tbinternet.ohchr.org/Treaties/CEDAW/Shared%20Documents/1_Global/INT_CEDAW_GEC_3731_F.pdf.

[9] *Ibid.*

[10] Eléonore Abou Ez, *LES pays d'Afrique du Nord et du Moyen-Orient sont les pires pour les droits des femmes, selon la Banque mondiale, France Info*, March 1, 2019, https://www.francetvinfo.fr/monde/afrique/societe-africaine/les-pays-d-afrique-du-nord-les-pires-pour-les-droits-des-femmes-selon-la-banque-mondiale_3211763.html.

[11] Juliette Gaté, *Women's Rights and Arab Revolutions,* La Revue des droits de l'homme, November 7, 2014, https://journals.openedition.org/revdh/929?lang=en#citedby.

[12] *Ibid. On stereotypes and the law, see also* generally Lubaale Emma Charlene, 'Confronting stereotypes as an entry point to realigning IAAF regulations with human rights and developments in Science' 17 *Gender and Behaviour,* (2019): 14413–14432.

It is to be conceded that presently, women in North Africa enjoy better protection of the law than they did twenty years ago. This progress is partly attributable to the emergence of dynamic feminist movements in the region during the 1980s and 1990s[13] which aimed at transforming the legal system and denouncing the dominant patriarchal model.[14] For example, the feminist movement in Morocco influenced reforms to the Family Code known as the 'Moudawana'. This Code 'constituted the locus of legal and civil discrimination against women.'[15] In addition, the research conducted by researchers such as Mernissi,[16] Lamrabet[17] and Maadi[18] has become a reference point to raise awareness of gender-based violence in the region. However, despite the critical role of such research, some loopholes are discernible. For example, some of the research conducted ignores the reality that 'gender roles, and even the division of labour, are neither prescribed nor ordered by nature but have historical origins.'[19] These historical dimensions need to be dismantled if women are to fully enjoy their rights in North Africa. For example, in many predominantly Muslim countries including Morocco and Egypt, women are considered minors by the justice system, thus, setting their civil rights up for violation and infringement.[20] Their status in society has created an environment for violence to thrive. By being reduced to

---

13 Fatima Sadiqi, *Les droits des femmes en Afrique du Nord au lendemain du printemps arabe*, IEMED Yearbook, Secteurs stratégiques, Société et Culture, https://www.iemed.org/observatori/arees-danalisi/arxius-adjunts/anuari/anuari-2014/Sadiqi_Droits_femmes_Printemps_arabe_Annuaire_IEMed_2014.pdf/.

14 Marguerite Rollinde, *Maghreb: quelles stratégies féministes à l'œuvre*, Genre en action, September 4, 2007, https://www.genreenaction.net/Maghreb-quelles-strategies-feministes-a-l-oeuvre.html.

15 Naciri Rabéa, 'Le mouvement des femmes au Maroc" 33 *Nouvelles Questions Féministes* (2014): 43–64.

16 Fatema Mernissi, *The Pride of Islamic Feminism in Modern Times—Obituary*, Muslim Institute, https://musliminstitute.org/freethinking/gender/fatema-mernissi-pride-islamic-feminism-modern-times-obituary.

17 Asma Lamrabet, *Islam et femmes: Emergence de nouvelles voies de libération pour les femmes en islam*, September 2014, http://www.asma-lamrabet.com/articles/l-emergence-de-nouvelles-voies-de-liberation-pour-les-femmes-en-islam/.

18 Mernissi *supra* note 16.

19 Zineb Maâdi, Al-Jassad al-unthawī wa-hulm al-tanmiyah, Casablanca: Le Fennec (2003).

20 Asma Lamrabet, Femmes et hommes dans le Coran: quelle égalité? (2012).

minors, they have been stripped of decision-making power and independence, thus, making them vulnerable to abuse. Other forms of violence that have thrived as a result of being reduced to minors include forced marriage, marital rape, female genital mutilation, feminicide and psychological violence.[21] Aside from this, religion is often advanced as a pretext to justify the superiority of men over women.[22] This strategy has been used to legitimise practices that are not dictated in religious texts. In fact, these problematic justifications often contradict the religious precepts.

In the context of Morocco, customs and traditions disregard the principle of consent during sexual intercourse in a matrimonial context.[23] This has left many women with the burden of marital rape as this act of violence is not considered a crime in the institution of marriage. Victims have had to resort to other offences such as the crime of assault to ensure that perpetrators are held to account.[24] In the North African country of Libya, government authorities are on record for failing to protect women from gender-based violence perpetrated by members of militias and armed groups.[25] Freedom House describes the Libyan society as being influenced by 'extremely conservative patriarchal traditions and tribal culture, which continue to foster gender discrimination.'[26] Furthermore, the United Nations Human Rights Council has noted that the Libyan culture contains 'entrenched discriminatory gender norms' which undermine the enforcement of women's rights.[27] The consequence of this cultural conservatism is that acts of gender-based violence such as rape,

---

21 *Ibid.*

22 See detailed discussion in Sect. 2.3 of this chapter.

23 Lara Deramaix and Julien Moriceau, *Quelle justice pour les femmes au Maroc? Analyse des parcours de justice, Avocats Sans Frontières*, (2019) 65, https://www.asf.be/wp-content/uploads/2019/12/ASF-justice-femmes-Maroc-2019-6-2.pdf.

24 PNUD Morocco, *Gender Justice and The Law: Assessment of Laws Affecting Gender Equality and Protection against Gender-Based Violence*, 2018, https://arabstates.unfpa.org/sites/default/files/pub-pdf/Morocco%20Country%20Assessment%20-%20English_0.pdf.

25 Martin Chave, *Libye, La guerre par le viol 3/4*, October 20 2018, https://www.notaweaponofwar.org/libye-la-guerre-par-le-viol-3-4/.

26 Freedom House, *Women's Rights in the Middle East and North Africa* (2010), www.freedomhouse.org.

27 United Nations Human Rights, *Integrating a Gender Perspective into Human Rights Investigations, Guidance and Practice*, (2016) 39, https://www.ohchr.org/Documents/Issues/Women/Publications/GenderIntegrationintoHRInvestigations.pdf.

domestic violence and assault are silenced.[28] Also notable in Libya is the fact that the use of rape as a weapon by armed groups has over the years been pervasive. Not surprisingly, in the cases currently before the International Criminal Court on the situation in Libya, counts of gender-based violence feature prominently.[29]

Aside from gender-based violence during peace times, situations of conflict and disaster have caused a surge in cases of gender-based violence in Northern African countries. In a study conducted by the United Nations Population Fund, it was demonstrated that the tensions accompanying epidemics have had the effect of amplifying already existing gender disparities, thus, increasing the risk of domestic violence and other forms of gender-based violence.[30] For example, violence against women has exploded globally due to the lockdown measures adopted by governments in different countries to curb the spread of the COVID-19 virus.[31] The surge in gender-based violence has been one of the unintended consequences of these lockdown measures,[32] with North African countries being no exception to the challenge. Especially disheartening are the health consequences of gender-based violence during these emergency situations. Studies show that the escalation in gender-based violence cases has caused a major threat to women's health.[33]

---

[28] Joint Submission to the United Nations Universal Periodic Review in the 22nd Session of the UPR Working Group, *The State of Libya Women's rights*, September 2014, https://www.upr-info.org/sites/default/files/document/libya/session_22_-_mai_2015/js3_upr22_lby_e_main.pdf.

[29] United Nations Population Fund, *Prise en charge de la violence basée sur le genre dans les situations d'urgence*, https://www.unfpa.org/sites/default/files/pub-pdf/GBV%20E-Learning%20Companion%20Guide_FRENCH.pdf.

[30] United Nations Population Fund, *Morocco: Pulling Together to Protect Women's Rights: Programming to Address Violence against Women: Ten Case Studies*, https://www.refworld.org/docid/469cd693c.html.

[31] International Planned Parenthood Federation, *COVID-19 and the Rise of Gender-Based Violence*, April 22, 2020, https://www.ippf.org/blogs/covid-19-and-rise-gender-based-violence; United Nations Development Programma, *Gender-Based Violence and COVID-19*, May 11, 2020, https://www.undp.org/content/undp/en/home/librarypage/womens-empowerment/gender-based-violence-and-covid-19.html.

[32] *Ibid*.

[33] World Health Organisation, *COVID-19 et violence à l'égard des femmes, Ce que le secteur et le système de santé peuvent faire*, April 7, 2020, https://apps.who.int/iris/bitstream/handle/10665/331762/WHO-SRH-20.04-fre.pdf?ua=1

All considered, gender-based violence remains rife across North Africa. Its pervasiveness feeds on deeply entrenched cultural and social norms which discriminate against women. Thus far, much has been written on the subject of gender-based violence across a number of North African countries.[34] However, no analysis engages with the subject from the perspective of access to criminal justice. In the light of this state of affairs, it is worth asking the question: to what extent do social norms limit the implementation of laws on gender equality and more specifically, criminal prosecution of cases of gender-based violence? Put differently, can the implementation of law, of itself, effectively ensure that gender-based violence is addressed? The main submission in this chapter is that the process of development and application of laws is determined by social norms. In addition, these norms shape laws. A question is therefore asked: To what extent can implementation of law, without ensuring a change in social norms, ensure the elimination of violence against women and gender equality? This question is answered by demonstrating that elimination of gender-based violence and effective criminal prosecution will require a change in attitudes and social behaviour. This is because gender-based violence is directly linked to social and cultural attitudes. Thus, it is critical to confront both social and legal norms. The chapter will demonstrate why this approach is critical by drawing on case studies from Morocco and Egypt.

[34] See, e.g., Selimovic JM and Larsson DM, 'Gender and Transition in Libya Mapping women's participation in post-conflict reconstruction' *The Swedish Institute of International Affairs*(2014): 1–33; Oussedik F, 'Religion, Gender, and Violence in Algeria' 6 *Brown Journal of World Affairs* (1996): 191–197; House PB, *Assaulted and accused sexual and gender-based violence in Tunisia, Amnesty International* (2015): 1–84; Naciri H, 'Gender-based Violence in Morocco: Domestic Violence as a Case in Point' 9 *Kultūra Ir Visuomenė. Socialinių Tyrimų Žurnalas* (2018): 51–66; Ambrosetti E, Amara NA and Condon S, 'Gender-Based Violence in Egypt: Analysing Impacts of Political Reforms, Social, and Demographic Change' 19 *Violence Against Women* (2013), https://doi.org/10.1177%2F1077801213486329.

2 Gender-Based Violence in Egypt and Morocco: The Law, Religion, Social Norms and Mentality Gaps

In the preceding section, the pervasive nature of gender-based violence across countries in North Africa including Morocco, Libya and Egypt has been highlighted. With the aim of this chapter being to investigate the interaction between access to justice and social norms, this section engages with this issue in the context of Morocco and Egypt based on three themes: 1. the various expressions of gender-based violence 2. the national and international framework on prevention of gender-based violence and 3. social norms and their implications on accountability for gender-based violence in Egypt and Morocco.

2.1 The Various Expressions of Gender-Based violence in Egypt and Morocco

Egypt is a country in North Africa headed by a president who serves both as a head of government and a head of state. The population of women in Egypt is estimated to be just over 50 million,[35] with this section of this Egyptian society considered to be an endangered species on account of gender-based violence.[36] Gender-based violence is reportedly one of the most pervasive human rights violations worldwide, with studies documenting that one-third of all women are affected by some form of violence in their lifetime.[37] Egypt has not been an exception to this scourge, with studies documenting alarming statistics on gender-based violence. In its 2018 report on 'Global Gender Gap', the World

---

[35] World Population Review, *Egypt Population* (2020), https://worldpopulationreview.com/countries/egypt-population/.

[36] Home Office, *Country Policy and Information Note Egypt: Women,* (2019): 1–49 https://assets.publishing.service.gov.uk/government/uploads/system/uploads/attachment_data/file/810875/Egypt_-_Women_-_CPIN_-_v2.0__June_2019__external.pdf.

[37] Devries K, Mak JY, García-Moreno C, Petzold M, Child JC, Falder G, Lim S, Bacchus LJ, Engell RE, Rosenfeld L, Pallitto C, Vos T, Abrahams N and Watts CH, *Global Health. The Global Prevalence of Intimate Partner Violence against Women* (2013): 1527–1528, http://www.ncbi.nlm.nih.gov/pubmed/23788730.

Economic Forum ranked Egypt in the 135th position out of 149 countries.[38] This ranking suggests that Egypt fairs badly in the advancement of gender equality. The report revealed a number of markers for this ranking including gaps in the labour force and political participation.[39] A 2017 survey by the Thomson Reuters Foundation also reported that of the 19 world's biggest megacities, Cairo (the capital city of Egypt) posed the most serious danger to women.[40] The Freedom House World Report of 2019 added voice to these disquieting statistics by documenting that 'domestic violence, sexual harassment and female genital mutilation are still among the most acute problems in the Egyptian society.'[41] The United Nations adds that up to 99.3% of Egyptian women in one of its surveys had experienced some form of sexual violence ranging from inappropriate body touches, verbal abuse, inappropriate looks, sexual harassment to rape.[42] Activist movements have in this regard noted that 'sexual harassment is a constant in the life of any Egyptian woman regardless of her social status or class.'[43] These figures come as no surprise given the various expressions of gender-based violence in Egypt.

Gender-based violence has found expression in the Egyptian society in multiple ways including rape, sexual assault, sexual harassment, verbal abuse, inappropriate looks, unwelcome physical and body touches, female genital mutilation, early and forced marriage, domestic violence, femicide and honour killings.[44] Honour killing, one of the most extreme form of violence against women, remains alive and well in Egypt.[45] It is often justified by women's failure to adhere to societal morals and

---

[38] World Economic Forum, *The Global Gender Gap Report 2018: Egyp*t, December 17, 2018, http://reports.weforum.org/global-gender-gap-report-2018/data-explorer/#economy=EGY.

[39] *Ibid*.

[40] Thomson Reuters Foundation, *The World's Most Dangerous Megacities for Women*, (2017), http://poll2017.trust.org/.

[41] Freedom House, *Freedom in the world*, (2019), https://freedomhouse.org/report/freedom-world/2019/egypt.

[42] United Nations, *Study on ways and methods to eliminate sexual harassment in Egypt*, (2013), http://harassmap.org/en/wp-content/uploads/2014/02/287_Summaryreport_eng_low-1.pdf.

[43] Jadaliyya Reports, *Sexual Violence against Women and the Increasing Frequency of Gang Rape in Tahrir Square and its Environs*, (2013), https://www.jadaliyya.com/Details/28108.

[44] Home Office *supra* note 36, 1–49.

[45] *Ibid*.

standards. Sexual harassment has been prevalent in all spheres be they private or public. The uprisings in Egypt, which in recent times date back to 2011 when former Egyptian President (Muhammad Mubarak) was ousted, have also led to the escalation and visibility of violence against women in the public space. During these protests, women were subjected to violence in its various forms including sexual harassment and rape.[46] Women activists were on the extreme end of the vulnerability continuum in as far as these attacks are concerned. Most of the women who have taken part in these protests have been targets in these attacks, with attackers seeking to humiliate and harass them to send a message that the political sphere is a preserve of men.[47] This systematic pattern of gender-based violence became so pervasive that women activist movement labelled them 'The Circles of Hell.'[48] Extremely disturbing is the fact that the State which should ideally be a guardian of women's rights has in many instances been at the centre of such violence. The Egyptian security forces have been implicated severally in atrocities against women through acts such as sexual violence in its various forms.[49] Chinkin draws on this state of affairs to conclude that sexual violence is inextricably linked to militarism in Egypt, with state agents manipulating unrest and peaceful protests to commit atrocious acts against women.[50]

Domestic violence is an often silenced form of violence in Egypt.[51] Despite its offensiveness, it remains an acceptable practice in most societies in Egypt. Even with its seriousness, current Egyptian laws do not criminalise it. Marital rape also remains un-criminalised. A cultural practice also rampant in Egypt is female genital mutilation. Although the

---

46 Kirollos Mariam, 'The daughters of Egypt are a red line' 24 *Sur—International Journal on Human Rights*, (2014): 137–153; Amnesty International, Egypt: Investigate attacks on women protesters, (2012), https://www.amnesty.org/en/latest/news/2012/06/egypt-investigate-attacks-women-protesters/.

47 *Ibid.*

48 *Ibid.*

49 McRobie Heather, 'Sexual violence and state violence against women in Egypt 2011–2014' 7 *CMI Insight* (2014): 1–6.

50 Chinkin Christine, 'Sexual Harassment: An International Human Rights Perspective' in MacKinnon Catharine and Siegel Reva (eds) *Directions in Sexual Harassment Law* (2003): 655.

51 Home Office *supra* note 36, at 1–49.

practice is slowly reducing in recent times, studies reveal that close to 90% of Egyptian women undergo this procedure.[52] Unfortunately, a number of women who have undergone the procedure have ended up living with the severe health consequences that come with it.[53] This practice continues to be rooted in cultural norms and practices, with many communities still practicing it on a large scale despite the enactment of a law which explicitly criminalises it. Aside from this cultural practice, violence against women has also found expression in economic disadvantage. For example, the inheritance rights of men and women in Egypt are not on par.[54] The various forms of economic exclusion in inheritance, ownership of property, securing of loans, etc., place many Egyptian women in vulnerable situations that make them susceptible to abuse.

The vulnerability of women in Morocco is not any different to that of Egyptian women. Morocco, another North African, is headed by a king.[55] While the legislative and executive roles in Morocco are vested in the parliament and executive, respectively, the king wields both legislative and executive power as he elects the head of the government and also reserves the power to issue decrees.[56] These decrees impact on the entire Moroccan population including women. Women constitute 51% of the Moroccan population of 36,915,188.[57] 99% of the Moroccan population is Islam[58] and the laws enacted by the legislative authority are directly inspired by Sharia law.

Women in Morocco continue to be victims of a wide range of abuse manifesting in various forms including sexual violence, domestic

---

[52] 28 Too Many, *Egypt: The law and FGM* (2018), https://www.28toomany.org/static/media/uploads/Law%20Reports/egypt_law_report_v1_(june_2018).pdf.

[53] *Ibid.*, see also World Health Organisation, Understanding and addressing violence against women: Female genital mutilation (2012); 1–8.

[54] Australian Department of Foreign Affairs and Trade, *Country information report Egypt* (2017), https://dfat.gov.au/about-us/publications/Documents/country-information-report-egypt.pdf.

[55] BBC News, Morocco profile—Leaders, October 26, 2013, https://www.bbc.com/news/world-africa-14121440.

[56] *Ibid.*

[57] Country Meters, *Morocco Population* (2020), https://countrymeters.info/en/Morocco.

[58] *Ibid.*

violence, female genital mutilation, psychological/economic/physical harm.[59] These disquieting expressions of gender-based violence have also been fuelled by a culture of victim-blaming; a climate of impunity; flaws in the criminal justice system and discriminatory social norms. The various expressions of gender-based violence in both Egypt and Morocco cannot be exhausted. Incontestable, however, is the fact that the scale of gender-based violence in both countries has reached alarming levels, with no section of women spared. Amidst such pervasiveness, a question could be raised—what is the law in Egypt and Morocco and what role does it play in elimination of gender-based violence and access to justice? This question is answered next.

2.2 International Commitments and National Legislative reforms in Morocco and Egypt

Laws are a major feature in all democratic societies. Klugman submits that they can 'play a symbolic role, by indicating that [gender-based violence] is socially unacceptable.'[60] He adds that where sanctions are effectively administered, laws may 'serve a deterrent function.'[61] In Egypt, progress has been registered, with some laws explicitly addressing gender-based violence. Progress can be gleaned from both the international and national legal regimes and activist movements in Egypt can be partly credited for this progress. Amidst the pervasiveness of gender-based violence, these movements have not remained silent. Organised groups of men and women, young and old, have been relentless in their demands for action to be taken in response to this plague.[62] Various activist movements, civil society organisations and individuals have not wavered in calling on the Egyptian government to address the

59 Morocco World News, *New Survey Shows High Rates of Violence Against Women in Morocco*, May 15, 2019, https://www.moroccoworldnews.com/2019/05/273120/survey-high-rates-violence-women-morocco/.

60 Klugman Jeni, *Gender Based Violence and the Law, World Development Report* (2017) 1.

61 *Ibid*.

62 Allam Nermin, 'Smoke and mirrors: State-sponsored feminism in post-uprising Egypt,' 86 *Social Research: An International Quarterly* (2019): 365–386.

alarming cases of gender-based violence. At the heart of these movements' campaigns have been calls to put an end to violence against women and for reforms to be made to laws with a view to ensuring that victims of violence access justice. These campaigns have seen the Egyptian government take action and indeed, there is evidence of some reforms being made including amendments to the constitution and criminalisation of sexual harassment.

Regarding Egypt's international legal framework, reference is made to treaties as a source of international law as it features prominently in the gender-based violence discourse. Generally, international treaties can play a role in standard-setting. Some treaties have provided comprehensive definitions to acts of violence against women and as such, provide a useful framework at the national level.[63] For activist movements, these instruments have formed a basis for advocacy and campaigns. In terms of Egypt's Constitution, Egypt is 'committed to the agreements, covenants, and international conventions of human rights that were ratified by Egypt. They have the force of law after publication in accordance with the specified circumstances.'[64] Effectively, Egypt is monist in terms of its reception of international treaties in its legal system. This means that the treaties ratified by Egypt do not require any further national enactment on the part of the country's legislative authority to have legal force in Egypt. In practice, however, the courts in Egypt have not been keen on directly applying treaties to criminal proceedings before them.

Egypt has ratified a host of treaties with a bearing on elimination of gender-based violence. These include the International Covenant on Civil and Political Rights of 1966, the United Nations Convention Against Torture 1987, the African Charter on Human and Peoples' Rights of 1981 and the CEDAW of 1979. A progressive interpretation of all these treaties places an obligation on Egypt to not just address violence against, but also eliminate it in all its forms. It is not feasible

[63] See e.g. the United Nations the Protocol to Prevent, Suppress and Punish Trafficking in Persons, Especially women and Children, supplementing the United Nations Convention against Transnational Organised Crime (2002). This Protocol has an explicit definition of 'human Trafficking' thus providing states parties without national legislation on human trafficking a useful framework at the national level.

[64] Constitution of Egypt (2014) 93.

to discuss all these treaties comprehensively. Therefore, focus is placed on a few issues pertaining to the CEDAW because this is the only international treaty on the rights of women that Egypt is party to. In terms of treaty law, Egypt is under obligation to enforce the provisions contained in the CEDAW in good faith.[65] The Committee on Elimination of Violence against Women, in its General Comment 19, mandates states 'to ensure that laws against family violence and abuse, rape, sexual assault and other gender-based violence give adequate protection to all women, and respect their integrity and dignity.'[66] This Committee has previously called on Egypt to take action on gender-based violence including 'the expeditious adoption of a comprehensive law criminalising all forms of violence against women, including domestic violence, marital rape, sexual violence, sexual harassment, institutional violence and crimes committed in the name of honor.'[67] This call has, however, hardly been implemented.

In light of the above mandate, the obligations on Egypt to protect women have been cut out. The above guidelines and many others issued by the Committee on Elimination of Discrimination against Women provide a useful framework for Egypt as a party to this treaty to prevent and hold perpetrators to account. However, the effectiveness of these standards has been undermined by the various reservations that Egypt has made to key provisions. Noteworthy reservations are article 2 which mandates states to 'condemn discrimination against women in all its forms'; article 9 on 'equal rights with men with respect of the nationality of their children'; article 16 on elimination of 'discrimination against women in all matters relating to marriage and family relations'; and

65 Vienna Convention on the Law of Treaties (1969) 26.

66 Committee on Elimination of Discrimination Against Women, General Recommendations adopted by the Committee on Elimination of Discrimination Against Women (General recommendation No. 19: Violence against women (1992) 24; see also Committee on the Elimination of Discrimination against Women, General recommendation No. 35 on gender-based violence against women, updating general recommendation No. 19 (2017).

67 Committee on the Elimination of Discrimination against Women, Concluding observations of the Committee.

on the Elimination of Discrimination against Women: Egypt, (2010), http://www.reproductiverights.org/sites/crr.civicactions.net/files/documents/CEDAW%20Concluding%20Observations%20Egypt.pdf.

article 29(2) on dispute resolution between states regarding the interpretation of provisions of the CEDAW. With all these being key provisions in advancing gender equality and criminal accountability, these reservations undermine the otherwise excellent enforcement standard enshrined in the CEDAW. Noteworthy, while there are other international treaties that would have had a reinforcing effect on criminal accountability for gender-based violence, Egypt has not ratified them. This is arguably deliberate as Egypt does not want to be bound by a women's rights regime that challenges its deeply entrenched social patterns of discrimination against women. Examples of such key treaties are the Protocol to the African Charter on Human and Peoples' Rights of Women in Africa (Maputo Protocol), which remains the most comprehensive treaty on issues of women in Africa.[68] Egypt has also not ratified the Rome Statute of the International Criminal Court which also offers a comprehensive framework for prosecution of international crimes relating to gender-based violence.[69]

At the national level, various commendable reforms are noticeable. Notably, in the Constitution, adopted in 2014, Egypt 'commits to protection of women against all forms of violence.'[70] The Constitution also guarantees equality regardless of a person's gender.[71] In terms of legislation, the Penal Code Act of Egypt criminalises various acts of gender-based violence including rape, sexual assault, sexual harassment and female genital mutilation.[72] This progress is indeed commendable. However, these laws can be criticised for not going far enough in addressing violence against women and ensuring that perpetrators of this type of violence are punished. For example, while sexual violence has been criminalised since 2014, it is notable that where there is no intent to obtain sexual benefits, no crime is committed and no charges can be preferred. The challenge with this kind of restrictive criminalisation is that it ignores the subtle acts of harassment against women such

68 Protocol to the African Charter on Human and Peoples' Rights of Women in Africa (2003).

69 Rome Statute of the International Criminal Court (1998).

70 Constitution of Egypt, 11.

71 *Ibid.*, Marginal note.

72 See Articles 267, 268, 269, 289 and 242 of the Egypt Penal Code No. 58 of 1937 relating to the crimes of rape, sexual assault, sexual harassment and female genital mutilation.

as verbal harassment and inappropriate looks. Such forms of violence, though subtle, are the most pervasive and when condoned, could escalate into more severe violations such as rape. Mackinnon explains that marginalisation of this kind persists because they are considered trivial and not worth pursuing.[73] In addition, despite the criminalisation of female genital mutilation, the definition of the crime leaves loopholes for abuse. For example, in terms of article 242 of the Penal Code act of Egypt, female genital mutilation means 'acts of female genital mutilation, by removing any of the external female genital organs, whether in part or in whole, or by inflicting any injuries to these organs without medical justification.' However, in the absence of a definition for 'medical justification,' the law becomes counterproductive. These provisions have been abused as they now constitute exceptional circumstances under which female genital mutilation occurs.[74] Furthermore, there are many acts of gender-based violence not criminalised by these laws including domestic violence, marital rape and human trafficking.

In Morocco, legal reforms have unquestionably been a crucial factor in the advancement of women's rights and the improvement of their status in society. For several decades, Morocco has been trying to amend its national laws with a view to promoting gender equality. Commitment to this goal has seen Morocco ratify several international human rights treaties with a bearing on gender equality. For example, Morocco is party to the International Covenants on Civil and Political Rights (ICCPR), the Economic, Social and Cultural Rights (ICESCR)[75] and the Convention on the Elimination of All Forms of Discrimination against Women (CEDAW).[76] In addition, Morocco has taken part in a number of regional and international conferences whose aim has been to

---

73 Mackinnon, cited in Kirollos *supra* note 46 at 140.

74 28 Too Many *supra* note 52 at 1–12.

75 International Covenant on Economic, Social and Cultural Rights, Rapport parallèle des ONG marocaines au quatrième rapport périodique du Gouvernement marocain sur la mise en oeuvre du Pacte International relatif aux Droits Economiques, Sociaux et Culturels, 2006–2012, https://tbinternet.ohchr.org/Treaties/CESCR/Shared%20Documents/MAR/INT_CESCR_CSS_MAR_21229_F.pdf.

76 UN Femmes Maghreb, *Le Maroc adopte le protocole facultatif à la CEDAW*, 27 août 2015, https://maghreb.unwomen.org/fr/actualites-evenements/actualites/2015/08/op-cedaw-maroc.

advance women's rights.[77] At the national level, the most recent Constitution of Morocco of 2011[78] establishes the primacy of international law in the domestic legal order and requires national laws to be harmonised with international standards in all areas including gender. Article 19 of the Constitution enshrines the principle of equal citizenship and establishes a body responsible for advancing progress in this area. Article 22 goes on to prohibit discrimination on the basis of sex. This provision also prohibits the practice of 'harming the physical or moral integrity of anyone, under any circumstances and by any person, private or public.' It adds that 'no one shall inflict on another, under any pretext whatsoever, cruel, inhuman or degrading treatment or punishment, or treatment which violates dignity.' With Morocco's commitment to international law and the very strong entrenchments in the Constitution, there is a reasonable expectation that its national legal framework should be up to speed with the international standards on women's rights.

Indeed, there is no denying that reforms to the Constitution and Morocco's commitment to international law have, to some extent, impacted on the national legal framework of Morocco. This can be gleaned from a number of national laws. For example, this progress is noticeable in the Penal Code Act of Morocco which now criminalises sexual harassment.[79] This Act also provides for increased penalties for the crime of rape against women.[80] This reform in the penal law of Morocco can be attributed partly to efforts by civil society organisations and parliamentary groups. The pressure mounted by these groups saw the Moroccan Parliament adopt a legislative amendment in 2014 which struck down article 475(2) of the Criminal Code. Prior to amendment, Article 475(2) provided that when the victim marries the perpetrator, 'he can no longer be prosecuted except by persons empowered to demand

[77] EUROMED Gender Equality Programme, *National Situation Analysis Report: Women's Human Rights and Gender Equality, Promoting Equality between Men and Women in the Euro-Mediterranean Region* (2008–2011), http://bnm.bnrm.ma:86/Reforme_de_la_constitution/EUROMED%20_%20Rapport%20national%20d'analyse%20de%20la%20situation%20_%20Rights%20human%20of%20women%20and%20equality%20between%20the%20sex.pdf.

[78] Constitution of Morocco July 1, 2011. Official Bulletin, 2011-06-17, No. 5952bis.

[79] EuroMed Rights, *Morocco: Situation report on violence against women* (2018) 1, https://euromedrights.org/wp-content/uploads/2018/03/Factsheet-VAW-Morocco-EN-Mar-2018.pdf.

[80] Penal Code, Article 88-1 and article 404.

the annulment of the marriage and then only after the annulment has been proclaimed.' With the repealing of this provision, rapists can no longer escape prosecution by choosing to marry their victims after they attain the age of eighteen.[81] With this framework in place, a good pace is set for accountability for violence against women in Morocco.

However, despite the above political and legal advances, several structural inequalities remain, particularly, in the Family Code, the Criminal Code, the Nationality Code and the Labour Code. In addition, the Penal Code is not comprehensive enough to cover the various expressions of violence against women in Morocco. There are limited legal provisions for the effective protection of women against violence and discrimination specifically directed against them on the basis of their gender. Notably, under articles 486 and 488, rape is considered a crime against morality and not a crime against the person.[82] Thus, marital rape and psychological violence are not criminalised because they are generally not considered to be against the morals of people in Morocco. This illustrates the persistence of a conservative and patriarchal posture. This posture determines the law and its application. There is therefore a link between social and legal norms in as far as gender equality in Morocco is concerned.

Despite the effort made by the government, there are several gaps in the legislative and regulatory framework. There is profound resistance especially when it comes to enforcement of these laws. As a result, there is an apparent gap between the legal framework and the actual practice.[83] This played out in Morocco with the enactment of the first Moroccan Personal Status Code (Moudawana) in 1957.[84] With this Status Code in place, Islamic doctrine and customary law were applied simultaneously by establishing 'a single code of positive law in conformity with Islamic

---

[81] Fadoua Benkhadda, *How NGOs helped change Moroccan law on rapists marrying their victims*, 7 février 2014, The Guardian, https://www.theguardian.com/global-development/poverty-matters/2014/feb/07/ngo-change-morocco-rape-law.

[82] EuroMed Rights, *supra* note 79.

[83] *Rapport analytique sur la situation des violences faites aux femmes et aux filles et des avancées réalisées au niveau du continent de l'Afrique*, November 2018, https://knowledge.uclga.org/IMG/pdf/africities_rapport_analytique_vef_23.11.2018_.pdf.

[84] The Moudawana: Dahirs of November 22, December 18, 1957, January 25, February 20 and April 4,1958.

law.'[85] In reality, this legal framework which was associated with religion only reinforced patriarchy and disparities between men and women. As a result, women were placed under the guardianship of husbands based on the assumption that husbands are the breadwinners in a home. It took relentless activism and advocacy by feminist movements and associations, accompanied by political will, to enact the Family Code (NCF) in 2004. It is the enactment of this Code that established a new balance between spouses and introduced the principle of gender equality. This was particularly evident in the definition of marriage.[86] This 2004 legislation on marriage and divorce is in keeping with the contemporary way of living of many Moroccans today. Thus, the law not only breathed life into the contemporary requirements of marriage; it also enshrined rules based largely on classical Muslim law.[87]

While the legal reforms are a representation of progress, there is a lack of monitoring and evaluation mechanisms of government policies on gender.[88] In addition, the protection provided by the 2004 Moudawana is subject to exceptions which undermine the good intentions of these laws and create loopholes for abuse of women.[89] For example, despite the prohibition of early and forced marriage in very strong terms, it is still practiced in exceptional circumstances. As already pointed out, while sexual violence by persons other than partners is effectively addressed, marital rape is still not a crime. The same challenge remains regarding the crime of sexual harassment. Sexual harassment remains pervasive and unabated in public places and other uncontrolled spaces because the current law defines harassment only in employer-employee settings. In addition, sexual violence by intimate couples has not been included in

[85] Kamal Mellakh, *De la Moudawwana au nouveau Code de la famille au Maroc: une réforme à l'épreuve des connaissances et perceptions ordinaires* (2005–2006), http://journals.openedition.org/anneemaghreb/78.

[86] *Ibid.*

[87] *Ibid.*

[88] Lara Deramaix, Julien Moriceau, *Quelle justice pour les femmes au Maroc ? Analyse des parcours de justice,* (2019) 8, https://www.asf.be/wp-content/uploads/2019/12/ASF-justice-femmes-Maroc-2019-6-2.pdf.

[89] EuroMed Rights *supra* note 79.

Law 103.13.[90] This law is known as the law 'to combat violence against women' and it came into force in September 2018. In addition, the government itself has made contradictory statements as to whether or not marital rape is a crime in Morocco. In November 2011, the Moroccan government told the United Nations Committee on Torture that marital rape is in fact a crime under Moroccan criminal law.[91] However, in a meeting with an alliance of Moroccan NGOs in 2013, the Minister of Justice stated that it was impossible to criminalise marital rape because 'you cannot deprive a man of what is rightfully his.'[92] These and many gaps have led to several protests among human rights organisations and feminist associations.[93]

Moreover, even with the laws in place in Morocco, there has hardly been any guidance for legal practitioners. This has resulted to recourse to arbitrariness by judicial officers in their interpretation of the Family Code.[94] Not coincidentally, the decisions of the courts highlight a trend in judicial opinion that is not systematically favourable to women.[95] The approach of these judicial officers should perhaps be less of a shock as the new law has not changed the old values of the family in which the mentalities of the judicial officers are anchored.[96] Morocco has indeed carried out several legislative reforms aimed at strengthening women's rights and gender equality within the legal system. This is the culmination of a long process to which feminist movements and associations have

---

[90] Law No. 103-13 on combating violence against women promulgated by Dahir No. 1-18-19 of 5 Jumada II 1439 (February 22, 2018); Bulletin Officiel No. 6688 of 21 Shawwal 1439 (July 5, 2018) 1384.

[91] Morocco: Submission to the Committee on Economic, Social and Cultural Rights Relating to the Economic, Social and Cultural Rights of Women, 56th Session, by the Advocates for Human Rights, https://www.theadvocatesforhumanrights.org/uploads/morocco_esc_shadow_report_august_2015.pdf.

[92] *Ibid.*

[93] *Ibid.*

[94] *Ibid.*

[95] Murgue Bérénice, *La Moudawana: les dessous d'une réforme sans précédent, Les Cahiers de l'Orient,* 2011/2 (N° 102) 15–29, https://www.cairn.info/revue-les-cahiers-de-l-orient-2011-2-page-15.htm.

[96] Lara Deramaix and Julien Moriceau, *Quelle justice pour les femmes au Maroc? Analyse des parcours de justice,* (2019) 48, https://www.asf.be/wp-content/uploads/2019/12/ASF-justice-femmes-Maroc-2019-6-2.pdf.

made a major contribution in the service of gender equality. However, the realities on the ground reveal that the implementation of these laws and women's access to justice are marred by discriminatory institutional and social practices.[97] This problem is even more daunting because of practical difficulties such as the imprecise nature of support and legal measures for women victims of violence. For example, the laws do not provide for financial assistance for survivors. They also don't clearly define the role of the government in providing support and services to victims of domestic violence, including shelter, health services, mental health care, legal advice and hotlines.[98] In addition to this, social and cultural barriers as well as economic dependence remain major obstacles to women's equality and their quest for justice. In a United Nations Women's report on justice, Naciri illustrates this position by giving the example of a woman who sues a family member or her spouse in court.[99] While this is a move she is to be commended for because of her boldness to ensure that justice is advanced, from a societal point of view, this is generally viewed as embarrassing and shameful. As a result, victims of gender-based violence continue to be socially misunderstood.[100]

There is therefore no denying that there are systematic barriers to women's quest for justice in Morocco.[101] To confirm this, a report recently published by the International Commission of Jurists has called

---

[97] EuroMed Rights *supra* note 79, at 3. See also Lubaale on the chronic gaps in legal framework on prosecution of criminal offences in Africa. Lubaale Emma Charlene, *Bridging the justice gap in the prosecution of acquaintance child sexual abuse: a case of South Africa and Uganda* (PhD Thesis, University of Pretoria 2015); Lubaale Emma Charlene, 'Admissibility of evidence presented by children in sex abuse prosecutions in Uganda: The case for reforms' *African Journal of Law and Criminology* 5(2015): 1–15; Lubaale Emma Charlene, 'The crime of attempted suicide in Uganda: the need for reforms to the law' (2017)(4)(1) *Journal of Law, Society and Development* 1–19; Lubaale Emma Charlene, 'Human rights reforms of criminal law in Africa' in Addaney M, Nyarko M and Boshoff E (eds) *Governance, Human Rights, and Political Transformation in Africa.* Palgrave Macmillan (2020) 149–171.

[98] Lucy Lamble, *UN Women report: Access to justice in Morocco*, The Guardian, July 6, 2011, https://www.theguardian.com/global-development/2011/jul/06/un-women-morocco-justice.

[99] Naciri Rebea, *The women's movement and political discourse in Morocco, United Nations Research Institute for Social Development Geneva*, 1–28 (1998), https://www.econstor.eu/bitstream/10419/148779/1/862525705.pdf.

[100] Naïma Chikhaoui, *Surpasser des obstacles en matière d'égalité: le cas du Maroc*, Quaderns de la Mediterrània, 2015, https://www.iemed.org/observatori/arees-danalisi/arxius-adjunts/qm22/94Quaderns_obstaclesFemmesMaroc_NChikhaoui.pdf.

[101] *Ibid.*

on Morocco to eradicate legal obstacles and discriminatory judicial attitudes that compromise women's access to justice for redress of sexual and gender-based violence.[102] Commendably, the parliament passed Law 103.13[103] in response to violence against women in 2018. The law has of course brought new protection measures for victims in the context of Morocco. Feminist associations, however, consider this law 'incomplete and ambiguous, leaving a wide margin of impunity for rapists.'[104] It has also been observed that the law does not provide a comprehensive definition for the various forms of violence against women. In addition, the law does not provide a definition of domestic violence and does not consider the criminalisation of marital rape. Violence against women also takes the form of psychological and economic abuse. However, all these acts of violence are not captured by this law. Moreover, while a number of women including single mothers, disabled women and migrant women are more vulnerable to abuse than others,[105] the law accords no regard to such vulnerability.

Regarding 'single mothers,' it is notable that they are generally considered by the Moroccan society as women who have children outside the framework of legal marriage. The children of these women are defined by law as illegitimate.[106] Until recently, these children and their mothers were not protected by law. Despite reforms regarding this issue, the application of the law is still largely imbued with Islamic Sharia. Of course, there have been some advances. For example, the Civil Status Act No. 37-99 of 2002 allows single mothers to choose a family name for their child. Similarly, the Family Code made it possible to recognise children born during the period of engagement. But even with these

---

102 International Commission of Jurists, *Morocco: Remove Obstacles to Women's and Girls' Access to Justice for Sexual and Gender-Based Violence—New ICJ Report*, June 28, 2019, https://www.icj.org/morocco-remove-obstacles-to-womens-and-girls-access-to-justice-for-sexual-and-gender-based-violence-new-icj-report/.

103 Dahir No. 1-18-19 of 5 Jumada II 1439 (February 22, 2018) enacting Act No. 103-13 on combating violence against women.

104 Laila Zerrour, La loi 103-13 entre en vigueur ce mercredi: Ce qui va changer, aujourdui.ma, 11 September 2018, https://aujourdhui.ma/societe/la-loi-103-13-entre-en-vigueur-ce-mercredi-ce-qui-va-changer.

105 EuroMed Rights *supra* note 79, 2.

106 Schlumpf E, 'The Legal Status of Children Born out of Wedlock in Morocco' 4 *Electronic Journal of Islamic and Middle Eastern Law* (2014): 1–26.

legislative reforms, the laws remain too weak to change the status quo.[107] Moreover, the texts of these reforms still remain inapplicable to cases of women who are raped or become pregnant as a result of consensual relations outside marriage. The exclusion suffered by such women increases their vulnerability to violence and makes it an uphill task for them to access justice.

Furthermore, Act No. 103-03 has certain shortcomings with regard to the provisions on protection, remedies and sanctions relating to domestic violence.[108] Although Morocco is a signatory to several international law conventions and recognises the primacy of international instruments over national legislation, the 2017 Universal Periodic Review (UPR) by the United Nations Human Rights Council noted several problems in its assessment of Morocco's human rights record,[109] partly due to gender bias. Notably, this legislation continues to consider traditional concepts without considering international standards relating to the definition of gender-based violence.[110] An example in this regard relates to the distinction in punishment of rape which is motivated by morality or honour and rape which is motivated by an attack on the physical and psychological integrity of the rape victim.[111] The former is punished less severely than the latter. As a result, women remain at risk of violence because certain forms of rape (such as honour rape) are considered less harmful that other forms of rape. Challenges also abound regarding effective access to justice and judicial remedies for victims of violence.

---

107 Asmaa Bassouri, *Maroc: la tourmente des mères célibataires*, Contrepoints, April 17, 2018, https://www.contrepoints.org/2018/04/17/314254-maroc-la-tourmente-des-meres-celibataires.

108 *Ibid*.

109 General Assembly United Nations, *National report submitted in accordance with paragraph 5 of the annex to Human Rights Council resolution* 16/2, A/HRC/WG.6/27/MAR/1, February 20, 2017, https://documents-dds-ny.un.org/doc/UNDOC/GEN/G17/037/94/PDF/G1703794.pdf?OpenElement.

110 Aïda Kheireddine, *Pourquoi la nouvelle loi marocaine contre la violence faite aux femmes n'est pas suffisante pour changer le Status quo*, Heinrich Böll Stiftung, April 13, 2018, https://ma.boell.org/fr/2018/04/13/pourquoi-la-nouvelle-loi-marocaine-contre-la-violence-faite-aux-femmes-nest-pas.

111 *Ibid*.

Overall, it is indisputable that the silence that historically surrounded violence against women in Morocco has been broken.[112] It is also notable that a framework for dialogue on issues of gender-based violence is gradually being established. The State has also promoted constructive engagement by including gender issues on its national political agenda. This has resulted in the implementation of various instruments women's rights. Furthermore, widespread awareness of violence against women continues to gain ground at different levels in society. In this regard, Moroccan feminists strive to promote women's empowerment through education on women's rights. In addition, they raise awareness of family law and the labour code through their Non-Government Organisations (NGOs) and community groups. Women's activist movements continue to contribute significantly to democracy in Morocco, due to their greater involvement in social and political affairs. Their influence has also been bolstered by their access to the media. The critical issues that these movements raise have opened up new avenues of reflection on issues of gender-based violence and other gender-related issues.[113]

It is also notable that in the past, victims of gender-based violence, especially sexual violence, suffered in silence for fear of their honour and that of their families being undermined. They were concerned about 'what people would say.' As a result, they did not dare to complain, besides, there was a legal vacuum for complaints to be made. Irrefutably, a lot has changed over the years in terms of women's willingness to report cases of gender-based violence. However, it should be stressed that gender-discriminatory social norms and attitudes continue to significantly hinder the realisation of justice for victims. It is undeniable that Egypt and Morocco have made progress despite the multiple flaws that have been identified. Even with these legal reforms, gender-based violence is rife and criminal accountability for this kind of violence remains a far-reaching goal. The next subsection engages with the social norms in Egypt and Morocco with a view to assessing their effect on the

---

[112] Safaa Monqid, *Violence against Women in Public Spaces: The Case of Morocco* (2012), http://journals.openedition.org/ema/3011.

[113] EuroMed Rights *supra* note 79 at 1.

law's effectiveness in ensuring criminal accountability and elimination of gender-based violence.

2.3 Social and Cultural Norms in Egypt and Morocco: Implication on Criminal Accountability for Gender-Based Violence

'It is a "natural duty to rape" women who wear revealing clothes in public places like ripped jeans.'[114] The foregoing statement was a comment by an Egyptian lawyer during a national debate aired on Egyptian national television. The lawyer made this remark during a discussion revolving around legal reforms to address gender-based violence in Egypt. At first glance, this would appear to be a random harsh statement. On closer scrutiny, however, the remark speaks volumes about Egypt's societal expectations of women as well as the power that men wield over women's behaviour. With statements such as this coming from a legal practitioner, who is expected to know better given his exposure to current legal standards, it is hard to fathom what the attitudes of those who are ignorant of the law would be.

Many African societies, as the case is elsewhere, are anchored in strong social morals and values. For many in Africa, life without allegiance to any form of social norm is no existence at all. Idang submits in this regard that 'the culture of a people is what marks them out distinctively from other human societies in the family of humanity.'[115] In traditional African societies, these norms shaped the society and though mostly unwritten, they set the standard for acceptable and unacceptable behaviour in the various African societies. Not all African cultures are the same, thus, it must be set out from the outset that there is a profound diversity in belief, traditions, norms, interpretations to religion and teachings on tradition. There are, however, a number of cross-cutting values that many traditional African societies subscribed to and still

[114] Selby Daniele, *Outrage Over Egyptian Lawyer Saying It's a 'Duty To Rape' Women* (2017), https://www.globalcitizen.org/en/content/egypt-rape-violence-against-women-lawyer-tv/.

[115] Idang Gabriel, *African cultures and values* 16 *Phronimon* (2015): 97.

invoke to this day. Noteworthy is the value of 'Ubuntu' which is literally interpreted to mean respect for 'humanity.' This value cuts across African societies and it has found various expressions across these respective societies. These and many other values have over the years crystalised to inform development of the customary laws across African countries. In most African countries, customary law forms part of the legal system and remains applicable to the extent that it is in agreement with human rights standards and the constitution.[116] It is to be conceded, however, that while African cultures, customs and norms continue to shape African societies, they have also been avenues through which violence against women thrives.

In the context of Egypt, as elsewhere, these customs have been embedded in social norms on gender roles. The Egyptian society is predominantly patriarchal and while patriarchy is an issue that cuts across continents, for many African societies it remains deeply entrenched. With this set-up, men are generally privileged.[117] They also assume power and authority over women and women's behaviour.[118] There is an expectation on men to provide for women in conformity to the gender stereotypes about masculinity. In turn, women are to submit to the authority of men and often, this is accompanied by abuse. In Egypt, these norms are a justification for acts of violence against women including domestic violence, marital rape, sexual harassment, wife battering and exclusion in the area of property ownership and inheritance.[119] Through these norms, various acts of gender-based violence have been normalised and this has contributed to the reluctance of the government to criminalise various acts such marital rape and domestic violence. This has further entrenched the culture of impunity in cases of gender-based violence.

Generally, gender-based violence is part of a larger problem of tolerance of discriminatory social norms. For instance, violence against

---

[116] See e.g. Section 39(2) of the Constitution of South Africa which provides that 'when interpreting any legislation, and when developing the common law or customary law, every court, tribunal or forum must promote the spirit, purport and objects of the Bill of Rights.'.

[117] Home Office *supra* note 36, at 18.

[118] McRobie, *Sexual violence and state violence against women in Egypt* (2014) 1–49.

[119] *Ibid*.

women in the name of 'having a good time' or 'entertaining' oneself remains a common practice in Egypt.[120] This has been at the expense of women who have in this regard become sources of such 'entertainment,' or rather, victimisation. Victimisation has been exacerbated by societal expectations on how women should behave. Failure to conduct oneself in accordance with expectations such as 'decent' dressing has often led to victim-blaming when violence occurs.[121] These norms have also condoned the practice of female genital mutilation which, as already alluded to, remains rife in Egypt. A practice that has been in existence for thousands of years, female genital mutilation persists mainly because of the social stigma that comes with failure to undergo it. Those who fail to undergo the procedure are considered to be impure, less feminine and unclean.[122] The failure to undergo it also reduces a woman's marriageability with some men keen on not committing to such women.[123] Many women therefore end up going through the procedure not out of will but to meet these expectations. One therefore gathers that the weight that social norms throw at women in Egypt is burdensome. Not coincidentally, the United Nations Rapporteur on Violence against women has aptly underscored that 'states must acknowledge that violence against women is not the root problem but that violence occurs because other forms of discrimination are allowed to flourish.'[124]

Peculiar to Egypt's discriminatory practices is the intersectionality between social norms and religion. Over 90% of Egypt's population is

[120] Kirollos *supra* note 46.

[121] Cairo Institute for Human Rights Studies, *Circles of hell from Tahrir to Zagazig?* April 4, 2017,
https://cihrs.org/egypt-circles-of-hell-from-tahrir-to-zagazig-when-will-the-normalization-of-sexual-violence-against-women-end/?lang=en.

[122] United Nations Development Programme, *Combatting Female Genital Mutilation in Egypt* (2015), http://www.undp.org/content/dam/undp/fgminegypt/index.html.

[123] *Ibid*.

[124] Rashida Manjoo, *Statement to the General Assembly*, October 3, 2011, http://www.un.org/womenwatch/daw/documents/ga66/RAPPORT_on_VAW.PDF.

Muslim[125] and Islam is recognised as the official national religion.[126] Most of the social norms that have founded a basis for gender-based violence in Egypt have been justified by religion. Linking these discriminatory social norms to the Islamic faith has, however, been questioned. Commentators warn that the interpretation that some religious practitioners give religious texts are to be taken cautiously as they may not always be a true representation of Sharia law.[127] Religious interpretations in justification of the subservient position of women in society abound. Noteworthy are interpretations which accord men the status of headship in the family and as breadwinners in the home.[128] Men are also to take responsibility of women and to exercise guardianship over their homes.[129] By virtue of these roles, they are to have authority over women and children. Aside from these general principles, various interpretations of the Quran have been relied on to justify acts of violence such as wife battering and marital rape.[130]

It is, however, notable that there are interpretations that have adopted alternative views to the same religious texts in the Quran and have in fact offered interpretations that are pro-women's rights.[131] In the light of such alternative approaches, some commentators have concluded that even states which subscribe to Islam as the national religion can hardly be justified in relying on Sharia to condone gender-based violence.[132] Commentators take the view that these governments maintain discriminatory social norms to legitimise themselves in political leadership rather

---

[125] United States of America Embassy-Egypt, *2018 Report on International Religious Freedom: Egypt* (2018), https://eg.usembassy.gov/2018-report-on-international-religious-freedom-egypt/; EuroMed Rights: Egypt, *Report on Violence against Women* (2018), https://euromedrights.org/wp-content/uploads/2018/11/201811-Gender-VAW-Factsheet-FR-PDF-MSH.pdf.

[126] The Constitution of Egypt (2014) 2. In terms of article 2 of the Egyptian Constitution 'Islam is the religion of the state and Arabic is its official language. The principles of Islamic Sharia are the principle source of legislation'.

[127] Hajjar Lisa, 'Religion, state power, and domestic violence in Muslim societies: A framework for comparative analysis' 29 *Law & Social Inquiry* (2004): 1–38.

[128] *Ibid.*

[129] *Ibid.*

[130] *Ibid.*

[131] *Ibid.*

[132] *Ibid.*

than to adhere to Sharia law.[133] Indeed, for many political leaders, the support that comes from a society that is deeply rooted in discriminatory norms is so appealing a benefit to be sacrificed on the altar of women's rights. This perhaps explains why, despite the well-established standards on women's rights, reforms to discriminatory laws and criminal accountability for gender-based violence in Egypt has proceeded at an extremely slow pace. Egypt continues to hold back in enacting comprehensive laws on redress of gender-based violence as to do so is to upset the majority population whose votes keep them in power.

The situation is not any different in Morocco. Indeed, since independence, the situation of women and perceptions about their status have undergone a significant evolution. This is partly attributable to the emergence of dynamic movements for the promotion and defines of women's rights. These organisations have campaigned for and sparked debates on issues of citizenship, modernity, equal rights and calls for improvement of the status of women in a society undergoing major reconfiguration.[134] In Morocco, social relations between the sexes have been historically and socially regulated in a hierarchical manner. The patriarchal system has had a major influence on such hierarchy. These social relations have mainly manifested themselves in spaces of socialisation in which the attributes of femininity and masculinity are defined. In this regard, men and women have been assigned gendered roles, with these roles generally placing women in positions of disadvantage. Thus, 'language, traditions, social norms and cultural representations work to confine each sex to its status, in a hierarchical configuration.'[135]

This model of the construction of gender social relations and power relations between classes has been discussed by sociologists and humanists. The first field surveys in this regard were carried out by Paul Pascon and his team in the 1970s.[136] The results of their work were published and they contributed to the genesis of a sociology on women in Morocco

---

[133] *Ibid.*

[134] Rahma Bourquia, *Gender and the Reconfiguration of Moroccan Society* (2015), http://books.openedition.org/cjb/1041.

[135] *Ibid.*

[136] Paul Pascon, cited by Hassan Rachik and Rahma Bourqia in *Sociology in Morocco: Theory and Research* (2011), http://journals.openedition.org/sociologies/3719.

which had earlier been initiated by Malika Belghiti in 1969.[137] At the end of the 1970s, a reflection led by a team of researchers was initiated on the issue of legal status and the family code.[138] Sociologist Fatima Mernissi initiated a new wave of research on feminist studies through her studies focusing on women in Moroccan Islamic tradition. From then on, women's rights issues emerged as a theme of academic research.[139] This trend has been reinforced by the funding from International Organisations. These organisations have over the years pushed for the development of research studies to serve as a basis for advocacy[140] and to inform law reform by decision-makers.[141] This is how work on deconstruction of the gender issues was initiated and continues to gradually gain ground in Morocco. On the whole, the redefinition othe legal framework on gender in Morocco stems from research, domestic activism and international pressure.

Despite the activism on women's rights, there is still a very strong denial of violence against women among representatives of civil society organisations. Recently, a guest on the set of a private television channel called Télé Maroc tried to explain rape. His explanation was not with a view to denouncing it or raising awareness, but rather, to legitimise it. He stated that 'rape exists because everyone has a sexual instinct. A desire that must be satisfied. When it is repressed, it gives rise to rape.'[142] The guest's views were an attack on victims and did nothing more than legitimise the pervasive crime of rape. But this is perhaps less surprising because according to Freedom House, violence perpetuated against women remains 'a problem that is sometimes justified in social or even religious terms.'[143] In addition to these justifications, a patriarchal

---

137 *Ibid*.

138 *Ibid.*

139 Rahma Bourquia *supra* note 134.

140 *Ibid*.

141 Dahir n° 1-04-22 of February 3,2004 promulgating law n° 70-03 on the Family Code. Official Gazette, 2005-10-06, n° 535.

142 'Video. A petition launched against a gynecologist who claims to understand rape' H24 Info, June 12, 2020, https://www.h24info.ma/maroc/video-une-petition-lancee-contre-un-gynecologue-qui-affirme-comprendre-le-viol/.

143 United States of America Embassy-Egypt, *2018 Report on International Religious Freedom: Egypt* (2018), https://eg.usembassy.gov/2018-report-on-international-religious-freedom-egypt/.

view of gender roles persists at different levels in society, thus, hindering the application of the principle of equality in all respects. Furthermore, there are aspects within the justice system which make women more vulnerable, thus, making it difficult for them to access justice.[144] In this regard, a study has shown that 'the way in which justice is thought out and put into practice undermines the idea of women's right.'[145] The study reveals 'a lack of means to enhance the spirit of the law and account for its effectiveness.'[146] It must be noted also that the religious framework, which was the only source of legislation on family law under the former Moudawana, leaves room for more relativism. Unfortunately, invoking relativism has not always worked to the benefit of women and to the advancement of their rights.[147]

All considered, laws have been enacted; Constitutions amended; and international treaties ratified; yet, criminal accountability and elimination of gender-based violence continue to be a challenge in both Egypt and Morocco. This state of affairs sends out a loud and clear message—elimination of all forms of violence against women in these countries requires more than legal enactments and criminal prosecution. It is a goal that calls for aggressive action to change the discriminatory social attitudes among the people in Morocco and Egypt. Legal reform and criminal prosecution are indeed relevant in the overall goal of elimination of violence against women. However, these strategies, by themselves, cannot deliver on this goal. If anything, they cannot take away the deeply entrenched social norms. Without fostering attitudinal change across societies in Egypt and Morocco, legal reform and criminal accountability will only go so far because gender-based violence is embedded in deeply rooted social norms. Incidentally, some of the practitioners at the centre of criminal justice including lawmakers, the judiciary, lawyers,

---

[144] Bernoussi Nadia and El Maslouhi Abderrahim, *Les chantiers de la bonne justice: Contraintes et renouveau de la politique judiciaire au Maroc, Revue française de droit constitutionnel* (2012) 479–510, https://www.cairn.info/revue-francaise-de-droit-constitutionnel-2012-3-page-479.htm.

[145] *Ibid.*

[146] *Ibid.*

[147] Houria Alami M'chichi, Malika Benradi, Mohamed Mouaqit, Fatima Zohra Boukaïssi and Rabha Zeidguy, *Le code de la famille, Perceptions et pratique judiciaire,* (2007) 281, https://www.fes.org.ma/common/pdf/publications_pdf/code_famille/code_de_la_famille.pdf.

social workers and the police are themselves caught up in these discriminatory social norms. Especially disheartening are reports revealing that some Egyptian judges (who ought to be the guardians of the law through objective interpretation and application of the law) have allowed social norms to influence decisions in criminal law cases on gender-based violence.[148] Reportedly, the decisions of some members of the police system in Egypt are also influenced by religious inclinations and social norms.[149] For example, cases of domestic violence are often not entertained by the police as they are considered socially acceptable.[150] Against this backdrop, a lot more needs to be done to address discriminatory social norms and attitudes.

3 Conclusion and Recommendations

From the discussion in the preceding sections on the two North African countries of Morocco and Egypt, a lot can be deduced. Notably, prevalence of gender-based violence is undeniable; there have been piecemeal legal reforms to address gender-based violence; there are, however, some gaps in the laws enacted; and there are serious gaps in criminal accountability for gender-based violence. It can also be gathered that despite the progress made in both countries, the deeply entrenched social norms constitute a major barrier to elimination of gender-based violence. While these norms have often been justified by Sharia law, there are some studies which suggest alternative interpretations, teachings and application of Sharia is viable.

Against the above backdrop, it is concluded that gender-based violence in both Morocco and Egypt is inextricably linked to discriminatory social norms. Thus, efforts to eliminate all forms of violence against women makes attitudinal change a prerequisite. It follows then that elimination of gender-based violence should focus on both criminal prosecution and strategies for changes in social attitude on issues of gender and gender

148 Hajjar *supra* note 127 at 9.

149 *Ibid.*

150 *Ibid.*

roles. Effective criminal prosecution can only be advanced in a society that is inclined towards respect for women's rights. In fostering a change in attitude, the relevant stakeholders cannot afford to make any assumptions as the least expected of individuals (including judges, lawyers, lawmakers and police) remain entangled in stereotypes that result from these discriminatory social norms.

One also gathers that in both Morocco and Egypt, religion has played a major role in shaping social norms. Often, however, religious texts have been subjected to problematic interpretations geared towards justifying discriminatory social norms. These flawed interpretations have had a ripple down effect on criminal accountability and the elimination of gender-based violence. In the light of this reality, religious leaders have their work cut out for them. Religion can be used as an entry point to foster a change in attitudes. Religion is a double-edged sword, having both a positive and negative edge to it. The positive edge of Sharia can be wielded creatively to foster society-wide change. With religious texts often founding a basis for laws in many societies, it is submitted that these texts constitute living law to be interpreted in the light of changing circumstances and human rights standards.

Activist movements have over the years played a prominent role in advocating for the rights of women in both Morocco and Egypt. With the deeply entrenched attitudes on issues of gender and equality, these movements have a lot to do in fostering change. This can be through research, advocacy and trainings. Various platforms including traditional media and social media constitute useful platforms for dissemination of information. The information disseminated should seek to question and dismantle the deeply rooted discriminatory attitudes, patterns and stereotypes.

In terms of law reform, both Egypt and Morocco should ratify the Maputo Protocol so that victims can have access to regional human rights institutions. These countries should also ratify the African Court Protocol and make a declaration under its article 34(6) to allow individuals and NGOs access to the court.[151]

---

[151] Protocol to the African Charter on Human and Peoples' Rights on the Establishment of an African Court on Human and Peoples' Rights 2004.

Suffice it to note that the norms in which gender-based violence in both Morocco and Egypt are embedded were not developed in one day. These norms have been in existence for thousands of years. It took time for them to crystalise, thus, it would be unrealistic to expect them to disappear through a mere enactment of law or criminal prosecution. This is not to suggest that legal reform and criminal prosecution is irrelevant. Rather, it is to put into perspective the critical need for attitudinal change. It is also critical to not lose sight of the progress made thus far. Every milestone needs to be documented as it not only informs subsequent strategic action but also contributes to the ultimate goal of elimination of violence against women. Some of these milestones may indeed be little, with some far from perfect, nonetheless, they will contribute to the overall goal of eliminating this plague on the African continent.

References

28 Too Many, *Egypt: The law and FGM*, June 2018, https://www.28toomany.org/static/media/uploads/Law%20Reports/egypt_law_report_v1(june_2018).pdf, October 5, 2020.

Abou Ez Eléonore, Les pays d'Afrique du Nord et du Moyen-Orient sont les pires pour les droits des femmes, selon la Banque mondiale, France Info, 1 March 2019, https://www.francetvinfo.fr/monde/afrique/societe-africaine/les-pays-d-afrique-du-nord-les-pires-pour-les-droits-des-femmes-selon-la-banque-mondiale_3211763.html, October 5, 2020.

African Committee of Experts on the Rights and Welfare of the Child, *Agenda 2040: Fostering an Africa fit for children* (2016).

African Union Commission, *Agenda 2063: The Africa We Want* (2015).

Alami M'chichi Houria, Benradi Malika, Mouaqit Mohamed, Boukaïssi Fatima Zohra and Zeidguy Rabha, *Le code de la famille, Perceptions et pratique judiciaire*, 2007, Fes Maroc, https://www.fes.org.ma/common/pdf/publications_pdf/code_famille/code_de_la_famille.pdf, October 5, 2020.

Allam Nermin, 'Smoke and mirrors: State-sponsored feminism in post-uprising Egypt' 86 *Social Research: An International Quarterly* (2019): 365–386.

Ambrosetti E, Amara NA and Condon S, *Gender-Based Violence in Egypt: Analysing Impacts of Political Reforms, Social, and Demographic Change*, 19 *Violence Against Women* (2013), https://doi.org/10.1177/1077801213486329, October 5, 2020.

Amnesty International, Egypt: *Investigate attacks on women protesters* (2012), https://www.amnesty.org/en/latest/news/2012/06/egypt-investigate-attacks-women-protesters/, October 5, 2020.

Annan Kofi, Secretary-General of the United Nations, *La violence à l'égard des femmes*, https://www.un.org/french/womenwatch/followup/beijing5/session/fiche4.html, October 5, 2020.

Australian Department of Foreign Affairs and Trade, *Country Information Report Egypt*, May 19, 2017, https://dfat.gov.au/about-us/publications/Documents/country-information-report-egypt.pdf, October 5, 2020.

Asma Lamrabet, *slam et femmes: Emergence de nouvelles voies de libération pour les femmes en islam*, September 2014, http://www.asma-lamrabet.com/articles/l-emergence-de-nouvelles-voies-de-liberation-pour-les-femmes-en-islam/, October 5, 2020.

Asma Lamrabet, Les droits de la femme en islam : une réflexion féministe, http://www.asma-lamrabet.com/articles/les-droits-de-la-femme-en-islam-une-reflexion-feministe/, October 5, 2020.

Asmaa Bassouri, Maroc : la tourmente des mères célibataires, Contrepoints, April 17, 2018, https://www.contrepoints.org/2018/04/17/314254-maroc-la-tourmente-des-meres-celibataires, 5 October 2020.

Bassouri Asmaa, *Maroc : la tourmente des mères célibataires, Contrepoints*, April 17, 2018, https://www.contrepoints.org/2018/04/17/314254-maroc-la-tourmente-des-meres-celibataires, October 5, 2020.

BBC News, *Morocco Profile—Leaders*, October 26, 2013, https://www.bbc.com/news/world-africa-14121440.

Benkhadda Fadoua, How NGOs Helped Change Moroccan Law on Rapists Marrying their Victims, February 7, 2014, The Guardian, https://www.theguardian.com/global-development/poverty-matters/2014/feb/07/ngo-change-morocco-rape-law, October 5, 2020.

Bernoussi Nadia and El Maslouhi Abderrahim, Les chantiers de la bonne justice Contraintes et renouveau de la politique judiciaire au Maroc, *Revue française de droit constitutionnel*, 2012/3 (n° 91), 479–510. https://doi.org/10.3917/rfdc.091.0479. https://www.cairn.info/revue-francaise-de-droit-constitutionnel-2012-3-page-479.htm, October 5, 2020.

Bourquia Rahma, Gender and the Reconfiguration of Moroccan society, 2015, http://books.openedition.org/cjb/1041, October 5, 2020.

Bugaighis Hala, El-Huni Ekram, Bugaighis Iman, Yusef Asma, *The Situation of Women in Libya*, Jussor Center for Studies and Development, 2018, https://docs.euromedwomen.foundation/files/ermwf-documents/7126_3.183.thesituationofwomeninlibyanreport2017-08.03.2017.pdf, October 5, 2020.

Cairo Institute for Human Rights Studies, *Circles of Hell from Tahrir to Zagazig?* April 2017, https://cihrs.org/egypt-circles-of-hell-from-tahrir-to-zagazig-when-will-the-normalization-of-sexual-violence-against-women-end/?lang=en, October 5, 2020.

Chave Martin, *Libye, La guerre par le viol 3/4*, October 20, 2018, https://www.notaweaponofwar.org/libye-la-guerre-par-le-viol-3-4/, October 5, 2020.

Chikhaoui Naïma, *Surpasser des obstacles en matière d'égalité: le cas du Maroc,* Quaderns de la Mediterrània, 2015, https://www.iemed.org/observatori/arees-danalisi/arxius-adjunts/qm22/94Quaderns_obstaclesFemmesMaroc_NChikhaoui.pdf, October 5, 2020.

Chinkin Christine, Sexual Harassment: An International Human Rights Perspective, in MacKinnon Catharine and Siegel Reva (eds) Directions in Sexual Harassment Law (2003).

Committee on Elimination of Discrimination against Women, General Recommendations adopted by the Committee on Elimination of Discrimination against Women (General recommendation No. 19: Violence against women).

Committee on the Elimination of Discrimination against Women, General Recommendation No. 35 on Gender-Based Violence against Women, Updating General Recommendation No. 19 (2017).

Committee on the Elimination of Discrimination against Women, Concluding Observations of the Committee on the Elimination of Discrimination against Women: Egypt, 2010, http://www.reproductiverights.org/sites/crr.civicactions.net/files/documents/CEDAW%20Concluding%20Observations%20Egypt.pdf, October 5, 2020.

Constitution of Egypt (2014). Constitution of Morocco of 1 July 2011. Official Bulletin (draft), 2011-06-17, No. 5952bis.

Constitution of South Africa (1996). Country Meters, Morocco Population, 2020, https://countrymeters.info/en/Morocco, October 5, 2020.

Dahir n° 1-04-22 of February 3, 2004 promulgating law n° 70-03 on the Family Code. Official Gazette, 2005-10-06, n° 535

Dahir No. 1-18-19 of 5 Jumada II 1439 (February 22, 2018) Enacting Act No. 103-13 on Combating Violence against Women.

Deramaix Lara, Moriceau Julien, *Quelle justice pour les femmes au Maroc? Analyse des parcours de justice,* Avocats Sans Frontières, April 2019, https://

www.asf.be/wp-content/uploads/2019/12/ASF-justice-femmes-Maroc-2019-6-2.pdf, October 5, 2020.

Devries K, Mak JY, García-Moreno C, Petzold M, Child JC, Falder G, Lim S, Bacchus LJ, Engell RE, Rosenfeld L, Pallitto C, Vos T, Abrahams N and Watts CH, *Global health. The Global Prevalence of Intimate Partner Violence against Women* (2013), http://www.ncbi.nlm.nih.gov/pubmed/23788730, October 5, 2020.

Egypt Penal Code No. 58 of 1937. EuroMed Rights: Egypt, *Report on Violence against Women*, 2018, https://euromedrights.org/wp-content/uploads/2018/11/201811-Gender-VAW-Factsheet-FR-PDF-MSH.pdf, October 5, 2020.

EuromedRights: *Morocco: Situation report on violence against women*, 2018, https://euromedrights.org/wp-content/uploads/2018/03/Factsheet-VAW-Morocco-EN-Mar-2018.pdf, October 5, 2020.

EUROMED Gender Equality Programme, National Situation Analysis Report: Women's Human Rights and Gender Equality, Promoting Equality between Men and Women in the Euro-Mediterranean Region (2008–2011), http://bnm.bnrm.ma:86/Reforme_de_la_constitution/EUROMED%20_%20Rapport%20national%20d'analyse%20de%20la%20situation%20_%20Rights%20human%20of%20women%20and%20equality%20between%20the%20sex.pdf, October 5, 2020.

Fadoua Benkhadda, *How NGOs Helped Change Moroccan Law on Rapists Marrying their Victims*, February 7, 2014, The Guardian, https://www.theguardian.com/global-development/poverty-matters/2014/feb/07/ngo-change-morocco-rape-law, October 5, 2020.

Fatema Mernissi, *The Pride of Islamic Feminism in Modern Times—Obituary*, Muslim Institute, https://musliminstitute.org/freethinking/gender/fatema-mernissi-pride-islamic-feminism-modern-times-obituary, October 5, 2020.

Fatima Sadiqi, *Les droits des femmes en Afrique du Nord au lendemain du printemps arabe*, IEMED Yearbook, Secteurs stratégiques, Société et Culture, https://www.iemed.org/observatori/arees-danalisi/arxius-adjunts/anuari/anuari-2014/Sadiqi_Droits_femmes_Printemps_arabe_Annuaire_IEMed_2014.pdf/, October 5, 2020.

Fatima Sadiqi, 'The Central Role of the Family Law in the Moroccan Feminist Movement' 35 *British Journal of Middle Eastern Studies* (2008): 325–337.

Freedom House, *Freedom in the world* 2019, https://freedomhouse.org/report/freedom-world/2019/egypt, October 5, 2020.

Gaté Juliette, *Women's Rights and Arab Revolutions*, La Revue des droits de l'homme, November 7, 2014, https://journals.openedition.org/revdh/929?lang=en#citedby, October 5, 2020.

General Recommendations Adopted by the Committee on the Elimination of Discrimination against Women, Eleventh Session (1992), General Recommendation No. 19: Violence against women, https://tbinternet.ohchr.org/Treaties/CEDAW/Shared%20Documents/1_Global/INT_CEDAW_GEC_3731_F.pdf, October 5, 2020.

Hajjar Lisa, 'Religion, State Power, and Domestic Violence in Muslim Societies: A Framework for Comparative Analysis' 29 *Law & Social Inquiry* (2004): 1–38.

Hala Bugaighis, Ekram El-Huni, Iman Bugaighis and Asma Yusef, *The Situation of Women in Libya*, Jussor Center for Studies and Development, 2018, https://docs.euromedwomen.foundation/files/ermwf-documents/7126_3.183.thesituationofwomeninlibyanreport2017-08.03.2017.pdf, October 5, 2020.

Hassan Rachik and Rahma Bourqia, *Sociology in Morocco: Theory and research*, 2011, http://journals.openedition.org/sociologies/3719, October 5, 2020.

Home Office, *Country Policy and Information Note Egypt: Women,* (2019) 1–49, https://assets.publishing.service.gov.uk/government/uploads/system/uploads/attachment_data/file/810875/Egypt_-_Women_-_CPIN_-_v2.0__June_2019__external.pdf, October 5, 2020.

House PB, Assaulted and Accused Sexual and Gender-Based Violence in Tunisia, Amnesty *International* (2015), 1–84.

Houria Alami M'chichi, Malika Benradi, Mohamed Mouaqit, Fatima Zohra Boukaïssi, Rabha Zeidguy, *Le code de la famille, Perceptions et pratique judiciaire,* 2007, Fes Maroc, https://www.fes.org.ma/common/pdf/publications_pdf/code_famille/code_de_la_famille.pdf, October 5, 2020.

Idang Gabriel, *African Cultures and Values. Phronimon* (2015) 16: 97–111.

Inter-Agency Standing Committee (IASC), *Directives en vue d'interventions contre la violence basée sur le sexe,* September 2005, https://interagencystandingcommittee.org/system/files/legacy_files/GBV%20Guidelines%20French.pdf, 5 October 2020.

International Commission of Jurists, *Morocco: Remove Obstacles to Women's and Girls' Access to Justice for Sexual and Gender-Based Violence—New ICJ Report,* June 28, 2019, https://www.icj.org/morocco-remove-obstacles-to-womens-and-girls-access-to-justice-for-sexual-and-gender-based-violence-new-icj-report/, October 22, 2020.

International Covenant on Economic, Social and Cultural Rights, Rapport parallèle des ONG marocaines au quatrième rapport périodique du Gouvernement marocain sur la mise en oeuvre du Pacte International relatif aux Droits Economiques, Sociaux et Culturels, 2006–2012, :https://

tbinternet.ohchr.org/Treaties/CESCR/Shared%20Documents/MAR/INT_CESCR_CSS_MAR_21229_F.pdf, 5 October 2020.

International Planned Parenthood Federation, *COVID-19 and the Rise of Gender-Based Violence*, April 22, 2020, https://www.ippf.org/blogs/covid-19-and-rise-gender-based-violence, September 30, 2020.

Jadaliyya Reports, Sexual Violence against Women and the Increasing Frequency of Gang Rape in Tahrir Square and its Environs, 2013, https://www.jadaliyya.com/Details/28108, October 5, 2020.

Joint Submission to the UN Universal Periodic Review 22 Session of the UPR Working Group, The State of Libya Women's rights, September 2014, https://www.upr-info.org/sites/default/files/document/libya/session_22__mai_2015/js3_upr22_lby_e_main.pdf, October 5, 2020.

Juliette Gaté, *Women's Rights and Arab Revolutions', La Revue des droits de l'homme*, November 7, 2014, https://journals.openedition.org/revdh/929?lang=en#citedby, October 5, 2020.

Kamal Mellakh, *De la Moudawwana au nouveau Code de la famille au Maroc: une réforme à l'épreuve des connaissances et perceptions ordinaires*, 2005–2006, http://journals.openedition.org/anneemaghreb/78, October 5, 2020.

Kirollos Mariam, The Daughters of Egypt are a Red Line, Sur—International Journal on Human Rights (2016) 24: 137–153.

Klugman Jeni, Gender based Violence and the Law, World Development Report (2017).

Kofi Annan, Secretary-General of the United Nations, *La violence à l'égard des femmes,* https://www.un.org/french/womenwatch/followup/beijing5/session/fiche4.html.

Lamble Lucy, UN Women Report: Access to Justice in Morocco, The Guardian, 6 July 2011, https://www.theguardian.com/global-development/2011/jul/06/un-women-morocco-justice, October 5, 2020.

Lamrabet Asma, *Islam et femmes: Emergence de nouvelles voies de libération pour les femmes en islam,* September 2014, http://www.asma-lamrabet.com/articles/l-emergence-de-nouvelles-voies-de-liberation-pour-les-femmes-en-islam/, October 5, 2020.

Lamrabet Asma, *Les droits de la femme en islam : une réflexion féministe*, http://www.asma-lamrabet.com/articles/les-droits-de-la-femme-en-islam-une-reflexion-feministe/, October 5, 2020.

Laila Zerrour, *La loi 103-13 entre en vigueur ce mercredi : Ce qui va changer*, aujourdui.ma, September 11, 2018, https://aujourdhui.ma/societe/la-loi-103-13-entre-en-vigueur-ce-mercredi-ce-qui-va-changer, October 5, 2020.

Lara Deramaix and Julien Moriceau, *Quelle justice pour les femmes au Maroc? Analyse des parcours de justice, Avocats Sans Frontières*, April 2019, https://www.asf.be/wp-content/uploads/2019/12/ASF-justice-femmes-Maroc-2019-6-2.pdf, October 5, 2020.

Lubaale Emma Charlene, 'Confronting stereotypes as an entry point to realigning IAAF regulations with human rights and developments in Science' 17 *Gender and Behaviour* (2019): 14413–14432.

Lubaale Emma Charlene, *Bridging the Justice Gap in the Prosecution of Acquaintance Child Sexual Abuse: A Case of South Africa and Uganda* (PhD Thesis, University of Pretoria 2015).

Lubaale Emma Charlene, 'Admissibility of Evidence Presented by Children in Sex Abuse Prosecutions in Uganda: The Case for Reforms' 5 *African Journal of Law and Criminology* (2015): 1–15.

Lubaale Emma Charlene, 'The Crime of Attempted Suicide in Uganda: The Need for Reforms to the Law' 4 *Journal of Law, Society and Development* (2017): 1–19.

Lubaale Emma Charlene, 'Human Rights Reforms of Criminal Law In Africa' in Addaney M, Nyarko M and Boshoff E (eds) *Governance, Human Rights, and Political Transformation in Africa* (2020) 149–171.

Manjoo Rashida, Statement to the General Assembly, October 3, 2011, http://www.un.org/womenwatch/daw/documents/ga66/RAPPORT_on_VAW.PDF, October 5, 2020.

Mellakh Kamal, *De la Moudawwana au nouveau Code de la famille au Maroc: une réforme à l'épreuve des connaissances et perceptions ordinaires*, 2005–2006, http://journals.openedition.org/anneemaghreb/78, October 5, 2020.

Monqid Safaa, *Violence against Women in Public Spaces: The Case of Morocco*, 2012, http://journals.openedition.org/ema/3011, October 5, 2020.

Marguerite Rollinde, *Maghreb: quelles stratégies féministes à l'œuvre, Genre en action*, September 4, 2007, https://www.genreenaction.net/Maghreb-quelles-strategies-feministes-a-l-oeuvre.html, October 5, 2020.

Martin Chave, *Libye, La guerre par le viol 3/4*, 20 October 2018, https://www.notaweaponofwar.org/libye-la-guerre-par-le-viol-3-4/, October 5, 2020.

McRobie Heather, 'Sexual Violence and State Violence against Women in Egypt' 7 *CMI Insight* (2014): 1–6.

Morocco World News, *New Survey Shows High Rates of Violence against Women in Morocco*, May 15, 2019, https://www.moroccoworldnews.com/2019/05/273120/survey-high-rates-violence-women-morocco/, October 5, 2020.

Murgue Bérénice, *La Moudawana: les dessous d'une réforme sans précédent, Les Cahiers de* (2011): 15–29, https://www.cairn.info/revue-les-cahiers-de-l-orient-2011-2-page-15.htm, October 5, 2020.

Naciri Rabéa, *Le mouvement des femmes au Maroc, Nouvelles Questions Féministes,* (2014): 43–64, https://www.cairn.info/revue-nouvelles-questions-feministes-2014-2-page-43.htm, October 5, 2020.

Naciri H, Gender-based Violence in Morocco: Domestic Violence as a Case in Point 9 Kultūra Ir Visuomenė. Socialinių Tyrimų Žurnalas (2018): 51–66.

Naïma Chikhaoui, *Surpasser des obstacles en matière d'égalité: le cas du Maroc,* Quaderns de la Mediterrània, 2015, https://www.iemed.org/observatori/arees-danalisi/arxius-adjunts/qm22/94Quaderns_obstaclesFemmesMaroc_NChikhaoui.pdf, October 5, 2020.

Office of the United Nations High Commissioner for Human Rights, Declaration on the Elimination of Violence against Women, https://www.ohchr.org/FR/ProfessionalInterest/Pages/ViolenceAgainstWomen.aspx, October 5, 2020.

Oussedik F, 'Religion, Gender, and Violence in Algeria' 6 *Brown Journal of World Affairs* (1996): 191–197.

PNUD Morocco, *Gender Justice and The Law, Assessment of Laws Affecting Gender Equality and Protection against Gender-Based Violence,* 2018, https://arabstates.unfpa.org/sites/default/files/pubpdf/Morocco%20Country%20Assessment%20-%20English_0.pdf, October 5, 2020.

Programme EUROMED Égalité Hommes-Femmes, *Rapport National d'Analyse de la Situation: Droits humains des femmes et Egalité entre les sexe,* Promouvoir l'égalité entre les hommes et les femmes dans la région euro-méditerranéenne, 2008–2011, http://bnm.bnrm.ma:86/Reforme_de_la_constitution/EUROMED%20_%20Rapport%20national%20d'analyse%20de%20la%20situation%20_%20Rights%20human%20of%20women%20and%20equality%20between%20the%20sex.pdf, October 5, 2020.

Protocol to the African Charter on Human and Peoples' Rights of Women in Africa (2003).

Rashida Manjoo, Statement to the General Assembly, October 3, 2011, http://www.un.org/womenwatch/daw/documents/ga66/RAPPORT_on_VAW.PDF, October 5, 2020.

Rome Statute of the International Criminal Court (1998).

Schlumpf E, 'The Legal Status of Children Born out of Wedlock in Morocco' 4 *Electronic Journal of Islamic and Middle Eastern Law* (2014): 1–26.

Selby Daniele, *Outrage Over Egyptian Lawyer Saying It's a 'Duty To Rape' Women*, 2017, https://www.globalcitizen.org/en/content/egypt-rape-violence-against-women-lawyer-tv/, October 5, 2020.

Selimovic JM and Larsson DM, Gender and Transition in Libya Mapping Women's *Participation in Post-Conflict Reconstruction*, The Swedish Institute of International Affairs (2014)

Thomson Reuters Foundation, The World's Most Dangerous Megacities for Women, 2017, http://poll2017.trust.org/, October 5, 2020.

UN, MONUSCO, *Gender et Violence*, https://monusco.unmissions.org/genre-et-violence, October 5, 2020.

United Nations, *Le Comité contre la discrimination à l'égard des femmes assigne une tâche prioritaire au Maroc: le changement des mentalités*, July 15, 2003, https://www.un.org/press/fr/2003/FEM1262.doc.htm, October 5, 2020.

United Nations Population Fund, *Morocco Pulling Together to Protect Women's Rights: Programming to Address Violence against Women: Ten Case Studies*, https://www.refworld.org/docid/469cd693c.html, October 5, 2020.

United Nations, *Convention on the Elimination of All Forms of Discrimination against Women*, https://www.un.org/womenwatch/daw/cedaw/, October 5, 2020.

United Nations Development Programme, *Combatting Female Genital Mutilation in Egypt*, (2015), http://www.undp.org/content/dam/undp/fgminegypt/index.html, October 5, 2020.

United Nations Development Program, Gender-Based Violence and COVID-19, May 11, 2020, https://www.undp.org/content/undp/en/home/librarypage/womens-empowerment/gender-based-violence-and-covid-19.html, September 20, 2020.

United Nations Human Rights, Integrating a Gender Perspective into Human Rights Investigations, Guidance and Practice, September 2016, https://www.ohchr.org/Documents/Issues/Women/Publications/GenderIntegrationintoHRInvestigations.pdf, October 5, 2020.

United Nations Protocol to Prevent, Suppress and Punish Trafficking in Persons, Especially Women and Children, Supplementing the United Nations Convention against Transnational Organised Crime (2002).

United Nations, Study on Ways and Methods to Eliminate Sexual Harassment in Egypt, 2013, http://harassmap.org/en/wp-content/uploads/2014/02/287_Summaryreport_eng_low-1.pdf, October 5, 2020.

United States of America Embassy-Egypt, 2018 Report on International Religious Freedom: Egypt, 2018, https://eg.usembassy.gov/2018-report-on-international-religious-freedom-egypt/, October 5, 2020.

Vienna Convention on the Law of Treaties (1969).

World Economic Forum, *The Global Gender Gap Report 2018: Egypt*, December 17, 2018, http://reports.weforum.org/global-gender-gap-report-2018/dataexplorer/#economy=EGY, October 5, 2020.

World Health Organisation, Understanding and Addressing Violence against Women: Female Genital Mutilation (2012).

World Health Organisation, *COVID-19 et violence à l'égard des femmes, Ce que le secteur et le système de santé peuvent faire*, April 7, 2020, https://apps.who.int/iris/bitstream/handle/10665/331762/WHO-SRH-20.04-fre.pdf?ua=1, October 5, 2020.

World Population Review, *Egypt Population 2020*, (2020). June 5, 2020, https://worldpopulationreview.com/countries/egypt-population/.

World Health Organisation, *Violence against Women*, November 29, 2017, https://www.who.int/news-room/fact-sheets/detail/violence-against-women, October 5, 2020.

9

The Right to Social Security as a Prerequisite to Access to Justice for Survivors of Sexual Violence in Zimbabwe

Untalimile Crystal Mokoena

1 Introduction

The realities of sexual violence against women have, for the past decades, been an issue of global concern.[1] International instruments like the Convention on the Elimination of all Forms of Discrimination Against Women (CEDAW), the Convention against Torture and Other Cruel,

[1] Mary J Osirim, 'Crisis in the State and the Family: Violence Against Women in Zimbabwe,' 7 *African Studies Quarterly* (2003): 2152–2448; Kate Dannies, *Sexual violence against women is a global crisis. Stop trying to make it a national one*, Quartz March 2, 2020, https://qz.com/1810434/the-way-we-talk-about-sexual-violence-is-only-making-it-worse/; United Nations Foundation, *A Global Issue We Can't Ignore: Violence Against Girls and Women*, https://unfoundation.org/blog/post/a-global-issue-we-cant-ignore-violence-against-girls-and-women/; UN News, *A Staggering One-in-Three Women, Experience Physical, Sexual Abuse*, https://news.un.org/en/story/2019/11/1052041.

U. C. Mokoena (✉)
Public Law University of Venda, Thohoyandou, South Africa
e-mail: crystal.mokoena@univen.ac.za

E. C. Lubaale and A. Budoo-Scholtz (eds.), *Violence Against Women and Criminal Justice in Africa: Volume I*, Sustainable Development Goals Series,
https://doi.org/10.1007/978-3-030-75949-0_9

Inhuman or Degrading Treatment or Punishment and the Protocol to the African Charter on Human and Peoples' Rights on the Rights of Women in Africa (Maputo Protocol) deal with such and other concerns relating to women's rights. Despite these measures, sexual abuse against women continues in Zimbabwe and other countries as well. Techniques, including strengthening access to justice, have frequently been adopted in an endeavour to address sexual violence against women. However, the rate of these degrading acts against women continues to rise, with an estimation that one-third of women in the world experience sexual violence.[2] Zimbabwe, on its own, is reported to have more than 100 girls abused sexually per day.[3] Literature indicates that these cases are prevalent in poor communities and among women of low income.[4] Important to note is that there is much more sexual violence that goes unreported, which further pushes the rate into great concern.

Sexual violence may be understood to include 'any form of non-consensual, sexual advance; sexual harassment or sexual assault'.[5] The World Health Organization (WHO) defines it as[6]:

[2] Kate Dannies, *Sexual Violence Against Women is a Global Crisis. Stop Trying to Make it a National One,* Quartz March 2, 2020, https://qz.com/1810434/the-way-we-talk-about-sexual-violence-is-only-making-it-worse/.

[3] Richard Nyamanhindi, *Hidden in Plain Sight: Child Sexual Abuse in Zimbabwe,* The Herald, February 4, 2015, https://www.herald.co.zw/hidden-in-plain-sight-child-sexual-abuse-in-zimbabwe/; Adeniyi F. Fagbamigbe, et al., 'Survival Analysis and Prognostic Factors Associated with the Timing of First Forced Sexual Act Among Women in Kenya, Zimbabwe and Cote d 'Ivoire' 4 *Scientific African* (2019): https://doi.org/10.1016/j.sciaf.2019.e00092.

[4] Fennie Mantula and Haroon Saloojee, 'Child Sexual Abuse in Zimbabwe' 25 *Journal of Child Sexual Abuse* (2016): https://doi.org/10.1080/10538712.2016.1234533; Simukai Shamu, et al., 'Does a History of Sexual and Physical Childhood ABUSE contribute to HIV Infection Risk in Adulthood? A Study Among Post-Natal Women in Harare, Zimbabwe,' 14 *PLOS One* (2019): e0198866. https://doi.org/10.1371/journal.pone.0198866; World report on Violence and Health, World Health Organisation, Geneva *Sexual Violence* (2002), https://www.who.int/violence_injury_prevention/violence/global_campaign/en/chap6.pdf?ua=1.

[5] http://www.phoenixrisen.org/what-is-sexual-violation.

[6] World Health Organization, Geneva, World Health Organization *Violence against Women—Intimate Partner and Sexual Violence Against Women* (2011), https://apps.who.int/iris/handle/10665/112325.

> Any sexual act, attempt to obtain a sexual act, unwanted sexual comments or advances, or acts to traffic or otherwise directed against a person's sexuality using coercion, by any person regardless of their relationship to the victim, in any setting, including but not limited to home and work.

For the purposes of this study, the term 'sexual violence' refers to all forms of sexual harassments and is used interchangeably with words such as rape, sexual abuse, sexual harassment, among others. Several crimes constitute sexual violence, and these include but not limited to: rape, attempted rape, sexual harassment, forced marriage/cohabitation, denial of use of contraception or protection against sexually transmitted diseases, coerced prostitution, child sexual abuse, forced abortion, indecent exposure, marital/partner rape, sexual exploitation, unwanted sexual contact.[7]

Amid various crimes, the criminal justice system is responsible for flattening the sexual violence curve through, among other means, arresting and prosecuting perpetrators.[8] This, however, becomes impossible in cases where abuse is unreported. Despite measures put in place to ensure access to justice, it remains vexing why survivors of sexual violence endure such demeaning gruesome treatment from men without laying charges. What has become apparent among scholars is that perpetrators of sexual violence are in many cases known or related to the survivors and hold positions of power or provision over the survivors.[9] Perpetrators

---

[7] Rachel Jewkes and others, 'Sexual Violence' in G Krug and others (eds) *World Report on Violence and Health* Etienne (2002) 147–182; Donna Greco and Sarah Dawgert 'Poverty and Sexual Violence: Building Prevention and Intervention Responses: A Guide for Counselors and Advocates' *Pennsylvania Coalition Against Rape* (2007) 2.

[8] Caleb Mutandwa, *How can Criminal Justice Work Constructively with Shona Justice to Provide Effective Remedies to Child Sexual Abuse Victims?* (2016), http://www.humanrights.dk/files/media/billeder/udgivelser/caleb_report_ok.pdf.

[9] Tichatonga J. Nhundu and Almon Shumba, 'The nature and frequency of reported cases of teacher perpetrated child sexual abuse in rural primary schools in Zimbabwe' 25 *Child Abuse and Neglect* (2001): 1517–1534; Osirim *supra* note 1; Eunice Njovana and Charlotte Watts, 'Gender violence in Zimbabwe: A need for collaborative action'4 *Reproductive Health Matters* (1996): https://doi.org/10.1016/S0968-8080(96)90005-1; Noel Garikai Muridzo, *An exploration of the phenomenon of child sexual abuse in Zimbabwe* (PhD thesis, University of Witwatersrand 2017) 16; Anthony S Musiwa, 'How Has the Presence of Zimbabwe's Victim-Friendly Court and Relevant Child Protection Policy and Legal Frameworks Affected the Management of Intrafamilial Child Sexual Abuse in Zimbabwe? The Case of Marondera District' *Journal of*

may be found responsible for the survivors' livelihoods, which encompass food, shelter and other general welfare needs. Few readings delve deep into exploring the impact of the social security-provider role played by a perpetrator on criminal/access to justice.

While various organisations (globally and regionally), as well as scholarly research, have focused on sexual violence and access to justice, little has been done on linking the two with social security. This chapter serves as an exploratory study of the nexus between sexual survivors' need to access justice while preserving their social security. This emanates from the understanding that the marginalised situation of women in Zimbabwe, including endurance in sexual violence, is exacerbated by the major economic crises that the country has plummeted into since the early 1990s.[10] As such, survivors of sexual violence may opt to protect perpetrators by not reporting crimes if they contribute to their own families' subsistence. It is against this backdrop that this work highlights the underlying challenges that exist in striving to advance both the rights to access to justice and social security for women survivors of sexual violence in Zimbabwe. In this way, this chapter begs the question; in what ways does social security affect access to justice for female sexual violence survivors? In addressing the said question, it is highlighted that survivors of sexual offences find themselves coerced to sacrifice their right to access to justice to safeguard their social security. Both rights are important and equally deserving of protection. Therefore, the government should endeavour to come up with various ways to set the survivors free from the fear of losing subsistence when they report the perpetrators. Empowerment programmes and various social security measures should be made available for survivors so that they may access justice without fear of prejudice on their social security.

Following this introductory part is a brief overview of access to justice in Zimbabwe. This indicates the measures put in place by the country to promote justice. The third section is on the legal protection of social

Interpersonal Violence (2018): 1752; Susan Rees and others, 'Believe #metoo: Sexual Violence and Interpersonal Disclosure Experiences Among Women Attending a Sexual Assault Service in Australia: A Mixed Methods Study' 6 *BMJ Open* (2019): e026773. https://doi.org/10.1136/bmjopen-2018-026773.

[10] Osirim *supra* note 1, 2152–2448.

security. An analysis of sexual violence in Zimbabwe follows wherein its extent and pattern are highlighted. Subsequently, a link among sexual violence, access to justice and social security is explored. The way these three influence or hinder the realisation of the other is demonstrated. Possible solutions to the dichotomy presented in safeguarding the two rights are then given. Lastly, the paper gives concluding remarks.

2 A Brief Overview of Access to Justice for Sexual Violence Survivors in Zimbabwe

Access to justice is viewed by the United Nations (UN) as a fundamental principle of the rule of law, which, if absent, it becomes impossible for people to either enjoy their human rights or have their voices heard.[11] In the same vein, Sustainable Development Goal (SDG) 16 is dedicated to peace, justice and strong institutions, and one of its targets is on the promotion of the rule of law to ensure access to justice for everyone.[12] In a bid to reach this target, an evaluation of a country's criminal justice system becomes obligatory. Attention to criminal justice systems is one of the key means of achieving access to justice; the two operate hand in glove. Hence, this study's reference to access to justice mainly focuses on criminal justice systems. Access to justice has also been addressed as an integral part of the Organisation for Economic Co-operation and Development (OECD) as its member states acknowledge it as essential to attaining inclusive growth.[13] Important to note is that Zimbabwe is among the OECD countries. Therefore, it must ensure access to justice

---

[11] United Nations and the Rule of Law, *Access to Justice,* https://www.un.org/ruleoflaw/thematic-areas/access-to-justice-and-rule-of-law-institutions/access-to-justice/.

[12] Target 16.3 of the UN General Assembly, *Transforming our world: The 2030 Agenda for Sustainable Development*, October 21, 2015, A/RES/70/1, https://www.refworld.org/docid/57b6e3e44.html.

[13] OECD Conference Centre, Paris, *Understanding Effective Access to Justice*, Workshop Background Paper (2016), https://www.oecd.org/gov/Understanding-effective-access-justice-workshop-paper-final.pdf.

within its borders. Also, in 2012, Zimbabwe partnered with the UN Development Programme on the enhancement of justice project.[14]

Yielding to this and other calls, the Zimbabwean Constitution (Constitution) grants the right to access to justice to everyone either individually or in groups.[15] Access to justice includes among others, the state's capacity to provide justice, the right to report a crime, access to courts, the right to be heard and to get fair results on a case. As a way of assisting sexual survivors to access this right, a Victim Friendly Unit was established in 1996 by the Zimbabwe Republic Police (ZRP).[16] This is a structure intended to offer support and conducive environment to survivors of sexual abuse. Its officers are placed in various police stations at district, provincial and national levels and currently, every police station has this unit.[17] The entity is also intended to help survivors access justice by offering friendly services and speedy handling of cases. Despite its promises of easing access to justice for sexual abuse survivors, the impact of the Victim Friendly Unit remains questionable as many cases go unreported. Only 20% of sexual crimes are said to be reported in Zimbabwe,[18] while survivors to the few reported cases do not seem to get the treatment/attention promised.

In *Mapingure v Minister of Home Affairs*, a rape survivor reported the crime but could not get medical help to prevent pregnancy as she had to wait until her rape trial was finalised.[19] The case was eventually finalised very late for safe termination of pregnancy. Interesting to note

[14] Aberdeen University Lawyers Without Borders, *Report on Access to Justice in Zimbabwe,* https://www.academia.edu/32030464/Report_on_Access_to_Justice_in_Zimbabwe.

[15] The Constitution of Zimbabwe Amendment (No. 20) Act, 2013.

[16] Zimbabwe Republic Police, *Victim Friendly Unit*, www.zrp.gov.zw/index.php?option=com_content&view=article&id=86&Itemid=741.

[17] International Federation of Red Cross and Red Crescent Societies, *Effective Law and Policy on Gender Equality and Protection from Sexual and Gender-Based Violence in Disasters*, (Geneva, 2017) https://reliefweb.int/sites/reliefweb.int/files/resources/Gender-SGBV-Report_-Zimbabwe.pdf.

[18] Zimbabwe National Statistics Agency, *Zimbabwe Demographic and Health Survey 2010–2011,* https://dhsprogram.com/pubs/pdf/FR254/FR254.pdf; Médecins Sans Frontières, *Untreated Violence: Breaking down the barriers to sexual violence care in Harare, Zimbabwe 2011–2017 Report,* https://samumsf.org/sites/default/files/2018-07/SGV%20Report_Harae%20Zimbabwe.pdf.

[19] SC 22–14-*Mapingure v Minister of Home Affairs* (2014).

is that the survivor had immediately approached a medical doctor for emergency contraceptives but could not get assistance in the absence of a police officer. Attempts to get a police officer on time proved futile until the prescribed time for emergency contraceptives lapsed. Given the poor rate of reporting of the cases of sexual violence, this case is probably the tip of an iceberg pointing out the failures in the criminal justice system. It is cases like these that discourage survivors from attempting to access justice. To add to this, the Victim Friendly Units face resource restraints just like other Zimbabwean institutions. The unit is also ill-capacitated and lacks resources like transport to deal with high volumes of rape cases.[20]

To intensify the plight of the survivors, Kelly, Lovett and Regan advance the view that of the few cases reported, police often drop the investigations too soon before the perpetrator is arrested.[21] This further lessens people's confidence in the criminal justice system and discourages reporting of such crimes. The insensitivity displayed by the judiciary in some sexual violence crimes leaves a discouraging message to the complainants. An example may be given of the case of *Nemukuyu v S*,[22] where the court sets out considerations for sentencing perpetrators of rape. This case which encouraged lenient sentences on rape cases is an indication of not only misconceptions but insensitivity around the crime. The fact that the court considered that the accused 'did not use a lot of force … [h]e simply overpowered the complainant, causing no further physical harm beside that he inflicted on her private parts'[23] is on its own a heartless humiliation to rape survivors which does not only trivialise sexual crimes but has the potential to deter pursuit of justice. In addition to these deterrents, survivors of sexual violence may fail to access justice because of costs associated with travelling to courts and police

[20] Ngonidzashe Mutanana and Douglas Gasva, 'Barriers to and Consequences of Reporting Rape in a Rural Community of Zimbabwe' 5 *Developing Country Studies* (2015): 15–21.

[21] Liz Kelly, Jo Lovett and Linda Regan, 'A Gap or a Chasm? Attrition in Reported Rape Cases' Home Office Research Study (2005) 293, https://www.researchgate.net/publication/238713283_Home_Office_Research_Study_293_A_gap_or_a_chasm_Attrition_in_reported_rape_cases.

[22] *Nemukuyu v S* [2010] JOL 26,232 (ZH).

[23] Paragraph 10, *Nemukuyu v S*.

stations.[24] This is aggravated by lengthy court procedures which usually require survivors to keep going back. Economic dependence on perpetrators makes it impossible for complainants to get financial assistance in matters against provider-perpetrators. Such economic dependence on perpetrators calls for an outline on the position of the Zimbabwean social security which follows hereinbelow.

3 The Protection of Social Security in Zimbabwe

Social security is a human right recognised by various international instruments and organisations including; the Universal Declaration of Human Rights (UDHR), International Covenant on Economic Social and Cultural Rights (ICESCR), the Convention on the Elimination of All Forms of Discrimination Against Women (CEDAW) and the International Labour Organisation (ILO).[25] In the same vein, Section 30 of the Constitution provides as follows[26]:

> The State must take all practical measures, within the limits of the resources available to it, to provide social security and social care to those who are in need.

The Constitution further guarantees the rights to education, health and food[27] which are part of the realisation of people's social security. Such provisions, however, do not imply that the notion of social security is new in the country. Just like other African countries, Zimbabwe's social security system dates back to the colonial era where it was characterised

[24] Noel G Muridzo and Victor Chikadzi, 'Some Impediments to Child Sexual Abuse Interventions and Corresponding Social Work Implications: Reflections on the Zimbabwean Victim Friendly System' *Journal of Human Rights and Social Work* (2020): https://doi.org/10.1007/s41134-020-00137-x.

[25] Universal Declaration of Human Rights, 1948, Article 22; ICESCR, Article 9; Article 11 of CEDAW; ILO Social Security (Minimum Standards) Convention, No. 102, 1952.

[26] The Constitution of Zimbabwe Amendment (No. 20) Act, 2013.

[27] Sections 75, 76, 77.

by discriminatory laws.[28] These had to be changed after the country attained its independence in 1980, and a National Social Security Act was enacted in 1989.[29] The Act was enacted mainly to provide for the establishment of social security measures to employees.[30] From the onset, the Act presented discriminatory coverage as it only protected employees, who ironically constitute a very small portion of the country's population.[31] The needs of the informally employed and the unemployed were ignored by the Act. Such a system pauses great challenges for the residents and is not helpful to a country tainted by extreme poverty and unemployment.[32]

The National Social Security Authority (NSSA) was given the mandate to come up with social security measures suitable for the needs of Zimbabweans. However, political and economic factors made it impossible for NSSA to introduce schemes comprehensive enough to cater for everyone.[33] In 1994, the government introduced social security schemes which covered the aged, disabled and provided for death benefits.[34] These were in the form of the Pensions and Other Benefits Scheme as well as the Accident Prevention and Workers Compensation Scheme. As directed by Section 3 of the National Social Security Act, the Pensions and other Benefits Scheme (POBS) was introduced.[35] This measure is

---

28 The laws regulating social security system during the colonial era were only a privilege of the elite which excluded the natives. Such system was meant to benefit the white settlers to the exclusion of the black natives.

29 The National Social Security Act (Chapter 17:04) of 1989.

30 Section 3(1) of the National Social Security Act (Chapter 17:04) of 1989.

31 Edwin Kaseke, 'Social Exclusion and Social Security: The Case of Zimbabwe' 18 *Journal of Social Development in Africa* (2003): http://digital.lib.msu.edu/projects/africanjournals/.

32 Chris Landsberg, 'African Solutions for African Problems: Quiet Diplomacy and South Africa's Diplomatic Strategy Towards Zimbabwe' 41 *Journal for Contemporary History* (2016): 126–148; Jephias Mapuva and Peter Makaye, 'Exploring Zimbabwe's Enduring Economic Challenges and Interventionist Strategies: Showcasing the Zimbabwe Agenda for Sustainable Socio-Economic Transformation (ZIMASSET)' 47 *African Journal of Development Studies*, 47 (2017): https://doi.org/10.25159/0304-615X/1249; Knocks T Zengeni, 'Zimbabwe: A Country Profile' 7 *Journal of International Studies* (2020): 157–169.

33 Norman Nhede, *The Social Security Policy of the Government of Zimbabwe: A Policy Analysis Overview* (PhD Dissertation, University of Pretoria 2016), https://repository.up.ac.za/bitstream/handle/2263/57163/Nhede_Social_2016.pdf?sequence=1&isAllowed=y.

34 Kaseke *supra* note 31, 35; Nhede *supra* note 33, 183.

35 National Social Security Authority (Pension and other Benefits Schemes), 1993. (S.I. No. 393 of 1993).

funded through employer-employee contributions and only covers the formally employed. POBS is meant to provide social protection in the event of retirement, disability or death of a breadwinner who contributed to the fund.[36] The Accident Prevention and Workers Compensation Scheme further safeguard workplace safety and is meant to prevent accidents therein. Both schemes are nevertheless, discriminatory as they do not cover those in informal sectors.

To cover the marginalised population which could not contribute towards any form of social insurance, non-contributory social security measures were introduced.[37] These were in the form of social or public assistance programmes which are means-tested and non-contributory.[38] The Social Welfare Assistance Act administers public assistance in Zimbabwe.[39] The Act aims to provide social welfare assistance to those in need. Section 3 thereof provides that[40]:

> Any destitute or indigent person or any person on his behalf may apply to the Director in the prescribed form for social welfare assistance in terms of this Act.

While this clause is coined as applicable to any indigent person, Section 6 indicates that for one to be eligible for such assistance, they should be over the age of 60.[41] This leaves the social welfare assistance catering only for the aged, disabled and those who suffer chronic illnesses. In circumstances where these reside far from service points, transport costs have left them discouraged to pursue the public social assistance as they

---

36 Section 3 of the National Social Security Act [Chapter 17:04] of 1989.

37 Edwin Kaseke, 'Informal Social Security in Southern Africa', *SASPEN and FES International Conference on Social Protection for those Working Informally, Birchwood Hotel, Johannesburg*, September 16–17, 2013. http://www.saspen.org/conferences/informal2013/Paper_Kaseke_FES-SASPEN-16SEP2013-INT-CONF-SP4IE.pdf.

38 Jotham Dhemba, 'Social Protection for the Elderly in Zimbabwe: Issues, Challenges and Prospects' 3 *African Journal of Social Work* (2013): 1–22; Edwin Kaseke, 'Social Exclusion and Social Security: The Case of Zimbabwe' 18 *Journal of Social Development in Africa* (2003): http://digital.lib.msu.edu/projects/africanjournals/.

39 Social Welfare Assistance Act (Chapter 17:06) of 1988.

40 Section 3 of the Social Welfare Assistance Act (Chapter 17:06) of 1988.

41 Social Welfare Assistance Act (Chapter 17:06) of 1988 Section 6(1)(a).

(transport costs) often become more than the grant itself.[42] Scholars also indicate awareness challenges, in that, a lot of Zimbabweans are not even aware of such assistance.[43] In addition to these limitations, the country's lack of resources put a strain on the sustainability of public assistance measures. This leaves a lot of destitute Zimbabweans without any form of social security.

Besides the afore-mentioned assistance, there are programmes such as the Basic Education Assistance Module (BEAM), Assisted Medical Treatment Order (AMTO) and food for work. The BEAM aims to support poor children with financial assistance in their education.[44] The challenges levelled against this kind of aid include late disbursement and unavailability of funds which often lead to students being taken out of schools.[45] The AMTO which is the form of free medical treatment to the needy requires one to pass a means test, which oftentimes involves lengthy processes like visiting the applicant's homes to verify the applicant's means as well as locating an AMTO officer since they are not housed within health facilities.[46] This presents shortcomings as one may be too sick for all the procedures needed for AMTO.

Also, the country's economic pandemic is putting a strain on the effectiveness of this form of assistance. To add to this, Nhede points out that officials tend to abuse AMTO to the point of depleting resources before the indigent benefit.[47] Similar challenges may also be identified in the food-for-work programme which is administered by local community leaders. The food availed by the government in exchange for working

---

42 Nhede *supra* note 33.

43 Dhemba *supra* note 38; UN Human Rights Council *Zimbabwe Policies Hitting Poor Hardest, say UN Rights Experts*, April 4, 2019, https://reliefweb.int/report/zimbabwe/zimbabwe-policies-hitting-poor-hardest-say-un-rights-experts.

44 Godfrey Kanyenze et al., *Beyond the Enclave: Towards a Pro-Poor and Inclusive Development Strategy for Zimbabwe* (2011).; Tawanda Masuka et al., 'Preserving the Future: Social Protection Programmes for Orphans and Vulnerable Children (OVC) in Zimbabwe' 2 *International Journal of Humanities and Social Sciences* (2012): 59–66.

45 Tawanda Masuka, 'The New Constitution of Zimbabwe and its Implication for Social Workers' 2 *Journal of Social Welfare and Human Rights* (2014): 29–40.

46 Stephen Buzuzi, et al., 'Impact of User Fees on the Household Economy in Zimbabwe' ReBUILD Working Paper No. 21, (2016), https://rebuildconsortium.com/media/1349/zimbabwe-user-fees-wp21-050516.pdf.

47 Nhede *supra* note 33.

in various projects may not be enjoyed by deserving people. Also, the local leaders' discretion on who works and benefit from the given projects may be unfair and villagers may be forced to gratify the leaders in ways involving tolerating unwanted sexual advances, in exchange for selection into food-for-work projects.

Given the socio-economic status of many Zimbabweans and the high unemployment rate, it is evident that most people are unprotected by the available social security measures as they are largely contributory and apply only to those formally employed. The non-contributory measures intended to cater for the majority are daunted with severe financial constraints, corruption as well as mismanagement allegations that they often leave deserving people with no coverage.[48] Although the measures are intended to assist the indigent population who live in dire poverty, the prevailing economic situation of Zimbabwe makes it difficult for the government to cope with the demands.[49] The schemes are, therefore, found non-viable as they are poorly funded and fail to cater for those in need.[50] This leaves a huge gap in the Zimbabwean social security system as the majority live in dire poverty.

Amidst all this, women and children are the most affected. In a study on children and women's socio-economic conditions, Zimbizi indicated that owing to the limited coping options, women and children become more vulnerable to the Zimbabwean economy which has slumped terribly.[51] The traditional family structures aggravate economic dependence on men as it becomes difficult for females to acquire resources needed to alleviate economic strain.[52] For instance, as elaborated, many Zimbabweans are left unemployed and living in poverty and unlike men, most women are not able to take diverse informal jobs away from their homes as they are mostly tasked with caring for children. The

[48] Kanyenze *supra* note 44.

[49] Nhede *supra* note 33.

[50] Dhemba *supra* note 38, 13.

[51] George Zimbizi, 'Study on Socio-economic Status of Children and Women on Commercial Farms, Mining and Peri-urban Areas' Report Prepared for UNICEF (2001), https://www.unicef.org/evaldatabase/files/ZIM_01-800_Part1.pdf.

[52] Carol Riphenburg, 'Women's Status and Cultural Expression: Changing Gender Relations and Structural Adjustment in Zimbabwe' 44 *Africa Today* (1997): 33–50.

current Covid-19 global pandemic has further exasperated the Zimbabwean socio-economic challenge. Although this scourge has attacked the globe, other countries were quick to offer economic support to their indigent communities, leaving poor countries like Zimbabwe lagged behind as they had to wait for international donors to assist in this regard.[53] Even when the long-anticipated assistance finally graced Zimbabwe, its amount and scope were very narrow to bring significant results to a poverty-stricken country.[54] For instance, at the time of conducting this study, vulnerable families from only eight urban areas became beneficiaries of money equivalent to US$12 per month donated by the United States through the United States Agency for International Development (USAID).[55]

All these factors and many more have made the socio-economic situation of women far worse than that of men. Such status quo compels those with no means of survival to be at the mercy of those who can provide, including survivors of sexual abuse who benefit from abusers. Mukamana et al. confirm that low economic status increases intimate partner violence which includes sexual violence.[56] Having said this, it is prudent to explore the Constitutional framework for sexual violence in Zimbabwe.

---

[53] Gift Dafuleya, 'Social and Emergency Assistance Ex-Ante and During COVID-19 in the SADC Region' 2 *The International Journal of Community and Social Development* (2020): 263.

[54] USAID, *USAID and WFP Provide Relief to over 100,000 Urban Dwellers During Covid-19*, September 30, 2020, https://www.usaid.gov/zimbabwe/press-releases/usaid-and-wfp-provide-relief-over-100000-urban-dwellers; Owen Gagare, *Zimbabwe: Caught Between the Pandemic and an Incapable State Good Governance Africa*, August 12, 2020, https://gga.org/zimbabwe-caught-between-the-pandemic-and-an-incapable-state/.

[55] USAID *supra* note 54.

[56] Jeanette I Mukamana, Pamela Machakanja and Nicholas K Adjei, 'Trends in prevalence and correlates of intimate partner violence against women in Zimbabwe, 2005–2015' 20 *International Health and Human Rights* (2020): https://doi.org/10.1186/s12914-019-0220-8.

4 The Constitutional Framework on the Prohibition of Sexual Violence

Section 2 of the Constitution states that the Constitution is supreme over all law and practice; as such any conduct not in line with it is invalid. The supremacy of the Constitution as well as gender equality are among the Constitution's founding values.[57] This means that all the provisions of the Constitution should be respected, protected and adhered to including women's right to freedom from all forms of violence. The Constitution provides that[58]:

> Every person has the right to bodily and psychological integrity, which includes the right—a. to freedom from all forms of violence from public or private sources.

All forms of violence are prohibited, including sexual violence.[59] Any form of sexual violence is a serious infringement on one's bodily and psychological integrity. Although such crimes are committed on the survivor's body, they also leave deep-rooted psychological effects;[60] thus, Section 51 pronounces against such violations. These crimes also transgress on a person's right to dignity as enunciated in Section 51 of the Constitution. Respecting one's dignity forms part of the founding principles of the Constitution.[61] The state is called upon to respect 'the inherent dignity and worth of each human being' including women. Sexual abuse is a direct infringement on the right to dignity and this being one of the Constitutional founding values, Zimbabwe should endeavour to eradicate all acts negatively impacting on the right to

---

[57] Section 3 of the Constitution.

[58] Section 52(a) of the Constitution.

[59] Section 52(a) of the Constitution.

[60] Rachel Jewkes and others, 'Sexual Violence' in Etienne G Krug et al. (eds) *World Report on Violence and Health* (2002)147–182; Noel G Muridzo and Victor Chikadzi, 'Some Impediments to Child Sexual Abuse Interventions and Corresponding Social Work Implications: Reflections on the Zimbabwean Victim Friendly System' *Journal of Human Rights and Social Work* (2020): https://doi.org/10.1007/s41134-020-00137-x.

[61] Section 3(e) of the Constitution.

dignity. Section 86(3) clearly articulates that the right to human dignity should not be violated by any person nor be constrained by any law.

Machakanja and others[62] contend that the present Constitution offers better protection to the rights of women than the former one. This is evident in Section 17 which mandates the state to 'take positive measures to rectify gender discrimination and imbalances resulting from past practices and policies'. Also, Section 80 guarantees women's equal dignity to men and further proscribes all legislation, traditions and practices that violate women's rights and safety. Acts such as child and forced marriages resulting in sexual violence and are prevalent on females are outlawed by the new Constitution as they perpetrate among other crimes, gender discrimination. Sexual crimes further impair on several Constitutional provisions, including the right to health, freedom from torture and ancillary rights.

Addressing sexual violence would help Zimbabwe safeguard many of its Constitutional provisions as the commission of this crime violates several rights entrenched in the Constitution. Having discussed the Constitutional framework on the prohibition of sexual assault, it is necessary to give an exploration of sexual violence in Zimbabwe including, the nature and extent of the crime. Therefore, the succeeding section is dedicated to the same.

5 An Analysis of Sexual Violence in Zimbabwe

Although sexual violence can occur against both males and females, it presents itself as a world-wide-problem for women.[63] Having mentioned this, only acts against women are referred to here. Worth noting also is that both adults and children may be exposed to this heinous crime.

---

[62] Pamela Machakanja and others, *The Constitutional and Legal Frameworks for the Protection of Women against Violence in Zimbabwe* 2016, https://zimlii.org/content/constitutional-and-legal-frameworks-protection-women-against-violence-zimbabwe.

[63] Maybe Zengenene and Emy Susanti, 'Violence against Women and Girls in Harare, Zimbabwe' 20 *Journal of International Women's Studies* (2019): 83–93.

However, this distinction is not maintained here, as abuse against both girls and women are discussed.

5.1 Nature of Sexual Violence in Zimbabwe

Sexual abuse in Zimbabwe takes various forms and dimensions within social, relational, cultural or political spheres. Although a significant portion of survivors of sexual crimes suffer these violations within their homes,[64] the abuses are generally divided into those committed by private persons, where the perpetrator is usually known and those committed by persons linked to the state as politically motivated rape.[65]

Rape in Zimbabwe has often been used as a political weapon dating back to the colonial era.[66] This form of sexual violence is directed at women because they are 'vulnerable and easy targets', owing to their political affiliations or their spouses or relatives'.[67] In 2008, the leading political party, the Zimbabwe African National Union-Patriotic Front (ZANU-PF), struck by the fear of losing elections, resorted to among other means, sexual violence to re-instil its political dominance.[68] Politically motivated rape cases are less likely to be reported as they are often committed by 'law enforcers' themselves. The Zimbabwean police and the Attorney General's Office have been reported as being reluctant to

---

[64] Central Statistical Office (CSO) and Macro International Inc Calverton, Maryland: CSO and Macro International Inc. *Zimbabwe demographic and health survey 2005–06*, 2007 https://dhsprogram.com/pubs/pdf/FR186/FR186.pdf.

[65] Douglas Coltart, 'Freedom from All Forms of Violence: Using Zimbabwe's New Constitution to Encourage Rape Law Reform' 50 *South African Crime Quarterly* (2014): 31–40.

[66] *Politically Motivated Rape in Zimbabwe* Report produced by the Women's Programme of the Research & Advocacy Unit, 2011, https://akcampaign.files.wordpress.com/2011/03/rau_politically_motivated_rape_110428.pdf; Obert Hodzi, 'Sexual Violence as Political Strategy in Zimbabwe: Transitional Justice Blind Spot? (2012), https://www.law.ox.ac.uk/sites/files/oxlaw/oberthodzi_zimbabwe_otjrdebates1.pdf; Douglas Coltart *supra* note 65.

[67] Rumbidzai Dube, *She Probably asked for it!' A Preliminary Study into Zimbabwean Societal Perceptions of Rape*, Research and Advocacy Unit, 2013, https://reliefweb.int/sites/reliefweb.int/files/resources/A-study-into-Zimbabwean-Societal-perception-of-rape.pdf.

[68] Obert Hodzi, *Sexual Violence as Political Strategy in Zimbabwe: Transitional Justice Blind Spot? Oxford Transitional Justice*, Research, Working Paper Series: Debates, 2012, https://www.law.ox.ac.uk/sites/files/oxlaw/oberthodzi_zimbabwe_otjrdebates1.pdf.

investigate and prosecute such crimes. Thus, survivors are denied access to justice where political rapes have taken place.[69]

Sexual abuse in Zimbabwe may take place within cultural belief contexts. A custom involving child pledging is sometimes practised. This involves the commitment to give a young girl in marriage to a rich man in exchange for material support.[70] This practice may also be performed on newborn girls, where the family enters into an agreement to care for the girl child with the help of the man who would become the child's husband.[71] The handing over usually takes place when the girl reaches teenage-hood. This custom promotes sexual abuse of young girls with the consent of their parents/guardians. The driving factor in this abuse is solely poverty as the child is exchanged in marriage for social security provision. There is also a view that some girls suffer sexual violence because of a myth that sexual intercourse with virgins brings wealth.[72] Such kinds of beliefs are also exacerbated by economic hardships within the country which compel people to go to extremes to secure an improved economic status.

As already elaborated, much of the sexual violence takes place within the survivors' homes perpetrated by either relatives or neighbours.[73] Shamu et al. indicate that the majority of the drivers of abuse in Zimbabwe emerge from 'family disorganisation and dysfunction often related to contexts of poverty and structural violence'.[74] The Zimbabwean economic challenges greatly contribute to family disintegration and

[69] *Ibid.*

[70] Noel Muridzo and Effie Malianga, 'Child Sexual Abuse in Zimbabwe: Prevention Strategies for Social Workers' 5 *African Journal of Social Work* (2015): 41–64; Symphorosa Rembe, et al., 'Child and Forced Marriage as Violation of Women's Rights, and Responses by Member States in Southern African Development Community' 25 *Agenda: Empowering Women for Gender Equity* (2011): 65–74.

[71] *Ibid*, 41–64.

[72] Mantula and Haroon *supra* note 4, 868.

[73] Isolde Birdthistle et al., 'Child Sexual Abuse and Links to HIV and Orphanhood in Urban Zimbabwe' 65 *Journal of Epidemiol Community Health* (2011): https://doi.org/10.1136/jech.2009.094359.

[74] Shamu et al. *supra* note 4, 2.

sexual abuse.[75] This also pushes young girls to drop out of school and be forced into marriages. Most families also suffer job losses which coerce them to rely on any available means of survival including tolerating sexual abuse.

5.2 The Extent of Sexual Violence

Sexual violence is one of the prevalent crimes in Zimbabwe. A survey conducted between 2010 and 2011 shows that 27% of women aged between 15 and 49 had encountered sexual abuse at some point in their life, with 49% being girls below 19 years of age.[76] Women from rural areas are more prone to sexual abuse compared to their urban counterparts.[77] Writing on child sexual abuse, Mantula and Saloojee also highlighted that sexual abuse among children is higher in poor communities and is often related to power relations.[78] This may be caused by poor social security; which places more rural women at risk of enduring and failing to report sexual violence where perpetrators contribute to their well-being.

In 2012, more than 41% of rape cases against children were perpetrated by neighbours.[79] This affirms reports of a study conducted in 2009 by Adult Rape Clinic that 67% of the reported cases were committed by relatives or neighbours.[80] While the figure presented in this brief outline may be worrisome, the Zimbabwe Demographic Health Survey, 2010–2011, buttressed the position that the number of gender-based violation and sexual violence is way more than what is reported.[81] This then calls

---

[75] Girl Child Network, *Gravity of Girl Child Sexual Abuse in Zimbabwe: Towards Creating a Culture of Prevention,* https://archive.kubatana.net/docs/sexual/gcn_sexual_abuse_zim_050517.pdf.

[76] Zimbabwe National Statistics Agency, *Zimbabwe Demographic and Health Survey 2010–2011,* Zimbabwe, https://dhsprogram.com/pubs/pdf/FR254/FR254.pdf.

[77] Central Statistical Office *supra* note 64.

[78] Mantula and Haroon *supra* note 4, 867.

[79] Hildegade Manzvanzvike, *Rape: When Society Lets Kids Down,* The Herald, December 26, 2012, https://www.herald.co.zw/rape-when-society-lets-kids-down/.

[80] Cited in Ngonidzashe and Gasva *supra* note 20, 15–21.

[81] Zimbabwe National Statistics *supra* note 76.

for an examination of the laws on sexual abuse and the protection of survivors in Zimbabwe.

5.3 Law on Sexual Violence

Rule 93 of the Customary International Law prohibits rape as well as any form of sexual violence.[82] Since it is made of obligations emanating from state practice, customary international law binds all states.[83] On a similar standing, the International Criminal Court Rome Statute describes rape as a crime against humanity.[84] Although Zimbabwe is not a party to the Rome Statute, the prohibition of rape has been afforded the *jus cogens* status,[85] meaning that all states must commit to fighting all forms of sexual violence and protecting the survivors.

On paper, Zimbabwe seems to be abiding by its international obligations of prohibiting sexual violence. Section 65(1) of the Zimbabwean Criminal Law (Codification and Reform) Act 2004 criminalises rape, which it describes as follows;

> sexual intercourse … with a female person and, at the time of the intercourse … the female person has not consented to it ...[86]

The same law points out that a child below 12 years is not capable of giving consent to sexual intercourse.[87] This implies that any person engaging in sexual activities with such a child is automatically guilty of a crime and cannot raise consent as a defence to the activity. The

---

[82] Customary International Law Database, https://ihl-databases.icrc.org/customary-ihl/eng/docs/home.

[83] John Dugard, *International Law: A South African Perspective* (2014) 27; Rebecca Crootof, 'Change without Consent: How Customary International Law Modifies Treaties' 41 *Yale Journal of International Law* (2016): 237–300.

[84] UN General Assembly, Rome Statute of the International Criminal Court (1998).

[85] David S Mitchel, 'The Prohibition of Rape in International Humanitarian Law as a Norm of Jus Cogens: Clarifying the Doctrine' 15 *Duke Journal of Comparative & International Law* (2005): 219–257.

[86] Criminal Law (Codification and Reform) Act 2004 Section 65(1).

[87] *Ibid*, Section 64(1).

Sexual Offences Act[88] is committed to dealing with sexual offences in Zimbabwe. Section 8 thereof criminalises rape. Other sexual offences are also listed and criminalised in the Act. Similarly, the Domestic Violence Act does not condone any form of sexual abuse.[89] Although not directly referring to sexual violence, the Constitution is clear on women rights protection.[90]

Despite the existence of all protective laws on sexual violence, Zimbabwe is performing poorly in implementing laws and policies safeguarding children against abuse and exploitation.[91] Sexual violence also continues to rise despite the legal framework in place.[92] As already indicated, social insecurity has a bearing on the high rates of sexual abuse and poor reporting in Zimbabwe. Hence, the following section explores the interconnection of these.

6 The Nexus Between Access to Justice and Social Security of the Survivors of Sexual Violence

Owing to the nature of sexual violence, it is apparent that women and children should be protected from this degrading crime. However, it is sad and unfortunate that sometimes, those tasked with protecting them contribute to the perpetuation of the crime either actively or passively.[93] Economic hardships aggravate this kind of behaviour. Perpetrators may be protected for the fear of losing social security benefits they provide. A report by the Girl Child Network affirmed that some mothers do not report their husbands who commit sexual abuse for the fear of

---

88 Sexual Offences Act (Chapter 9:21).

89 The Domestic Violence Act (Chapter 5:16) 24 of 2006.

90 Constitution, Section 80.

91 Mantula and Haron *supra* note 4, 870.

92 International Federation of Red Cross and Red Crescent Societies, *Effective law and policy on gender equality and protection from sexual and gender-based violence in disasters,* Geneva, (2017), https://reliefweb.int/sites/reliefweb.int/files/resources/Gender-SGBV-Report_-Zimbabwe.pdf.

93 Ngonidzashe and Gasva *supra* note 20, 15–21.

losing a breadwinner to prison.[94] This shows that when faced with sexual violence and the fear of losing social security, people would most likely choose to safeguard their right to social security.

In a study conducted by Mutanana and Gasva, one of the interviewed survivors of sexual abuse indicated that the relatives of the perpetrator, who was her uncle, discouraged her from reporting the abuser alluding that no one was going to take care of her if her uncle (perpetrator) was arrested.[95] This implies that the survivors' intentions of reporting the crime got thwarted by the need to protect her social security since she had to choose between pursuing justice for the crime committed against her and losing her subsistence. Such prejudiced decisions are encountered by many sexual abuse survivors in Zimbabwe and the country's economic situation exacerbates the aforesaid. Failure to have reliable social security measures perpetuates and forces a connection between the perpetrator and survivor as abusers may be the sole source of provision.

In situations where rape cases are reported, they may be settled out of court with the perpetrator required to compensate the family of the survivor or to marry her.[96] These kinds of marriages are said to be prevalent during the drought seasons where poverty and food insecurities are rife.[97] Despite the cruel foundation of these marriages, parents continue to give their daughters in such marriages as they eradicate social insecurities in two ways which are: (1) reducing the number of dependents in a household; and (2) using lobola (bride price) to cater for the family needs.

Understandably, economically well-off families would less likely choose financial compensation over justice or choose to have their daughters married off to rapists. Such decisions are often persuaded by economic needs. Perpetrators also tend to be protected when they hold breadwinner position in the survivor's family. Chikwiri and Lemmer argue that owing to the fear of losing financial support, some parents or

---

94 Girl Child Network, *Gravity of Girl Child Sexual Abuse in Zimbabwe: Towards Creating A Culture of Prevention*', https://archive.kubatana.net/docs/sexual/gcn_sexual_abuse_zim_050517.pdf.

95 Ngonidzashe and Gasva *supra* note 20.

96 Mantula and Haroon *supra* note 4, 868.

97 International Federation of Red Cross *supra* note 92.

guardians prevent children from reporting sexual violence committed by breadwinners.[98] Thus, a nexus exists between the right to access to justice and the need to safeguard one's social security right. Unfortunately, the pressing human demands on social security always triumph over access to justice. Such realities render legal frameworks on access justice a fallacy for survivors of sexual violence.

The nexus between access to justice and social security was affirmed by Nyenti in mentioning that, 'the right of access to justice and social cannot be seen in isolation'.[99] This means that it is not enough to simply have police stations, courts and other structures in place for the survivors of sexual violence without paying attention to the external factors which have a direct and great impact on their freedom to access justice. In this case, it is evident that socio-economic factors greatly strain access to justice, therefore measures must be put in place to address such challenges.

A report by the International Federation of Red Cross states that the socio-economic dependence of women on men acts as a huge challenge in law enforcement.[100] Women indicated in the same report that their reliance on men for sustenance as well as the fear of being unable to provide for their children hinder them from seeking justice for the abuse they suffer. To buttress this, women of higher wealth status seem to experience less domestic and sexual violence within their homes.[101]

As sexual abuse is 'an epitome of unequal power between males and females',[102] there is a great need to safeguard women's social security as this would help in remedying the inequality between sexes and eventually free them from the chains of injustice. Written from an understanding that a clash often arises between sexual abuse survivors' need to protect

---

[98] Elizabeth Chikwiri and Eleanor M Lemmer, 'Gender-Based Violence in Primary Schools in the Harare and Marondera Districts of Zimbabwe' 5 *Journal Sociology Social Anthropology* (2014): 95–107.

[99] Mathias Nyenti, 'Access to Justice in the South African Social Security System: Towards a Conceptual Approach' 46 *De Jure* (2013): 901–916.

[100] International Federation of Red Cross *supra* note 92.

[101] Central Statistical Office *supra* note 64.

[102] Regis Chireshe and Excellent Chireshe, 'Sexual Harassment of Female Students in Three Selected High Schools in Urban Masvingo Zimbabwe' 23 *Agenda* (2009): 88–96.

their source of well-being and the need for justice, it is important to give a brief overview of some feasible ways of dealing with this challenge. Thus, the following section is devoted to that.

7 Possible Solutions to the Dilemma

Based on the discussion above, it is without doubt that for access to justice to be effective, it should go beyond the mere implementation of criminal justice mechanisms. Thus, the first solution to the challenge presented may be to extend the meaning and understanding of access to justice. Writing from a South African perspective, Nyenti posits that access to justice has since acknowledged a broader perspective which includes social justice, economic justice and environmental justice.[103] Access to justice has a close link with social security. Literature, however, has mainly presented the connection between access to justice and social security within the ambit of failure to access justice due to financial constraints, for instance, difficulties in paying legal fees.[104] This work, however, stretches that link to encompass socio-economic dependence on the perpetrator as a barrier to accessing justice. Hence, access to justice cannot be looked at in isolation, its assessment and realisation are dependent on other related rights.

It is also associated with social development and economic growth.[105] In this way, it is viewed as people's engine (especially the poor and vulnerable) to enjoy their socio-economic rights. The implication herein is that other rights are also important in the realisation of access to justice.[106] On that account, a mere implementation of structures and institutions for access to justice without paying attention to other external factors,

---

[103] Nyenti *supra* note 99, 901–916.

[104] *Ibid*.

[105] Marcus Manuel and Clare Manuel, *Achieving equal access to justice for all by 2030: Lessons from global funds*, Overseas Development Institute, Working paper (2018) 537, https://www.odi.org/sites/odi.org.uk/files/resource-documents/12307.pdf;

OECD Conference Centre, Paris, *Understanding Effective Access to Justice: Workshop Background Paper* (2016), https://www.oecd.org/gov/Understanding-effective-access-justice-workshop-paper-final.pdf.

[106] Nyenti *supra* note 99, 901–916.

which may hinder effective justice, may not yield the desired results. Thus, no matter how comprehensive the structures for accessing justice may be, human beings are highly unlikely to make use of them if using them would result in their only source of livelihood taken away or affected. In other words, vulnerable people would likely choose to preserve their social security over accessing justice, especially if such justice or government would not put food on their table or pay their bills. As such, it is high time that access to justice takes into consideration other factors like the survivor's social security. In the same way, that the law recognises injustice occasioned by the failure to afford legal services to the poor, the socio-economic being of the vulnerable must be acknowledged as an obstruction to justice. Such endeavours would also assist in Zimbabwe's achievement of SDGs.

The SDGs among other issues place emphasis on the need for all states to ensure access to justice. It is worth noting that both access to justice and social security are acknowledged as achievable goals for sustainable development. SDGs 1 and 2 are dedicated to eradicating poverty, ending hunger as well as achieving social security and SDG 16 is committed among others, to access justice for all. Target 3 of SDG 16 relates to the promotion of 'the rule of law at the national and international levels and to ensure equal access to justice for all' by 2030.[107] This study, thus, indicates that the dynamics involved in sexual violence may hinder the attainment of access to justice for all as desired among other frameworks by the SDGs.

For instance, the outcry that some of the abused children are prevented from reporting crimes committed against them out of the fear of having no one to care for them if the provider (also perpetrator) could be sentenced may be alleviated by the availability of children's homes. The government of Zimbabwe may establish more children's homes to help care for children left with no one to care for them. The viability of this recommendation is seen in a study conducted in Hurungwe District in Mashonaland West province, where the available children's

[107] Target 16.3 of the UN General Assembly, *Transforming our World: The 2030 Agenda for Sustainable Development*, October 21, 2015, A/RES/70/1, https://www.refworld.org/docid/57b6e3e44.html.

home was found to be overwhelmed and could not measure up, given the prevalence of children in need of help in the area.[108]

Since sexual violence is more pervasive in poor communities, attempts to empower females economically may have a bearing on the reduction of the crime. Improved socio-economic structures through programmes and policies which strengthen females' education and employment may assist in preventing sexual abuses.[109] More policies aimed at uplifting women in workplaces, for instance, may be considered. Bursaries aimed at supporting and advancing female education may also encourage many females to advance their studies. These measures may help increase social security among females which may, in turn, prevent them from tolerating sexual violence in exchange of socio-economic provision from perpetrators. Income-generating options may also be introduced to Zimbabwean women. This may be in the form of trainings offered by the government as a way of economically empowering females to enable them to fend for themselves and their dependants.

Increased support systems for survivors of sexual violence may be one of the strategies to reduce the prevalence of the crime in Zimbabwe. These may include provision of well-equipped and resourced safe houses for survivors. Such safe houses may offer, among other supports, counselling, trainings on self-development on how survivors may conquer stigma and blame from their societies while empowering them on how to lead a normal and better life after the ordeal. These may come in handy as most survivors become incapacitated to seek justice because of fear of judgement and further victimisation by their own families and communities at large. Where necessary, such assistance may be offered not only to the survivor of sexual violence but also to her dependants and those depending on the perpetrator. Where the whole family looks up to the perpetrator for subsistence, ways of empowering such a family to live without the perpetrator may be explored.

Sexual violence is deep-rooted in gender stereotypes and discrimination against women in societies. In this way, the UN Women envisages

---

[108] Ngonidzashe and Gasva *supra* note 20, 15–21.

[109] Kathleen Basile and others, *Stop SV: A Technical Package to Prevent Sexual Violence: Centers for Disease Control and Prevention* (2016) 12.

that sexual violence may be prevented through offering education to both girls and boys at an early stage on issues of gender equality and respectful relationships.[110] Such preventative programmes are of importance as the goal is to prevent sexual violence from happening in the first place. Zimbabwe may benefit having more of these training programmes as boys would grow up knowing how to avoid acts amounting to sexual violence, whereas girls may be trained on knowing what actions to accept or to not condone. Girls may also be taught self-defence measures to help protect themselves from any acts of sexual violence. In this regard, lessons may be drawn from Kenya's Ujamaa No means No Worldwide project which teaches high school girls tactics on self-defence.[111] The focal point of this programme is on girls' strengths to maintain and protect their rights.

In addition, investing in a wide range of teachings on stopping sexual violence may yield desirable outcomes. Both males and females may be taught about managing healthy and safe relationships. These trainings may include, teaching females independence in all aspects instead of viewing males as their sole source of provision. This would help eliminate vulnerability to perpetuated sexual violence by intimate partners. In the same vein, females may be trained in leadership roles and available opportunities.

Awareness programmes on sexual violence may be increased in Zimbabwe. Given a wide scope of what constitutes sexual violence, it should never be taken for granted that everyone understands what these entail. Some forms of sexual crimes may not be necessarily considered as such in some communities. Thus, continuous awareness should be conducted throughout the country. These should not just be on the knowledge of the crimes but also different structures available for survivors and their families. Programmes should also address defective social norms which normalise or condone sexual violence. Norms including but not limited to gender and cultural norms need to be

---

[110] UN Women, *Focusing on Prevention to Stop the Violence,* https://www.unwomen.org/en/what-we-do/ending-violence-against-women/prevention.

[111] *Reducing Sexual Assault through the Empowerment of High School Girls: New Tactics in Human Rights*, https://www.newtactics.org/tactic/reducing-sexual-assault-through-empowerment-high-school-girls.

tackled about sexual violence. Instead of rigid gender and cultural norms which may perpetrate violence against women, societies may be educated on adapting into a protective culture.[112] In this way, males may be educated on becoming allies against sexual violence rather than being perpetrators or accomplices.

Zimbabwe may approach various donors or sponsors to assist them to alleviate the plight of female sexual crimes. Donors like World Bank, United Nations Children's Fund (UNICEF), Department for International Development (DFID) and the World Food Program usually assist in social security.[113] Although these may be assisting the country in other areas, there is a possibility of them extending their support to help eradicate sexual violence crimes against women.

8 Conclusion

In a nutshell, a connection between social security and the right to access to justice places the indigent survivors of sexual violence in Zimbabwe in a compromising position which forces them to forfeit one right for the other. The dire economic conditions in the country compel most survivors to protect perpetrators who provide for their livelihood. This is driven by fear or being left socially insecure. Such harsh and detrimental decisions greatly impact on most women's access to justice. The mere implementation of laws against sexual violence and establishing justice institutions have proven insufficient as rape statistics continue to skyrocket.

As such, a strong recommendation, herein, is on strengthening social security systems since desperate dependence on perpetrators for livelihood often hinder crime reporting. Thus, addressing social security is important for Zimbabwe as it would not only help in the advancement of people's socio-economic rights but also the realisation of women's right to justice. This kind of approach is also essential in the current times where

[112] Basile and others *supra* note 109, 15.

[113] Marina Dodlova, Anna Giolbas and Jann Lay, 'Non-contributory social transfer programs in developing countries: A new dataset and research agenda' 16 *Data in Brief* (2018): 51–64.

the world is in the final decade of the realisation of the global SDGs, as failure to address one right would negatively impact on the achievement of several SDGs.

References

Aberdeen University Lawyers Without Borders, *Report on Access to Justice in Zimbabwe*, https://www.academia.edu/32030464/Report_on_Access_to_Justice_in_Zimbabwe.

Basile Kathleen C and others, *Stop SV: A Technical Package to Prevent Sexual Violence.* (2016).

Birdthistle Isolde J and others, Child Sexual Abuse and Links to HIV and Orphanhood in Urban Zimbabwe, 65 *Journal of Epidemiol Community Health*, https://doi.org/10.1136/jech.2009.094359 (2011).

Central Statistical Office (CSO) and Macro International Inc Calverton, Maryland: CSO and Macro International Inc, *Zimbabwe Demographic and Health Survey 2005–06*, (2007), https://dhsprogram.com/pubs/pdf/FR186/FR186.pdf, June 12, 2020.

Chikwiri, Elizabeth and Lemmer, Eleanor M, 'Gender-Based Violence in Primary Schools in the Harare and Marondera Districts of Zimbabwe,' 5 *Journal Sociology Social Anthropology* (2014): 95–107.

Chireshe Regis and Chireshe Excellent, 'Sexual Harassment of Female Students in Three Selected High Schools in Urban Masvingo, Zimbabwe,' 23 *Agenda* (2009): 88–96.

Coltart Douglas, 'Freedom from all forms of violence: Using Zimbabwe's new Constitution to encourage rape law reform' 50 *South African Crime Quarterly* (2014): 31–40.

Constitution of Zimbabwe Amendment (No. 20) Act, 2013.

Criminal Law (Codification and Reform) Act 2004.

Crootof Rebecca, 'Change without Consent: How Customary International Law Modifies Treaties,' 41 *Yale Journal of International Law* (2016): 237–300.

Customary International Law Database. https://ihl-databases.icrc.org/customary-ihl/eng/docs/home, June 12, 2020.

Dannies Kate, *Sexual Violence against Women is a Global Crisis. Stop Trying to Make it a National One*, Quartz March 2, 2020, https://qz.com/1810434/the-way-we-talk-about-sexual-violence-is-only-making-it-worse/, June 12, 2020.

David S Mitchel, 'The Prohibition of Rape in International Humanitarian Law as a Norm of Jus Cogens: Clarifying the Doctrine,' 15 *Duke Journal of Comparative & International Law* (2005): 219–257.

Dhemba Jotham, 'Social Protection for the Elderly in Zimbabwe: Issues, Challenges and Prospects,' 3 *African Journal of Social Work* (2013): 31–22.

Dugard John, *International Law: A South African perspective* (2014).

Fagbamigbe Adeniyi F and others, 'Survival Analysis and Prognostic Factors Associated with the Timing of First Forced Sexual Act Among Women in Kenya, Zimbabwe and Cote d'Ivoire' 4 *Scientific African* (2019): 1–14.

Gift Dafuleya, 'Social and Emergency Assistance Ex-Ante and During COVID-19 in the SADC Region,' 2 *The International Journal of Community and Social Development* (2020): 251–268.

Girl Child Network, *Gravity of Girl Child Sexual Abuse in Zimbabwe: Towards Creating A Culture of Prevention*, http://archive.kubatana.net/docs/sexual/gcn_sexual_abuse_zim_050517.pdf, June 12, 2020.

Greco Donna and Dawgert Sarah *Poverty and Sexual Violence: Building Prevention and Intervention Responses: A Guide for Counselors and Advocates* (2007).

Hodzi Obert, *Sexual Violence as Political Strategy in Zimbabwe: Transitional Justice Blind Spot? Oxford Transitional Justice* Research, Working Paper Series: Debates (2012), https://www.law.ox.ac.uk/sites/files/oxlaw/oberthodzi_zimbabwe_otjrdebates1.pdf.

International Federation of Red Cross and Red Crescent Societies, Geneva, *Effective law and policy on gender equality and protection from sexual and gender-based violence in disasters* (2017), https://reliefweb.int/sites/reliefweb.int/files/resources/Gender-SGBV-Report_-Zimbabwe.pdf, June 12, 2020.

Jewkes Rachel and others 'Sexual Violence' in Etienne G Krug and others (eds) *World Report on Violence and Health* (2002).

Kanyenze Godfrey and others *Beyond the Enclave: Towards a Pro-Poor and Inclusive Development Strategy for Zimbabwe* (2011).

Kaseke Edwin, 'Social Exclusion and Social Security: The Case of Zimbabwe,' 18 *Journal of Social Development in Africa* (2003): 33–48.

Kelly Liz, Lovett Jo and Regan Linda, *A Gap or a Chasm? Attrition in Reported Rape Cases*, Home Office Research Study 293, (2005), https://www.researchgate.net/publication/238713283_Home_Office_Research_Study_293_A_gap_or_a_chasm_Attrition_in_reported_rape_cases, June 12, 2020.

Landsberg Chris, 'African Solutions for African Problems: Quiet Diplomacy and South Africa's Diplomatic Strategy Towards Zimbabwe,' 41 *Journal for Contemporary History* (2016): 126–148.

Mantula Fennie and Saloojee Haroon, 'Child Sexual Abuse in Zimbabwe,' 25 *Journal of Child Sexual Abuse* (2016): 866–880.

Manuel Marcus and Manuel Clare, *Achieving Equal Access to justice for all by 2030: Lessons from Global Funds*, Overseas Development Institute, Working Paper 537, 2018, https://www.odi.org/sites/odi.org.uk/files/resource-documents/12307.pdf, June 12, 2020.

Manzvanzvike Hildegade, *Rape: When society lets kids down,* The Herald, December 26, 2012, https://www.herald.co.zw/rape-when-society-lets-kids-down/, 12 June 2020.

Mapingure v Minister of Home Affairs (2014).

Mapuva Jephias and Makaye Peter, 'Exploring Zimbabwe's Enduring Economic Challenges and Interventionist Strategies: Showcasing the Zimbabwe Agenda for Sustainable Socio-Economic Transformation (ZIMASSET),' 47 *African Journal of Development Studies* (2017).

Masuka Tawanda and others, 'Preserving the Future: Social Protection Programmes for Orphans and Vulnerable Children (OVC) in Zimbabwe,' 2 *International Journal of Humanities and Social Sciences* (2012): 59–66.

Masuka Tawanda, 'The New Constitution of Zimbabwe and its Implication for Social Workers,' 2 *Journal of Social Welfare and Human Rights* (2014): 29–40.

Maybe Zengenene and Emy Susanti, 'Violence against Women and Girls in Harare, Zimbabwe,' 20 *Journal of International Women's Studies* (2019): 83–93.

Médecins Sans Frontières, *Untreated Violence: Breaking Down the Barriers to Sexual Violence Care in Harare, Zimbabwe 2011–2017 Report*, https://samumsf.org/sites/default/files/201807/SGV%20Report_Harae%20Zimbabwe.pdf, June 12, 2020.

Mukamana Jeanette I, Machakanja Pamela and Adjei, Nicholas K, 'Trends in prevalence and correlates of intimate partner violence against women in Zimbabwe, 2005–2015,' 20 *International Health and Human Rights* (2020): https://doi.org/10.1186/s12914-019-0220-8.

Muridzo Noel G and Chikadzi Victor, 'Some Impediments to Child Sexual Abuse Interventions and Corresponding Social Work Implications: Reflections on the Zimbabwean Victim Friendly System' *Journal of Human Rights and Social Work* (2020): https://doi.org/10.1007/s41134-020-00137-x.

Muridzo Noel G, *An exploration of the phenomenon of child sexual abuse in Zimbabwe* (PhD Thesis, University of Witwatersrand 2017).

Muridzo Noel G and Malianga Effie, 'Child Sexual Abuse in Zimbabwe: Prevention Strategies for Social Workers,' 5 *African Journal of Social Work* (2015): 41–64.

Musiwa Anthony, 'How Has the Presence of Zimbabwe's Victim-Friendly Court and Relevant Child Protection Policy and Legal Frameworks Affected the Management of Intrafamilial Child Sexual Abuse in Zimbabwe? The Case of Marondera District,' *Journal of Interpersonal Violence* (2018): 1748–1777.

Mutanana Ngonidzashe and Gasva Douglas, 'Barriers to and Consequences of Reporting Rape in a Rural Community of Zimbabwe' 5 *Developing Country Studies* (2015): 15–21.

National Social Security Act of 1989.

National Social Security Authority (Pension and other Benefits Schemes), 1993. (S.I. No. 393 of 1993).

New Tactics in Human Rights, *Reducing Sexual Assault through the Empowerment of High School Girls*, https://www.newtactics.org/tactic/reducing-sexual-assault-through-empowerment-high-school-girls, June 12, 2020.

Nhundu Tichatonga and Shumba Almon, 'The nature and frequency of reported cases of teacher perpetrated child sexual abuse in rural primary schools in Zimbabwe' 25 *Child Abuse and Neglect* (2001): 1517–1534.

Njovana Eunice and Watts Charlotte, 'Gender Violence in Zimbabwe: A Need for Collaborative Action' 4 *Reproductive Health Matters* (1996): 46–55.

Norman Nhede, The Social Security Policy of the Government of Zimbabwe: A Policy, *Analysis Overview* (PhD Dissertation, University of Pretoria 2016), https://repository.up.ac.za/bitstream/handle/2263/57163/Nhede_Social_2016.pdf?sequence=1&isAllowed=y, June 12, 2020.

Nyamanhindi Richard, *Hidden in Plain Sight: Child Sexual Abuse in Zimbabwe*, The Herald, February 4, 2015, https://www.herald.co.zw/hidden-in-plain-sight-child-sexual-abuse-in-zimbabwe/, June 12, 2020.

Nyenti Mathias, 'Access to Justice in the South African Social Security system: Towards a Conceptual Approach' 46 *De Jure* (2013): 901–916.

OECD Conference Centre, *Understanding Effective Access to Justice, Workshop Background Paper* (2016).

Osirim, Mary J, 'Crisis in the State and the Family: Violence Against Women in Zimbabwe' 7 *African Studies Quarterly* (2003): 153–169.

Owen Gagare, *Zimbabwe: Caught Between the Pandemic and an Incapable State*, Good Governance Africa, August 12, 2020 https://gga.org/zimbabwe-caught-between-the-pandemic-and-an-incapable-state/, June 12, 2020.

Rees Susan and others, 'Believe #metoo: Sexual Violence and Interpersonal Disclosure Experiences among Women Attending a Sexual Assault Service in Australia: A Mixed Methods Study' 6 *BMJ Open* (2019): e026773. https://doi.org/10.1136/bmjopen-2018-026773.

Report Produced by the Women's Programme of the Research & Advocacy Unit, *Politically Motivated Rape in Zimbabwe* (2011), https://akcampaign.files.wordpress.com/2011/03/rau_politically_motivated_rape_110428.pdf, June 12, 2020.

Riphenburg Carol, 'Women's Status and Cultural Expression: Changing Gender Relations and Structural Adjustment in Zimbabwe' 44 *Africa Today* (1997): 33–50.

Rome Statute of the International Criminal Court (1998).

Rumbidzai Dube, *She probably asked for it! A Preliminary Study into Zimbabwean Societal Perceptions of Rape*, Research and Advocacy Unity (2013), https://reliefweb.int/sites/reliefweb.int/files/resources/A-study-into-Zimbabwean-Societal-perception-of-rape.pdf, June 12, 2020.

Shamu Simukai and others, 'Does a History of Sexual and Physical Childhood Abuse Contribute to HIV Infection Risk in Adulthood? A Study among Post-natal Women in Harare, Zimbabwe' 14 *PLOS One* (2019): e0198866. https://doi.org/10.1371/journal.pone.0198866.

Symphorosa Rembe and others, 'Child and forced marriage as violation of women's rights, and responses by member states in Southern African Development Community' 25 *Agenda: Empowering Women for Gender Equity* (2011): 65–74.

Transforming Our World: The 2030 Agenda for Sustainable Development. UN General Assembly.

UN Human Rights Council, *Zimbabwe Policies Hitting Poor Hardest, say UN Rights Experts*, April 4, 2019, https://reliefweb.int/report/zimbabwe/zimbabwe-policies-hitting-poor-hardest-say-un-rights-experts, June 12, 2020.

UN News, *A Staggering One-in-Three Women, Experience Physical, Sexual Abuse*, https://news.un.org/en/story/2019/11/1052041.

UN Women, *Focusing on Prevention to Stop the Violence*, https://www.unwomen.org/en/what-we-do/ending-violence-against-women/prevention, June 12, 2020.

United Nations Foundation, *A Global Issue We Can't Ignore: Violence Against Girls and Women*, https://unfoundation.org/blog/post/a-global-issue-we-cant-ignore-violence-against-girls-and-women/, June 12, 2020.

USAID, *USAID and WFP Provide Relief to over 100,000 Urban Dwellers During Covid-19,* September 30, 2020, https://www.usaid.gov/zimbabwe/press-releases/usaid-and-wfp-provide-relief-over-100000-urban-dwellers, June 12, 2020.

World Health Organisation, *Sexual Violence*: World Report on Violence and Health (2002), https://www.who.int/violence_injury_prevention/violence/global_campaign/en/chap6.pdf?ua=1, June 12, 2020.

World Health Organization, *Violence Against Women—Intimate Partner and Sexual Violence against Women*, (2011), https://apps.who.int/iris/handle/10665/112325, June 12, 2020.

Zengeni Knocks, 'Zimbabwe: A Country Profile' 7 *Journal of International Studies* (2020): 157–169.

Zimbabwe National Statistics Agency Harare, *Zimbabwe Demographic and Health Survey 2010–2011*, https://dhsprogram.com/pubs/pdf/FR254/FR254.pdf, June 12, 2020.

Zimbabwe Republic Police, *Victim Friendly Unit*, www.zrp.gov.zw/index.php?option=com_content&view=article&id=86&Itemid=741, 12 June 2020.

Zimbizi George, *Study on Socio-economic Status of Children and Women on Commercial Farms, Mining and Peri-urban Areas*, Report Prepared for UNICEF, (2001), https://www.unicef.org/evaldatabase/files/ZIM_01-800_Part1.pdf, June 12, 2020.

10

Roots Revisited: Barriers to Justice for Survivors and Victims of Female Genital Mutilation in The Gambia

Raeesa Rajmohamed

1 Introduction

Female Genital Mutilation (FGM), a common violent assault against women in Africa,[1] flourishes in The Gambia.[2] The nation's failure to eradicate the practice demonstrates, amongst others, the judiciary's failure in the face of gender-based violence. The national legislation which prohibits the practice has rendered itself meaningless in its five

[1] World Health Organization, *Female Genital Mutilation (FGM)*, https://www.who.int/reproductivehealth/topics/fgm/prevalence/en/.

[2] Note that: *The Gambia: Multiple Indicator Cluster Survey (MICS) 2018* is the primary survey used within this chapter to report FGM rates in The Gambia. This survey is also used to report the *attitudes* towards domestic violence. It is used in conjunction with domestic violence rates and FGM rates reported in the *Demographic and Health survey (DHS) 2013*, as all subsequent available DHS surveys do not include FGM or domestic violence; The Gambia Bureau of Statistics (GBOS) and International Community Foundation (ICF) International, *The Gambia Demographic and Health Survey: Key Indicators 2019–2020* (Rockville, MD: GBOS and ICF International, July 2020), https://dhsprogram.com/pubs/pdf/PR127/PR127.pdf.

R. Rajmohamed (✉)
University of The Gambia, Serrekunda, The Gambia
e-mail: Raeesa@UTG.edu.gm

University of Bristol, Bristol, England

E. C. Lubaale and A. Budoo-Scholtz (eds.), *Violence Against Women and Criminal Justice in Africa: Volume I*, Sustainable Development Goals Series,
https://doi.org/10.1007/978-3-030-75949-0_10

years as the practice of Type III FGM, FGM's rarest[3] and most severe form,[4] persists.[5] The Gambian government remains at the mercy of a culture favouring the practice. It sublimates external resistance; in itself becoming what Kurt Lewin deems the 'resistor': the force preventing necessary social paradigm shifts.[6] According to Lewin, a *cultural* movement against the practice *must* manifest to garner adequate support to challenge FGM and achieve transitional justice; yet The Gambia offers none. The governmental and national 'resistors' to FGM-abolishment face no threat, rendering it impossible to fulfil Lewin's opposing ends of the equilibrium. The country is thus static, trapped in a state of deceit. The government superficially pleases the international sphere by performing 'bare minimum' expectations, *appearing* incentivised to eradicate FGM and spark change when it is instead hindering the cause. Ultimately, the government encourages the practice through a perceived apathy, allowing tradition to prosper and creating a roadblock against social transformation.

FGM has been a common topic for scholarly discussion, academic scrutiny and NGO/political activism. Most publications on the subject are qualitative studies,[7] systematic reviews[8] and demographic surveys.[9]

---

[3] Type III FGM is FGM is undergone only 10% of the time globally; Heather Sipsma, Peggy Chen, Angela Ofori-Atta, Ukwuoma Ilozumba, Kapouné Karfo and Elizabeth H. Bradley, 'Female Genital Cutting: Current Practices and Beliefs in Western Africa,' 90 *Bulletin of the World Health Organization* (2012): 124.

[4] The Gambia Bureau of Statistics (GBOS) and International Community Foundation (ICF), *supra* note 2, 220; 28 Too Many, *The Gambia: The Law and GFM* (Online: Thomson Reuters Foundation, 2018), https://www.28toomany.org/static/media/uploads/Law%20Reports/gambia_law_report_v1_september_2018.pdf.

[5] The Gambia Bureau of Statistics (GBOS) International Community Foundation (ICF) International, *supra* note 2; 28 Too Many, *The Gambia: The Law and GFM supra* note 4.

[6] Kurt Lewin, 'Frontiers in Group Dynamics: Concept, Method and Reality in Social Science; Social Equilibria and Social Change,' 1 *Human Relations* (1947): 15.

[7] Asresash Demissie Abathun, Johanne Sundby and Abdi A. Gele, 'Attitude Toward Female Genital Mutilation Among Somali and Harari People, Eastern Ethiopia,' 8 *International Journal of Women's Health* (2016): 557–569.

[8] Rigmor C. Berg and Eva Denison, 'A Tradition in Transition: Factors Perpetuating and Hindering the Continuation of Female Genital Mutilation/Cutting (FGM/C) Summarized in a Systematic Review,' 34 *Health Care for Women International* (2013): 837–859.

[9] The Gambia Bureau of Statistics (GBOS) International Community Foundation (ICF) International, *The Gambia Demographic and Health Survey 2013* (Rockville, MD: GBOS and ICF International, September 2014), https://dhsprogram.com/pubs/pdf/FR289/FR289.pdf.

However, there is a lack of academic analysis of the practice *and* societal methods to achieve transitional justice. Ultimately, the literature often considers FGM on a global scale, with little focus given to The Gambia specifically. Equally, FGM literature is usually confined to affirming speculation that FGM is intrinsically woven within practising societies,[10] like Berg and Denison's 2013 systematic review of FGM.[11] This literature is valuable as they succeed in providing a 'necessary first step' towards eradicating FGM by identifying forces underpinning and perpetuating its existence. Nevertheless, any broad scope cannot consider country-specific variables.

There has also been country-specific literature which tends to revolve around societal motivation without consideration of access to justice, such as the work of Abathun and others' study on members of the Somali and Harari community in Ethiopia.[12] Abathun and others strongly identify regional differences amongst views towards FGM, as well as the cultural and gender-based motivations towards strengthening and exacerbating the practice. However, their conclusion echoes in other 'culturally analytical' FGM literature,[13] and broadly recommends 'collaborative and strong effort amongst government, local organisations, community and religious leaders to play a major role in the process to bring behavioural change.'[14] Literature on FGM often suggests governmental and organisational incentives to spark change, without acknowledging the hurdles to be overcome as a precursor to transitional justice being achieved. Outside of blogs and articles, which still only briefly review the ban in its early stage,[15] scholarly FGM literature on The Gambia tends to tackle the

[10] Patricia Broussard, 'Female Genital Mutilation: Exploring Strategies for Ending Ritualized Torture; Shaming, Blaming, and Utilizing the Convention Against Torture,' 15 *Duke Journal of Gender Law & Policy* (2008): 19–47; Rigmor and Denison, *supra* note 8.

[11] Berg, Rigmore C. and Eva Denison, 'Effectiveness of Interventions Designed to Prevent Female Genital Mutilation/Cutting: A Systematic Review,' 43 *Studies in Family Planning* 43 (2012): 135–146.

[12] Asresash Demissie Abathun, Johanne Sundby and Abdi A. Gele, 'Attitude Toward Female Genital Mutilation Among Somali and Harari People, Eastern Ethiopia,' 8 *International Journal of Women's Health* (2016): 557–569.

[13] Rigmore and Denison, *supra* note 11.

[14] Asresash et al., *supra* note 12, 568.

[15] Satang Nabaneh, 'Banning Female Circumcision in The Gambia Through Legislative Change: The Next Steps,' AfricLaw, January 19, 2016.

topic by offering a male perspective on the subject.[16] Although beneficial in adding breadth to the greater Gambian perception of the practice, it fails to give focus to FGM *victims* and their inability to access justice. Any existing FGM literature that does specifically focus on The Gambia *and* progressing the society, is outdated and thus unable to consider the country's 2015 criminalisation. Hernlund and Shell-Duncan's analysis of FGM in The Gambia and Senegal, for example, vitally identifies the more prominent grey area that occurs between ideologies in favour of the practice and ideologies opposed to the practice.[17] Though they argue the existence of a constant and fluid fluctuation of opinions and views towards FGM, their range is also still limited to discussing communal/cultural perspectives. They also call for the examination of 'the manner in which behaviour change occurs and the factors that alter or deter readiness for change… within the social contexts [of FGM].'[18] However, it does so in 2007, long before the country legally prohibited FGM.

Despite criminalisation in 2015, FGM prevails within Gambian borders, frustrating the aspirations of non-governmental organisations (NGOs) lobbying for the practice's eradication. Victims of FGM often do not view themselves as victims. Instead they are encouraged and celebrated for undergoing the practice,[19] shunned if they reject it[20] and pressured and coerced to engage in its propagation due to societal expectation and tradition.[21] Consequently, they are unable to seek help or retribution for their suffering[22] (see Section 3.3). Justice is thus inaccessible for women of The Gambia.

---

[16] Adriana Kaplan, Babucarr Cham, Lamin A. Njie, Ana Seixas, Sandra Blanco and Mireia Utzet, 'Female Genital Mutilation/Cutting: The Secret World of Women as Seen by Men,' *Obstetrics and Gynaecology International* (2013): 1–11; Inger-Lise Lien, 'The Perspectives of Gambian Men on the Sexuality of Cut and Uncut Women,' 20 *Sexualities* (2017): 521–534.

[17] Ylva Hernlund and Bettina Shell-Duncan, 'Contingency, Context, and Change: Negotiating Female Genital Cutting in The Gambia and Senegal,' 53 *Africa Today* (2007): 43–57.

[18] Ibid., 55.

[19] Ibid., 52.

[20] Ibid.

[21] Ibid., 53.

[22] Stated in the testimony of a Madinka woman; Ylva and Shell-Duncan, *supra* note 17, 49 and 48.

This chapter seeks to expand upon the existing literature by utilising them in a country-specific analysis of The Gambia. It analyses whether illegality, one of the identified deterrents to FGM, can truly constitute as an FGM 'hindrance' when popular attitudes accept the practice. It intends to fill the scholarly gap by specifically addressing barriers in access to justice for FGM survivors in The Gambia. It further scrutinises the government's covert role in perpetuating the practice alongside identifying the necessary actions the government must take to achieve transitional justice.

2 Prevalence of Female Genital Mutilation

The term 'prevalence' is often used in this chapter concerning FGM. It is crucial to note that the term is an expression of the total number of victims as a *proportion* of the given population of women.[23] The practice of FGM is undergone in Yemen,[24] Iraq,[25] Indonesia,[26] other Middle-Eastern and Asian countries, and at least 28 African countries,[27] primarily concentrated throughout Western and Northeast Africa.[28] However, over the last three decades, various countries in Africa have

23 UNICEF, 'Indicator Profiles: Percentage of Girls and Women (aged 15–49 years) Who Have Undergone Female Genital Mutilation (FGM),' https://data.unicef.org/indicator-profile/PT_F_15-49_FGM/.

24 Yemen Ministry of Public Health and Population and Central Statistical Organization, *Yemen National Health and Demographic Survey 2013* (Rockville, MD, July 2015), 163, https://dhsprogram.com/pubs/pdf/FR296/FR296.pdf.

25 MICS, 2018*Multiple Indicator Cluster Survey (MICS6) Briefing* (2018) 53, https://reliefweb.int/sites/reliefweb.int/files/resources/English_7.pdf.

26 Though FGM in Indonesia is 'understudied', see WHO and Ministry of Health Republic of Indonesia, *State of Health Inequality Indonesia* (World Health Organization 2017), xiv and 41, https://www.who.int/docs/default-source/gho-documents/health-equity/state-of-inequality/12-dec-final-final-17220-state-of-health-inequality-in-indonesia-for-web.pdf?sfvrsn=54ae73ea_2.

27 28 Too Many, *supra* note 4.

28 World Health Organization, Sexual and Reproductive Health: Female Genital Mutilation: Prevalence of FGM (2013), https://www.who.int/reproductivehealth/topics/fgm/prevalence/en/#:~:text=Prevalence%20of%20FGM,female%20genital%20mutilation%20every%20year.

evidenced a gradual shift against FGM,[29] with governments continuously choosing to criminalise the practice. Most recently, in 2020, Sudan joined the trend,[30] although locals reportedly fear the practice will continue underground.[31] Nevertheless, East African countries have progressed substantially throughout this time. Uganda successfully reduced its FGM prevalence to 0%,[32] dropping the victim number to 0.3% of women[33] (as noted, 'prevalence' is distinct from the number of victims and refers to the *proportion* of victims in relation to the population of women). Uganda's neighbouring countries have also done well in efforts to eradicate the practice[34] with the United Republic of Tanzania having a drop of 10% in FGM prevalence over the last twenty years.[35] Kenya was also applauded by UNICEF for its substantial progress towards abandoning FGM,[36] despite having a prevalence rate that is over double Tanzania's with a figure of 21%.[37]

However, while this improvement is also observed in countries like Chad, Cote d'Ivoire, Ethiopia, Nigeria, Ghana, the Congo, Cameroon

---

29 Ngianga-Bakwin Kandala, Martinsixtus Ezejimofor and Paul Komba, 'Secular Trends in the Prevalence of Female Genital Mutilation/Cuttings Among Girls: A systematic Analysis,' 5 *BMJ* (2019): 1–7.

30 Penal Code of 1991 (amendment) Law No. 12 of 2020, article 141(a).

31 BBC News, *Sudan Criminalises Female Genital Mutilation (FGM)*, BBC News, May 1, 2020, https://www.bbc.com/news/world-africa-52502489.

32 UNICEF, *Female Genital Mutilation (FGM)*, February 2020, https://data.unicef.org/topic/child-protection/female-genital-mutilation/; Uganda Bureau of Statistics, *Uganda Demographic and Health Survey 2016* (2018): 148, https://dhsprogram.com/pubs/pdf/FR333/FR333.pdf.

33 Ibid.

34 Tanzania had multifaced educational campaigns with promising results; Moses Galukande, Joseph Kamara, Violet Ndabwire, Elisabeth Leistey, Cecilia Valla and Sam Luboga, 'Eradicating Female Genital Mutilation and Cutting in Tanzania: An Observational Study,' 15 *BMC Public Health* (2015): 1–10.

35 18% in 1996 to 10% in 2016; National Bureau of Statistics, *Tanzania Demographic and Health Survey 2010* (Calverton, MD, April 2011): 295, https://dhsprogram.com/pubs/pdf/FR243/FR243 June; Ministry of Health, Community Development, Gender, Elderly and Children et al., *Tanzania Demographic and Health Survey and Malaria Indicator Survey 2015–2016: Final Report*, (2016): 359 https://dhsprogram.com/pubs/pdf/FR321/FR321.pdf.

36 Kenya's progress towards abandoning FGM is strong compared to other countries in Eastern and Southern Africa: UNICEF, *A Profile of Female Genital Mutilation in Kenya*, https://reliefweb.int/report/kenya/profile-female-genital-mutilation-kenya.

37 Kenya National Bureau of Statistics et al., *Kenya Demographic and Health Survey 2014* (2015): 333, https://www.dhsprogram.com/pubs/pdf/FR308/FR308.pdf.

and Sierra Leone,[38] it has remained static in others. Studies have shown that, for the past 30 years, FGM prevalence has remained 'high and stable' in both Mali and The Gambia.[39] Yet, unlike Mali, which has not criminalised FGM and shares a border with a fellow nation of high FGM prevalence,[40] The Gambia maintains FGM support despite both legally prohibiting the practice *and* the country's geography. Low FGM rates exist in The Gambia's neighbouring country, Senegal.[41] It is this discrepancy that brings The Gambia to the forefront of discussion.

The Gambia, although the sixth smallest African country, houses one of the continent's highest number of FGM victims below and over 14 years of age,[42] with 75.5% of all women 14–49 having suffered FGM.[43] Distribution-wise, the *majority of all* women within *each* Gambian region are FGM survivors, with the exception of the country's busiest and most diverse capital city, Banjul- still, this percentage is only slightly below half.[44] Within ethnic groups, the Wolof community is the only Gambian community who do not engage with the practice[45]: only 13% of Wolof women are FGM victims versus 96.3% of Mandinka

38 Alissa Koski and Jody Heymann, 'Thirty-year Trends in the Prevalence and Severity of Female Genital Mutilation: a Comparison of 22 Countries,' 2 *BMJ Global Health* (2017): 6.

39 Ibid.

40 Guinea; Institut National de la Statistique et Ministère du Plan et du Développement Economique, *Enquête Démographique et de Santé, République de Guinée 2018 (Guinea Demographic and Health Survey 2018)*, (2019): 353, https://dhsprogram.com/pubs/pdf/FR353/FR353.pdf.

41 Agence Nationale de la Statistiqueet de la Démographie (ANSD), *Sénégal: Enquête Démographique et de Santé Continue (EDS-Continue) 2017* (2018): 324, https://dhsprogram.com/pubs/pdf/FR345/FR345.pdf.

42 76%: UNICEF Data, 'Female Genital Mutilation: Percentage of girls who have undergone FGM (2020),' https://data.unicef.org/topic/child-protection/female-genital-mutilation.

43 MICS, *The Gambia: Multiple Indicator Cluster Survey 2018* (2019): 354, https://mics-surveys-prod.s3.amazonaws.com/MICS6/West%20and%20Central%20Africa/Gambia/2018/Survey%20findings/The%20Gambia%202018%20MICS%20Survey%20Findings%20Report_English.pdf.

44 Ibid.

45 Adriana Kaplan, Mary Forbes, Isabelle Bonhoure, Mireia Utzet, Miguel Martín, Malick Manneh, and Haruna Ceesay, 'Female Genital Mutilation/cutting in The Gambia: Long-term Health Consequences and Complications During Delivery and for the Newborn,' 5 *International Journal of Women's Health* (2013): 328.

women and 94% of Sarahule women.[46] Across almost all spectra of Gambian life, most Gambian women are FGM victims.

In The Gambia, FGM is implemented without anaesthesia, antibiotic or any form of medication. Neither prior nor post criminalisation, medical guidelines or regulations have not existed surrounding the 'procedure,' nor is it performed by trained medical practitioners. Instead, it is 'often practiced by an old woman using an instrument that does not facilitate high precision in cutting,'[47] such as rusty knives, razors or scissors.[48] Therefore, even if Type I FGM is intended, what sometimes results is Type II or III.[49] This may account for the inconsistent reports detailing the most common *type* of FGM undergone nationally, with some detailing Type II, and others citing Type III. Similarly, there may be a lack of understanding of the severity of the cutting performed or endured.

3 FGM as a Form of Gender-Based violence

FGM is often referred to as female 'cutting' or female 'circumcision' despite a gross severity in harm that is not *typically* found in the practice of its 'male counterpart.'[50] A *true* male equivalent would be the

[46] MICS, *supra* note 43.

[47] Kaplan, *supra* note 45, 329.

[48] Nawal Nour, *Female Genital Cutting (circumcision)* UpToDate, January 13, 2020, https://www.uptodate.com/contents/female-genital-cutting-circumcision?search=female%20genital%20mutilation&source=search_result&selectedTitle=1~27&usage_type=default&display_rank=1.

[49] Kaplan, *supra* note 45, 329.

[50] Zuhdi Jasser, Waqas Khan, and Shaaz Mahboob, *Comparisons Between Female Genital Mutilation and Male Circumcision are False and Dangerous,* Uncommon Ground, February 26, 2018, https://uncommongroundmedia.com/comparisons-female-genital-mutilation-male-circumcision-false-dangerous/.

complete amputation of the penis,[51] arguably[52] rendering the current female practice incomparable to any circumcision. FGM often causes severe and irreversible physical *and* mental consequences, such as haemorrhaging, extreme blood loss, trauma and post-traumatic stress disorder (PTSD), alongside potential permanent damage to future offspring such as birth asphyxia and brain damage.[53] FGM thus represents a persistent and pervasive issue of global public health.

The World Health Organization (WHO) classifies the specific forms of FGM into four main types, with the severity of assault increasing with each category. Type I (clitoridectomy) is 'the partial or total' extraction of the visible portion of the clitoral glans (Type Ia). Removing the clitoral hood, also known as the prepuce, also fits within this category (the removal of both classifies Type Ib). Type II (excision) refers to the partial or *complete* removal of the inner folds of the vulva, the clitoral glans and the labia minora (extraction of the labia minora only represents Type IIa, removal of both represents Type IIb). This may also occur when the outer folds of the vulva, the labia majora, are cut (which represents Type IIc FGM). Type III (infibulation) describes the process by which the labia minora and/or the labia majora are cut, extracted, rearranged, brought together and stitched ('infibulation') to completely narrow the vaginal orifice. Type IV encompasses all other remaining destructive 'procedures to female genitalia for non-medical purposes, such as piercing, incising,' pricking, cauterisation and scraping.[54]

The vulva, the sex-specific genitalia, is the target of the amputation,[55] thus basing the 'necessity' of this maiming entirely on the sex

---

[51] The glans penis, the male equivalent of the female clitoris, is distinct from the prepuce (foreskin) which is typically removed in male circumcision: Brian Caldwell, *Techniques for neonatal circumcision*, UpToDate, (2020), https://www.uptodate.com/contents/techniques-for-neonatal-circumcision?search=male%20circumcision&source=search_result&selectedTitle=3~150&usage_type=default&display_rank=3.

[52] Robert Darby and Steven Svoboda, 'A Rose by Any Other Name?: Rethinking the Similarities and Between Male and Female Genital Cutting,' 21 *Medical Anthropology Quarterly* (2007): 301–323.

[53] Nahid Toubia, 'Female Circumcision as a Public Health Issue,' 331 *The New England Journal of Medicine* (1994): 712–716.

[54] World Health Organization, Types of Female Genital Mutilation (2020), https://www.who.int/sexual-and-reproductive-health/types-of-female-genital-mutilation.

[55] Nour, *supra* note 48.

of the child. Significantly, the majority of *all* FGM victims around the world have had their genital flesh extracted instead of 'only' suffering mutilating slashes.[56] Correspondingly, the term 'gender-based violence' refers to violence inflicted upon someone because of their gender; it is frequently based on the corresponding expectations of that gender's role in society.[57] FGM, as physical and emotional harm inflicted upon coerced children and women, based on the sexual organs associated with their gender-at-birth, and undergone with the purpose to *mutilate* those organs, evidently fulfils multiple criteria to constitute gender-based violence. Acts of 'gender-based violence' are issues of public health and societal discrimination, encompassing mental, physical and sexual abuse, murder, control, deprivation of liberty and the delegating of blame for 'undesired' outcomes on someone based solely on their gender.[58] Often, gender-based violence is 'inherently rooted' in a societal power dynamic which views men as hierarchically superior to women[59] The motivations behind FGM, which usually encompass an intention to *regulate* a woman's sexuality, reinforces this claim. FGM is thus referred to as an act of gender-based violence throughout this chapter.

[56] Alissa Koski and Jody Heymann, 'Thirty-year Trends in the Prevalence and Severity of Female Genital Mutilation: A Comparison of 22 Countries,' 2 *BMJ Global Health* (2017): 1–8.

[57] Pragna Patel, Elliot Raizes and Laura Broyles, 'Human Immunodeficiency Virus Infection' in Edward T Ryan, David R Hill Tom Solomon, Naomi E Aronson and Timothy P Endy (eds.) *Hunter's Tropical Medicine and Emerging Infectious Diseases* (2020): 232–266.

[58] 'Violence that results in, or is likely to result in, physical, sexual or psychological harm or suffering to women, including threats of such acts, coercion or arbitrary deprivation of liberty, whether occurring in public or in private life' (United Nations Human Rights Office of the High Commissioner): United Nations Human Rights Office of the High Commissioner, *Declaration on the Elimination of Violence against Women* (Proclaimed by General Assembly resolution 48/104 of December 20, 1993), https://www.ohchr.org/EN/ProfessionalInterest/Pages/ViolenceAgainstWomen.aspx; Rachel Jewkes and Liz Dartnall, 'Sexual Violence' in Harald Kristian Heggenhougen and Stella Quah (eds.) *International Encyclopedia of Public Health* (2008): 723–731.

[59] 'They often include expectations that women and girls will be under the control of men; that men have sex as a right within marriage; that women should not have sexual desires or a right to sexual pleasure; that sexually aroused men cannot control themselves; and that women and girls are responsible for ensuring that they do not arouse inappropriate sexual desires in men. A nexus of power and control lies at the heart of explanations of why men rape'; Jewkes and Dartnall, *supra* note 58.

This chapter makes an analogy with Alex Huxley's *Roots: The Saga of an American Family*[60] a revolutionary[61] piece of literature, and a subsequent miniseries,[62] which documented the journey of a Gambian sold into slavery. The story garnered critical acclaim from inception.[63] Notwithstanding academic debate over 'historical memory,'[64] and speculated genealogical errors,[65] *Roots* served to directly engrave the ghastly history of colonial and racial exploitation of The Gambia.[66] At present, there remains an internally motivated sex-based exploitation in the country: FGM. The practice is a severe human rights violation that mimics the horror and cruelty of the slave trade, and it prospers in The Gambia. Thus, in this analysis of violence against women, *Roots*, in its stripped essence, is revisited: acts of horror are accepted, practised and flourishing within The Gambia's borders with culpability lying almost entirely in its own culture and control. Significantly, unlike slavery, FGM and violence against women *have* been accepted and welcomed within The Gambia's culture, posing an internal cultural challenge.

---

60 Alex Haley, *Roots: The Saga of an American Family* (1976).

61 The miniseries adaptation 'pushed African nations to publicly come to grips with slavery's brutal history; their often-complicated relationships with the worldwide African diaspora; and their own contemporary struggles with inequality within their borders': Cynthia Greenlee, *How 'Roots' Reverberated in Africa*, The American Prospect, May 30, 2016, https://prospect.org/culture/roots-reverberated-africa/.

62 *Roots*. TV Miniseries. Marvin J. Chomsky, John Erman, David Greene and Gilbert Moses. USA: Warner Brothers Television (1977).

63 The New York Times, 1976 A Selection of Noteworthy Titles, *The New York Times*, December 5, 1976, https://www.nytimes.com/1976/12/05/archives/1976-a-selection-of-noteworthy-titles.html; The New York Times, Critics Circle Nominates 20 Books by US Authors, *The New York Times*, December 13, 1976, https://www.nytimes.com/1976/12/13/archives/critics-circle-nominates-20-books-by-us-authors.html; Kenneth K. Hur and John P. Robinson, 'The Social Impact of 'Roots," 55 *Journalism Quarterly* 55, (1978): 19–83.

64 Wright, prior to Haley's publication, struggled to find Gambians who recalled life before or during the slave trade, this changed post Root: Greenlee *supra* note 61; Donald R. Wright, 'The Effects of Alex Haley's Roots on How Gambians Remember the Atlantic Slave Trade,' 38 *History in Africa* (2011): 295–318.

65 Jesse T. Moore, 'Alex Haley's Roots: Ten Years Later,' 18 *The Western Journal of Black Studies* (1994): 70.

66 Through a balance of 'remembering' and 'forgetting,' remembering specifically through the suffering of specific people, such as Kunta Kinte in Haley's story: Alice Bellagamba, 'Back to the Land of Roots: African American Tourism and the Cultural Heritage of the River Gambia,' 1 *Cahiers d'études africaines* (2009): 453–476; Ziya Meral, 'A Duty to Remember? Politics and Morality of Remembering Past Atrocities,' 5 *International Politics Anthropology* (2012): 29–50.

4 Causes of FGM in The Gambia

Gender-based violence is pervasive within The Gambia, trapped within a firm grip of a hierarchical power dynamics, fear of retaliation, stigma, discrimination and societal pressure, all of which represent firm cultural obstacles to access justice.[67] This cultural hold is prevalent in almost all facets of Gambian life, thus entering intimate and private settings, ultimately influencing the treatment of female sex-workers[68] and fostering domestic violence.[69] There is a tendency for these victims to suffer in silence due to the ongoing cultural ideologies accepting, acknowledging and permitting abusive behaviour by men and *husbands*.[70] Subsequently, the vast majority of cases go unreported.[71] Thus, there exists reasonable speculation that numbers highly exceed those documented in national surveys. Regardless, in 2013, just over one in four ever-married women reported having experienced a form of violence from their spouse in the previous 365 days.[72] Of Gambian women aged 15–49, 41% have experienced physical violence at least once after reaching the age of 15 years old, and 10% had experienced violence as recently as within 12 months prior to the survey. There is, however, an expressed confidence in the country's *declared* efforts to end domestic violence, assured by the United Nations Development Programme (UNDP), United Nations Children's Fund (UNICEF), United States Agency for International Development (US AID), the United Nations Population Fund (UNFPA) and the

---

[67] The Gambia Bureau of Statistics (GBOS) International Community Foundation (ICF) International, *The Gambia Demographic and Health Survey 2013* (2014): 225, https://dhsprogram.com/pubs/pdf/FR289/FR289.pdf.

[68] Jennifer A. Sherwood, Ashley Grosso, Michele R. Decker, Sarah Peitzmeier, Erin Papworth, Daouda Diouf, Fatou Maria Drame, Nuha Ceesay and Stefan Baral, 'Sexual Violence Against Female Sex Workers in The Gambia: A Cross-sectional Examination of the Associations Between Victimization and Reproductive, Sexual and Mental Health,' 15 *BMC Public Health* (2015).

[69] Patrick Idoko, Emmanuel Ogbe, Oley Jallow and Amaka Ocheke, 'Burden of Intimate Partner Violence in The Gambia—A Cross Sectional Study of Pregnant Women,' 12 *Reproductive Health* (2015): 1–6.

[70] 49.9% of Gambian women 'believe a husband is justified in beating his wife' in any of the following scenarios: if she goes out without telling him, neglects the children, argues with him, *refuses sex with him* or burns the food while cooking: MICS, *supra* note 43.

[71] The Gambia Bureau of Statistics, *supra* note 67, 225.

[72] Ibid.

World Health Organization (WHO).[73] Unfortunately, despite the 2015 amendment to the Women's Act 2010, there is yet to be confidence in the country's *actual* efforts to eradicate FGM.

Although The Gambia is similar to other African countries practising FGM in many respects, its desire to continue FGM differ since it is uniquely integral to its communal structure. Whereas other African communities may uphold FGM due to tradition, religion and coercion,[74] Gambian culture intrinsically honours *familial* customs and pride, interpersonal to their bloodline.[75] This distinction means that either the criminalisation of FGM, shallow education of associated harms or an encouragement to abandon the practice, directly challenges the honour and pride of a Gambian's bloodline. Convincing a local Gambian to question the presence and practice of FGM becomes convincing one to dishonour an elder and their custom.[76] Societal ramifications for a Gambian refusing FGM are thus severe. Mothers who have not undergone FGM are sometimes: denied the right to provide an opinion in family matters,[77] cannot interfere in the FGM outcome of their child, are banned from the ceremony and cannot visit their daughters post FGM when in seclusion.[78] A Wolof woman, a member of Gambia's

---

[73] Ibid.

[74] Rigmor and Denison, *supra* note 8, 843.

[75] Binta Colley, 'Community and Family Involvement in Gambia, West Africa,' in Diana HiattMichael (ed.) *Promising Practices for Family Involvement in Schooling Across the Continents* (2005); Abdoulaye Saine, *Culture and Customs of Gambia* (2012); Godfrey Mwakikagile, *Ethnic Diversity and Integration in The Gambia: The Land, the People and the Culture* (2010); Sonalde Desai, 'Children at Risk: The Role of Family Structure in Latin America and West Africa,' 18 *Population and Development Review* (1992): 694; Jukka Jouhki and Luara Stark, *Causes and Motives of Early Marriage in The Gambia: Is New Legislation Enough?* (2017); Laurie Hatcher, 'Female Circumcision in The Gambia,' in Bill Roberts and Bala Saho (eds.) *Tubaab Two: From Baobab to the Bantaba* (1998): 62–63.

[76] Although no religion condones FGM, the ritual ceremony has religious justification, and women are seen as failing their God if denying the practice: Nour, *supra* note 48; Isatou Touray, the current Vice-President of The Gambia and FGM activist, mirroring many other FGM victims was surprised to learn it was not mentioned in the Qur'an; members of her community are continuously informed her otherwise: Emma Batha, 'From Prisoner to Hero: Activist Persuades Gambia to Ban FGM,' *Thomas Reuters Foundation*, March 25, 2010, https://news.trust.org/item/20130325105400-mxd9h/.

[77] Ylva and Shell-Duncan, *supra* note 17, 52.

[78] Ibid.

ethnic community least likely to partake in FGM, recounted her experience as an 'uncut' mother in 2007 survey. She described how societal exclusion inevitably drove her to undergo FGM as an adult.[79] Similarly, young girls bully peers who have not been subjected to FGM, bestowing upon them the derogatory nickname 'solema.'[80] Like the account of the Wolof woman, this all drives those who escaped being a victim of FGM to weigh any *known* harmful outcome of FGM (often excused as being 'the will of God'[81]) against the real social benefits of community acceptance.[82] In The Gambia, 'dichotomising those who retain and those who abandon [FGM] oversimplifies the complexity of contemplation and decision-making.'[83]

FGM is often justified as a means to guarantee a women's sexual abstinence due to the resulted pain from intercourse,[84] continuing the traditional expectation of female subservience. These rationalisations illustrate the cultural view of a woman's role in society through misinformation: many believe FGM pleases a woman's husband,[85] eases labour to safeguard procreating[86] and renders intercourse more enjoyable for the man, despite many men in the community not having the experience to challenge this claim.[87] As these values are so intrinsically instilled, Gambian FGM survivors, despite the extreme pain, still 'fulfil their sexual obligations with their husbands.'[88] Undoubtedly, FGM not

---

79 Ibid.

80 Ibid., 53.

81 Stated in the testimony of a Madinka woman: Ylva and Shell-Duncan, *supra* note 17, 49 and 48; Witnessing death or trauma does not prevent the continuation of the practice.

82 'Existing hierarchies within communities foster the violation of the rights of individuals who are in a vulnerable position, yet these individuals are unable to challenge such discrimination and marginalization in the interest of safeguarding the power position of the community': Ambika Satkunanathan, 'The Politics of Reconciliation in Transitional Justice,' *The International Journal of Transitional Justice* (2014): 182; Ylva and Shell-Duncan, *supra* note 17, 48.

83 Ylva and Shell-Duncan, *supra* note 17, 55.

84 UNFPA, *A Holistic Approach to the Abandonment of Female Genital Mutilation/Cutting* (2020), https://www.unfpa.org/sites/default/files/pub-pdf/726_filename_fgm.pdf.

85 Nour, *supra* note 48.

86 Ylva and Shell-Duncan, *supra* note 17, 48.

87 Lien, *supra* note 16, 532–533.

88 Ibid, 530.

only '*appears* fundamentally and irredeemably violent, debilitating, and misogynistic,'[89] it *is*.

The hierarchical dynamic of 'male dominance' thus remains at the root of Gambian culture and family life.[90] Knowledge of this dynamic is significant when considering micro initiatives to achieve transitional justice after Lewin's Theory of Change is fulfilled and society 'unfrozen' (*as explored below in 6 The Methodology to Achieve Change*). The Gambia is not yet at this stage of consideration. However, when it is, if this value is not considered, the focus can unproductively move away from disassembling the hierarchy, and instead wrongly view FGM as an issue of 'sameness' and equality.[91] Notably, FGM is not an issue of gender *discrimination*, instead, it is one of *gendered societal control*. Framing FGM as 'sexist' within a culture that is yet to address equality in the same way as the Global North, may be unproductive if the aim is to urgently eliminate the practice. Addressing woven traditions of FGM as an issue of liberal ideologies commonly associated with the Global North, such as sexism, will only trigger safeguarding tradition from external pressures and stunt transitional justice. Further analysis of the perception of women in society is needed and can also serve to illustrate the cause of the dominance of domestic abuse in The Gambia.[92] However, as a micro issue, it does not fall within the scope of this chapter.

---

[89] Audrey Macklin, 'The Double-Edged Sword: Using the Criminal Law Against Female Genital Mutilation in Canada,' in Abusharaf, Rogaia Mustafa (ed.) *Female Circumcision: Multicultural Perspectives* (2007): 208.

[90] Sulayman S.S. Jammeh, Chieh-Yu Liu, Su-Fen Cheng and Jane Lee-Hsieh, 'Community Based Study on Married Couples' Family Planning Knowledge, Attitude and Practice in Rural and Urban Gambia,' 14 *African Health Sciences* (2014): 273–280.

[91] Catharine Mackinnon, 'Difference and Dominance: On Sex Discrimination,' in Anne Phillips (ed.) *A Feminism and Politics* (1998): 307.

[92] The Gambia Bureau of Statistics, *supra* note 5.

5 Effects of FGM

FGM in its severest form may lead to death, often due to blood loss.[93] Yet, in more 'mild' cases, FGM causes a cluster of devastating and irreversible lifelong complications. FGM Types I–III often lead to dyspareunia, dysmenorrhea, chronic bladder and vaginal infections, sebaceous cysts, vulvar abscesses, fibrosis, voiding difficulties, keloids, infertility, as well as chronic pain and difficulties during: sexual intercourse, pelvis movement/examinations, and vaginal delivery.[94] Likewise, risks associated with the unsterilised tools used for the cutting[95] may lead to infection and even the transfer of Human Immunodeficiency Virus (HIV).[96] At the time of the 'procedure,' the extreme pain may cause shock, haemorrhaging, and 'acute urinary retention, infection and abscesses, a failure to heal, injury to the adjacent tissues, fractures and dislocation.'[97]

Specifically in The Gambia, pregnant FGM survivors who seek obstetric care, are four times more likely to suffer unnecessary complications during childbirth, such as perineal tearing and prolonged labour.[98] Furthermore, due to FGM, their new-borns are four times more likely to suffer health complications such as foetal distress, birth asphyxia, caput succedaneum and even stillbirth.[99] Significantly, this study represents women who sought medical care, which represents only 30% of

---

93 'Shot-term complications of female circumcision [include] hemorrhage, anemia, hypotension, oliguria, shock and death': Nour, *supra* note 48.

94 Ibid. Mass Waltham, *Clinicians in 139 Countries Turn to Wolters Kluwer's UpToDate Advanced to Deliver High-Quality Care*, Business Wire, July 11, 2019, https://www.businesswire.com/news/home/20190711005521/en/Clinicians-139-Countries-Turn-Wolters-Kluwer%E2%80%99s-UpToDate; 'More than 1.9 million clinicians in 190 + countries rely on UpToDate…the only resource associated with improved patient outcomes and hospital performance;' 'About US,' UpToDate, accessed June 30, 2020, https://www.uptodate.com/home/about-us.

95 Nour, *supra* note 48.

96 UNFPA, *supra* note 84.

97 Ibid., 4.

98 Kaplan et al., *supra* note 45.

99 Ibid.

Gambian pregnancies.[100] It is not unreasonable to then conclude FGM obstetric complications in The Gambia are often more severe, as they commonly occur without medical assistance.

Finally, the psychological impact of FGM, excluding the emotional effect of adverse obstetric outcomes, are similarly extreme, leading to 'psychosomatic disorders which, in turn, affect eating, sleeping, moods, cognition ...[including] post-traumatic stress.'[101] Partners of FGM survivors in The Gambia have also noted that survivors acquire a lifelong fear of *any* form of physical affection or intimacy.[102] Notably, however, nearly 72% of Gambian men are unaware of *any* negative impact FGM has on the health and well-being of girls and women,[103] inadvertently encouraging them to uphold the practice.

The harms of FGM extend beyond 'gender-based torture,'[104] reaching as far as the public health sector.[105] The 'procedure' burdens The Gambia's already limited medical resources[106] and, due to complications during childbirth, can cause long-term strain when new-borns suffer from birth asphyxia and permanent brain damage. The public health

---

[100] Mamady Cham, Johanne Sundby and Siri Vangen, 'Availability and Quality of Emergency Obstetric Care in Gambia's Main Referral Hospital: Women-users' Testimonies,' 6 *Reproductive Health* (2009): 1–8.

[101] UNFPA, *supra* note 84.

[102] 'Cut women were afraid of men touching them and that the lack of sexual feeling spilt over into ordinary life. A cut woman would not be as affectionate on a daily basis as an uncut woman would be': Lien, *supra* note 16, 530.

[103] Kaplan, *supra* note 16, 10.

[104] Adeyinka M. Akinsulure-Smith and Adeyinka M. Akinsulure-Smith, 'Exploring Female Genital Cutting Among Survivors of Torture,' 19 *Journal of Immigrant and Minority Health* (2017): 769–773.

[105] 'Aside from health-related, ethical, and moral consequences of FGM, it has been estimated by the World Health Organization (WHO) that the annual cost of obstetric complications is more than $3.7 million': Elliot Klein, Elizabeth Helzner, Michelle Shayowitz, Stephan Kohlhoff and Tamar A Smith-Norowitz, 'Female Genital Mutilation: Health Consequences and Complications—A Short Literature Review,' *Obstetrics and Gynecology International* (2018): 1–7; David Bishai, Yung-Ting Bonnenfant, Manal Darwish, Taghreed Adam, Heli Bathija, Elise Johansen, Dale Huntington, *Estimating the Obstetric Costs of Female Genital Mutilation in Six African Countries*, World Health Organization, https://www.who.int/bulletin/volumes/88/4/09-064808-ab/en/.

[106] Sunkaru Touray, Baboucarr Sanyang, Gregory Zandrow, Fatoumatta Dibba, Kaddy Fadera, Ebrima Kanteh, Madikoi Danso, Landing N Sanyang, Masirending Njie, Grey Johnson, Awa Sanyang and Awa Touray, 'An Assessment of Critical Care Capacity in The Gambia,' 47 *Journal of Critical Care* (2018): 245–253.

crises necessitate upstream solutions.[107] However, in this instance, the only proactive resolution is the complete eradication of FGM—there is no method of performing FGM which does not result in severe medical complications. Whether the perspective is from a human rights context or public health initiative, the sole solution *is,* and can only be, the elimination of FGM.

6 The Methodology to Achieve Change: The Shift to a Gambia Without Violence Against Women

To alter the status quo, denounce FGM and offer survivors access to justice, it is necessary to first consider how one may achieve change within the society in question. In The Gambia, adjusting the status quo and rejecting FGM is not welcome. In eight years, the percentage of women who have undergone FGM has only decreased by 0.6%,[108] and in 2019, the country was deemed to face 'major challenges' in progressing towards gender equality.[109] Like many other FGM practising countries, the criminalisation of the practice remains inconsistent with a long-understood culture of tradition, ritual and religion.[110] Senegal, as

[107] John McKinlay, 'A Case for Refocusing Upstream: The Political Economy of Illness,' in Peter Conrad and Rochelle Kern (eds.) *The Sociology of Health and Illness: Critical Perspectives* (1986): 489; Keith Syrett, 'Doing "Upstream" Priority-Setting for Global Health with Justice: Moving from Vision to Practice?' 11 *Public Health Ethics* (2018): 265.

[108] Republic of The Gambia, *The Gambia: Voluntary National Review, a Report on the Progress of Implementation of SDGs* (2020), annex page 40, https://sustainabledevelopment.un.org/content/documents/263072020GambiaVNR.pdf.

[109] J. Sachs, G. Schmidt-Traub, C. Kroll, G. Lafortune and G. Fuller, *Sustainable Development Report 2019* (2019): 205; Garry Blight, Liz Ford, Frank Hulley-Jones, Niko Kommenda and Lydia McMullan, Climate, Inequality, Hunger: Which Global Problems Would You Fix First?: Country Choice The Gambia, *The Guardian*, January 15, 2020, https://www.theguardian.com/global-development/ng-interactive/2020/jan/15/environment-inequality-hunger-which-global-problems-would-you-fix-first.

[110] Akin-Tunde Odukogbe, Bosede Afolabi, Oluwasomidoyin Bello and Ayodeji Adeyanju, 'Female Genital Mutilation/Cutting in Africa,' 6 *Translational Andrology and Urology* (2017): 138.

the only country sharing a border with The Gambia, bears a comparatively low[111] and declining FGM presence[112] while the number of FGM victims in The Gambia have remained high. In fact, The Gambia is the *only* African state to have a large number of FGM victims without sharing a border with a country that bears a similar FGM prevalence.[113] The proximity of a country where FGM is far less common, and thus less culturally intrinsic, appears to have little influence on Gambian FGM attitudes. Therefore, transforming the nation to openly encourage and embrace a shift *away* from FGM and finally accept pre-existing laws requires radical societal change. Achieving a social paradigm shift is the sole method in which FGM can effectively be transitioned out of the practice. An effective method to do so must be examined.

The interrelation between social, economic and political life demonstrates that tradition need not always stunt social change.[114] In the same vein, *political* change does not guarantee nor facilitate *social* change. The law itself, as seen in The Gambia, does not, and cannot, precipitate social change, it merely acts to enhance and safeguard an already evolving shift. Thus, the law in isolation will never be effective unless culture *adapts* to (and does not conflict with) progression.[115] The success of Gambian Dropping Knife ceremonies,[116] in which communities perform a symbolic and cultural ritual declaring the end of FGM

---

[111] UNICEF, *Female Genital Mutilation (FGM): At Least 200 Million Girls and Women Alive Today Living in 31 Countries Have Undergone FGM* (2020), https://data.unicef.org/topic/child-protection/female-genital-mutilation/#_edn1; 'Rising Up for Rights for Women and Girls Abandoning Female Genital Mutilation and Cutting in the Fouta of Senegal,' UNFPA 2017, last accessed June 20, 2020, https://www.unfpa.org/sites/default/files/pub-pdf/Fouta%20Booklet.pdf.

[112] 28.2% in 2005 versus 24% in 2020: Ndiaye Salif and Mohamed Ayad, *Senegal DHS, 2005—Final Report* (2005); UNICEF, *supra* note 111; Ngianga-Bakwin Kandala and Bettina Shell-Duncan, 'Trends in Female Genital Mutilation/Cutting in Senegal: What Can We Learn from Successive Household Surveys in Sub-Saharan African countries?' 18 *International Journal for Equity in Health* (2019).

[113] Observed the colour-coded prevalence map of Africa found after expanding 'read more,' under subheading: 'The prevalence of FGM varies greatly across countries with data' found at UNICEF, 'Female genital mutilation (FGM),' February 2020, https://data.unicef.org/topic/child-protection/female-genital-mutilation/.

[114] Joseph R. Gusfield, 'Tradition and Modernity: Misplaced Polarities in the Study of Social Change,' 72 *American Journal of Sociology* (1967): 352.

[115] Ibid., 356.

[116] *Dropping the Knife in The Gambia*, 28 Too Many, December 21, 2015, https://www.28toomany.org/blog/dropping-the-knife-in-the-gambia-guest-blog-by-jacqueline-hoover/.

practice, is an example of how the combination of respect for cultural practice along with progressive ideology, successfully permits change, although this occurs long before the ceremony takes place. The Gambia has accepted and practised FGM throughout its history; its termination necessitates an irresistible alteration of the external and internal environment.[117] The challenge lies in attempting to achieve this on a macro scale.

Kurt Lewin's theory of change is useful in analysing the environment and internal factors necessary in order to achieve successful growth on a national level.[118] Lewin describes processes like culture as an ever-evolving matter, a quasi-stationary process.[119] To achieve societal change, he refers to a quasi-stationary equilibrium, in which certain social forces will resist any suggestion of change, reversing progress.[120] To succeed, a force is required to break the social habit and 'unfreeze' the custom-igniting a need to respond to that force. Once unfrozen, reactions in favour of the status quo (resisting forces) should not be capable of outpowering those forces favouring progression. 'One should not think in terms of the *goal to be reached* but rather in terms of a change *from the present level to the desired one*;'[121] thus these levels can only be attained if resisting forces fail to inhibit progress.

The 'unfreezing' of society then allows the opportunity for transitional justice,[122] the final and vital component in achieving a social paradigm shift. This broad concept considers all approaches associated

[117] Michael Fullan, *Leading in Change* (2004): 39.

[118] Edgar Schein, 'Kurt Lewin's Change Theory in the Field and in the Classroom: Notes Toward a Model of Managed Learning,' 9 *Systems Practice* (1996): 27; Syed Talib Hussain, Shen Lei, Tayyaba Akram, Muhammed Jamal Haider, Syed Hadi Hussain and Muhammad Ali, 'Kurt Lewin's Change Model: A Critical Review of the Role of Leadership and Employee Involvement in Organizational Change,' 3 *Journal of Innovation & Knowledge* (2018): 123.

[119] Kurt Lewin, 'Frontiers in Group Dynamics: Concept, Method and Reality in Social Science; Social Equilibria and Social Change,' 1 *Human Relations* (1947): 15.

[120] Ibid., 16.

[121] Ibid., 32.

[122] 'Transitional justice processes need to respond to the specific and different concerns that arise in transitions from identity-based conflict': Ambika Satkunanathan, 'The Politics of Reconciliation in Transitional Justice,' *The International Journal of Transitional Justice* (2014): 182.

with a society accepting and addressing a history of human rights violations to achieve justice, reconciliation and accountability.[123] It is a strategic approach for a country emerging from atrocity[124] and respects both judicial and non-judicial measures.[125] According to the notion, to reach the desired long-lasting societal change, any transition must heed political factors[126] and only consider *internal* and subjective national approaches.[127] It is necessary to have a societal acceptance that an atrocity has occurred—in this instance, acknowledging FGM as an act of gender-based violence. Yet, this acknowledgement can only happen if the country has both the ability and partisan *will* for this reform.[128] Governmental stance is critical as the whole community must acknowledge the abuse and exploitation to begin societal healing. A joint consensus on the adequate 'micro' way to move forward is then necessary, while still adapting to the 'contextual particularities that have existed'[129] as to prevent backlash to profound change. Once stipulated, the process of resolution and transformation can begin, with the country now wanting to, and succeeding in, holding wrongdoers accountable[130]—in this instance, through successfully enforcing laws criminalising FGM (unlike current practice). Presently, a form of Gambian transitional justice *is* in progress: The Gambian Truth, Reconciliation and Reparations Commission (TRRC) which demonstrates a national effort to address human rights abuses under the country's previous dictator.[131] In an attempt for reconciliation, the TRRC is creating a shift away from society under the preceding authoritarian rule. However, the scope of the TRRC is limited to human rights offences committed by the previous regime. It does not consider FGM—an offence committed by both citizens and the state.

---

[123] Report of the UN Secretary General, *The Rule of Law and Transitional Justice in Conflict and Post-conflict Societies*, United Nations Security Council, UN Doc. S/2004/616 (2004), 4, paragraph 8.

[124] Kirsten Fisher and Robert Stewart, *Transitional Justice and the Arab Spring* (2014): 1.

[125] Ibid.

[126] Ambika, *supra* note 122.

[127] Report of the UN, *supra* note 123, 1.

[128] Ibid.

[129] Fisher and Stewart, *supra* note 124.

[130] Ibid., 4.

[131] 'Truth, Reconciliation and Reparations Commission,' 2018 http://www.trrc.gm/.

Reverting back to Lewin's theory, a force is required to break the social habit in question. In The Gambia, something significant must be done to unfreeze the country's current state of FGM practice and acceptance, despite the discomfort which may consequently arise. As Lewin notes, to 'break open the shell of complacency and self-righteousness, it is sometimes necessary to [deliberately] bring about an emotional stir-up.'[132] However, this can only be done upon the deconstructing of resisting forces. Only then can the country gradually enter the necessary stages of transitional justice to overcome the current atrocities of FGM. The resistors that prevent The Gambia from 'unfreezing' the status quo are found in a complacency towards violence against women in the form of FGM and the governments wish to maintain the practice. The efficacy of national law, its public perception, absence of government prioritisation and deep routed cultural value will serve to describe Lewin's warned resistors. For the elimination of FGM, these obstacles must be acknowledged and understood so an efficient call for action may be created.

7 Criminal Without Accountability—The Law Against FGM in The Gambia[133]

7.1 A Mere Check in the Box

Culture, as examined above, is a naturally anticipated resistor against social paradigm shifts and was one anticipated by Lewin himself. However, Lewin viewed culture as embodying two opposing forces within itself, those in favour of the intended eliminated practice, and those against, creating a necessary equilibrium which overtime achieves change. The Gambia provides a distinct case with less inspiring

---

132 Lewin, *supra* note 119, 35.

133 The Criminal Code and the Children's Act 2005 may also be read in conjunction with the Women's (Amendment) Act by further enforcing the protection of women and girls against harm. These harms can be argued to encompass FGM, much like the protection against harm in the constitution and draft constitution, although this reasoning has never occurred in a court of law.

outcomes. Though NGOs, activists, medical practitioners and organisations against FGM exist, they only represent the opinions of the few. The lack of legal enforcement and national initiative proves these small bodies are only specks in a larger sphere of FGM tolerance. The resistors face no resistance.

Arguably, the existence of Gambian legislation prohibiting FGM contradicts this claim. *Surely*, the argument goes, *if the country is willing to impose laws against an action, they must be demonstrating some national stance against the practice- would not that alone constitute one of Lewin's 'forces*?' The law *does* address *some* elements of FGM (as examined below). However, it is ultimately mediocre and blatantly ineffective to the extent of being counterproductive. Upon further investigation, it becomes clear that there never existed a governmental intention to enforce the law; the law did not arise as a means for women to access justice. Criminalisation was a political move to silence NGOs who had garnered global attention, a mere *check in the box* to gain international praise.

7.2 Analysis of the Law

Under the then 'dictator'[134] Yahya Jammeh,[135] and after considerable international efforts by internationally renowned activist Jaha Dukureh,[136] alongside her partnership with United Kingdom news outlet *The Guardian*,[137] The Gambia historically criminalised FGM in 2015.[138] The pre-existing Women's Act 2010 was amended through

---

134 BBC News, *Profile: Former Gambian President Yahya Jammeh*, BBC News Africa, January 22, 2017, https://www.bbc.com/news/world-africa-24383225.

135 Human Rights Watch, 'Yahya Jammeh,' https://www.hrw.org/tag/yahya-jammeh.

136 UN Women, 'Regional UN Ambassador Jaha Dukureh,' https://www.unwomen.org/en/partnerships/goodwill-ambassadors/jaha-dukureh.

137 Mae Ryan, Jaha Dukureh's Story of FGM Survival: 'I'm Not Going to Let Fear Deter Me from Doing Anything Now'—Video, *The Guardian*, May 12, 2014, https://www.theguardian.com/society/video/2014/may/12/jaha-dukureh-female-genital-mutilation-video.

138 Kate Lyons, The Gambia Bans Female Genital Mutilation, *The Guardian*, November 24, 2015, https://www.theguardian.com/society/2015/nov/24/the-gambia-bans-female-genital-mutilation.

the inclusion of Section 32A,[139] forming the Women's (Amendment) Act. However, criminalisation through an *amendment* alone alludes to a lack of driving force against FGM. A representative of the Department of Social Welfare noted that a robust and more 'sensitive' Ministry of Justice would have enacted a separate bill to give adequate weight to the issue.[140] Members of The Gambian public also perceived the amendment as a political pronouncement, as the legislation itself appears to be an afterthought.[141] Ultimately, in accordance with the country's previous national moves, the nation was cheated out of any genuine effort to end FGM—many of the country's previous national actions have been to keep 'international appearances' rather than spark a societal shift. Gambians themselves then fail to take governmental actions seriously.

The 2015 Act's inclusion of FGM is a 'side note.' For its length, it is a decent piece of legislation. The amendment fully defines FGM[142] and describes the methods and materials which may be used for stitching during infibulation.[143] Furthermore, it does not shy from biological terms and removes ambiguity over the extent of harm. Sentencing is firm: perpetrators face three-year imprisonment and a possible fine of fifty thousand dalasi (roughly $966 USD),[144] a considerable amount considering it is one of the poorest countries in the world (bearing a gross national income per capita of $2,168 USD).[145] Equally, if FGM

[139] The Women's (Amendment) Act 2015, Section 32A.

[140] Fanta Bai Secka in 'Activity Report: Key Persons Interview on Bottlenecks of the FGM Law in The Gambia,' July 7, 2017, https://www.safehandsforgirls.com/our-reports.

[141] Alagie Jarju of the National Youth Council in 'Activity Report: Key Persons Interview on Bottlenecks of the FGM Law in The Gambia,' July 7, 2017, https://www.safehandsforgirls.com/our-reports.

[142] The Women's (Amendment) Act 2015, Section 32A (3)a–f.

[143] Ibid.

[144] As of November 17, 2020, 17:15 Coordinated Universal Time.

[145] The Gambia is ranked as 172 out of 189 in the Human Development Index and has a gross national income per capita of only $2,168: United Nations Development Programme, *Human Development Report 2020: The Next Frontier; Human Development and the Anthropocene*, 345, http://hdr.undp.org/sites/default/files/hdr2020.pdf; United Nations Development Programme: Human Development Reports, *Human Development Index*, http://hdr.undp.org/en/content/human-development-index-hdi; The World Bank, *GDP (current US$): All Countries and Economies*, https://data.worldbank.org/indicator/NY.GDP.MKTP.CD.

leads to death, it garners life imprisonment.[146] Additionally, the legislation is somewhat thorough by criminalising the promotion, abetting and requesting of FGM as well as the failure to notify authorities if it has taken place or is anticipated. The former incites the same fine of fifty thousand dalasi and the latter a fine of ten thousand dalasi, (roughly $193 USD[147]).[148] Yet, FGM victims seem to be neglected entirely throughout the amendment. If the perpetrator is not prosecuted, or the crime unreported, the statute is meaningless.

Alternatively, however, Uganda, the country with the more successful FGM eradication, as discussed earlier in this chapter, has a different approach. It's FGM ban is through an *independent* statute (as opposed to an amendment to pre-existing law) and achieves everything The Gambia's criminalisation ought to have done in order to place victims, and their retribution, at the forefront of it's legislation. The Prohibition of the Female Genital Mutilation Act 2010 (PFGM)[149] is Uganda's eight-page statute criminalising FGM. The legislation not only accomplishes everything The Gambian amendment accomplishes, it far exceeds its limitations. The PFGM not only promises access to justice through criminalisation, it proactively offers *protection from injustice*, allowing anyone fearful that they themselves, or a woman they know, may become victim to FGM to apply for a court order.[150] The legislation sets out methods for victims to also receive compensation[151] and stretches its reach by assisting Ugandan victims who are even harmed *outside* Uganda.[152] The Act thus places the harm and suffering *of victims*, and their ability to access justice, at the heart of criminalisation. Furthermore, although the prevalence of Gambian FGM is not a direct result of inadequate legislation, it is worth considering the effect an *independent* piece of legislation may have had on the public's understanding of the gravity of FGM. By assenting the PFGM, which did not alter any previous statute and thus

146 The Women's (Amendment) Act 2015, Section 32A (2)a–b.

147 As of November 17, 2020, 17:15 Coordinated Universal Time.

148 The Women's (Amendment) Act 2015, Section 32B.

149 Prohibition of the Female Genital Mutilation Act 2010.

150 Ibid., 14(1).

151 Ibid., 13.

152 Ibid., 15.

stood independently as the will of parliament, the Ugandan government made their stance against FGM clear. The same cannot be said for The Gambia. Ultimately, the inefficacy of Gambian law limits any of the amendment's positives, such as its clarity and fines.

Since criminalisation, there are only two reported FGM cases in The Gambia,[153] both with unknown conclusions.[154] One of the cases was publicised,[155] taking place just two months after the enactment of the Women's Amendment Act, when The Gambia was still in the international spotlight—it reaped global praise.[156] Yet, in the following years, the courts and government have been silent on the topic. During the 2019 redraft of the national constitution, the government loudly endorsed FGM through that silence. The Gambia had a unique opportunity to permanently stand against the practice by entrenching its criminalisation. The redrafting of the Constitution of Gambia (1996)

153 UNFPA-UNICEF Joint Programme on Female Genital Mutilation/Cutting, *2016 Annual Report of the UNFPA-UNICEF Accelerating Change by the Numbers: Joint Programme on Female Genital Mutilation/Cutting: Accelerating Change* (Online: July 2017) 38, https://reliefweb.int/sites/reliefweb.int/files/resources/UNFPA_UNICEF_FGM_16_Report_web.pdf.

154 28 Too Many, *supra* note 5.

155 Women's UN Report Network (WUNRN), *Gambia- New Legislation on FGM Applied in Gambian Court: The Gambia Committee on Traditional Practices Affecting the Health of Women and Children (GAMCOTRAP)*, WUNRN, March 21, 2016, https://wunrn.com/2016/03/gambia-new-legislation-on-fgm-applied-in-gambian-court/.

156 The case was viewed as 'express[ing] the importance and seriousness of the State in taking legal stand in the protection of children from FGM': WUNRN, *supra* note 155; UNFPA-UNICEF, *supra* note 153.

gave false[157] hope[158] of a new constitution[159] which would forever entrench and protect the prohibition of FGM.[160] However, the Constitutional Review Commission (CRC), when faced with the opportunity to disavow FGM in the highest form, opted instead to publicly remove FGM from its scope of consideration.[161]

The Gambia's approach and outlook alone is a stark contrast to Uganda's *successful* mindset and method of eradicating FGM. The practice in Uganda was arguably previously protected by article 37 of the Constitution, *the right to culture and similar rights*.[162] However, the Constitutional Commission[163] and the Constituent Assembly in 1994 both agreed 'the State has a right to protect its citizens, *especially*

---

[157] The draft did not give any mention to FGM. Instead, much like the previous constitution, the draft Constitution's Section 53's Rights of Women focused on a brief assurance of equal treatment and opportunity. Section 53, the Rights of Children, elaborates to describe the right to protect children 'from abuse, neglect, all forms of violence, inhuman treatment and punishment, and hazardous or exploitative labour' and Section 40 stipulated the right to be free from the subjection of torture and violence, all of which could be used to describe prohibiting FGM. However, FGM is not explicitly mentioned: *Gambia (The)'s Draft Constitution of 2019*, Draft of November 12, 2019, https://www.constituteproject.org/constitution/Gambia_2019D.pdf?lang=en.

[158] The Constitutional Review Commission allowed the public to submit comments and suggestions of the Draft Constitution to the Secretariat for consideration; Constitutional Review Commission, *Report of the Constitutional Review Commission on the Draft Constitution for the Third Republic of The Gambia*, March 30, 2020: 68 https://crc220.org/wp-content/uploads/2015/12/CRC-FINAL-REPORT-ON-THE-DRAFT-CONSTITUTION.pdf; 'Clarifications Concerning Certain Provisions of the CRC Draft Constitution' *Constitutional Review Commission*, Press Release, December 28, 2019, https://crc220.org/clarifications-concerning-certain-provisions-of-the-crc-draft-constitution/.

[159] Unfortunately, much like the draft Constitution 2019, the Constitution of Gambia (1996) gave no mention of FGM, despite describing the right for women to be assured equality (Article 28) and the right of the children (Article 29) to be protected from harm.

[160] Constitutional Review Commission, *supra* note 158.

[161] A common suggestion was the inclusion of FGM, however, the CRC responded by stating it 'was not an issue for the Constitution.

[162] Whether article 37 can be used to protect FGM was discussed by the Constituent Assembly; Constitution of Uganda 1995, article 37; *Proceedings of the Constituent Assembly (Official Report)* (Uganda Printing and Publishing Corporation: 1994), 2009; Emphasis added, *Proceedings of the Constituent Assembly (Official Report)* (Uganda Printing and Publishing Corporation: 1994), 2013.

[163] *The Report of the Uganda Constitutional Commission: Analysis and Recommendations* (Uganda Printing and Publishing Corporation 1992) paragraph 7.69.

when cultures are harmful and oppressive.'[164] Ultimately, this cultural outlook set the scene for a smooth and steady cultural transition into FGM prohibition; a perspective The Gambia has historically lacked. Over a decade following the statement, the NGO Law and Advocacy for Women in Uganda petitioned the Uganda Constitutional Court to clarify and declare FGM as inconsistent to the country's 'supreme authority.'[165] Uganda thus publicly and nationally deemed FGM as unconstitutional.[166] The Attorney General's acceptance of the NGO's application was interpreted as the *government* agreeing with the petition, 'that indeed the custom and practice of FGM violated the … constitution.'[167] The declaration coincided with a governmental consultative tour to FGM prevalent areas in Uganda (which, in its subsequent report, called for the criminalising of the practice),[168] and the creation of the 2010 PFGM.[169] The government had not only declared the practice unconstitutional, but also took measures to study its prevalence in the country when banning it as an independent offence. Ultimately, the Ugandan government's firm stance on the matter is and has always been, vividly clear. Thus, The Gambia's inability to do the same is a clear resistor to change, and an indicator that the country as a whole still favours FGM. To the men and women of The Gambia, FGM is seen as a tradition that does not carry penalty in practice,[170] an idea enforced by The Gambian government avoiding any opportunity to stand against it.

---

164 Emphasis added, *Proceedings of the Constituent Assembly (Official Report)* (Uganda Printing and Publishing Corporation: 1994), 2011.

165 Constitution of Uganda 1995, article 2.

166 *Law Advocacy for Women in Uganda v Attorney General* (Constitutional Petition No 8 of 2007), [2010] UGCC 4 (July 28, 2010).

167 Jamil Ddamulira Mujuzi, 'Female Genital Mutilation in Uganda: A Glimpse at the Abolition Process,' 56 *Journal of African Law* (2012): 139–150; *Law and Advocacy for Women in Uganda v Attorney General* (constitutional petition no 8 of 2007) [2010] UGCC 4 (July 28, 2010) at 4.

168 'Report of the Committee on Gender, Labour and Social Development on Female Genital Mutilation Bill 2009' (2009) cited in Ddamulira, *supra* note 167.

169 Prohibition of the Female Genital Mutilation Act 2010.

170 *Activity Report: Key Persons Interview on Bottlenecks of the FGM Law in The Gambia*, July 7, 2017 https://www.safehandsforgirls.com/our-reports.

8 Barriers to Access to Justice

8.1 The Government as a Resistor to Change

Within The Gambia, support for the FGM status quo far exceed forces resisting it, unbalancing Lewin's equilibrium for successful change. The legal failures are twofold. Firstly, cases of FGM remain unreported and without penalty, with officials actively ignoring its illegality. Secondly, the two cases which have been reported were not seen to their conclusion. In layman's terms: *no one cares*. This is of course attributable to both the government's lack of enforcement and the cultural backdrop for an 'FGM-favouring' environment. The two feed upon each other. The Gambian government appears to be a pawn *led* by culture, covertly surrendering to national societal norms while pandering to international expectation. It is then the government itself which represents a large macro obstacle, reinforcing archaic cultural ideals, creating hurdles for NGOs and acting as the guardian of the status quo.

The sole purpose of The Gambia's 2015 FGM criminalisation was the attainment of international clout and silencing international FGM objectors, whilst still nationally preserving and maintaining the practice. This has been evidenced for years. The country signed, ratified and acceded numerous international and regional treaties detailing the need to eliminate FGM *decades* before its criminalisation. Through the ratification process, the Convention on the Elimination of all Forms of Discrimination Against Women (CEDAW),[171] the CRC,[172] the African Charter,[173] the Maputo Protocol[174] and the Cairo Declaration on the Elimination of FGM (Cairo Declaration),[175] which comprises 17 recommendations

[171] The Convention on the Elimination of all forms of Discrimination Against Women (1979) (CEDAW).

[172] Convention on the Rights of the Child (1989) (CRC).

[173] African Charter on Human and Peoples' Rights (1981) (ACHPR).

[174] Maputo Protocol, Article 5(b).

[175] Cairo Declaration on the Elimination of FGM (2003).

to prohibit FGM,[176] were all legally effective within its borders, yet FGM still prevailed. Furthermore, the country had signed the Convention Against Torture and Other Cruel, Inhuman or Degrading Treatment or Punishment,[177] and acceded both the ICCPR[178] and the ICESCR.[179] Instead of change, however, religious clerics at the time denied FGM's existence to the global community.[180] Six years later, in 2015 and upon finally acknowledging the presence of FGM through legal prohibition, the country adopted the United Nations (UN) Sustainable Development Goal (SDG) (Agenda 2030),[181] pledging once again to end FGM.[182] However, the *first* National Voluntary Review was only submitted *five* years later in 2020.[183] There appears to be is a tendency for the country to do what is necessary to alleviate international pressure without 'following through' on promises made.

The Gambia's deceit[184] is most visible when compared to Somalia's transparency. Somalia holds the highest prevalence of FGM in the

[176] The National Council for Childhood and Motherhood, *Afro-Arab Expert Consultation Legal Tools for the Prevention of Female Genital Mutilation* (2003), http://www.sexarchive.info/ECR6/pdf_fgm_cairo2003_eng.pdf.

[177] Convention Against Torture and Other Cruel, Inhuman or Degrading Treatment or Punishment (1984).

[178] The International Covenant on Civil and Political Rights (1966).

[179] International Covenant of Economic, Social and Cultural Rights (1966).

[180] 'Senior Muslim clerics in The Gambia have previously denied the existence of FGM in The Gambia saying instead that was is practiced is 'female circumcision': Kate Lyons, The Gambia Bans Female Genital Mutilation, *The Guardian*, November 24, 2015, https://www.theguardian.com/society/2015/nov/24/the-gambia-bans-female-genital-mutilation.

[181] United Nations, *Transforming Our World: The 2030 Agenda for Sustainable Development* (A/RES/70/1), https://sustainabledevelopment.un.org/content/documents/21252030%20Agenda%20for%20Sustainable%20Development%20web.pdf.

[182] Goal 5.3; United Nations, *Transforming Our World: The 2030 Agenda for Sustainable Development* (A/RES/70/1), https://sustainabledevelopment.un.org/content/documents/21252030%20Agenda%20for%20Sustainable%20Development%20web.pdf; Lesley Connolly and Cheryl He, *Toward a New Gambia: Linking Peace and Development* (2018): 2.

[183] Republic of The Gambia, *The Gambia: Voluntary National Review, a Report on the Progress of Implementation of SDGs* (June 2020), https://sustainabledevelopment.un.org/content/documents/263072020GambiaVNR.pdf.

[184] Thomas Reuters Foundation, 'The Law and FGM an Overview of 28 African Countries September 2018' http://www.trust.org/contentAsset/raw-data/1e5a2969-bd56-4fc3-8034-5409fd161175/file.

world[185] and, like The Gambia, practices FGM Type III.[186] Yet, Somalia has not criminalised the practice,[187] has not acceded, signed or ratified the CEDAW and has not adopted the Cairo Declaration. The country has only *signed* the Maputo Protocol, has not ratified the African Charter and denies the jurisdiction of the African Court on Human and Peoples' Rights. Although abandoning its female citizens and grossly failing to protect women from FGM,[188] the country has given no expectation of change nor been deceitful of its national practice, allowing a path for more international accountability and a clear indication of the necessary progress.

It appears as though The Gambia is neither capable of admitting its shortcomings, nor does it have an overseeing body to expose them. For decades, it has failed to uphold the rule of law,[189] avoiding transparency and accountability in all accounts.[190] In 2016, the president promised resignation after three years in power,[191] a promise he ignored in 2019[192] in the absence of any public means of appeal. In 2020, *The Gambian*

---

185 UNICEF, *supra* note 111.

186 UNICEF, *Statistical Country Profile on Female Genital Mutilation/Cutting: Somalia*, December 2013, https://data.unicef.org/wp-content/uploads/country_profiles/Somalia/FGMC_SOM.pdf.

187 Rupa Shenoy, *Despite Recent Historic Gains in Ending FGM, Somalia Sees Dramatic Increase*, The World, June 3, 2020, https://www.pri.org/stories/2020-06-03/despite-recent-historic-gains-ending-fgm-somalia-sees-dramatic-increase.

188 Siobhán O'Grady, *Most Girls in Somalia Experience Genital Mutilation. The Ritual Just Killed a 10-year-old*, The Washington Post, July 20, 2018, https://www.washingtonpost.com/news/worldviews/wp/2018/07/20/most-girls-in-somalia-experience-genital-mutilation-the-ritual-just-killed-a-10-year-old/; The Guardian, Huge FGM Rise Recorded in Somalia During Coronavirus Lockdown, *The Guardian*, May 18, 2020 https://www.theguardian.com/world/2020/may/18/fgm-risk-in-somalia-heightened-by-coronavirus-crisis.

189 Specifically, 'no man is above the law': Albert Venn Dicey, *Introduction to the Study of the Law of the Constitution* (1982): 115.

190 The 2019 US Department of State report deemed that even the country's expenditure was 'not subject to adequate oversight or audit': *U.S. Department of State 2019 Fiscal Transparency Report* (Pursuant to Section 7031(b)(3) of the Department of State, Foreign Operations and Related Programs Appropriations Act, 2019 (Div. F, P.L. 116–6) [FY 2019 SFOAA]), August 15, 2019, https://www.state.gov/2019-fiscal-transparency-report/.

191 BBC News, *Gambia's Jammeh Loses to Adama Barrow in Shock Election Result*, BBC News, December 2, 2016, https://www.bbc.com/news/world-africa-38183906.

192 Ruth Maclean and Saikou Jammeh, Gambia's Joy Gives Way to Sinking Distrust as Barrow Clings to Power, *The Guardian*, September 23, 2019, https://www.theguardian.com/global-development/2019/sep/23/gambia-joy-gives-way-to-sinking-distrust-adama-barrow-clings-to-power.

Times criticised the country for its inability to measure progress[193] and meet a twenty-year goal,[194] much like its goals to eradicate FGM.[195] The country fails to have what the UN specifies should *already* exist in a society hoping to eliminate human right violations[196] despite attempts to claim otherwise.

International scrutiny *does* appear to precipitate tangible change, notwithstanding the inefficacy of that change. It was not until Dukureh, and *the Guardian UK* brought FGM into international limelight that the national FGM atrocity was finally acknowledged and legal change effected. However, the taxing contribution of nine national groups,[197] and a variety of NGOs[198] working over nearly a *decade*, only led to an increase of 1.9% of Gambian women *favouring* the eradication of FGM.[199] Arguably, the only mechanism to achieve governmental change is international coercion as the country panders to the international

---

[193] The Gambia Times, *Vision 2020, Is The Gambia Worst Off than Before?* The Gambia Times, January 1, 2020, https://www.thegambiatimes.com/vision-2020-is-the-gambia-worst-off-than-before/.

[194] Ibid.

[195] The Chief Executive of The Gambia Committee on Traditional Practices (GAMCOTRAP), an organisation aiming to end 'gender-based violence,' anticipated having an FGM free country by 2020. Yet, in 2020, GAMCOTRAP's server ID address of www.gamcotrap.gm cannot be found; Republic of The Gambia, *The Gambia: Voluntary National Review, a Report on the Progress of Implementation of SDGs* (June 2020) 31, https://sustainabledevelopment.un.org/content/documents/263072020GambiaVNR.pdf.

[196] In The Gambia, 'all persons, institutions and entities, public and private, including the State itself' are *not* 'accountable to laws that are publicly promulgated' they are not 'equally enforced and independently adjudicated' and are thus inconsistent 'with international human rights norms and standards': Report of the UN Secretary General, *The Rule of Law and Transitional Justice in Conflict and Post-conflict Societies* (United Nations Security Council, UN Doc. S/2004/616 [2004]) 4.

[197] Including the National Steering Committee of FGM and Gender-Based Violence which, '(established in 2009), is the national coordination mechanism for work on FGM/C': UNFPA-UNICEF, *supra* note 153.

[198] The NGO Safe Hands for Girls provides school outreach, training, and hosts days that focus on women's rights and FGM, such as Zero Tolerance Day and its associated conferences; Safe Hands for Girls (2020) https://www.safehandsforgirls.com/our-work.

[199] 64.2% in 2010 to 62.3% in 2018; MICS, *The Gambia: Multiple Indicator Cluster Survey 2010* (UNICEF Final Report, June 2012), https://catalog.ihsn.org/index.php/catalog/6776/download/81358; and MICS, *The Gambia: Multiple Indicator Cluster Survey 2018*, (Survey Findings Report, July, 2019): 357, https://mics-surveys-prod.s3.amazonaws.com/MICS6/West%20and%20Central%20Africa/Gambia/2018/Survey%20findings/The%20Gambia%202018%20MICS%20Survey%20Findings%20Report_English.pdf.

sphere. Yet, due to the lack of transparency and any deep scrutiny, this has only led to the country making false claims.[200] The country cannot improve *internally* if it consistently denies the gravity of the problem.

One may speculate that because international pressure has instigated *all* previous FGM 'commitments,' The Gambia can *only* progress if strong-armed by the global community. However, this logic will only further precipitate the repeated failure of Gambian 'efforts.' The Women's (Amendment) Act 2015, the ratification of international treaties, the 'commitment' to Agenda 2030, amongst others, have all been hollow promises sprung from a will to silence undesired international pressure. Denigration of FGM is already commonly viewed by Gambians as the unwanted influence of 'the West' attempting to 'destroy' their country and tradition;[201] there is no need for more fuel to stunt progress. One must remember that transitional justice must be internally based and is dependent upon a society's *will* to change. As Fisher and Stewart note, 'the focus of pressures and direct interventions by external, international actors... could undermine any sort of organic [transition to a] liberal democracy.'[202] To truly achieve transitional justice and societal healing, The Gambia must first internally *welcome* a progression of their culture denouncing the practice. As seen by its consistent failure, this cannot be forced externally. Incentive must come from within the country itself to avoid half-hearted commitments and truly achieve national condemnation.

[200] A '2020 UNICEF The Gambia and UNFPA' press release wrongly claimed that young girls are at a 'much lower risk' of falling victim to FGM than their mothers due to national efforts to eradicate the practice; however, the data is misleading. Girls between the ages of 0–14 are often less likely to undergo FGM in The Gambia because they have not yet reached the pubescent age during which FGM is performed. The resulting discrepancy in incidence between age groups may have been purposefully utilised to mislead and create the impression that national improvement had occurred. It quoted the gap between FGM victims aged 0–14 years and women aged 15–49: 50% versus 75%.': Joint statement by UNFPA, UNICEF on International Day of Zero Tolerance for Female Genital Mutilation,' https://www.unicef.org/gambia/press-releases/joint-statement-unfpa-unicef-international-day-zero-tolerance-female-genital; MICS *supra* note 43. 'It is important to remember that prevalence data for girls age 0–14 years reflect their current—not final—FGM status, since many of them may not have reached the customary age for FGM at the time of the survey;' MICS, *supra* note 199, 353.

[201] Ylva and Shell-Duncan, *supra* note 17.

[202] Fisher and Stewart, *supra* note 124, 6.

8.2 Public Perceptions

The most damning consequence of the government's lax approach towards FGM is the perpetuation of a cycle:

> Gambian culture values FGM → the government does not bestow significance to its criminalisation → the law is not enforced → the people culturally believe the law is of no significance → practice continues → Gambian culture values FGM, and so on.

In Senegal, studies have revealed that highly publicised cases are enough to generate widespread fear of prosecution,[203] reducing its practice. There is no opportunity for this to exist in The Gambia. As described by a local Gambian, the people 'know [FGM] is happening, the police know it is happening, the legal system knows it is happening, but no one is taking the lead to enforce the law.'[204] The cultural predisposition supporting FGM is only further enhanced by the government's careless attitude. Additionally, a bias against the FGM criminalisation was *already* robust due to the legislations enactment under Jammeh's dictatorship; the law is viewed as a remnant of the previous dictatorial regime.[205] In 2018, a woman justified subjecting her daughter to FGM because she believed their new 'democratic' society, free from Jammeh's dictatorship, would allow her to act as she wished without consequence. She similarly expected President Barrow to remove the law.[206] The government's silence on the matter has created the impression that it *is* 'unjust' debris left over from the previous rule.[207] Even the police question whether the government supports the law.[208] There is a dire need for the government

---

[203] Ylva and Shell-Duncan, *supra* note 17, 48.

[204] Alagie Jarju of the National Youth Council in *Activity Report: Key Persons Interview on Bottlenecks of the FGM Law in The Gambia,* July 7, 2017, https://www.safehandsforgirls.com/our-reports.

[205] Activity Report, *supra* note 204.

[206] Nellie Peyton and Lamin Jahateh, *With New Found Democracy, Gambia Faces Resurgence in FGM and Child Marriage*, Thomas Reuters, January 23, 2018, https://uk.mobile.reuters.com/article/amp/idUSKBN1FC0XA.

[207] Fanta Jatta from Action Aid in Activity Report, *supra* note 204, 12.

[208] Ibid.

to be outspoken about the illegality and seriousness of FGM as their inactivity perpetuates the cycle.

9 Conclusion

The exploitation of women is currently embedded within Gambian culture as exemplified by FGM despite its illegality. In essence, this female torture is a cultural issue, eerily reminiscent of Gambian's suffering from colonial slavery, history immortalised in Alex Haley's Roots. However, where slavery was largely[209] an external threat thrust upon Gambians, and thus the need for a societal shift was starkly clear, FGM comes from within. Kurt Lewin'stheory of change is then vital to understand how The Gambia may achieve progression. Lewin dictates a need to outweigh any 'resistors against change' with forces favouring evolution. Yet, this proves difficult when the government acts as the greatest resistor towards FGM eradication. FGM is scrutinised at an international level for causing extreme physical and emotional mutilation to its victims. It is an issue of both public health and human rights. However, unlike Somalia, whose government has been transparent in its encouragement of FGM, The Gambian government has deceived the global community into believing it wishes to eradicate the practice in an attempt to evade international condemnation. The Gambian public is well aware of the disconnect between the law and culture, and of the betrayal of its female citizen. A cycle presents itself, and FGM flourishes.

Society must be unwoven to create a radical shift that condemns FGM. Nevertheless, the current governmental stance stunts any opportunity to challenge these archaic practices and beliefs. Society cannot be 'unfrozen' unless a macro mechanism presents an equal or greater opposition to the governmental resistance, or the government resistance ceases to exist. Previous 'hollow promises' reveal that The Gambian government cannot be incentivised by global pressure to publicly embrace progression

---

[209] Adaobi Tricia Nwaubani, 'When the Slave Traders Were African' *Wall Street Journal*, September 20, 2019, https://www.wsj.com/articles/when-the-slave-traders-were-african-11568991595.

and cause the necessary societal 'unfreezing.' Ultimately, the motivation must come from within the country itself. In order to achieve change and remove the barriers preventing access to justice, the government must be compelled to undergo a complete re-evaluation of national priorities while truly welcoming them. As accomplished in Uganda, The Gambia must publicly condemn FGM, rigorously incorporate the condemnation in all facets of Gambian law, visibly enforce the laws already in existence and develop micro-level plans to address and deconstruct the 'frozen' culture. The culture of FGM encouragement and acceptance must then be unhemmed to adequately identify a method whereby the country can effectively *adapt* progression through transition instead of *force* a sudden change. The Gambia must thus undergo the process of transitional justice. To do this, following the change in law, the role of women within society, and the historical need for control and ownership surrounding them, must be addressed and denounced at a national level in a way that respects the cultural norm. More discussion on how this may be achieved is necessary. Micro methods to achieve societal change must involve more in-depth analysis of the hierarchical structure. However, in order to attain the required societal shift, FGM must *first*, on a macro scale, publicly be given the importance it necessitates. Until then, while the legal prohibition of FGM in The Gambia remains, the absence of its enforcement leads to a failure to offer access to justice for its victims. FGM thus persists as a criminal act without accountability.

References

28 Too Many, *Dropping the Knife in The Gambia* (December 21, 2015). https://www.28toomany.org/blog/dropping-the-knife-in-the-gambia-guest-blog-by-jacqueline-hoover/, October 20, 2020.

28 Too Many, *The Gambia: The Law and GFM* (Online: Thomson Reuters Foundation, 2018).

28 Too Many, *The Law and FGM: An Overview of 28 African Countries* (Thomson Reuters Foundation: September 2018). https://www.28toomany.

org/static/media/uploads/Law%20Reports/the_law_and_fgm_v1_(september_2018).pdf, October 20, 2020.

Activity Report: Key Persons Interview on Bottlenecks of the FGM Law in The Gambia (July 7, 2017). https://www.safehandsforgirls.com/our-reports, 20 October 2020.

Abathun, Asresash Demissie, Johanne Sundby and Abdi A Gele, 'Attitude Toward Female Genital Mutilation Among Somali and Harari People, Eastern Ethiopia,' 8 *International Journal of Women's Health* (2016): 557–569.

African Charter on Human and Peoples' Rights (1981).

Agence Nationale de la Statistique et de la Démographie (ANSD), *Sénégal: Enquête Démographique et de Santé Continue (EDS-Continue) 2017* (2018). https://dhsprogram.com/pubs/pdf/FR345/FR345.pdf, October 20, 2020.

Akinsulure-Smith, Adeyinka M. and Adeyinka M. Akinsulure-Smith 'Exploring Female Genital Cutting Among Survivors of Torture,' 19 *Journal of Immigrant and Minority Health* (2017): 769–773.

Ali Nimco, *We Will End Female Genital Mutilation only by Backing Frontline Activists* (The Guardian, February 6, 2020). https://www.theguardian.com/global-development/2020/feb/06/we-will-end-female-genital-mutilation-only-by-backing-frontline-activists, October 20, 2020.

Baldwin Robert, Martin Cave and Martin Lodge, *Understanding Regulation: Theory, Strategy, and Practice* (2012).

Batha Emma, *From Prisoner to Hero: Activist Persuades Gambia to Ban FGM* (Thomas Reuters Foundation, March 25, 2010). https://news.trust.org/item/20130325105400-mxd9h/, October 20, 2020.

BBC News, *Profile: Former Gambian President Yahya Jammeh* (BBC News Africa, January 22, 2017). https://www.bbc.com/news/world-africa-24383225, October 20, 2020.

BBC News, *Sudan Criminalises Female Genital Mutilation (FGM)* (BBC News, May 1, 2020). https://www.bbc.com/news/world-africa-52502489, October 20, 2020.

Bellagamba Alice, 'Back to the Land of Roots: African American Tourism and the Cultural Heritage of the River Gambia,' 1 *Cahiers d' études africaines* (2009): 453–476.

Berg Rigmor and Eva Denison, 'A Tradition in Transition: Factors Perpetuating and Hindering the Continuance of Female Genital Mutilation/Cutting (FGM/C) Summarised in a Systematic Review,' 34 *Health Care for Women International* (2013): 837–859.

Berg Rigmore and Eva Denison, 'Effectiveness of Interventions Designed to Prevent Female Genital Mutilation/Cutting: a Systematic Review,' 43 *Studies in Family Planning* (2012): 135–146.

Bishai, David, Yung-Ting Bonnenfant, Manal Darwish, Taghreed Adam, Heli Bathija, Elise Johansen, Dale Huntington, *Estimating the obstetric costs of female genital mutilation in six African countries*, World Health Organization, https://www.who.int/bulletin/volumes/88/4/09-064808-ab/en/, October 20, 2020.

Blight Garry, Liz Ford, Frank Hulley-Jones, Niko Kommenda and Lydia McMullan, *Climate, Inequality, Hunger: Which Global Problems Would You Fix First?: Country Choice 'The Gambia'* (The Guardian, January 15, 2020). https://www.theguardian.com/global-development/ng-interactive/2020/jan/15/environment-inequality-hunger-which-global-problems-would-you-fix-first, October 20, 2020.

Broussard Patricia, 'Female Genital Mutilation: Exploring Strategies for Ending Ritualised Torture; Shaming, Blaming, and Utilising the Convention Against Torture,' 15 *Duke Journal of Gender Law & Policy* (2008): 19–47.

Cairo Declaration on the Elimination of FGM (2003) (CDEFGM).

Caldwell Brian, *Techniques for Neonatal Circumcision*, UpToDate, https://www.uptodate.com/contents/techniques-for-neonatal-circumcision?search=male%20circumcision&source=search_result&selectedTitle=3~150&usage_type=default&display_rank=3, October 20, 2020.

Catharine Mackinnon, 'Difference and Dominance: On Sex Discrimination,' in Anne Phillips (ed.) *Feminism and Politics* (1998): 295–312.

Cham Mamady, Johanne Sundby and Siri Vangen, 'Availability and Quality of Emergency Obstetric Care in Gambia's Main Referral Hospital: Women-users' Testimonies,' 6 *Reproductive Health* (2009): 1–8.

Colley Binta, 'Community and Family Involvement in Gambia, West Africa,' in Diana Hiatt Michael (ed.) *Promising Practices for Family Involvement in Schooling Across the Continents* (2005).

Connolly Lesley and Cheryl He, *Toward a New Gambia: Linking Peace and Development* (2018).

Constitution of Uganda (1995).

Constitutional Review Commission, *Report of the Constitutional Review Commission on the Draft Constitution for the Third Republic of The Gambia*, March 30, 2020, https://crc220.org/wp-content/uploads/2015/12/CRC-FINAL-REPORT-ON-THE-DRAFT-CONSTITUTION.pdf, October 20, 2020.

Constitutional Review Commission: Press Release, *Clarifications Concerning Certain Provisions of the CRC Draft Constitution*, December 28, 2019. https://crc220.org/clarifications-concerning-certain-provisions-of-the-crc-draft-constitution/, October 20, 2020.

Convention Against Torture and Other Cruel, Inhuman or Degrading Treatment or Punishment (1984) (CTOCIDTIP).

Convention on the Rights of the Child (1989) (CRC).

Darby Robert and Steven Svoboda, 'A Rose by Any Other Name?: Rethinking the Similarities and Between Male and Female Genital Cutting,' 21 *Medical Anthropology Quarterly* (2007): 301–323.

Ddamulira Mujuzi Jamil, 'Female Genital Mutilation in Uganda: A Glimpse at the Abolition Process,' 56 *Journal of African Law* (2012): 139–150.

Declaration on the Elimination of Violence against Women (Proclaimed by General Assembly resolution 48/104 of December 20 1993) https://www.ohchr.org/EN/ProfessionalInterest/Pages/ViolenceAgainstWomen.aspx, October 20, 2020.

Desai Sonalde, 'Children at Risk: The Role of Family Structure in Latin America and West Africa,' 18 *Population and Development Review* 18 (1992): 689–717.

Dicey Albert Venn, *Introduction to the Study of the Law of the Constitution* (1982).

First African Summit on Female Genital Mutilation and Child Marriages: Report, June, 2019, http://www.Users/Ray/Downloads/1st%20African%20Summit%20on%20FGM%20and%20Child%20Marriage%20-%20June%202019-%20Final%20Report.pdf, October 20, 2020.

Fisher Kirsten and Robert Stewart, *Transitional Justice and the Arab Spring* (2014).

Fullan Michael, *Leading in Change* (2004).

Galukande Moses, Joseph Kamara, Violet Ndabwire, Elisabeth Leistey, Cecilia Valla and Sam Luboga, 'Eradicating Female Genital Mutilation and Cutting in Tanzania: An Observational Study,' 15 *BMC Public Health* (2015): 1–10.

Gambia's Jammeh Loses to Adama Barrow in Shock Election Result (BBC News, December 2, 2016). https://www.bbc.com/news/world-africa-38183906.

Gambia's Draft Constitution of 2019, Draft of November 12, 2019. https://www.constituteproject.org/constitution/Gambia_2019D.pdf?lang=en, October 20, 2020.

Greenlee Cynthia, *How 'Roots' Reverberated in Africa* (The American Prospect, May 30, 2016). https://prospect.org/culture/roots-reverberated-africa/, October 20, 2020.

Gusfield, Joseph, 'Tradition and Modernity: Misplaced Polarities in the Study of Social Change,' 72 *American Journal of Sociology* (1967): 356.

Haley Alex, *Roots: The Saga of an American Family* (1976).

Hatcher Laurie, 'Female Circumcision in The Gambia,' in Bill Roberts and Bala Saho (eds.) *Tubaab Two: From Baobab to the Bantaba* (1998) 59–64.

Hernlund, Ylva and Bettina Shell-Duncan, 'Contingency, Context, and Change: Negotiating Female Genital Cutting in The Gambia and Senegal,' 53 *Africa Today* (2007): 43–57.

Huge FGM Rise Recorded in Somalia During Coronavirus Lockdown (The Guardian, May 18, 2020). https://www.theguardian.com/world/2020/may/18/fgm-risk-in-somalia-heightened-by-coronavirus-crisis, October 20, 2020.

Human Rights Watch, *Yahya Jammeh*. https://www.hrw.org/tag/yahya-jammeh, October 20, 2020.

Hur Kenneth and John Robinson, 'The Social Impact of 'Roots," 55 *Journalism Quarterly* (1978): 19–83.

Hussain Syed Talib, Shen Lei, Tayyaba Akram, Muhammed Jamal Haider, Syed Hadi Hussain and Muhammad Ali, 'Kurt Lewin's Change Model: A Critical Review of the Role of Leadership and Employee Involvement in Organisational Change,' 3 *Journal of Innovation & Knowledge* (2018): 123–127.

Idoko Patrick, Emmanuel Ogbe, Oley Jallow and Amaka Ocheke, 'Burden of Intimate Partner Violence in The Gambia—A Cross Sectional Study of Pregnant Women,'12 *Reproductive Health* (2015): 1–6.

Institut National de la Statistique et Ministère du Plan et du Développement Economique, *Enquête Démographique et de Santé, République de Guinée 2018 [Guinea Demographic and Health Survey 2018]*, (2019). https://dhsprogram.com/pubs/pdf/FR353/FR353.pdf, October 20, 2020.

International Covenant of Economic, Social and Cultural Rights (1966) (ICESCR).

Jammeh Sulayman, Chieh-Yu Liu, Su-Fen Cheng, and Jane Lee-Hsieh, 'Community based study on married couples' family planning knowledge, attitude and practice in rural and urban Gambia,' 14 *African Health Sciences* (2014): 273–280.

Jasser Zuhdi, Waqas Khan, and Shaaz Mahboob, *Comparisons Between Female Genital Mutilation and Male Circumcision are False and Dangerous, Uncommon Ground* (February 26, 2018) https://uncommongroundmedia.com/comparisons-female-genital-mutilation-male-circumcision-false-dangerous/, October 20, 2020.

Jewkes Rachel and Liz Dartnall, 'Sexual Violence' in Harald Kristian Heggenhougen and Stella Quah (eds.) *International Encyclopedia of Public Health* (Elsevier Inc., 2008): 723–731.

Joseph Gusfield, 'Tradition and Modernity: Misplaced Polarities in the Study of Social Change,' 72 *American Journal of Sociology* (1967): 352.

Jouhki Jukka and Luara Stark, *Causes and Motives of Early Marriage in The Gambia: Is New Legislation Enough?* (Finland: Poverty and Development Working Papers, 2017).

Kandala Ngianga-Bakwin and Bettina Shell-Duncan, 'Trends in Female Genital Mutilation/Cutting in Senegal: What Can We Learn from Successive Household Surveys in Sub-Saharan African Countries?,' 18 *International Journal for Equity in Health* (2019).

Kandala Ngianga-Bakwin, Martinsixtus Ezejimofor and Paul Komba, 'Secular trends in the Prevalence of Female Genital Mutilation/Cuttings Among Girls: a Systematic Analysis,' 3 *BMJ* (2019): 1–7.

Kaplan Adriana, Babucarr Cham, Lamin Njie, Ana Seixas, Sandra Blanco, and Mireia Utzet, 'Female Genital Mutilation/Cutting: The Secret World of Women as Seen by Men,' *Obstetrics and Gynaecology International* (2013): 1–11.

Kaplan Adriana, Mary Forbes, Isabelle Bonhoure, Mireia Utzet, Miguel Martín, Malick Manneh, and Haruna Ceesay, 'Female Genital Mutilation/Cutting in The Gambia: Long-term Health Consequences and Complications During Delivery and for the New-Born,' 3 *International Journal of Women's Health* (2013): 323–321.

Kenya National Bureau of Statistics et al., *Kenya Demographic and Health Survey 2014* (December 2015), https://www.dhsprogram.com/pubs/pdf/FR308/FR308.pdf, October 20, 2020.

Klein Elliot, Elizabeth Helzner, Michelle Shayowitz, Stephan Kohlhoff and Tamar A. Smith-Norowitz, 'Female Genital Mutilation: Health Consequences and Complications—A Short Literature Review,' *Obstetrics and Gynecology International* (2018): 1–7.

Koski Alissa and Jody Heymann, 'Thirty-year Trends in the Prevalence and Severity of Female Genital Mutilation: A Comparison of 22 Countries,' 2 *BMJ Global Health* 2017 (2017): 1–8.

Law and Advocacy for Women in Uganda v Attorney General (Constitutional Petition No 8 of 2007), [2010] UGCC 4 (July 28, 2010). https://www.refworld.org/cases,UGA_CC,4cf3a53f2.html, October 20, 2020.

Law Advocacy for Women in Uganda v Attorney General (Constitutional Petitions no 13 /05 /& 05 /06) (2007) UGCC 1 (April 5, 2007).

Lewin Kurt, 'Frontiers in Group Dynamics: Concept, Method and Reality in Social Science; Social Equilibria and Social Change,' 1 *Human Relations* (1947): 5–47.

Lien Inger-Lise, 'The Perspectives of Gambian Men on the Sexuality of Cut and Uncut Women,' 20 *Sexualities* (2017): 521–534.

Lyons Kate, *The Gambia Bans Female Genital Mutilation* (The Guardian, November 24, 2015). https://www.theguardian.com/society/2015/nov/24/the-gambia-bans-female-genital-mutilation, October 20, 2020.

Macklin Audrey, 'The Double-Edged Sword: Using the Criminal Law Against Female Genital Mutilation in Canada,' in Abusharaf Rogaia Mustafa (ed.) *Female Circumcision: Multicultural Perspectives* (2007).

Maclean Ruth and Saikou Jammeh, *Gambia's Joy Gives Way to Sinking Distrust as Barrow Clings to Power* (The Guardian, September 23, 2019). https://www.theguardian.com/global-development/2019/sep/23/gambia-joy-gives-way-to-sinking-distrust-adama-barrow-clings-to-power, October 20, 2020.

Maputo Protocol (2003).

Meral Ziya, 'A Duty to Remember? Politics and Morality of Remembering Past Atrocities,' 5 *International Politics Anthropology* (2012): 29–50.

McKinlay John, 'A Case for Refocusing Upstream: The Political Economy of Illness,' in Peter Conrad and Rochelle Kern (eds.) *The Sociology of Health and Illness: Critical Perspectives* (1986).

MICS, *2018 Multiple Indicator Cluster Survey (MICS6) Briefing* (2018), https://reliefweb.int/sites/reliefweb.int/files/resources/English_7.pdf, October 20, 2020.

MICS, *The Gambia: Multiple Indicator Cluster Survey 2018* (Survey Findings Report, July, 2019). https://mics-surveys-prod.s3.amazonaws.com/MICS6/West%20and%20Central%20Africa/Gambia/2018/Survey%20findings/The%20Gambia%202018%20MICS%20Survey%20Findings%20Report_English.pdf, October 20, 2020.

MICS, *The Gambia: Multiple Indicator Cluster Survey 2010 (UNICEF Final Report, June 2012).* https://catalog.ihsn.org/index.php/catalog/6776/download/81358, October 20, 2020.

Ministry of Health, Community Development, Gender, Elderly and Children et al., *Tanzania Demographic and Health Survey and Malaria Indicator Survey 2015–2016: Final Report*, (December 2016). https://dhsprogram.com/pubs/pdf/FR321/FR321.pdf, October 20, 2020.

Montgomery Eric, 'Polygyny in The Gambia,' in Bill Roberts and Bala Saho (eds.) *Tubaab Two: From Baobab to the Bantaba* (1998): 65–70.

Moore Jesse, 'Alex Haley's Roots: Ten Years Later,' 18 *The Western Journal of Black Studies* 18 (1994).

Mwakikagile Godfrey, *Ethnic Diversity and Integration in The Gambia: The Land, the People and the Culture* (2010).

Nabaneh Satang, *Banning Female Circumcision in The Gambia Through Legislative Change: The Next Steps* (AfricLaw, January 19, 2016).

Naldi Gino, 'Future Trends in Human Rights in Africa: The Increased Role OF THE OAU? in Malcolm Evans and Rachel Murray (eds.) *The African Charter on Human and Peoples' Rights: The System of Practice, 1986–2000* (2002).

National Bureau of Statistics, *Tanzania Demographic and Health Survey 2010* (Calverton, MD, April 2011). https://dhsprogram.com/pubs/pdf/FR243/FR243.pdf [June 24, 2011], October 20, 2020.

Naylor Larry, *Culture and Change: An Introduction* (Westport, CO: Bergin & Garvey, 1996).

Nour Nawal M., 'Female Genital Cutting (circumcision),' (UpToDate, January 13, 2020). https://www.uptodate.com/contents/female-genital-cutting-circumcision?search=female%20genital%20mutilation&source=search_result&selectedTitle=1~27&usage_type=default&display_rank=1, October 20, 2020.

Nwaubani Adaobi Tricia, When the Slave Traders Were African (*The Wall Street Journal*, September 20, 2019). https://www.wsj.com/articles/when-the-slave-traders-were-african-11568991595.

Odukogbe Akin-Tunde, Bosede Afolabi, Oluwasomidoyin Bello and Ayodeji Adeyanju, 'Female Genital Mutilation/Cutting in Africa,' 6 *Translational Andrology and Urology* (2017).

O'Grady Siobhán, *Most Girls in Somalia Experience Genital Mutilation. The Ritual Just Killed a 10-year-old* (The Washington Post, July 20, 2018). https://www.washingtonpost.com/news/worldviews/wp/2018/07/20/most-girls-in-somalia-experience-genital-mutilation-the-ritual-just-killed-a-10-year-old/, October 20, 2020.

Ortiz-Ospina Esteban, *Global Health* (Our World in Data 2016, June 30, 2020).

Patel Pragna Elliot Raizes and Laura Broyles, 'Human Immunodeficiency Virus Infection' in Edward Ryan, David Hill Tom Solomon, Naomi Aronson and Timothy Endy (eds.) *Hunter's Tropical Medicine and Emerging Infectious Diseases* (2020): 232–266.

Penal Code of 1991 (amendment) Law No. 12 of 2020.

Peyton Nellie and Lamin Jahateh, *With New Found Democracy, Gambia Faces Resurgence in FGM and Child Marriage* (Thomas Reuters, January 23, 2018). https://uk.mobile.reuters.com/article/amp/idUSKBN1FC0XA, October 20, 2020.

Proceedings of the Constituent Assembly (Official Report) (Uganda Printing and Publishing Corporation: 1994).

Prohibition of the Female Genital Mutilation Act (2010).

Republic of The Gambia, *The Gambia: Voluntary National Review, a Report on the Progress of Implementation of SDGs,* https://sustainabledevelopment.un.org/content/documents/263072020GambiaVNR.pdf, October 20, 2020.

Roots, TV Miniseries—Marvin Chomsky, John Erman, David Greene and Gilbert Moses: USA, Warner Brothers Television (1977).

Ryan Mae, *Jaha Dukureh's Story of FGM Survival: 'I'm Not Going to Let Fear Deter Me from Doing Anything Now'—Video* (The Guardian, May 12, 2014). https://www.theguardian.com/society/video/2014/may/12/jaha-dukureh-female-genital-mutilation-video, October 20, 2020.

Sachs J., G. Schmidt-Traub, C. Kroll, G. Lafortune and G. Fuller, *Sustainable Development Report 2019* (2019).

Safe Hands for Girls, https://www.safehandsforgirls.com/our-work, October 20, 2020.

Saine Abdoulaye, *Culture and Customs of Gambia* (2012).

Salif Ndiaye and Mohamed Ayad, *Senegal DHS, 2005—Final Report* (2005).

Satkunanathan Ambika, 'The Politics of Reconciliation in Transitional Justice,' *The International Journal of Transitional Justice* (2014): 171–182.

Schein, Edgar, 'Kurt Lewin's Change Theory in the Field and in the Classroom: Notes Toward a Model of Managed Learning,' 9 *Systems Practice* (1996): 27–47.

Scraton Phil, *Power, Conflict and Criminalisation* (2007)

Shenoy Rupa, *Despite Recent Historic Gains in Ending FGM, Somalia Sees Dramatic Increase* (The World, June 3, 2020). https://www.pri.org/stories/2020-06-03/despite-recent-historic-gains-ending-fgm-somalia-sees-dramatic-increase, October 20, 2020.

Sherwood Jennifer, Ashley Grosso, Michele Decker, Sarah Peitzmeier, Erin Papworth, Daouda Diouf, Fatou Maria Drame, Nuha Ceesay and Stefan Baral, 'Sexual Violence Against Female Sex Workers in The Gambia: A Cross-sectional Examination of the Associations Between Victimisation and Reproductive, Sexual and Mental Health,' 15 *BMC Public Health* (2015).

Sipsma Heather, Peggy Chen, Angela Ofori-Atta, Ukwuoma Ilozumba, Kapouné Karfo and Elizabeth Bradley, 'Female Genital Cutting: Current

Practices and Beliefs in Western Africa,' 90 *Bulletin of the World Health Organization* (2012): 77–156.
Syrett Keith, 'Doing "Upstream" Priority-Setting for Global Health with Justice: Moving from Vision to Practice?' 11 *Public Health Ethics* (2018): 265.
The Convention on the Elimination of all forms of Discrimination Against Women (1979) (CEDAW).
The Gambia Bureau of Statistics (GBOS) International Community Foundation (ICF) International, *The Gambia Demographic and Health Survey 2013* (2014).
The Gambia Bureau of Statistics (GBOS) and International Community Foundation (ICF), *The Gambia Demographic and Health Survey: Key Indicators 2019–2020* (2020).
The Gambia Times, *Vision 2020, Is The Gambia Worst Off than Before?* (The Gambia Times, January 1, 2020).
The Gambia: Voluntary National Review: A Report on the Progress of SDGs (June, 2020). https://sustainabledevelopment.un.org/content/documents/263072020GambiaVNR.pdf, October 20, 2020.
The Girl Generation, *The Gambia Committee on Traditional Practices Affecting the Health of Women and Children (GAMCOTRAP).* https://www.thegirlgeneration.org/organisations/gambia-committee-traditional-practices-affecting-health-women-and-children-gamcotrap, October 20, 2020.
The International Covenant on Civil and Political Rights (1966).
The National Council for Childhood and Motherhood, *Afro-Arab Expert Consultation Legal Tools for the Prevention of Female Genital Mutilation* (2003). http://www.sexarchive.info/ECR6/pdf_fgm_cairo2003_eng.pdf, October 20, 2020.
The New York Times, *1976 A Selection of Noteworthy Titles* (The New York Times, December 5, 1976). Archive, https://www.nytimes.com/1976/12/05/archives/1976-a-selection-of-noteworthy-titles.html, October 20, 2020.
The New York Times. *Critics Circle Nominates 20 Books by US Authors.* (The New York Times, December 13, 1976). Archive, https://www.nytimes.com/1976/12/13/archives/critics-circle-nominates-20-books-by-us-authors.html, October 20, 2020.
The Report of the Uganda Constitutional Commission: Analysis and Recommendations (1992, Uganda Printing and Publishing Corporation).
The Women's (Amendment) Act 2015.

The World Bank: *Data: Life Expectancy at Birth, Total (years)—Sub-Saharan Africa* (2018). https://data.worldbank.org/indicator/SP.DYN.LE00.IN?locations=ZG, October 20, 2020.

The World Bank, *GDP (current US$): All Countries and Economies*, https://data.worldbank.org/indicator/NY.GDP.MKTP.CD, October 20, 2020.

Thomas Reuters Foundation, *The Law and FGM an Overview of 28 African Countries September 2018*, http://www.trust.org/contentAsset/raw-data/1e5a2969-bd56-4fc3-8034-5409fd161175/file22, October 20, 2020.

Toubia Nahid, 'Female Circumcision as a Public Health Issue,' 331 *The New England Journal of Medicine* (1994): 712–716.

Touray Sunkaru, Baboucarr Sanyang, Gregory Zandrow, Fatoumatta Dibba, Kaddy Fadera, Ebrima Kanteh, Madikoi Danso, Landing Sanyang, Masirending Njie, Grey Johnson, Awa Sanyang and Awa Touray, 'An Assessment of Critical Care Capacity in The Gambia,' 47 *Journal of Critical Care* (2018): 245–253.

Truth, Reconciliation and Reparations Commission (2018). http://www.trrc.gm/.

Uganda Bureau of Statistics, *Uganda Demographic and Health Survey 2016*, (2018). https://dhsprogram.com/pubs/pdf/FR333/FR333.pdf, October 20, 2020.

UN Women, *Regional UN Ambassador Jaha Dukureh*, https://www.unwomen.org/en/partnerships/goodwill-ambassadors/jaha-dukureh, October 20, 2020.

UNFPA, *A Holistic Approach to the Abandonment of Female Genital Mutilation/Cutting*, https://www.unfpa.org/sites/default/files/pub-pdf/726_filename_fgm.pdf, October 20, 2020.

UNFPA-UNICEF Joint Programme on Female Genital Mutilation/Cutting, *2016 Annual Report of the UNFPA-UNICEF Accelerating Change by the Numbers: Joint Programme on Female Genital Mutilation/Cutting: Accelerating Change* (2017).

UNICEF, *A Profile of Female Genital Mutilation in Kenya*, https://reliefweb.int/report/kenya/profile-female-genital-mutilation-kenya.

UNICEF Data, *Female Genital Mutilation: Percentage of Girls Who Have Undergone FGM* (February, 2020). https://data.unicef.org/topic/child-protection/female-genital-mutilation, October 20, 2020.

UNICEF, *Female Genital Mutilation (FGM): At Least 200 Million Girls and Women Alive Today Living in 31 Countries Have Undergone FGM*, https://data.unicef.org/topic/child-protection/female-genital-mutilation/#_edn1, October 20, 2020.

UNICEF, *Female Genital Mutilation (FGM)* (February, 2020). https://data.unicef.org/topic/child-protection/female-genital-mutilation/, October 20, 2020.

UNICEF, *Female Genital Mutilation (FGM): The Prevalence of FGM Varies Greatly Across Countries with Data*, https://data.unicef.org/topic/child-protection/female-genital-mutilation/#_edn1, October 20, 2020.

UNICEF, *Indicator Profiles: Percentage of Girls and Women (Aged 15–49 years) Who Have Undergone Female Genital Mutilation (FGM)* (May 20, 2020). https://data.unicef.org/indicator-profile/PT_F_15-49_FGM/, October 20, 2020.

UNICEF, *Joint Statement by UNFPA, UNICEF on International Day of Zero Tolerance for Female Genital Mutilation* (February 6, 2020). https://www.unicef.org/gambia/press-releases/joint-statement-unfpa-unicef-international-day-zero-tolerance-female-genital, October 20, 2020.

UNICEF, *Statistical Country Profile on Female Genital Mutilation/Cutting: Somalia* (December 2013). https://data.unicef.org/wp-content/uploads/country_profiles/Somalia/FGMC_SOM.pdf, October 20, 2020.

United Nations, *About the Sustainable Development Goals*, https://www.un.org/sustainabledevelopment/sustainable-development-goals/, October 20, 2020.

United Nations, *Country Profile: The Gambia* (Economic Commission for Africa 2017).

United Nations Development Programme, *Human Development Report 2020: The Next Frontier; Human Development and the Anthropocene*, http://hdr.undp.org/sites/default/files/hdr2020.pdf, October 20, 2020

United Nations Development Programme: Human Development Reports, *Human Development Index (HDI)*, http://hdr.undp.org/en/content/human-development-index-hdi, October 20, 2020.

United Nations, *The Sustainable Development Agenda*, https://www.un.org/sustainabledevelopment/development-agenda/, October 20, 2020.

United Nations, *Transforming Our World: The 2030 Agenda for Sustainable Development* (A/RES/70/1), https://sustainabledevelopment.un.org/content/documents/21252030%20Agenda%20for%20Sustainable%20Development%20web.pdf, October 20, 2020.

UN Secretary General Report, *The Rule of Law and Transitional Justice in Conflict and Post-conflict Societies* (United Nations Security Council, UN Doc. S/2004/616 [2004]).

UpToDate, *About US*, https://www.uptodate.com/home/about-us, October 20, 2020.

US Department of State 2019 Fiscal Transparency Report (Pursuant to Section 7031(b)(3) of the Department of State, Foreign Operations and Related Programs Appropriations Act, 2019 (Div. F, PL 116–6) (FY. 2019 SFOAA)) (August 15, 2019). https://www.state.gov/2019-fiscal-transparency-report/, October 20, 2020.

Waltham Mass, *Clinicians in 139 Countries Turn to Wolters Kluwer's UpToDate Advanced to Deliver High-Quality Care* (Business Wire, July 11, 2019). https://www.businesswire.com/news/home/20190711005521/en/Clinicians-139-Countries-Turn-Wolters-Kluwer%E2%80%99s-UpToDate, October 20, 2020.

Women's UN Report Network (WUNRN), *Gambia- New Legislation on FGM Applied in Gambian Court: The Gambia Committee on Traditional Practices Affecting the Health of Women and Children (GAMCOTRAP),* WUNRN, https://wunrn.com/2016/03/gambia-new-legislation-on-fgm-applied-in-gambian-court/, October 20, 2020.

World Health Organization and Ministry of Health Republic of Indonesia, *State of Health Inequality Indonesia* (2017), https://www.who.int/docs/default-source/gho-documents/health-equity/state-of-inequality/12-dec-final-final-17220-state-of-health-inequality-in-indonesia-for-web.pdf?sfvrsn=54ae73ea_2, October 20, 2020.

World Health Organization, *Female Genital Mutilation (FGM)*, https://www.who.int/reproductivehealth/topics/fgm/prevalence/en/, October 20, 2020.

World Health Organization, *Sexual and Reproductive Health: Female Genital Mutilation: Prevalence of FGM* (2013), https://www.who.int/reproductivehealth/topics/fgm/prevalence/en/#:~:text=Prevalence%20of%20FGM,female%20genital%20mutilation%20every%20year, October 20, 2020.

World Health Organization, *Types of Female Genital Mutilation* (2020), https://www.who.int/sexual-and-reproductive-health/types-of-female-genital-mutilation, October 20, 2020.

Wright Donald, 'The Effects of Alex Haley's Roots on How Gambians Remember the Atlantic Slave Trade,' 38 *History in Africa* (2011): 295–318.

Yates Jennifer, 'Tubab in a Land Cruiser: A Study of Maternal Child Health Care in The Gambia from an American Student's Perspective,' in Bill Roberts and Bala Saho (eds.) *Tubaab Two: From Baobab to the Bantaba* (1998): 13–28.

Yemen Ministry of Public Health and Population and Central Statistical Organization, *Yemen National Health and Demographic Survey 2013* (2015), https://dhsprogram.com/pubs/pdf/FR296/FR296.pdf, October 20, 2020.

11

Access to Justice by Victims of Violence Against Women and Girls in Tanzania: A Social Legal Perspective

Cecilia Ngaiza and Asina Omari

1 Introduction

The term violence has received varying definitions from different authors depending on the context addressed. Since, this chapter addresses various types of violence to women and girls, the authors opt for a rather general definition by *Mhoja* and *Bisimba* who define violence against women (including girls) as[1]:

---

[1] Monica Mhoja and Hellen-Kijo Bisimba, 'Tanzanian Customary Laws of Inheritance: A Case of Cultural Violence Against Women,' in Ludgera Klempf (ed.) *Women Challenging Violence: Experiences from Eastern and Southern Africa* (1994): 2.

C. Ngaiza (✉) · A. Omari
University of Dar es Salaam School of Law, Dar es Salaam, Tanzania

A. Omari
e-mail: asinaomari@udsm.ac.tz

E. C. Lubaale and A. Budoo-Scholtz (eds.), *Violence Against Women and Criminal Justice in Africa: Volume I*, Sustainable Development Goals Series,
https://doi.org/10.1007/978-3-030-75949-0_11

> …any act, omission or conduct by means of which physical, sexual or mental suffering is inflicted directly or indirectly, through threat, coercion, or any other means on any woman (or girl) with the purpose or effect of intimidating, punishing or humiliating her or of maintaining her in sex stereotyped roles or of undermining the security of her person, her self respect or of diminishing her physical or mental capacities.

Considering the fact that the above discussion covers violence against women and girls (VAWG)[2] in Tanzania, the description of the term violence by Tanzania's Ministry of Health, Community Development, Gender, Elderly and Children is also considered; this includes but not limited to:

> … infringement of women and girls' basic human rights on basis of their gender that occasions adverse health, demographic, and economic consequences to the victims and the entire society… An example can be considered in a matrimonial setting where seven in ten ever married women face spousal violence in form of physical or emotional attacks. These incidents include cuts, bruises, broken bones or teeth and deep wounds among other injuries.[3]

The incidents are generally common to societies where enforcement of human rights standards in relation to women and girls are exposed to plural legal orders coupled with cultural practices, societal stereotypes, religious beliefs and ignorance of law.[4]

Over the years, legal researchers have attempted to get to the bottom of VAWG in Tanzania through analytical accounts of legal, policy and institutional framework relevant to protecting the rights of women and girls in the country. While others see the gaps in the policy and legal

---

[2] See the Committee on the Elimination of Discrimination against Women, General recommendation No. 35 on Gender-Based Violence against Women, *Updating General Recommendation No. 19*, (2017), 5–6; for a further discussion on forms of gender-based violence.

[3] Ministry of Health, Community Development, Gender, Elderly and Children et al., *Tanzania Demographic and Health Survey and Malaria Indicator Survey* (2016): 367.

[4] International Council on Human Rights Policy, *When Legal Worlds Overlap: Human Rights, State and Non-State Law* (2009): 73.

framework as the major cause for continued existence of VAWG,[5] we argue that giving a blind eye to the social aspect of the problem equally contributes to the inadequacy in the efforts to uprooting the ancestry nature of VAWG in Tanzanian societies. A deeper understanding of why the current legal and policy interventions are not working has to be associated with a rather neglected socio-legal perspective of looking at VAWG. In the end, it will become evident that additional actions to curb VAGW apart from adopting laws, policies and establishing relevant institutions is needed despite the reality that the same has existed, albeit far from perfect.[6] In a nutshell, setbacks to fighting VAWG including the obstacles in reporting and seeking justice by the victims of VAWG, has to be understood in the context of not only the existing gaps in the policy and legal framework but also the socio-economic and cultural factors that inhibit reporting and justice.[7]

Given the fact that VAWG is a complex issue, the chapter tackles it by first providing a historical background to VAWG in Tanzania with the intent to establish the chain of events and circumstances that have led to subsistence of this intricate conundrum in Tanzania. Going forward, the discussion provides the corresponding locally and internationally inspired measures taken by Tanzania to combat VAWG. Such measures that include the most recent developments reflect the legal environment set up to provide remedies to victims of VAWG in the country. This segment links the discussion on socio-cultural and economic origins of VAWG in Tanzania to their legal and policy remedies. The chapter extends to challenges of access to justice by victims of VAWG despite the existing initiatives developed to check this problem. This is to highlight the extent to which further efforts and different approaches are required to tackle the existing problem in the country. Finally, the chapter wraps up with the prospects of combating VAWG in Tanzania.

---

[5] See generally Tanzania Women Lawyers Association (TAWLA), *Review of Laws and Policies Related to Gender Based Violence of Tanzania Mainland* (2014).

[6] Human Development Trust, *Gaps in Policies and Laws That Perpetuate Gender Based Violence in Tanzania: An Analysis and Synthesis* (2011).

[7] Jennifer McCleary-Sills et al., *Help-Seeking Pathways and Barriers for Survivors of Gender-based Violence in Tanzania: Results from a Study in Dar es Salaam, Mbeya, and Iringa Regions* (2013).

2 Background to Socio-cultural and Economic Violence Against Women in Tanzania

The premises from which VAWG in Tanzania emanates are connected to social, cultural and economic conditions surrounding women in both rural and urban areas. These conditions have been carried out over the years and have taken different shapes depending on each era's prevailing circumstances. This section gives a clearer background of how the three aforementioned spheres have historically contributed to the persistent problem of VAWG in Tanzania as it scans through the pre-colonial, colonial, independence and post-independence periods in the country.

2.1 The Pre-Colonial Era

Gender was one of the very important aspects in the pre-colonial societies. The rationale is that, gender encompassed more than just an individual. It was afforded importance just like it was for the case of tasks and rituals.[8] Women and girls were defined by their roles in the society considering the prevailing cultural and traditional circumstances.[9] Some societies mostly in the coastal areas followed the matrilineal system on one hand. In the matrilineal societies, women were not prejudiced and had voices in their families. This haven lasted until when such system met some patriarchal elements introduced to the coastal areas by among other factors, Islam.[10] On the other hand, the patrilineal system

---

[8] Signe Arnfred, 'Reflection on Family, Trends of Change, Lobola and Polygyny Women and Law in Southern Africa,' in Women and Law in Southern Africa (WLSA) (ed.) *Changing Families: Changing Laws, Working Paper No.9.* (1994): 38.

[9] Ophelia Mascarenhas and Marjorie Mbilinyi, *Women in Tanzania: An Analytical Bibliography* (1983): 35.

[10] Marja-Liisa Shwantz, *Women in Development: A Creative Role Denied?* (1985): 19. Also See Sherene Razak, 'Imperilled Muslim Women, Dangerous Muslim Men and Civilised Europeans: Legal and Social Responses to Forced Marriages,' 12 *Feminist Legal Studies* (2004): 129 who argues that, social responses to violence against women in Muslim communities are culturally oriented i.e. the violence in the said religion has built up over the years from cultural practices of communities professing such religion and the practices transmitted to elsewhere where the religion got spread.

existed in the rest of the interior societies which practiced inequalities between boys and girls from childhood through adulthood. Children were trained to occupy their social pre-existing positions and gender roles, whereby; male children were oriented to become aggressive and dominant, while female children were trained to remain submissive and accustomed to inferior positions in their families without resistance.[11] Generally, women were swimming in the pool of a deep-rooted patriarchal system and unbalanced gender roles. It is however argued that, data related to women's roles in the pre-colonial period has remained scarce due to their conventional insignificance position in the traditional society.[12]

2.2 The Colonial Era

The situation for women shifted from bad to worse with the coming into place of colonial regimes in Tanzania. Colonialism introduced capitalist economy to the country which added weight on women's shoulders in relation to undertaking their primary gender roles as well as engaging in colonial economic activities such as production of cash crops. In addition, when capitalist economy entered societies with bride wealth traditions, husbands gained more control of their wives' labour per the amount of bride wealth they could afford to pay.[13] This was a typical advent of violence against women in households. All these new additions to the then colonial Tanganyika (now mainland Tanzania) destabilised social relationships in various communities.[14] Despite the foregoing, women had throughout this period accepted male-biased gender ideologies for the sake of forging 'peaceful' co-existence with men.[15]

---

[11] Bart Rwezaura, 'Domestic Application of International Human Rights Norms in Protecting the Rights of the Girl Child in Eastern and Southern Africa,' in Welshman Ncube (ed.) *Culture Tradition and Children's Rights in Eastern and Southern Africa* (1998): 32.

[12] Els Baerends, *Changing Kinship, Family and Gender Relationships in Sub-Sahara Africa* (1994): 20.

[13] Ibid., 41 and 66.

[14] Ibid., 1.

[15] Ibid., 18.

2.3 The Independence Era

At independence, the idea of emancipating women and girls from the purportedly cultural violence were curtailed by the pre-existing perception that women naturally belong in the domestic domain.[16] However, there are records of women who were not only vocal but very instrumental in the independence struggle.[17] In the late 1960s, it had gradually become of the government's concern that, there was a big wave of girls' non-enrolment to schools and others dropping out from schools by pregnancies.[18] Therefore, some religions, customs and traditions favoured early marriages to avoid pre-marital pregnancies.[19] This situation led to high illiteracy rates among women apart from other socio-economic issues. Nevertheless, it was not of the government's interests to tackle human rights issues at this particular period. The country was grappling with post-colonial challenges. Efforts were directed to building the country's economy as well as putting into action development policies and strategies. The centre of attention was on issues like agricultural development, industrial expansion and labour stabilisation.[20]

2.4 The Post-Independence Era

Moving far from the first decade of independence, the country was yet to adopt the Bill of Rights in the national Constitution. This occasioned a functional discriminatory justice system. For instance,

---

[16] Ibid., 69.

[17] For a further description of the role of women in the independence struggle in Tanganyika see *inter alia* Susan Gaiger, *TANU Women: Women and Culture in the Making of Tanganyika Nationalism 1955–1965* (1997).

[18] Mascarenhas and Mbilinyi, *Women in Tanzania: An Analytical Bibliography* (1983): 36.

[19] Stella Bendera, E. Maro and Mary Mboya, 'A Gender Perspective on Violence: Its Form and Consequences for Education of Primary School Pupils in Tanzania,' in S. J. Bendera and S. W. Mboya (eds.) Gender *and Education in Tanzanian Schools* (1996): 35. Also, see the Law of Marriage Act, 1971, Section 23 (1) that back up this position by setting the minimum statutory age of marriage for girls to be 15 years or below 15 years per the Court's consent.

[20] Felician Tungaraza, 'Changes in Traditional Social Security and Their Impact on Women in Tanzania,' in Ludgera Klemp (ed.) *Gender and Social Policy: Experiences of Tanzania* (1994): 12–34, 21.

courts could still render inequitable judgments backing cultural VAWG. Some judges applied the law as it was, however, discriminatory.[21] This involved, but not limited to, probate cases governed by the prejudiced customary inheritance law.[22] Such law, *interalia,* deprived and still does deprive women and girls of inheriting properties like clan land, assigning them only usufruct rights thereto that terminates in the event they marry or die.[23] In a separate incident, a mother is not at all featured in the customary rules addressing situations when children lose their father (impliedely, a woman losing her husband).[24] This is an open form of cultural violence.

Later, in a sharp socialist Tanzania, women oppression at homes was regarded as an 'attribute to capitalism' whereby family is a private institution.[25] For socialists, women were 'expected' to live as equal to their fellow citizens, that is, men.[26] Hence, violence against women was regarded a 'myth' in a socialist Tanzania. This state of affairs persisted and resulted into the government placing less focus on tackling the VAWG that existed in the society by then. VAWG was not considered a social problem of great concern. Omar addresses a 'social problem' as a condition considered by the majority inappropriate and that, the same calls for relevant remedy.[27]

---

[21] Mhoja and Bisimba, *supra* note 1, 2.

[22] See the cases of *Felista Ishekampora v Martin Banyuka*, 1968 [H.C.D] 12 where the High Court applied the codified Customary Law, Para 27 and 77 of the Local Customary Law (Declaration) (No.04) Order, 1963 and ordered the shift of a childless widow's share of inheritance to her step son. Adding insult to injury, the High Court in the case of *Verdiana Kyabuje v Gregory Kyabuje* (1968) HCD no 459 stated that, it is not upon the Court to effect customary change no matter how far it can sympathise with the violence occasioned to women by the customary law. These deep-rooted customary convictions led to a prolonged trend of this judicial practice even after entrenchment of the Bill of rights in the Constitution. To this effect, see the case of *Scolastica Benedict v Martin Benedict*, 1988 [H.C.D] 499, whereby a widow was ordered by the Court to give a vacant possession of her matrimonial home to her stepson.

[23] Local Customary Declaration Law (Declaration) (No.04) Order, 1963, Rule 20 and 27.

[24] See the case of *Donatila Exavery v. Perekinas Twamgabo* (1989) cited in Mhoja and Bisimba, 'Tanzanian Customary Laws of Inheritance,' 3.

[25] Mascarenhas and Mbilinyi, *supra* note 18, 16.

[26] Julius Kambarage Nyerere, *Socialism and Rural Development* (1967): 3.

[27] Cuthbert Omar, 'Explaining Social Problems,' in Cuthbert Omari and Leonard Shaidi (eds.) *Social Problems in Eastern Africa* (1991): 1.

The succeeding capitalism regime in Tanzania considered family issues as 'private' matters. Family grievances (including VAWG) are preferred to be resolved at the family level. The 'privacy' practice that has been and is still entertained erodes women's rights to protection against violence.[28] Research suggests that family is the basis for legitimising basic cultural fingerprinting in any society.[29] Thus, if the culture of VAWG emanates from the family level, the problem requires extra initiatives to uproot.

In relation to girls, there are still basic issues at home leading to their psychological and physical violence. Some of them are; withdrawal of a girl child from studies by her parents to participate in puberty rites (some of which entail female genital mutilation) and unbalanced subjection of school girls to performing domestic chores at home or for income (with the risk of exposure to sexual harassment and assaults). This impacts negatively girl's rights as compared to their male counterparts.[30] A rather recent and concrete example relates to the incidents of rape and early marriages affecting girls in regions like Shinyanga, Arusha, Geita and Mbeya Districts who stayed home per the government's order as an initiative to break the COVID-19 pandemic chain at schools.[31]

3 Responses to Violence Against Women and Girls in Tanzania

Having gone through the trail of historical grounds for subsistence of VAWG in Tanzania, it is imperative to take a step further and delve deep into the issue of how Tanzania has responded to this problem. Apparently, Tanzania has not assumed a low-key position in devising means to counter VAWG going on in the country. Such means include

---

[28] Fareda Banda, *Women, Law and Human Rights: An African Perspective* (2005): 159.

[29] Welschman Ncube, 'The African Cultural Fingerprint: The Changing Concept of Childhood,' in Welschman Ncube (eds.) *Law, Culture Tradition and Children's Rights in Eastern and Southern Africa* (1998): 13.

[30] Rwezaura, *supra* note 11, 35.

[31] Maduhu Marco, *Wapata Ujauzito Likizo ya Corona*, 25 May 2020, https://www.ippmedia.com/sw/habari/wapata-ujauzito-likizo-ya-corona; Zaya Elizabeth, *Wanafunzi 100 Wapata Mimba Kipindi cha Corona*, 17 June 2020, https://www.ippmedia.com/sw/habari/wanafunzi-100-wapata-mimba-kipindi-corona.

adopting policies, strategies, action plans, laws as well as setting up and strengthening institutions to respond to the problem. The foregoing discussion provides an analysis of such initiatives while complimenting the socio-legal perspective opted for the general discussion of the chapter. This segment is very crucial as the laws adopted in the country reflect the social realities captured by the policies, strategies, action plans; and international commitments made by Tanzania to curtail VAWG.

3.1 Policies, Strategies and Action Plans

In 1996, Tanzania adopted the Community Development Policy of which, *inter alia*, targets to change cultural orientations with negative impacts on women and girls. This was followed by the Women and Gender Development Policy of 2000 that aims at creating legal environment free from gender discrimination, among other things. This Policy is complemented by the National Strategy for Gender Development of 2005 which is meant to speed up implementation of Women and Gender Development Policy as well as the implementation of national, regional and international commitments on gender equality and empowerment of women in the country. Further, the National HIV/AIDS Polices and Multi Sectoral Framework on HIV/AIDS have been adopted to initiate programmes with and by men to promote male responsible behaviour in sexual and family relations so as to reduce the recurring incidents of irresponsible parenthood and domestic violence.[32] Additionally, the National Strategy for Growth and Reduction of Poverty (MKUKUTA II) of 2010 was devised to guarantee solutions to problems facing women and girls like discriminatory practices among others. The National Plan of Action for Prevention and Eradication of Gender-Based Violence against Women of 2001–2015 that envisioned a society free of physical, psychological, emotional and sexual violence against women and children by the year 2015 was also adopted to this effect. This plan has been extended through the National Plan of Action to End

[32] See the *Tanzania National HIV/AIDS Policy and the National Multisectoral Framework on HIV/AIDS* (2003–2007): 29; also the Second Edition (2008–2012).

Violence against Women and Children in Tanzania 2017/18–2021/22 as the backbone strategy to eliminate VAWG in the country.

3.2 Laws

3.2.1 International Legal Framework

Tanzania (then Tanganyika) demonstrated her commitment to international human rights obligation as soon as she obtained her independence on 9 December 1961. For instance, on 30 January 1962, mainland Tanzania then Tanganyika, ratified the Abolition of Forced Labour Convention and the Convention Concerning Forced or Compulsory Labour.[33] This was meant, among other things, to guarantee protection to women and girls working under forced labour conditions. Afterwards, on 11 June 1976, Tanzania acceded to the International Covenant on Civil and Political Rights (ICCPR) and the International Covenant on Economic Social and Cultural Rights (ICESCR), both of the year 1966.[34] The Covenants guarantee every person's right to equality to enjoy civil and political rights as well as economic, social and cultural rights.[35] Particularly, the ICCPR guarantees every person's right to life, liberty and security of person, protection against torture, cruelty, slavery, inhuman and degrading treatment, right to dignity of a person, equality before judicial and *quasi*-judicial bodies, equal recognition by the law, privacy, family, honour and reputation, freedom of thought, opinion, conscience, religion and association and the right to marry with free consent upon the marriageable age. The ICCPR also recognises family as the basic unit in the society, earning the entitlement to be protected by the society and the state. Moreover, the ICCPR provides for children's right to fair treatment as minors with no distinction whatsoever.[36]

---

[33] (ILO Convention No. 105), 320 U.N.T.S. 291 and (ILO Convention No. 29), 39 U.N.T.S. 55, respectively.

[34] Website of the United Nations, *Treaty Collection (Depository): International Covenant on Civil and Political Rights and International Covenant on Economic, Social and Cultural Rights*, https://treaties.un.org/pages/ViewDetails.aspx?src=TREATY&mtdsg_no=IV-11&chapter=4&lang=en.

[35] See the ICCPR and ICESCR generally.

[36] ICCPR, articles 6–10, 14, 16–19, 22–24 and 26.

The ICESCR guarantees the rights to equality, to enjoy work and equal opportunity to earn a living, right to work in favourable conditions and equal reward of one's labour, right to free consent in marriage and reasonable treatment of women before and after giving births, right to enjoy the highest standard of physical and mental health as well as everyone's right to education.[37] Under these Covenants, state parties (including Tanzania) are under the obligation to submit reports to the Human Rights Council and the Committee on Economic, Social and Cultural Rights, respectively, via the Secretary General of the United Nations, on the measures taken so far and the progress made in achieving the rights guaranteed under the Conventions. Such reports are also shared with the specialised agencies of relevancy to the reports submitted.[38]

On 17 July 1980, Tanzania signed the International Convention on Elimination of All Forms of Discrimination against Women (CEDAW) and ratified the same on 20 August 1985.[39] In its totality, the CEDAW addresses and places emphasis on the equality of gender in all aspects surrounding women, be it social or economic. The CEDAW provides for equality across genders in the field of education, employment and healthcare. It also specifically mentions rural women and the role they play in economic activities to ensure stability and survival of their families. In this sense, the CEDAW stresses their right to be considered equal in terms of access to opportunities related to economic development with a view to ending the prevailing economic exploitation and violence to women brought by unequal participation in production activities.[40] Likewise, the CEDAW addresses other rights in relation to equality between men and women, equality before the law, equal treatment in family affairs and responsibilities as well as in matrimonial and property rights.[41] It obliges the state parties to it to ensure elimination of prejudices, customary and practices that put women in inferior position

---

37 ICESCR, articles 3, 6–12.

38 ICCPR, article 40 and ICESCR, article 16.

39 Website of the United Nations, *Treaty Collection (Depository): Convention on the Elimination of All Forms of Discrimination Against Women,* https://treaties.un.org/pages/ViewDetails.aspx?src=TREATY&mtdsg_no=IV-11&chapter=4&lang=en.

40 CEDAW, articles 10–14.

41 CEDAW, article 16.

in the society hence, exposing them to several forms of violence.[42] Just like in the foregoing international treaties, Tanzania has to adhere to the provisions of the CADAW and the periodic reports from the CEDAW Committee regarding the rights of women in Tanzania.[43]

With the view to protecting a girl child, Tanzania has signed the Convention on the Rights of the Child 1989 (CRC) on 1 June 1990 and ratified the same on 10 June 1991.[44] The CRC requires the State to ensure a child is protected from all forms of discrimination or punishment basing on the status, activities, opinions or beliefs of his or her parents, legal guardians or family members.[45] On this trend, Tanzania has undertaken the obligation to ensure all appropriate legislative, administrative, social and educational measures are taken to protect the child from all forms of physical or mental violence while in the care of parent(s), legal guardian(s) or any other person who has the care of the child. Moreover, Tanzania has the obligation to submit periodic reports to the Committee on the Rights of the Child measures she has taken to realise maximum protection of children's (girls) rights domestically.[46]

3.2.2 Regional Agreements

Tanzania, being a member of the African Union, is party to several African regional human rights agreements that protect the rights and welfare of women and girls. The country has signed and ratified the African Charter on Human and Peoples' Rights 1981 (Banjul Charter) on 31 May 1983 and ratified the same on 18 February 1984.[47] Among other things, the African Charter recites the civil and political rights and economic, social and cultural rights as provided for under the ICCPR

[42] Ibid., article 5.

[43] Ibid., article 18,

[44] Website of the United Nations, *Treaty Collection (Depository): Convention on the Rights of the Child*, https://treaties.un.org/pages/ViewDetails.aspx?src=TREATY&mtdsg_no=IV-11&chapter=4&lang=en.

[45] Convention on the Rights of the Child, 1989, article 2.

[46] Ibid., article 19 and 44.

[47] Website of the African Commission on Human and Peoples' Rights, *Ratification Table: African Charter on Human and Peoples' Rights*, https://www.achpr.org/ratificationtable?id=49.

and the ICESCR, specifically the right to respect of one's dignity. It also prohibits acts of exploitation, degradation, slavery, torture, cruel, inhuman or degrading punishment and treatment to the citizens of parties to the Charter.[48] Under the Charter, Tanzania has committed itself to submitting to the African Commission on Human and Peoples' Rights reports on the status of implementation of the obligations assumed under the Charter.

The country took a step further by signing the Protocol to the African Charter on the Rights of Women in Africa 2003 (Maputo Protocol) on 5 November 2003 and subsequently ratifying the same on 3 March 2007.[49] Based on this move, Tanzania consented to fulfilling the obligation of ensuring that women and girls' rights are realised in the country. The Maputo Protocol also protects women and girls from discrimination and harmful practices such as early marriages (marriages below the age of eighteen years). It further protects women's sexual reproductive health rights including the right to make decisions for the safety of their health. The Protocol also provides for the right to food security and property rights particularly in instances of inheritance. Tanzania has further undertaken to protect the rights of widows, elderly women, women with disabilities and those living in distress, including their right to receive legal aid.[50]

Additionally, on 23 October 1998, Tanzania signed the African Charter on the Rights and Welfare of the Child of 1990 (ACRWC) and ratified the same on 23 March 2003.[51] Tanzania is tasked under this Charter to update the African Committee of Experts on the Rights and Welfare of the Child (African Children's Committee) on the progress made in ensuring implementation, protection and enjoyment of *inter*

---

[48] Banjul Charter, article 5.

[49] Website of the African Union, *List of the Countries that Have Signed, Ratified and Acceded to the Protocol to the African Charter on Human and Peoples' Rights on the Rights of Women in Africa*, https://au.int/sites/default/files/treaties/37077-sl.PROTOCOL%20TO%20THE%20AFRICAN%20CHARTER%20ON%20HUMAN%20AND%20PEOPLE%27S%20RIGHTS%20ON%20THE%20RIGHTS%20OF%20WOMEN%20IN%20AFRICA.pdf.

[50] Maputo Protocol (2003), articles 2–6, 8, 10, 14, 15 and 20–24.

[51] Website of the African Committee of Experts on the Rights and Welfare of the Child, *Ratification Table: African Charter on the Rights and Welfare of the Child*, https://www.acerwc.africa/ratifications-table/.

alia the rights of a girl child as provided for in the ACRWC.[52] Such rights include the right to protection against discrimination, child labour with resultant effects to physical, mental, spiritual, psychological, moral or social development, torture, abuse and harmful socio-cultural practices, right to education, parental care and protection and fair treatment while in conflict with the law.[53]

Going an extra mile, on 9 March 2010, Tanzania signed a declaration accepting the jurisdiction of the African Court on Human and Peoples' Rights (the African Court) and subsequently deposited it with the African Union per article 34(6) of the Protocol to the African Charter on Human and Peoples' Rights on the Establishment of an African Court on Human and Peoples' Rights of 1998. This bold move enabled individuals, groups or non-governmental organisations with observer status with the African Commission on Human and Peoples' Rights to directly file cases regarding, among other things, violation of women and girls' rights in Tanzania to the African Court. Regrettably, such declaration was withdrawn on 14 November 2019, leaving individuals, groups and non-governmental organisation with an option to access the Court via the African Commission on Human and Peoples' Rights.[54]

3.2.3 Sub-Regional Agreements

At the East African Community (EAC) level, Tanzania signed the Treaty for the Establishment of the East African Community of 1999 on 30 November 1999 together with other primary EAC Partner states. The Treaty entered in force on July 2000 having received ratification by its signatories; i.e. Kenya, Tanzania and Uganda.[55] The Treaty places an obligation on Tanzania to[56]:

(a)…

[52] African Charter on the Rights and Welfare of the Child (1990), article 43.

[53] Ibid., articles 11, 15, 16, 17, 19 and 20.

[54] African Court Protocol, articles 5 (1) (a) and 34 (6).

[55] Website of the East African Community (EAC), *History of the EAC*, https://www.eac.int/eac-history.

[56] EAC Treaty, article 121.

> (b) abolish legislation and discourage customs that are discriminatory against women;
> (c) promote effective education awareness programmes aimed at changing negative attitudes towards women;
> (d) ...
> (e) take such other measures that shall eliminate prejudices against women and promote the equality of the female gender with that of the male gender in every respect.

Also, being a member state to the Southern African Development Community (SADC), Tanzania has signed the SADC Protocol on Gender and Development, as amended (SADC Gender Protocol) on 17 August 2008.[57] The SADC Gender Protocol contains specific provisions addressing the rights of women and girls. Article 6(2) directs State Parties to the Protocol to enact and enforce legislation that eliminates among other things, violence against women.[58] Article 11 further obligates member states to protect girls from economic exploitation, trafficking and all forms of violence including sexual abuse.[59]

3.2.4 National Legislation

There exists no specific law addressing VAWG in Tanzania. Notwithstanding this fact, several provisions of the law are scattered in different pieces of legislation that address VAWG. The Marriage Act of 1971[60] prevents a spouse from imposing corporal punishment on the other.[61] This is, however, not sufficiently addressed as corporal punishment is not expressly stated as an offence in the Act. Other forms of violence like marital rape, psychological and economic violence in the matrimonial setting are not covered by this Act. Additionally, the Act directs courts

---

[57] Website of the Southern African Development Community, '*Protocols: SADC Protocol on Gender and Development*, https://www.sadc.int/files/8713/5292/8364/Protocol_on_Gender_and_Development_2008.pdf.

[58] SADC Protocol on Gender and Development (2008) article 6 (2) (d).

[59] Ibid., article 11 (1) (d).

[60] CAP 29, Revised Edition, 2019.

[61] Law of Marriage Act, CAP 29 Revised Edition, 2019, Section 66.

to have regard to the parties' prevailing customs and traditions while distributing matrimonial assets.[62] This is the case given the historical trail and multi-cultural nature of Tanzanian societies. It is therefore upon the prevailing Judge to exercise care and discretion regarding human rights standards to filter the customs and traditions that threaten the rights of women and girls.

Another major legal initiative which was rather general was brought by the inclusion of the Bill of Rights in the Constitution of the United Republic of Tanzania of 1977 in the year 1984. Article 13(5) of the Constitution prohibits discrimination on the basis of sex among other criteria. The rights asserted in the Constitution were made enforceable through the enactment of the Basic Rights and Duties Enforcement Act (BRADEA),[63] which vests the High Court with the mandate to receive and determine cases of human rights violations.[64] Although the current Tanzania Constitution does not specifically prohibit violence against women and girls, it prohibits discrimination on the basis of gender or sex.

The Sexual Offence Special Provisions Act (SOSPA) of 1998 was enacted in a manner that offers broader proscription of sexual offences and stricter penalties to perpetrators. This Act largely amended and repealed provisions in the Penal Code[65] with regard to violence against women and children. Specific provisions were adopted that responded to the prevailing status of VAWG in the country. Some of them concern rape, attempted rape, sexual exploitation, harassment, physical and indecent assault, grave sexual abuse, gross indecency, women or girls' defilement, trafficking, unnatural offences and cruelty to children (in this case girls) including female genital mutilation.[66] SOSPA also amended the Criminal Procedure Act (the CPA)[67] by introducing a mandatory fine to the convicted as compensation for the injuries sustained by the VAWG

[62] Ibid., Section 114 (2) (a).

[63] CAP 3, Revised Edition, 2019.

[64] BADEA, Sections 4 and 8.

[65] CAP 16, Revised Edition, 2019.

[66] Penal Code, Sections 130, 131, 131 A, 132, 135, 138A, 138B, 138C, 138D, 139A, 140, 154, 155 and 169A.

[67] CAP 20, Revised Edition, 2019.

victims, in addition to any penal punishment imposed on any sexual offence committed.[68] In addition, the CPA is amended to the effect that, the High Court may impose a greater punishment on sexual offences than the one imposed by the subordinate courts if the High Court is exercising its revisionary or appellate jurisdiction.[69]

Subsequently, in the year 2001, an Act to domesticate the Treaty for the Establishment of the East African Community was passed in Tanzania. Section 121 of the Act discourages all prejudices existing against women in Tanzania and calls for government action to promote equality of rights between men and women. Moreover, the Anti-Trafficking in Persons Act of 2008 was enacted to extend protection to women and children (girls) who have been suffering violence through acts of recruitment or abduction for purposes of domestic exploitation overseas, slavery, involuntary servitude, sexual exploitation, prostitution, forced marriages to foreigners and debt bondage, just to mention a few.[70] In 2009, the Law of the Child Act[71] was enacted to provide, promote, protect and maintain the welfare of a child with a major intention of giving domestic effect to the global and regional conventions on the rights and welfare of children to which Tanzania is a party. This Act provides for children's (in this case girls below 18 years) right to be protected against discrimination, rights to parental property, personal opinion, protection against harmful employment, torture and ill treatment.[72] The Act also imposes upon parents an obligation to ensure that a child's dignity is respected and protected by overseeing that he or she is not exposed to any kind of neglect, discrimination, violence, oppression, abuse, physical or moral perils.[73]

---

[68] Criminal Procedure Act, Section 348A.

[69] Criminal Procedure Act, Section 373.

[70] Anti-Trafficking in Persons Act, 2008, Section 4.

[71] Act No.21 of 2009, CAP 13, Revised Edition, 2019.

[72] Law of the Child Act, Sections 5 and 10–14.

[73] Ibid., Section 9.

3.3 Institutions

3.3.1 Ministries

There have been several initiatives at the institutional level in Tanzania to respond to VAWG. These include but are not limited to gender focal points in every ministry. Apart from this, some individual ministries and non-governmental organisations have taken further steps as discussed below.

(a). The Ministry of Health, Community Development, Gender, Elderly and Children

This Ministry ensures the general wellbeing of women and children in the country. Having ratified the CEDAW in the year 1985, the Government took its first step of creating a Women and Children's Division within the Department of Community Development in the then Ministry of Community Development, Culture, Youth and Sports. Further, in October 1990, the Department of Community Development was upgraded to a full Ministry of Community Development, Women Affairs and Children.[74] The said Ministry's nomenclature has evolved to the current Ministry of Health, Community Development, Gender, Elderly and Children with now a designated gender department which has a specific section on women affairs.[75] Such section specifically deals with all matters pertaining to women's welfare. This includes formulating policies, strategies and action plans which are women and girls friendly and advising the Government on the same issues. The Ministry also responds to international human rights' treaty(ies) obligations to ensure protection of the rights of women and girls in the country. This includes submitting periodic reports to relevant international bodies (Committees) on Tanzania's progress in implementation of women and girls' rights

[74] Olekambaine, *Gender and Social Policy: Experiences from Tanzania* (1994): 55–56.

[75] See the Website of the Ministry of Health, Community Development, Gender, Elderly and Children, *Departments*, http://www.mcdgc.go.tz/index.php/departments/category/gender/.

at the national level. Last but not least, the Ministry is involved in training gender focal points established in all ministries on the ministerial gender mainstreaming and budgeting.[76]

(b). The Ministry of Constitution and Legal Affairs

This Ministry, through the Law Reform Commission, has conducted several studies that have came up with viable recommendations for reforming the laws that perpetuate VAWG in Tanzania. Such studies include identification of the codified customary laws from the patrilineal societies which are against the principles of human rights and natural justice. This study culminated into a report that was submitted to the then Minister of Constitutional Affairs and Justice with suggestions to expunge from the codified Local Customary Law Orders all those customary laws that are offensive to Constitutional provisions and natural justice. The Report was submitted to the Minister responsible in March 2009.[77] Also, the Ministry through the established National Commission for Human Rights and Good Governance (CHRAGG) has run several projects and developed initiatives to address human rights violations in the country including development of National Human Rights Action Plan 2013–2017. The objectives of the latter are to, *inter alia,* facilitate domestication of the CEDAW by enacting a domestic law on violence, review other discriminatory legislation, promote public awareness on the harmful impact of sexual and domestic violence and provide psychosocial counselling, shelter and vocational support to victims of gender-based and domestic violence as well as female genital mutilation. Another initiative that has been taken by CHRAGG is the establishment of a free complaint online site for people in Tanzanian with human rights complaints including complaints related to VAWG which can be submitted to the 'special groups section'. Here, the complainants submit their claims and addresses for the Commission's

[76] USAID, *Gender Violence in Tanzania, An Assessment of Policies, Services and Promising Interventions* (2008): 21.

[77] Law Reform Commission of Tanzania, 'The Review of Customary Laws Project,' 4 *The Law Reformer Journal* (2013): 86.

assistance.[78] More importantly, the judiciary that operates under this Ministry has made commendable steps to ensure justice for victims of VAWG in different aspects including domestic violence, sexual offences and discrimination. The most recent and ground-breaking judgments by the higher Courts in Tanzania, that is, the High Court and the Court of Appeal of Tanzania, have finally drawn a demarcation for the minimum age of marriage for both boys and girls to be 18 years in the famous *Rebeca Gyumi case*.[79] The Courts went further and called upon the government to amend the Law of Marriage Act to reflect these decisions.

(c). The Ministry of Home Affairs

Apart from investigating and prosecuting offences related to VAWG in the country, the Tanzania Police Force under this Ministry of Home Affairs has instituted reforms in its structure to accommodate gender issues, including the acts of violence facing women and girls. Out of this initiative, the Tanzania Police Female Network (TPFNet) was instituted after the creation of Gender and Children Desks in police stations across the country.[80] By the year 2012, a total number of 417 Gender and Children Desks had been established at the districts level. The desks are structurally managed from the top-level leadership with clearly formulated Standard Operation Procedure (SOPs) and Guidelines for proper handling of claims of violence.[81]

The Gender and Children Desks have the main objective of ensuring that all the cases and complaints about gender-based violence and child abuse are solved timely, and the offenders are taken to court. The desks' activities include encouraging survivors and victims of violence to report such incidents and responding accordingly to all sexual and gender-based cases as well as cases involving child abuse and other related complaints

[78] See the Website of the Tanzanian Commission on Human Rights and Good Governance, *Projects*, https://www.chragg.go.tz/index.php/81-various-projects/current-projects/517-sms-for-human-rights-project.

[79] See the cases of *The Attorney General v Rebeca Z. Gyumi*, Civil Appeal No.204 of 2017, in the Court of Appeal of Tanzania at Dar es Salaam (Unreported).

[80] The detailed role of the police gender desks is discussed in the next subsection.

[81] Tanzania Women Lawyers Association, *Report on the Review of Laws and Policies Related to Gender Based Violence of Tanzania Mainland*, 42 and 43.

Table 1 Tanzania Police Force, Report, 2017.

	Offence (that forms part of VAWG)	Number of incidences in 2017
1	Assault	8,659
2	Rape	8,039
3	Bodily Harm	7,219
4	Grievous Bodily Harm	4,861

brought to the police stations.[82] Furthermore, they are tasked with keeping records of all incidents as they are reported, for monitoring and evaluation purposes. The desks also collaborate with other actors to assist, secure and protect survivors by giving them appropriate services including, health interventions, legal aid and accommodation. In doing all this, the gender desks strive to ensure that all cases based on gender violence and child abuse are reduced and eventually eliminated.[83]

Nevertheless, the most recent crime statistics report of 2017 displays an increase of gender-based crimes in the country as compared to the preceding year. The year 2017 saw a total of 41,416 incidences of sexual and gender-based violence as compared to 31,996 recorded in the year 2016, which is a 29.4 percent increase.[84] Noteworthy is the fact that some of the offences that generally constitute VAWG would be considered as offences against persons. The offences that have stood out (for adults) are depicted in the Table 1.

The above statistics are prima facie evidence that the afore-explained policies, legal and institutional responses to overcome VAWG in Tanzania have not succeeded in eradicating the problem. The factors weighing down these aggressive initiatives feature in the proceeding discussion.

[82] Ministry of Home Affairs, *Tanzania Police Force, Guidelines for the Establishment of Police Gender and Children's Desk* (2012) Unpublished, 7.

[83] Ministry of Home Affairs, *Tanzania Police Force, Guidelines for the Establishment of Police Gender and Children's Desk*, 7.

[84] Tanzania Police Force and The National Bureau of Statistics, *Takwimu za Hali ya Uhalifu na Matukio ya Usalama Barabarani Januari—Desemba 2017* (2018), https://www.nbs.go.tz/nbs/takwimu/trade/TakwimuHaliYaUhalifuJan-Dec2017.pdf.

4 Challenges

Despite the very well-crafted legal, policy and institutional responses by Tanzania as discussed above, VAWG remains pervasive, with challenges remaining regarding accessing justice by the victims. The conventional obstacle in legal practice has been lack of a specific law on VAWG. One would always have to refer to the Penal Code and various other statutes when incidents of violence occur.[85] Nevertheless, this is not the major challenge *per se*. As elaborated at the beginning of the chapter, one persistent challenge is lack of reporting by majority of the survivors and victims. There are several factors that contribute to this state of affairs. These factors can be looked at from various perspectives including the cultural attitudes in Tanzania. For both survivors and people around them, reporting and seeking justice (outside the family) is invariably seen as airing dirty laundry in public and bringing shame to the family.[86] Thus, the family and community structures (including local government leaders) remain the available pathways for survivors to seek justice. This leads to conciliatory processes which normally end up with forgiveness for the sake of protecting the family's honour.[87]

The cultural attitudes also affect service providers and practitioners such as the police and other members of the justice systems. Many in the society believe that pursuing justice by the victims of VAWG is a departure from a particular societal norms.[88] As the police, judges, magistrates and local government leaders are part and parcel of the traditional Tanzanian societies, some of them fail to separate their cultural inclinations from their line of duty. This affects the victims of VAWG when the incidents of violence particularly domestic violence reach their offices. In many instances, parties are requested to return home and reconcile with perpetrators or sort out their differences without invoking

[85] See generally Kipobota Clarence, *A Comprehensive Study on the Efficiency of the Enforcement of the Penal Code, CAP. 16 Against the Gender Based Violence in Tanzania Mainland* (2012) for an extensive discussion on this challenge.

[86] Some initiation ceremonies for girls who have reached puberty place emphasis on this kind of submission that a female should carry around to protect the family(ies)'s honour.

[87] McCleary-Sills et al., *Help-Seeking Pathways and Barriers for Survivors of Gender-based Violence in Tanzania*, 50.

[88] Ibid., 50.

the legal arm that could have provided a permanent solution to the problem. The Police Gender and Children Desks with trained officers constitute avenues to curb this problem. This platform was expected to bring justice closer to the community. Another related method devised to encourage victims of VAWG to keep pursuing justice and relief was the introduction of One Stop Centres as a medico-legal linkage to deal with VAWG and related offences; to offer medical and legal support to the victims of VAWG at a fast-tracked pace.[89] However, due to lack of awareness and fear instilled in women and girls in the society, reluctance by many victims of VAWG has persisted, thus, restraining them from accessing services which are at their disposal.[90] It is important to underscore that, in the absence of the aforementioned One Stop Centres, victims of violence such as physical assaults are required to seek a specific police form (commonly known as a PF 3) which is the primary legal document for reporting and evidence collection. Victims have to subsequently present the same to the public health facility in order to obtain medical treatment. This is a rather complicated and prolonged procedure which discourages VAWG victims from seeking help from formal institutions.[91]

Another challenge is poverty.[92] Women earning low to no income are usually affected by low mobility in order to save money. Therefore, going to the police station to report an incident of violence or seeking legal assistance becomes too cumbersome specifically for those living away from the police stations, hence, victims choose to forego that part, especially when they consider the injuries 'not too serious'.[93] Legal aid centres which seek to assist, among other groups, women of low income, could

[89] These are centres where a survivor gets services of a health care worker (doctor), the police and a social welfare officer. In some instances, the centres partner with legal aid providers, so that, legal aid is also available at the post where necessary. The Information obtained from the Social Welfare Officer at Amana Regional Hospital where the first one stop centre was piloted states thatasof2019 there were 15 one stop centres country wide.

[90] McCleary-Sills et al., *supra* note 87, 36.

[91] Information obtained from a Legal Aid Officer at the University of Dar es Salaam School of Law, Legal Aid Committee–Clinic on 01.10.2020.

[92] McCleary-Sills et al., *supra* note 87, 45.

[93] Information obtained from a Legal Aid Officer at the University of Dar es Salaam School of Law, Legal Aid Committee–Clinic on 02.10.2020. Also see Jennifer McCleary-Sills et al., Ibid., 34.

have been a proper remedy for the aforementioned challenge. However, when it comes to criminal cases, the legal aid field holds its own set of challenges regarding cases of VAWG. The first being that, cases of a criminal nature are prosecuted by the Republic. Therefore, legal aid becomes self-inhibited based on the assumption that the victims need no legal aid as all the necessary procedures to access justice fall in the hands of the Republic. Secondly, legal aid in the criminal justice system is still a fairly less invested phenomenon in the country and hence even the seasoned and inexperienced legal aid officers are grappling with it. However, there are some legal aid providers who give counselling, watch briefs in court and provide advice to victims who seek legal aid services.[94]

Further, corruption or the perception of VAWG within law enforcement and the criminal justice system is another factor that hinders victims from obtaining justice.[95] Some of them either have the perception that the perpetrators who are wealthier than them are willing to pay off the officials in the justice system or that they are likely to be asked for bribes to smoothen the process of obtaining justice.[96] This is also the case for those who would consider reporting incidents of VAWG to the community and local government leaders.[97] This stems from the lack of trust in the criminal justice system. Lastly, for the unmarried victims of VAWG, there is the moral challenge of the taboo of not exposing informal intimate relations before marriage.[98] Young girls and unmarried victims are more likely to not report incidents of violence if they have been committed by a sexual partner since it would be hard for them to explain the relationship to their families or authorities. In these instances, friends become the support system.[99]

[94] Information obtained from a Legal Aid Officer at the University of Dar es Salaam School of Law, Legal Aid Committee–Clinic on 02.10.2020.

[95] McCleary-Sills et al., *supra* note 87, 51.

[96] Tanzania Women Lawyers Association (TAWLA), *Review of Laws and Policies Related to Gender Based Violence of Tanzania Mainland* (2014), 32.

[97] McCleary-Sills et al., *supra* note 87, 51.

[98] Ibid., 36.

[99] Ibid., 25.

5 Prospects

As initiatives to end VAWG in Tanzania gain momentum with the positive power of the media in exposing the available avenues to prevent and solve this problem, the same is gradually being uprooted. The primary step is the Government's commitment and the implementation of sustainable programmes to educate women and girls on how they can overcome the problem from within. This includes knowing what to not tolerate. Also, as Tanzanians remain the most valuable asset for national development, the government invests in an evidence-based awareness raising programs against VAWG. This however is dependable on sufficient and monitored budgets. To ensure that the work done by relevant stakeholders is achievable, the government needs to adopt initiatives to end VAWG. The government needs to include all relevant stakeholders in devising such initiatives including, government officials from the village to the central government level, the Police Force—Gender and Children Desks, judges, magistrates, lawyers and advocates, prosecutors, paralegals, paramedics, doctors, teachers, traditional and religious leaders (community gate keepers), financial institutions and non-governmental organisations.

Vibrant non-governmental organisations with objectives to fight against VAWG have over the years, increased across the country. They are involved in advocacy, awareness raising programmes and litigation for the interests of women and children. These include but are not limited to: the Legal Aid Committee of the University of Dar es Salaam School of Law, the Tanzania Women Lawyer's Association (TAWLA), Women Legal Aid Centre (WLAC), the Legal and Human Rights Centre (LHRC) and the Tanganyika Law Society. Media organisations like the Tanzania Media Women Association (TAMWA) and recently Wanawake Live, in Partnership with the Haki za Wanawake (HAWA) Foundation, have narrowed and dedicated their focus on women and children's rights advocacy through the media to reach the wider audience across the county. Also, paralegals[100] and other legal aid providers have been

[100] Paralegals in Tanzania have now been recognised as official legal aid providers under the Legal Aid Act, 2017.

at the frontline to ensure that victims of VAWG access justice from the grassroots level. Non-governmental organisations further engage on policy development and law reforms processes. They also prepare shadow reports to state reports submitted by Tanzania to the international human rights bodies to paint a real picture of Tanzania's implementation of international human rights obligations. This is a positive indication that the government of Tanzania is well backed-up in the fight against VAWG and is hence in a better position to gradually eliminate VAWG from the Tanzanian societies.

As VAWG by and large occurs and is dealt with in community settings; any programme aimed at reducing and eliminating VAWG whether by the government or other actors has to fully engage the community. It is only efforts that consider the social and community aspects which will be able to look into the social factors that perpetuate VAWG and tackle the social cultural barriers that hinder reporting and accessing justice by women and girls that will be feasible.[101] In other words, joint efforts of all the actors including communities and community gate keepers that will produce better results in the bid to eliminate VAWG.

6 Conclusion

It takes the 'whole village' to end VAWG in Tanzania. It is not a one man or woman's business. This is because the problem is deeply rooted in the society with historical, cultural and religious justifications. Mere adoption of national legislation and ratification of human rights instruments will not halt this. Actions and initiatives that have been taken by the government at the policy, law and institutional level are not to remain on paper. They should be reflected in the society via continuous deliberate actions to eradicate VAWG. When the society joins efforts with the government to end VAWG in Tanzania, this nightmare experienced by women and girls may one day be put to rest.

---

[101] McCleary-Sills et al., *supra* note 87, 54.

References

African Commission on Human and Peoples' Rights, *Ratification Table: African Charter on Human and Peoples' Rights*, https://www.achpr.org/ratification table?id=49, November 25, 2020.

African Union, *List of the Countries That Have Signed, Ratified and Acceded to the Protocol to the African Charter on Human and Peoples' Rights on the Rights of Women in Africa*, https://au.int/sites/default/files/treaties/37077-slPROTOCOL%20TO%20THE%20AFRICAN%20CHARTER%20ON%20HUMAN%20AND%20PEOPLE%27S%20RIGHTS%20ON%20THE%20RIGHTS%20OF%20WOMEN%20IN%20AFRICA.pdf, November 25, 2020.

Bart Rwezaura, 'Domestic Application of International Human Rights Norms in Protecting the Rights of the Girl Child in Eastern and Southern Africa,' in Welshman Ncube (ed.), *Culture Tradition and Children's Rights in Eastern and Southern Africa* (1998): 28–46.

Commission on Human Rights and Good Governance, *Projects*, https://www.chragg.go.tz/index.php/81-various-projects/current-projects/517-sms-for-human-rights-project, June 20, 2020.

Committee on the Elimination of Discrimination against Women, General Recommendation No. 35 on Gender-Based Violence against Women, Updating General Recommendation No. 19 (2017).

Cuthbert Omar, 'Explaining Social Problems,' in Cuthbert Omari and Leonard Shaidi (eds.), *Social Problems in Eastern Africa* (1991): 1–11.

East African Community (EAC), *History of the EAC*, https://www.eac.int/eac-history, November 25, 2020.

Els Baerends, *Changing Kinship, Family and Gender Relationships in Sub-Sahara Africa* (1994).

Fareda Banda, *Women, Law and Human Rights: An African Perspective* (2005).

Felician Tungaraza, 'Changes in Traditional Social Security and Their Impact on Women in Tanzania,' in Ludgera Klemp (ed.), *Gender and Social Policy: Experiences of Tanzania* (1994): 12–34.

Human Development Trust, *Gaps in Policies and Laws That Perpetuate Gender Based Violence in Tanzania: An Analysis and Synthesis* (2011).

International Council on Human Rights Policy, *When Legal Worlds Overlap: Human Rights, State and Non-State Law* (2009).

Jennifer McCleary-Sills et al., *Help-Seeking Pathways and Barriers for Survivors of Gender-based Violence in Tanzania: Results from a Study in Dar es Salaam, Mbeya, and Iringa Regions* (2013).

Julius Kambarage Nyerere, *Socialism and Rural Development* (1967).

Kipobota Clarence, *A Comprehensive Study on the Efficiency of the Enforcement of the Penal Code, CAP. 16 Against the Gender Based Violence in Tanzania Mainland* (2012).

Law Reform Commission of Tanzania, 'The Review of Customary Laws Project,' 4 *The Law Reformer Journal* (2013).

Maduhu Marco, *Wapata Ujauzito Likizo ya Corona*, May 25, 2020, https://www.ippmedia.com/sw/habari/wapata-ujauzito-likizo-ya-corona, June 20, 2020.

Marja-Liisa Shwantz, *Women in Development: A Creative Role Denied* (1985).

Ministry of Health, Community Development, Gender, Elderly and Children et al., *Tanzania Demographic and Health Survey and Malaria Indicator Survey* (2016).

Ministry of Health, Community Development, Gender, Eldery and Children, *Departments*, http://www.mcdgc.go.tz/index.php/departments/category/gender/, June 9, 2020.

Ministry of Home Affairs, *Tanzania Police Force, Guidelines for the Establishment of Police Gender and Children's Desk*, (2012) Unpublished.

Monica Mhoja and Hellen-Kijo Bisimba, 'Tanzanian Customary Laws of Inheritance: A Case of Cultural Violence Against Women,' in Ludgera Klempf (ed.), *Women Challenging Violence: Experiences from Eastern and Southern Africa* (1994).

Ophelia Mascarenhas and Marjorie Mbilinyi, *Women in Tanzania: An Analytical Bibliography* (1983).

Sherene Razak, 'Imperilled Muslim Women, Dangerous Muslim Men and Civilised Europeans: Legal and Social Responses to Forced Marriages,' 12 *Feminist Legal Studies* (2004): 129–174.

Signe Arnfred, 'Reflection on Family, Trends of Change, Lobola and Polygyny Women and Law in Southern Africa,' in Women and Law in Southern Africa (WLSA) (ed.), *Changing Families: Changing Laws, Working Paper No.9*. (1994): 36–47.

Southern African Development Community, *Protocols, SADC Protocol on Gender and Development*, https://www.sadc.int/files/8713/5292/8364/Protocol_on_Gender_and_Development_2008.pdf, November 25, 2020.

Stella Bendera, E. Maro and Mary Mboya, 'A Gender Perspective on Violence: Its Form and Consequences for Education of Primary School Pupils in

Tanzania,' in S. J. Bendera and S. W. Mboya (eds.), Gender *and Education in Tanzanian Schools* (1996): 31–58.

Susan Gaiger, *TANU Women: Women and Culture in the Making of Tanganyika Nationalism 1955–1965* (1997).

Tanzania National HIV/AIDS Policy and the National Multisectoral Framework on HIV/AIDS (2003–2007), 29.

Tanzania Police Force and The National Bureau of Statistics, *Takwimu za Hali ya Uhalifu na Matukio ya Usalama Barabarani Januari - Desemba 2017* (2018), https://www.nbs.go.tz/nbs/takwimu/trade/TakwimuHaliYaUhalifuJan-Dec2017.pdf, June 15, 2020.

Tanzania Women Lawyers Association (TAWLA), *Review of Laws and Policies Related to Gender Based Violence of Tanzania Mainland* (2014).

United Nations, *Treaty Collection (Depository): Convention on the Elimination of All Forms of Discrimination Against Women*, https://treaties.un.org/pages/ViewDetails.aspx?src=TREATY&mtdsg_no=IV-11&chapter=4&lang=en, November 25, 2020.

United Nations, *Treaty Collection (Depository): International Covenant on Civil and Political Rights and International Covenant on Economic, Social and Cultural Rights*, https://treaties.un.org/pages/ViewDetails.aspx?src=TREATY&mtdsg_no=IV-11&chapter=4&lang=en, November 25, 2020.

USAID, *Gender Violence in Tanzania, An Assessment of Policies, Services and Promising Interventions* (2008).

United Nations, *Treaty Collection (Depository): Convention on the Rights of the Child*, https://treaties.un.org/pages/ViewDetails.aspx?src=TREATY&mtdsg_no=IV-11&chapter=4&lang=en, November 25, 2020.

Website of the African Committee of Experts on the Rights and Welfare of the Child, *Ratification Table: African Charter on the Rights and Welfare of the Child*, https://www.acerwc.africa/ratifications-table/, November 25, 2020.

Welschman Ncube, 'The African Cultural Fingerprint? The Changing Concept of Childhood,' in Welschman Ncube (ed), *Law, Culture Tradition and Children's Rights in Eastern and Southern Africa* (1998): 11–27.

Zaya Elizabeth, *Wanafunzi 100 Wapata Mimba Kipindi cha Corona*, June 17, 2020, https://www.ippmedia.com/sw/habari/wanafunzi-100-wapata-mimba-kipindi-corona, June 20, 2020.

Index

E. C. Lubaale and A. Budoo-Scholtz (eds.), *Violence Against Women and Criminal Justice in Africa: Volume I*, Sustainable Development Goals Series,
https://doi.org/10.1007/978-3-030-75949-0

R

S

The manufacturer's authorised representative in the EU is Springer Nature Customer Service Centre GmbH, Europaplatz 3, 69115 Heidelberg, Germany. If you have any concerns regarding our products, please contact ProductSafety@springernature.com

Printed and bound by CPI Group (UK) Ltd, Croydon, CR0 4YY
30/09/2026
02225700-0015